PLOTINUS

PLOTINUS

Myth, Metaphor, and Philosophical Practice

STEPHEN R. L. CLARK

THE UNIVERSITY OF CHICAGO PRESS

CHICAGO AND LONDON

The University of Chicago Press, Chicago 60637
The University of Chicago Press, Ltd., London
© 2016 by The University of Chicago
All rights reserved. Published 2016.
Paperback edition 2018
Printed in the United States of America

27 26 25 24 23 22 21 20 19 18   2 3 4 5 6

ISBN-13: 978-0-226-33967-2 (cloth)
ISBN-13: 978-0-226-56505-7 (paper)
ISBN-13: 978-0-226-33970-2 (e-book)

DOI: https://doi.org/10.7208/chicago/9780226339702.001.0001

Library of Congress Cataloging-in-Publication Data

Names: Clark, Stephen R. L., author.
Title: Plotinus: myth, metaphor, and philosophical practice / Stephen R. L. Clark.
Description: Chicago ; London : The University of Chicago Press, 2016. | Includes
    bibliographical references and index.
Identifiers: LCCN 2015037892 | ISBN 9780226339672 (cloth : alk. paper) | ISBN
    9780226339702 (e-book)
Subjects: LCSH: Plotinus. | Philosophy, Ancient.
Classification: LCC B693.Z7 C55 2016 | DDC 186/.4—DC23
LC record available at http://lccn.loc.gov/2015037892

♾ This paper meets the requirements of ANSI/NISO Z39.48–1992 (Permanence of
Paper).

Let us fly to our dear country. What then is our way of escape, and how are we to find it? We shall put out to sea, as Odysseus did, from the witch Circe or Calypso—as the poet says (I think with a hidden meaning)—and was not content to stay though he had delights of the eyes and lived among much beauty of sense. Our country from which we came is There, our Father is There. How shall we travel to it, where is our way of escape? We cannot get there on foot; for our feet only carry us everywhere in this world, from one country to another. You must not get ready a carriage, either, or a boat. Let all these things go, and do not look. Shut your eyes, and change to and wake another way of seeing, which everyone has but few use.

—Plotinus, *Ennead* I.6 [1].8, 16–28

CONTENTS

vii

PREFACE

This volume had its beginnings in a Leverhulme Trust–funded project (2002–3) whose aim was to examine Plotinus's use of metaphor, with the working assumption that this could be identified as philosophically "constructive" rather than merely ornamental or rhetorical. My colleague Panayiota Vassilopoulou and I shared a conviction that Plotinus's work was more than a compendium of abstract arguments, and that it could be understood only by those willing at least to *try* to follow its advice (just as a poem is understood only by reciting it, a play by its performance, or a philosophy by arguing about it). Our original intention was to write a joint study of these issues, and in what follows I continue to be influenced by my colleague's thoughts and studies. Other events, responsibilities, and projects have delayed us both, and this volume, in consequence, is written only by myself, with all the appropriate thanks both to Panayiota and to other friends, students, and acquaintances.

By "constructive," I mean that these images and metaphors were intended to be spiritual or imaginative exercises, which could be expected to have a transformative effect on those willing to follow them through: "dynamic" in two ways at least, in that they develop as one contemplates them, and that their enjoyment changes one's underlying mind-set. The project offered to the Trust was to see how this approach could enrich our understanding of Plotinus and how it could be applied in current pedagogic practice. We aimed first to identify prominent and recurring metaphorical images in Plotinus's philosophical system and to read these metaphors with attention to their root, or "literal," meaning in the context of his times and to their previous philosophical associations. In this way, we aimed to follow and adopt Plotinus's own method when engaging with his predecessors and thus to establish new ways of grasping and using the Plotinian texts.

When read carefully, these metaphors are more than superficial ornaments. By changing the "metaphors we live by,"[1] we can begin to change the way we live. Plotinus's goal was both to clarify our thinking and to facilitate our virtuous living.

The Trust's support also helped to make it possible to hold the 2004 meeting of the International Society for Neoplatonic Studies at Liverpool—a meeting which both helped to clarify our ideas and led to the publication of essays first tried out at that conference by enthusiastic scholars and philosophers (Vassilopoulou and Clark, *Late Antique Epistemology*). A further conference, organized by Michael McGhee and John Spencer in 2004, "Philosophy as a Way of Life," has also resulted in an edited volume of essays, in honor of Pierre Hadot (Chase, Clark, and McGhee, *Philosophy as a Way of Life*). I learned much from reading and helping to edit these papers. Panayiota and I have ourselves delivered papers relating to the theme of this work at international conferences and seminars in Oxford, Cambridge, San Francisco, Liverpool, Quebec, New Orleans, Athens, Chester, Manchester, and Victoria, and I acknowledge help given us there by many scholars, philosophers, and friends.[2]

The project has precedents. Dillon, commenting on the imagery of V.8 [31].9,[3] remarks that "here we are being called upon to use our imagination creatively, to attain to a purely intellectual conception," and suggests that the exercise works as Plotinus says.[4] Hadot describes Plotinus's treatises as "spiritual exercises in which the soul sculpts herself."[5] Shaw suggests that Plotinus's images were intended as "theurgic" in effect: not merely talk about the gods but a way of invoking them, without the overt rituals that philosophers like Iamblichus preferred but in the same spirit.[6] Rappe likewise: "decoding these texts involves seeing them as something like meditation manuals rather than mere texts. The non-discursive aspects of the text—the symbols, ritual formulae, myths, and images—are the locus of

---

1. See Lakoff and Johnson, *Metaphors We Live By.*

2. Relevant papers by Panayiota Vassilopoulou include "Creation or Metamorphosis"; "From a Feminist Perspective"; "Sages of Old, Artists Anew"; "Teaching Philosophy through Metaphor"; introduction to Vassilopoulou and Clark, *Late Antique Epistemology*; "Plotinus' Aesthetics"; "Plotinus and Individuals"; and, with Jonardon Ganeri, "Cathartic Potion"; "Metaphor of Life"; and "Geography of Shadows."

3. Throughout, I use a standard format for citing the *Enneads.* Here V.8 [31].9 means book V, treatise 8 [31st in chronological order of writing], section 9. Line numbers, when they are given, will follow the section numbers, as in IV.3 [27].25, 13–4.

4. Dillon, "Plotinus and the Transcendental Imagination," 58–9.

5. Hadot, *Plotinus; or, the Simplicity of Vision,* 22.

6. Shaw, "Eros and Arithmos."

this pedagogy. Their purpose is to help the reader to learn how to contemplate, to awaken the eye of wisdom."[7] Of the passage cited by Dillon, Rappe remarks that "it is fair to call [it] a meditation because it involves two features often employed in meditation techniques: the active but directed use of the imagination, and the sustained presence of this imaginative construction as a method of changing habitual modes of thought or self-awareness."[8] And again: "to read the text as an ideal reader is to take part in a theurgic ritual."[9] Plotinus's myths and metaphors are "spiritual exercises."[10] To understand them better it is necessary to learn how Plotinus could reasonably have expected them to be practiced by his contemporaries and how they have affected later creative thought.

There are also many modern studies, chiefly in psychiatry and psychotherapy, of the role that stories, myths, and metaphors play in constructing or reconstructing troubled minds: whether or not there are really "demons" of the sort that Plotinus's contemporaries and followers supposed, the image of those demons may be forcefully present, and it may also be possible to interrogate, domesticate, or at last expel them. Many therapists employ some version of guided imagery to assist the program. The scholarly and popular literature is so extensive that any particular examples will be almost arbitrary, but among the most helpful I have found are Corthright's *Psychotherapy and Spirit*, Hillman's *Re-visioning Psychology*, Lawley and Tompkins's *Metaphors in Mind*, and Abram's *Spell of the Sensuous*. I have also learned from Tolle (especially *The Power of Now*) and from Taylor's *Waking from Sleep*. Therapists often refer back to Jung's work, especially his *Psychology and Alchemy*. Material in the philosophy (and anthropology) of religion is also relevant, from Durkheim's *Elementary Forms of the Religious Life* and James's *Varieties of Religious Experience* onward.

Because Plotinus's images are thus protreptic they need not be judged, cannot be judged, as if they were intended merely to describe the world or our experience of it. We may describe a cake without being any closer to creating it. A cake recipe is not a description, though it may sometimes

---

7. Rappe, *Reading Neoplatonism*, 3. See also Kupperman, *Living Theurgy*, 8: "the contemplative and theurgical practices espoused by the Neoplatonists, from Plotinus through Ficino, effectively bring about changes in the practitioner, regardless as to the divine or psychological, or both, causes of those changes."

8. Rappe, *Reading Neoplatonism*, 79.

9. Ibid., 173, on Proclus.

10. In Hadot's words, "voluntary personal practices intended to cause a transformation of the self" (*What Is Ancient Philosophy?*, 179). On a parallel development in Indian thought and practice, see Dalton, "Development of Perfection." My thanks to Paul Williams for this reference.

involve descriptions ("stir the mixture till it thickens"); rather, it is a set of instructions on how to bake a cake that do not in any helpful sense resemble the eventual cake. And the instructions have no effect unless we follow them. So it is with much of Plotinus's argument. One serious problem for this sort of philosophy is of course that it is difficult to follow the instructions, whether because our desires get in the way or because we cannot manage the intensity of concentration that the images require. There is a prior problem: what exactly do the instructions mean? What is it, for example, "to think away the spatiality" (or the bulk) of material things (V.8 [31].9)? What state of consciousness is being recommended when Plotinus speaks of love or drunkenness or nakedness (VI.7 [38].22; VI.7 [38].35; I.6 [1].7)? What sort of stars or starlike consciousness is intended when he declares that we once were stars, or are eternally (III.4 [15].6)? What does it mean to say that the soul goes round God, like the stars (II.2 [14].2, 15; VI.9 [9].8), or that we should expect transformed "spherical" bodies (IV.4 [28].5, 18ff.)? In what sense can Plotinus hope to ask the Muses—or Time itself—how Time came to be (III.7 [45].11)? If we are to "bring the god in us back to the god in the all" (as Plotinus's deathbed instruction reads),[11] how do we even get started without knowing what those gods may be? "It does no good at all to say 'Look to God,' unless one also teaches how one is to look" (II.9 [33].15, 33–4). What is it that is not being said in all these questions because it was obvious? If the recipe for the cake requires us to add two eggs to the mix, might not the novice neglect to break them and discard the shells?[12]

One further problem is that no particular interpretation can be fully justified from the text. Honest scholars have therefore sometimes insisted that scholarly exegesis must be confined to "what the text says," and all further speculation be reckoned fable (or perhaps philosophy). This may indeed be a proper response to readings that seize upon some phrase or half-examined argument and develop this in the light of modern interests: Aristotle as an "ordinary language" philosopher, for instance! But scholarly exegesis simply of "the text" cannot be all we do, for at least five reasons. First of all, it is obvious that all philosophers have more beliefs than they

11. *Porphyry on the Life of Plotinus* 2.25, in Plotinus, *Enneads*, trans. Armstrong, vol. 1, (hereafter cited as Porphyry, *Life*).

12. See Luhrmann, *When God Talks Back*, 173: "What remains to us of [Ignatius Loyola's] *Spiritual Exercises* are notes, not much better than early cookbooks by Apicius or Mrs. Beeton, with their lists of ingredients and vague instructions, intelligible only to those who already know how to cook." As Luhrmann observes, there is at least an unbroken *oral* tradition of interpretation and practice "within the Jesuit fold." The Plotinian tradition, by contrast, has to be reinvented every few centuries!

write down, beliefs which may influence their arguments. Plotinus, for example, wouldn't explain why he wouldn't talk about his childhood, nor why he wouldn't join Amelius's tour of temples, and left his friends and followers to guess. Such guesses may be good or bad, but we cannot avoid proposing them. The point, indeed, is not only that no one ever writes down everything he or she believes but also that there was a strong tradition precisely against doing so, or at least against revealing such writings:

> It was not only the Pythagoreans and Plato that concealed many things; but the Epicureans too say that they have things that may not be uttered, and do not allow all to peruse those writings. The Stoics also say that by the first Zeno things were written which they do not readily allow disciples to read, without their first giving proof whether or not they are genuine philosophers. And the disciples of Aristotle say that some of their treatises are esoteric, and others common and exoteric. Further, those who instituted the mysteries, being philosophers, buried their doctrines in myths, so as not to be obvious to all.[13]

Erennius, Origen, and Plotinus, it is said, had agreed not to reveal their master Ammonius's doctrines: "Erennius was the first to break the agreement, and Origen followed his lead."[14] Plotinus eventually began to base his lectures on Ammonius's teachings—and fell silent when Origen turned up, saying that "it damps one's enthusiasm for speaking when one sees that one's audience knows already what one is going to say"![15] Do we know that he wrote all the teachings down? Obviously, we do not.

Second, none of these philosophers considered themselves to be wholly original: they were writing and arguing within an ancient oral tradition. Flo-

13. Clement of Alexandria, *Stromata* 5.9. Eunapius of Sardis (fl. AD 380), *Lives*, 357, remarks that though "some philosophers hide their esoteric teachings in obscurity, as poets conceal theirs in myths, *Porphyry* praised clear knowledge as a sovereign remedy" (and therefore revealed both his own near suicide and Plotinus's arguments against the plan).

14. Porphyry, *Life* 3.24–35.

15. Ibid., 14.21–5. If this event happened during Porphyry's time in Rome (in the 260s), then this Origen cannot have been the Christian theologian, who died during the Decian persecutions in the 250s. But nothing in the *Life* requires that Porphyry was present: he may have been told about it. It may be more significant that the Christian Origen wrote voluminously, while only two texts are explicitly mentioned as the work of an Origen who might be a different, pagan writer (or only two were not clearly Christian?). Porphyry (Eusebius, *History*, 158–60 [6.19.6–7]) identifies the Christian as a mere *akroates* of Ammonius, while the one who turned up in Rome was a member of the inner circle, a *zelotes*. None of this is conclusive! "Origen" (dual or single) was influenced in either case by Ammonius's Platonism and probably his hermeneutical techniques. See Martens, *Origen and Scripture*, 36–7.

rovsky's rebuke, in an essay on early Christian writings, also applies (with appropriate reservations) to pagan Platonists:

> There is a tendency among some scholars to assume that if something is not mentioned in a text, the author had no knowledge of it. This is a fundamentally erroneous presupposition and hence an erroneous methodology. The assumption of this methodological approach or perspective misses the prime reality—a living Church was already in existence since Pentecost and that living Church knew the deposit about which they preached, knew the tradition, which they had received and continued to impart in their missionary activity.[16]

Christians might insist that the Holy Spirit was guiding their debates, and would not permit them to lapse into egregious error, whereas the pagans could have had no such reasonable assurance (though Porphyry suggested that Plotinus was divinely guarded against error).[17] But in both cases more was debated—and more assumed—than was ever written down.

Third, the "living voice" was to be preferred to any written text, as it was only—or at least principally—from such a voice, such a living presence, that we could hope to pick up the things that cannot be said but only shown. This was a notion shared by both pagan and Christian writers: Papias recorded that he "did not imagine that things out of books would help me as much as the utterances of a living and abiding voice."[18] This does not, of course, preclude the use of texts and textual commentaries: Plotinus's seminars took their start from these. But even now the discipline of philosophy—like carpentry or surgery—is learned in a long apprenticeship to some master, and not just "from books."

A fourth reason to go beyond the text must apply even to the most literary of traditions, the least reliant on oral transmission and on unvoiced assumptions. We cannot ever understand "the text" at all without making our own assumptions about what it might reasonably say: Plotinus's Greek was idiosyncratic, and even his contemporaries found it difficult. It is hard enough to follow modern philosophers, writing in familiar languages and available for further questions. Thinking that "what Plotinus said" is obvious is at least optimistic. We understand any such text when we can make

16. Florovsky, *Byzantine Fathers*, chap. 4.
17. Porphyry, *Life* 23.19–21: "he wrote what he wrote under [the gods'] inspection and supervision."
18. Eusebius, *History, 102* [3.39]; see L. Alexander, "Living Voice."

plausible additions to it, or at least have some guess as to how the author might respond to an objection. And this leads to the fifth reason why mere exegesis cannot be enough. Darwinian theory—to take a more modern and more familiar case—is not just what Darwin said: Darwin himself believed (for example) in the inheritance of acquired characteristics, a theory that we now contrast with Darwinism. Darwinism or Darwinian theory takes its beginnings from his writings, but it has developed in ways that he might not have recognized (though the more hagiographical of his successors sometimes seem to suggest that every later development is "really" in the texts). Refusing to develop Darwinism beyond what Darwin said would amount to saying that Darwin's ideas were so utterly mistaken as not even to be a beginning. Refusing to develop Plotinian theory, so to speak, beyond the explicit text is to say that he (and by extension Plato and all other "Platonists") was as wrong as Nostradamus.[19] It is possible that this is what some scholars and philosophers believe: their investigations are still of great value,[20] but they were perhaps too quick to dismiss the theory.[21]

Darwinism, of course, can be checked, and has been checked, against our growing knowledge of the world. Some exegetes assume, for whatever reason, that Plotinian or Platonic theory cannot thus be checked, and so is a dead theory: one to be expounded only by the repetition or reordering of selected passages. I aim to rebut that notion, by attempting to develop and to check the texts against our own experience of the world and the evidence of other—seemingly similar—traditions. But even if Plotinian theory were a wholly false account of things, it might be worth developing. There was never a man named Sherlock Holmes in Baker Street: this has not prevented authors and film directors from developing the character and the tales.[22] Not all such efforts become canonical, any more than every performance of a play or piece of music is worth recalling. Past phi-

19. The point is made by Deck, *Nature, Contemplation, and the One,* 81: "If we wish to treat Plotinus as merely a historical curiosity, it is enough for us to repeat what he himself has said in somewhat similar language. . . . If, however, we wish to take him seriously as a philosopher . . . we must go a step further and try to 'make sense' of his account for ourselves."

20. See, e.g., Lloyd, *Anatomy,* for a short, dry, and reliable account of Neoplatonic logic and metaphysics by a philosopher who seems to have thought it nonsense.

21. Plotinus himself certainly did not think it enough merely to collate and repeat what the ancient philosophers had said: "we must consider that some of the blessed philosophers of ancient times have found out the truth, but it is proper to investigate which of them have attained it most completely, and how we too could reach an understanding about these things" (III.7 [45].1).

22. See also W. R. Stanford, *Ulysses Theme,* on the figure of Odysseus as it has been developed over the centuries; and Galinsky, *Heracles Theme,* similarly on Heracles.

losophies, even if they were wholly unrealistic, may still have an afterlife, and the importance of that life is judged by other criteria than their truth content—or lack of it. Their contribution may be better appreciated by the impact these philosophies still have on changing the world as we know it: just repeating the play as written, or the last performance that the producer saw, is no good use of theatrical talent. So also with the *Enneads*: we shall not understand them till we can make a worthwhile guess about what is not said, and develop them in ways Plotinus did not, quite possibly, intend. To change the world can be a matter of ethical, political, educational, or aesthetic practice. In all these directions, the relevance of Plotinus's philosophy is gradually being recognized in recent years, despite the fact that Plotinus himself did not explicitly divide his philosophy in this or any other way.[23] On one account, a reading of the *Enneads* in this light will be like developing Darwinian theory; on another, like sketching the backstory or future life of Holmes. If we do neither, why bother with the *Enneads* at all? Even discussing them as part of our intellectual history requires that we see them through the eyes of their interpreters and devotees: that is, we have to see how they were and might be developed. But if we do both, as Plotinus himself did when speaking even of his own favored philosopher (Plato), we may better understand how we cannot know the world and ourselves except by changing them.

My own qualifications for attempting this work are partly academic and partly personal. My hope, from the beginning of my academic life, was to maintain my interest in the classical world as a whole, as philosopher, historian, and literary critic. That hope, as I found myself employed in philosophy departments in Glasgow and in Liverpool, proved unrealistic. I can no longer claim the fluency in reading and writing Greek and Latin that I once possessed, nor have I kept up with innovations and discoveries in mainstream classical scholarship: for those I must rely upon my friends and colleagues. I have, on the other hand, been able to interest myself in other issues, including the biological underpinnings of our ethical and religious attitudes, the moral status of (nonhuman) animals, the nature of mental disorders, and the philosophy of religion. Almost all my academic work has included references to Plotinus or Porphyry, and I have had much enjoyment, since my retirement from paid employment, in rediscovering many classical and other antique texts—culminating in an introduction to ancient

---

23. Dillon, "Ethic for the Late-Antique Sage"; O'Meara, *Platonopolis*; Miles, *Plotinus on Body and Beauty*.

Mediterranean philosophy intended to break open the artificial boundaries around "classical philosophy."[24] In my present work I hope to break down the barriers between scholarly and esoteric examination of Neoplatonic philosophy: this is not to disparage or dismiss the work of either scholars or esotericists, not even the most text-based of scholars and the most fanciful of esotericists. On the contrary, it is to acknowledge and to honor both!

My personal qualifications for daring to write about reforming our mental habits, and for offering guidance on a spiritual path, are still more limited. I have been a professing—Anglican—Christian since late adolescence, and even once hoped to join the nonstipendiary ministry of the Scottish Episcopal Church (an ambition or vocation overtaken by events). In common with other children of the sixties, I imagined that it was up to us to make up our own rules about many personal matters in the new age dawning— only to discover that many of the old rules still applied! Much more to the point, I have also myself endured cancer, surgery, and postoperative depression and have observed the effects of depression—notoriously, the "academic disease"—and of other serious illness in my friends and colleagues. I also have at least as many vices as Zopyrus the physiognomist identified in Socrates.[25] The exercises I describe—whether directly from Plotinus's texts or from extrapolated or associated themes—have often proved useful. Many are ones that people in many times and places have invented for themselves, especially advice about breathing, silencing obsessive voices (whether or not these are demons), summoning the images of virtue, and redirecting our attention. Others are more peculiar to Plotinus or his day and need imaginative reworking before they can be used by us here-now. I have also been assisted, personally and professionally, by being asked to consider theological work within the Greek Orthodox tradition, especially Evagrius, Maximus the Confessor, and Gregory Palamas. My aim has been to bring these many elements together in a unified account, keeping an eye, as Plotinus urges, on our leader (VI.9 [9].8, 39). My likely failure may at least provide material for a better view.

---

24. S. Clark, *Ancient Mediterranean Philosophy.*

25. Phaedo of Elis, in his *Zopyrus*, recorded that Zopyrus, a foreign physiognomist, inferred from the shape of his head and neck that Socrates was "a dim-witted lecher." Socrates agreed that he had these vices, but that he had cast them out "through the discipline that comes from philosophy." I make no such personal claim but note—again—that this discipline was what "Philosophy" once meant. See Cicero, *On Fate*, 419 (chap. 10); Alexander of Aphrodisias, *On Fate*, 48 (6.171), 130. On Porphyry's view of Socrates, his initial character, and his reformation, see Johnson, *Religion and Identity*, 40-1.

ACKNOWLEDGMENTS

I have addressed many of the themes in the following pages in earlier published papers. This earlier work includes "Waking-Up: A Neglected Model for the After-life," *Inquiry* 26 (1983): 209–30; "Where Have All the Angels Gone?," *Religious Studies* 28 (1992): 221–34; "Plotinus: Body and Mind," in *Cambridge Companion to Plotinus*, edited by Lloyd Gerson (Cambridge: Cambridge University Press, 1996), 275–91; "Thinking about How and Why to Think," *Philosophy* 71 (1996): 385–404; "A Plotinian Account of Intellect," *American Catholic Philosophical Quarterly* 71 (1997): 421–32; "The Cosmic Priority of Value (Aquinas Lecture, Leuven)," *Tijdschrift voor filosofie* 62 (2000): 681–700; "*To synonthyleuma, i omorfia kai i Platoniki fantasia*" [Rubble, beauty, and the Platonic imagination], in *Oikologikes axies* [*Ecological values*], edited by K. Boudouris (Athens: International Center for Greek Philosophy and Culture, 2002), 61–75; "Plotinus—The Enneads," in *Central Works of Philosophy*, vol. 1, edited by J. Shand (London: Acumen, 2005), 119–39; (with Panayiota Vassilopoulou) "How Not to Love Nature," in *Proceedings XVI Congress of Philosophy: Philosophy, Competition and the Good Life* (in Greek, trans. Constantinos Athanasopoulos), vol. A (Athens: Spetses, 2005), 77–98; "Going Naked into the Shrine: Herbert, Plotinus and the Constructive Metaphor," in *Platonism at the Origins of Modernity*, edited by D. Hedley and S. Hutton (Dordrecht: Springer, 2008), 45–61; "What Has Plotinus's One to Do with God?," in *Philosophers and God*, edited by Michael McGhee and John Cornwell (London: Continuum, 2009), 21–37; conclusion to *Late Antique Epistemology: Other Ways to Truth*, edited with Panayiota Vassilopoulou (Basingstoke: Palgrave Macmillan, 2009), 289–301; "Plotinian Dualisms and the 'Greek' Ideas of Self," *Journal of Chinese Philosophy* 36 (2009): 554–67; "Plotinus: Charms and Counter-Charms," in *Conceptions of Philosophy*, edited by Anthony O'Hear, *Royal Institute of Philosophy Supplementary Volume 65* (Cambridge: Cambridge University Press, 2010), 215–31; "Therapy and Theory Reconstructed," in *Philosophy as Therapy*, edited by Clare Carlisle and Jonardon Ganeri, *Royal Institute of Philosophy Supplementary Volume 66* (Cambridge: Cambridge University Press, 2010), 83–102; "How to Become Unconscious," in *The Metaphysics of Consciousness*, edited by Pierfrancesco Basile, Julian Kiverstein, and Pauline Phemister, *Royal Institute of Philosophy Supplementary Volume 67* (Cambridge: Cambridge University Press, 2010), 21–44; "*The Mind Parasites*: Wilson, Husserl, Plotinus," in *Around the Outsider: Essays Presented to Colin Wilson*, edited by Colin Stanley (Alresford: O-Books, 2011), 42–62; "Moments of Truth: The Marginal and the Real," *European Legacy* 17, no. 6 (2012): 769–78; "Personal Identity and Identity Disorders," in *Oxford Handbook of Philosophy and Psychiatry*, edited by K. W. M. Fulford et al. (Oxford: Oxford University Press, 2013), 911–28; "Discerning the Spirits: Healing and the Moral Problems of Efficacy," in *Spiritual Healing: Science, Meaning, and Discernment*, edited by Sarah Coakley (Grand Rapids, MI: Eerdmans, forthcoming); "Plotinus on Remembering and Forgetting," in *Greek Memories*, edited by Luca Castagnoli and Paola Ceccarelli (Cambridge: Cambridge University Press, forthcoming); "Silence in the Land of Logos," in *Papers on Gregory Palamas*, edited by Constantinos Athanasopoulos (forthcoming).

My earlier books on these and related topics include *Aristotle's Man: Speculations upon Aristotelian Anthropology* (Oxford: Clarendon Press, 1975; pbk., 1983); *From Athens to Jerusalem* (Oxford: Clarendon Press, 1984); *The Mysteries of Religion* (Oxford: Blackwell, 1986); *Civil Peace and Sacred Order* (Oxford: Clarendon Press, 1989); *A Parliament of Souls* (Oxford: Clarendon Press, 1990); *God's World and the Great Awakening* (Oxford: Clarendon Press, 1991); *God, Religion and Reality* (London: SPCK, 1998); *Understanding Faith: Religious Belief and Its Place in Society*, St. Andrews Studies in Philosophy and Public Affairs (Exeter: Imprint Academic, 2009); *Ancient Mediterranean Philosophy* (London: Bloomsbury, 2013).

All passages from Plotinus are—except when I have entered a small disagreement—reprinted by permission of the publishers and Trustees of the Loeb Classical Library from Plotinus, *The Enneads*, 7 vols., Loeb Classical Library, vols. 440–5 and 468, translated by A. H. Armstrong (Cambridge, MA: Harvard University Press, copyright © 1966–88, by the President and Fellows of Harvard College). Loeb Classical Library® is a registered trademark of the President and Fellows of Harvard College. The physical volumes that I have employed were a present from Professor Armstrong himself (sadly, without additional annotations); my debt to him is very much greater. The Loeb Classical Library is also the best source of English versions of many other ancient authors quoted throughout this volume. Passages from Plato are drawn either from Benjamin Jowett's *Dialogues of Plato Translated into English with Analyses and Introductions* (Oxford: Oxford University Press, 1892) or else from Edith Hamilton and Huntington Cairns's *Collected Dialogues of Plato, including the Letters* (Princeton, NJ: Princeton University Press, 1982).

To all my friends, colleagues, students, and occasional critics I owe many thanks, and especially to Constantinos Athanasopoulos, Jay Bregman, Gillian Clark, Sarah Coakley, Kevin Corrigan, John Dillon, Douglas Hedley, Michael McGhee, John Spencer, and Panayiota Vassilopoulou. In the last months of writing I was saddened by the death of my former colleague Gillian Howie, who approached her own disease and death in the proper spirit of self-examination and philosophical invention, as well as arranging matters as well as could be for the benefit of her bereaved family. She would find much to disagree with in the monograph that follows, but perhaps also something of interest. It is my hope that others may do so too.

I should also acknowledge my debts to the University of Liverpool and to the University of Bristol: both have permitted me continued access to their libraries and other online resources. Implicit in that acknowledgment is a further debt, to the inventers and sustainers of the World Wide Web, which serves—in addition to its practical advantages—as a working image, *eikon aei eikonizomene* ("an image always reimagining itself"; after II.3 [52].18, 17), of the Plotinian Intellect.

PART I

Prolegomena

CHAPTER ONE

Why Read Plotinus?

Plotinus was born in Egypt, possibly in Lycopolis (whether Asyut in the Thebaid in Upper Egypt[1] or its colony in the Delta is uncertain), in about AD 204, studied under the philosopher Ammonius Saccas in Alexandria, joined the young emperor Gordian's ill-fated expedition against the Persians (being eager—it was said—to learn about the Persian and Indian philosophical traditions),[2] escaped to Antioch when Gordian was assassinated (AD 244), migrated to Rome, and spent the rest of his life leading philosophical discussions in the Platonic tradition. This brief account from Porphyry may conceal more than it reveals. Why, after all, did Plotinus go to Rome? The likelier thought is that he went back with the army led by Philip the Arab (who had arranged the coup) to claim authority in Rome (and perhaps Plotinus was more closely involved in this struggle than Porphyry ever knew).[3] Coups and countercoups followed rapidly, part of the Senate's struggle with the legions over the power to appoint new emperors. Philip was followed by Decius, Gallus, Aemilian, and at last by Valerian, who hung on long enough to make war on Persia and be humiliatingly cap-

---

1. Eunapius identifies his birthplace only as "Lyco," and this has usually been taken to mean the city in Upper Egypt that was the home of Alexander of Lycopolis, a third-century Christian bishop who wrote philosophically against the Manichaeans (Migne, *Patrologia Graeca* 18.409–48), and Meletius, another Christian bishop (d. AD 325), known for his refusal to allow back into communion those who renounced their Christian faith in the face of persecution.

2. M. Edwards, *Culture and Philosophy*, 31, plausibly proposes that it was *Porphyry* who had those interests (attested by his own frequent reference to Brahmans or Samanaeans).

3. Porphyry, after all, spent only a few years in Plotinus's company, and we have only his word (*Life* 7.51–2) that Plotinus "entrusted to [him] the editing of his writings." We might think differently about Plotinus if we had Amelius's account or Eustochius's. It is sadly plausible that Porphyry wrote, in part, to elevate his own importance in Plotinus's circle: see Bauckham, *Jesus and the Eyewitnesses*, 137–45.

tured and enslaved by Shapur I.[4] Valerian's son Gallienus favored Plotinus
but was judged to have fallen, after a good beginning, "into every vice, losing
his hold on the state through unforgivable apathy and despair."[5] In Gallienus's time the Gallic provinces seceded (and were reconquered), and the brief
empire of Palmyra served first as a buffer against the Parthians and then as
a force judged hostile to Rome's interests. Gallienus was murdered by his
legionaries in another coup and was succeeded by Claudius, "a thrifty man,
modest, tenacious in pursuit of justice . . . who nonetheless succumbed
to illness"[6] in the same year, AD 270, as Plotinus (and, possibly, Shapur).
Porphyry was away from Rome in Sicily at the time and had been invited
to join his former master Longinus back in Syria[7] (under Palmyrene rule),
where Amelius—Plotinus's other editor—was already resident (in Apamea).[8]
What happened when Aurelian (Claudius's successor) conquered Palmyra
(and incidentally executed Longinus, who had been Zenobia's adviser)[9] we
don't know in detail. Porphyry at least survived.

We know nothing about Plotinus's ancestry or early childhood. He does
refer to native Egyptian practices and theories, but probably no more knowl-
edgeably than should be expected of a resident of Egypt educated in the Hellenic tradition. It has been suggested that some of his linguistic peculiarities
are a sign of a Coptic upbringing, and that he might have been affected—if
only to disagreement—by contact with Sethian Gnostics and other esoteric
speculators.[10] Though Porphyry says that Plotinus planned to visit India, having heard rumors about Indian philosophy (at that time, both Hindu and Buddhist), he did not arrive there, and it seems in any case an odd and inefficient

4. See Zosimus, *New History*, 6–15 (chaps. 18–47).

5. Hekster, *Rome and Its Empire*, 104; Eutropius, *Breviarum* 9.8. See also Hekster, *Rome and Its Empire*, 100; Sextus Aurelius Victor, *Book of the Caesars* 33. According to the *Historia Augusta*, vol. 3, 43–5 (13.1–5), Zenobia of Palmyra "ruled for a long time, not in feminine fashion or with the ways of a woman, but surpassing in courage and skill not merely Gallienus, than whom any girl could have ruled more successfully, but also many an emperor" (cited by Hekster, *Rome and Its Empire*, 98). Eusebius, on the other hand, praised Gallienus as one who ended Valerian's persecution of Christians: *History*, 231–2, 238 (7.13, 7.23). Both versions may have some truth in them. On Gallienus, see further Blois, *Policy of Gallienus*, 175–94.

6. Hekster, *Rome and Its Empire*, 105; Eutropius, *Breviarum* 9.11.

7. Porphyry, *Life* 19.4–8. Porphyry doesn't say that he *accepted* the invitation. Where he went after Sicily we don't know.

8. "Here the long-robed philosophers paced beneath the colonnades that still extend for more than a mile through fields of asphodel and anemone, the barley sugar twisting of the col-umns reflecting the intricacies of their thought" (Stoneman, *Palmyra and Its Empire*, 132). See also Bowersock, "Hellenism of Zenobia"; Teixidor, "Palmyra in the Third Century."

9. Zosimus, *New History*, 18 (chap. 56). See also A. Watson, *Aurelian and the Third Cen-tury*, 78–84.

10. See MacCoull, "Plotinus the Egyptian?"

stratagem. There was probably some intellectual contact between the different traditions: the Mauryan emperor Aśoka had sent out Buddhist missionaries some centuries earlier, and Clement of Alexandria's teacher Pantaenus (c. 182–c. 212), a convert to Christianity from Stoicism, had visited India and found a Christian community already there.[11] But there is no solid reason to suppose that Plotinian philosophy was strongly influenced by such rumors as reached Rome or Egypt: his inspiration was drawn from the Platonic texts and from the long tradition of Hellenic speculation, including the Peripatetic, Skeptical, and Stoic schools. Discussions in Plotinus's seminars in Rome often began from readings of Plato, Aristotle, Numenius of Apamea, Alexander of Aphrodisias, and other Aristotelian commentators, and rambled thereafter.[12]

We don't know much about Plotinus's beginnings, because he wouldn't tell. Porphyry ascribed Plotinus's unwillingness to give details of his ancestry and early life to his "being ashamed of being in a body,"[13] and this judgment—along with familiar aphorisms describing philosophy as "the flight of the alone to the Alone"[14]—suggests to some that he was a solitary depressive or (worse still) a mystic.[15] Thus, Louth, speaking for many, contrasts the Plotinian goal with Augustine's conviction "that it is with others, in some kind of *societas*, that we are to seek God."[16] But is that not what Plotinus himself did, living among friends in Rome and drawing on their philosophical insights? It is likely that *Porphyry* was depressive: he records that Plotinus spotted his condition and ordered him away from Rome to Sicily to recover.[17] Plotinus himself was more robust. If he avoided the public

11. Eusebius, *History, 156* [4.10], cited by Chadwick, *Early Christian Thought*, 32. Cf. Philo, *Quod omnis probus liber sit* 14.93–6 (*Collected Works*, vol. 9, 63), on the refusal of Calanos the gymnosophist to be bullied into accompanying Alexander back to Greece. The anecdote traveled further than Calanos himself.

12. See Porphyry, *Life* 3.37–8.

13. Ibid., 1.2.

14. This is the phrase with which Porphyry elected to close the *Enneads*, though the treatise is the ninth in chronological order: VI.9 [9].11, 51 (MacKenna's translation). Armstrong (*Enneads, vol. 7*, 345) prefers "escape in solitude to the solitary." The meaning, as I shall argue later, has little to do with solitude or loneliness: the soul needs to be stripped of desires, opinions, and the like—"*monotheisa*" (see I.6 [1].5, 58)—not of companionship.

15. Note that "the fourth-century philosopher Themistius chastised [Neoplatonists] for leading an overly contemplative life in which they did not deign to emerge from their couches and secluded spots" (E. Watts, *City and School*, 17, citing Themistius, *Oration* 28.341d). Watts goes on to point out that Themistius's criticism is "unrepresentative of the historical reality," and that even those "most dedicated to a life of contemplation acted in accordance with the norms of conduct expected of men in their social position."

16. Louth, "Augustine," 137.

17. Eunapius has a slightly different story, though it is not clear where he had heard it: Porphyry "conceived a hatred of his own body and of being human," traveled to Lilybaeum in

baths or public rituals, this need not be because he was either shy or arrogant. Maybe he was following Seneca's advice!

> I have lodgings [wrote Seneca] right over a bathing establishment. So picture to yourself the assortment of sounds, which are strong enough to make me hate my very powers of hearing! When your strenuous gentleman, for example, is exercising himself by flourishing leaden weights; when he is working hard, or else pretends to be working hard, I can hear him grunt; and whenever he releases his imprisoned breath, I can hear him panting in wheezy and high-pitched tones. Or perhaps I notice some lazy fellow, content with a cheap rubdown, and hear the crack of the pummelling hand on his shoulder, varying in sound according as the hand is laid on flat or hollow. Then, perhaps, a professional comes along, shouting out the score; that is the finishing touch. Add to this the arresting of an occasional roysterer or pickpocket, the racket of the man who always likes to hear his own voice in the bathroom, or the enthusiast who plunges into the swimming-tank with unconscionable noise and splashing. Besides all those whose voices, if nothing else, are good, imagine the hair-plucker with his penetrating, shrill voice,—for purposes of advertisement,—continually giving it vent and never holding his tongue except when he is plucking the armpits and making his victim yell instead. Then the cakeseller with his varied cries, the sausageman, the confectioner, and all the vendors of food hawking their wares, each with his own distinctive intonation. . . . You may be sure that you are at peace with yourself, when no noise readies you, when no word shakes you out of yourself, whether it be of flattery or of threat, or merely an empty sound buzzing about you with unmeaning din. "What then?" you say, "is it not sometimes a simpler matter just to avoid the uproar?" I admit this. Accordingly, I shall change from my present quarters. I merely wished to test myself and to give myself practice. Why need I be tormented any longer, when Ulysses found so simple a cure for his comrades even against the songs of the Sirens?[18]

Sicily, and began starving himself to death. "But great Plotinus 'kept no vain watch' on these things, and either followed in his footsteps or inquired for the youth who had fled, and so found him lying there; then he found abundance of words that recalled to life his soul, as it was just about to speed forth from the body. Moreover he gave strength to his body so that it might contain his soul" (Eunapius, *Lives*, 343).

18. Seneca, *Moral Epistles*, vol. 1, 373–5, 381.

Plotinus also preferred not to join a religious friend (Amelius) in visits to "the temples at the New Moon and the feasts of the gods," saying that "they ought to come to me, not I to them."[19] The response has been interpreted as a rejection of those gods, but it is more likely that he meant that they could not be commanded, that it was for them to descend (see V.5 [32].8, 3). One of his complaints against "the Gnostics," after all, was—exactly—that they thought themselves superior to the gods (II.9 [33].9, 53–64). So also Plato distinguished magic and true religion "in that magic makes every effort to persuade the gods, whereas the truly religious behavior is to leave the gods a free choice, for they know better than we do what is good for us."[20] Porphyry tells us, concerning Plotinus, that "it seems that the gods often set him straight when he was going on a crooked course 'sending down a solid shaft of light,' which means that he wrote what he wrote under their inspection and supervision."[21] We should not chase after that light, however, "but wait quietly till it appears, preparing oneself to contemplate it, as the eye awaits the rising of the sun" (V.5 [32].8).[22] Consider also the advice of Zosimus of Panopolis, the alchemist:

> Do not roam about searching for God; but sit calmly at home, and God, who is everywhere, and not confined in the smallest place like the daemons, will come to you. And being calm in body, also calm your passions, desire and pleasure and anger and grief and the twelve portions of death. In this way, taking control of yourself, you will summon the divine [to come] to you, and truly it will come, that which is everywhere and nowhere.[23]

19. Porphyry, *Life* 10.34–41. M. Edwards, *Neoplatonic Saints*, 86n202, speaks, quite without warrant, of Plotinus's "contempt for cultic piety," but it is true that Proclus made more of such public ceremonial than—according to Porphyry—Plotinus did.

20. Graf, *Magic in the Ancient World*, 27, after Plato, *Laws* 10. E. Clarke, *Iamblichus' "De mysteriis,"* 23–4, points out that Iamblichus, now remembered for preferring theurgic rituals to philosophy, also insisted that the initiative must lie with God, and that those rituals were not magical techniques.

21. Porphyry, *Life* 23.18–21.

22. See Hadot, *Plotinus; or, the Simplicity of Vision*, 61.

23. Cited by Fowden, *Egyptian Hermes*, 122. Zosimus, born in the late fourth century AD, employed alchemical images (chopping, boiling, braising) to describe self-transformation, echoing stories about shamanic initiations (Jung, *Psychology and Alchemy*). These don't seem to be imaginative techniques favored by Plotinus: he advocates scrubbing our selves and our internal statues—not flaying them or breaking them in pieces. But see Plato, *Euthydemus* 285c, where Socrates offers himself to Dionysodorus: "he may put me in the pot, like Medea the Colchian, kill me, boil me, if he will only make me good."

This is what Plotinus probably intended.

Plotinus was trusted to manage the persons and estates of orphans left in his charge, "so his house [actually, the house of an aristocratic Roman widow] was full of young lads and maidens."[24] He kept his head in the jealous atmosphere of Rome's intellectual cliques and military feuds. He drew lessons—as did Marcus Aurelius,[25] but to a different end—from sculpture, dances, and athletic competitions, as well as from rumors about Egyptian priests and, maybe, Indian gymnosophists and from the works of Plato and Aristotle. "In answering questions he made clear both his benevolence to the questioner and his intellectual vigour."[26] When he began to suffer from the disease that killed him,[27] his friends avoided him, because he was still inclined to greet everyone with a kiss (a standard greeting for family and friends).[28] In character, in brief, he was more sanguine than melancholic, and readier than most philosophers to listen and to learn.[29]

That this brief summary of Plotinus's life and character is now needed is odd. Most philosophers—and in later years most Christian theologians—were members of an educated elite who were expected to take on social duties, as well as to be able to control their moods and tempers, and to use

24. Porphyry, *Life* 9.10.
25. "Consider song, dance, wrestling as metaphors for life as a whole, and bring the same analytic process to bear on life also" (Aurelius, *Meditations* 11.2), but Aurelius uses this to suggest that we should despise the bits that go to make up the whole. See J. Miller, *Measures of Wisdom*, 176: "Marcus will talk himself into a state of morbid melancholy or complete contempt for the world without knowing how to cure himself, without assuming that a cure exists." See also Sellars, "Aurelius and the Tradition of Spiritual Exercises."
26. Porphyry, *Life* 13.10.
27. Scholars have suggested that this was either tuberculosis or leprosy—but the much more obvious solution is that it was the "plague of Cyprian," which struck the Mediterranean world between 251 and 270. Porphyry (*Life* 2.6–10) himself links Plotinus's disease with the onset of that plague and adds that it grew worse once his masseurs died and he was no longer getting his daily massage. McNeil, *Plagues and People*, 131–2, suggests that this (and also the Antonine plague a century earlier) was either smallpox or measles. Grmek, *Diseases in the Ancient World*, suggests that it was typhus; see also Grmek, "Les maladies et la mort."
28. And perhaps he had another reason to withdraw from Rome, and his acquaintances had another reason to avoid him after Gallienus's assassination. We can guess that many moved from the city at that time of plague and disorder, to escape infection as well as senatorial vengeance, and to gain some quiet. A country *villa* was, conventionally at least, a more private and casual place than the urban *domus*, where associates and dependents could expect to be made welcome; see Hales, *Roman House*, 20–3.
29. See also Ousager, *Plotinus on Selfhood*, for a serious attempt to read the *Enneads* within a political context. Ousager perhaps exaggerates the political significance of some Plotinian anecdotes and phrases (see esp. 224), but he is right to remind us of the political backdrop.

their wealth—such as it was—with proper generosity.[30] The *Enneads* were for centuries the channel through which the Platonic tradition was passed to Christian, Jewish, Islamic, and early-modern philosophers, and they had enormous influence also outside the philosophical academies, in art, poetry, and the nonacademic esoteric tradition.[31] Twentieth-century commentators were inclined to place him in the supposed decay of rational, Hellenic thought, though they gave him a little credit for avoiding the excesses, as they thought, of Iamblichus and the *Hermetic Corpus*. The truth is otherwise. Art, science, and philosophy owe Platonists, and "Neoplatonists," a lot, and may yet owe more.

The text we know as the *Enneads* would nowadays be called *The Collected Works of Plotinus of Alexandria, Edited by Porphyry of Tyre*. Plotinus wrote at speed, without troubling to reread or correct his work (his eyesight being too weak), and the resulting treatises varied considerably in length. Thirty years after Plotinus's death, Porphyry produced what became the standard edition by reordering the treatises into six volumes, each of nine separate treatises, in obedience to some numerological (Pythagorean) fancy. Sometimes he broke up one long piece into several or included some scrappy notes as a single treatise. The whole provides a reasonable order in which to tackle the texts, but modern readers may prefer to concentrate on single treatises or at any rate to begin—for example—with the very first that Plotinus wrote, "*On Beauty*" (I.6 [1]).[32]

Plotinus's world, the social and imaginative world of third-century Rome, is certainly not ours. Sadly, we have no reliable narrative about the place and period and must piece our picture together from passing references in later writings, which usually have an agenda. Briefly, it was a time of recurrent plagues, earthquakes, mutinies, slave revolts, and invasions (though none, as yet, that reached down into Italy). It was "a time of the most calamitous instability," "one of the darkest periods of Roman history."[33] There was a newly revived *Persian* Empire to the east, beyond

---

30. E. Watts, *City and School*, 17–9. See, e.g., M. Edwards, *Neoplatonic Saints*, 77–83 (*Life of Proclus* 14–7).

31. See Merlan, *From Platonism to NeoPlatonism*; Merlan, *Monopsychism, Mysticism, Metaconsciousness*; Adamson, *Arabic Plotinus*. On Plotinus's religious and aesthetic influence, see Balthasar, *Glory of the Lord*, 280–313.

32. I shall rely almost entirely on Armstrong's version for the Loeb Classical Library. The most popular Anglophone version was a lifelong labor by MacKenna. Other Anglophone selections include O'Brien, *Essential Plotinus*; Uzdavinys, *Heart of Plotinus*; Corrigan, *Reading Plotinus*. See also the Francophone series of commentaries, beginning with Plotin traités 1–6, ed. Brisson and Pradeau.

33. Blois, *Policy of Gallienus*, 1.

the former frontiers of the Roman Empire, and brief Gallic and Palmyrene Empires to the north and east, even within those older boundaries. Emperors, usually brought to power by their armies and sluggishly endorsed by the Senate, did not have long reigns. Christians were sometimes persecuted, at the whim of local magistrates or occasional imperial dictat, but were also often ignored. Theorists, artists, and engineers of one school or another came from all around the Mediterranean basin, and beyond, but there seem to have been few inventions or innovations in medicine or engineering. What educated people mostly believed was that the earth was spherical (but that the Antipodes were beyond our reach), that the fixed and wandering ("planetary") stars revolved around the earth, that there were demons loose among us, and that there was an intelligible order to the cosmos (i.e., that there was indeed a *cosmos* rather than a jumble of disconnected bits).

Plotinus could suppose that each of us, upon our first entry to the natural universe, was and is incarnate as a star (IV.4 [28].5),[34] and that such troubles as we suffer here and now are often, though not always, retribution for the crimes we committed in past lives. "There is no accident in a man's becoming a slave, nor is he taken prisoner in war by chance, nor is outrage done on his body without due cause, but he was once the doer of that which he now suffers; and a man who made away with his mother will be made away with by a son when he has become a woman, and one who has raped a woman will be a woman in order to be raped" (III.2 [47].13, 11–3). There are still people, even philosophers, prepared to believe in karmic reincarnation, but I know none who seriously think that their own higher selves are still embodied in the stars of heaven, which we now conceive as very distant and indifferent suns, not as the innumerable eyes of night. Most educated Westerners doubt the existence of *daimones* or the power of magic (but accept the existence of intangible forces which we can often put to work for us, and increasingly rely on gadgets controlled by verbal commands and ciphers). We Westerners know, or at least must strongly believe, much more about the biochemistry of love than ever Plotinus knew, and we much more easily believe that such love is an obsessive madness, functioning only to bind us, briefly, as breeders.[35] We know, or at least we think we know, that there need never be a single goal, a good that serves all natures and desires. We

---

34. See Scott, *Origen and the Stars*, for a history of this and related ideas about the stars.

35. Some moderns even seem to be endorsing Lucretius's judgment that "casual sex" is better if it is not contaminated by erotic passion, still less romantic love: "Nor doth that man who keeps away from love / Yet lack the fruits of Venus; rather takes / Those pleasures which are free of penalties. / For the delights of Venus, verily, / Are more unmixed for mortals sane-of-soul / Than for those sick-at-heart with love-pining" (Lucretius, *On the Nature of Things* 4.1026–8).

know, or think we know, that human intelligence has emerged from common animal intelligence, by neo-Darwinian accident, and isn't an angelic visitor to the world of nature. And unlike most Hellenic thinkers, we think pity is a virtue,[36] and for grown men to love boys a vice. What has Plotinus, or the Platonic tradition, to do with us and our necessities? "It was all so unimaginably different, and all so long ago."[37]

One answer might simply be that we Westerners might, after all, be wrong. To modify a remark of Chesterton's, it is the main purpose of historical or comparative philosophy to show that humanity can be great and even glorious under conditions, and with beliefs, quite different from our own.[38] When modernists deny even the possibility of metempsychosis or of nonrational intelligence or of the thought that we are indeed asleep and dreaming, they restrict our options—and create great difficulties for their own, unreflective theories. If it is truly *impossible*, for example, that S has been a woman, or G a man, it is also absurd to ask us to imagine what we would feel if we variously were, and so absurd to demand of us the moral imagination that is the root of justice.[39] If it were impossible to conceive that we're asleep and dreaming, it would also be impossible to conceive that there is a real world independent of our feelings and experience. If the only intelligence were strictly rational (i.e., founded only in self-evident truth and purely logical inference), none of us would ever know a thing. If human intelligence is only a modified "animal intelligence" (and animals are, like us, seed-scattering robots controlled by "selfish genes"), then we have no reason to expect our reasonings to have the power and range we think they do.[40] The commoner opinions of humankind (which may be closer to Plo-

36. See Ferwerda, "Pity in Plotinus," for a balanced account of Plotinus's opinion of pity.

37. McNeice, "Autumn Journal" (1938) (*Poems*, 139). The factor that McNeice found most alien was the accepted presence of slaves—people stripped of honor and dignity.

38. See Chesterton, *Fancies versus Fads*, 176.

39. The point here is that those who reject the mere *possibility* of metempsychosis do so in the conviction that my identity is indissolubly linked to my actual physical being: no one born in any other form could *possibly* be me. It may be a mere "matter of fact" that I have never been a bush and a bird and a dumb fish in the sea (any more than I have ever lived in Japan or been a candidate for high office in the church or in the state). But that is not to reject the notion that I "could have been." For this and related issues, see Madell, *Idea of the Self*, who deploys an ingenious argument that if—as seems intuitively reasonable—I *could* have been one of two identical twins (but, obviously, not both), then I am not simply identical with a particular physical being. See also Taliaferro, *Golden Cord*, 54–6.

40. "With me the horrid doubt always arises whether the convictions of man's mind, which have been developed from the mind of the lower animals, are of any value or are at all trustworthy. Would anyone trust in the convictions of a monkey's mind, if there are any convictions in

tinus's than to those of the modern intelligentsia) might be correct, even
when they contradict our fashionable theories.

We might be wrong, and Plotinus, even if occasionally in error, might
be mostly right. Oddly, modern scientists and mathematicians, including
Gödel and Bohr, have been more sympathetic to Platonic ideas than the
philosophers who rejected them, supposedly in the name of science.[41] But
even if he were totally wrong, it would still be worth considering what he
has to say. How else shall we understand our own ideas if we have no notion
of the possibilities we are denying? And even if we could, somehow, understand ourselves, how shall we understand any others? Plotinus is especially
important for us to understand, since his influence, and the influence of
Platonists and "Neoplatonists," have been so significant for centuries, in
Western and Eastern Christendom, in Muslim thought, and Jewish. The
medieval and early-modern philosophers most often studied in philosophy
departments themselves knew what they owed to Platonists. Students of
modern philosophy who have forgotten this (or never been informed) will
often misread the very authors they prefer: Leibniz, Spinoza, Berkeley,
Kant, and Hegel rephrase Plotinian ideas; even the founders of twentieth-
century analytical philosophy, such as Moore and Frege, repeat Plotinian
and Platonic arguments, not always with acknowledgment. Nor is it only
"Western" philosophy that is illuminated by an understanding of ancient
Western history. It isn't necessary to think that Plotinus was influenced by
Indian or any other Eastern philosophers,[42] as some twentieth-century commentators thought: everything he wrote can be understood within the tradition of Hellenic philosophy (which was itself open to other influences). But
many commentators have testified that there are at least some similarities
with Indian or Chinese thought, and that those traditions, therefore, are not
wholly alien to "Western" sensibilities. To read and even partly understand
Plotinus, therefore, is to have a key to much of the human philosophical
tradition. My hope is that anyone sufficiently exasperated or intrigued by
the following monograph will at least be inspired to read some few of the

---

such a mind?" (Darwin, *Life and Letters*, vol. 1, 315–6). I have addressed this issue repeatedly in
other volumes; see, most recently, "Folly to the Greeks."

41. "The Platonistic view is the only one tenable. Thereby I mean the view that mathematics describes a non-sensual reality, which exists independently of the human mind and is
only perceived, and probably perceived very incompletely, by the human mind" (Gödel, "Basic
Theorems on the Foundations of Mathematics," 322–3). For further discussion, see Spencer,
Eternal Law.

42. Numenius of Apamea (*Fragmenta*, frag. 1), however, whom some accused Plotinus
of copying (Porphyry, *Life* 17.16–25), makes mention of "Brachmanes, Ioudaioi, Magoi and
Aiguptes."

Enneads: they will then discover that for all his subtlety and high ideals Plotinus was also calmly commonsensical—and often very funny.

And of course the fact remains that he might actually be right.

All contemporary writers share to some extent the contemporary outlook—even those, like myself, who seem most opposed to it. Nothing strikes me more when I read the controversies of past ages than the fact that both sides were usually assuming without question a good deal which we should now absolutely deny. They thought that they were as completely opposed as two sides could be, but in fact they were all the time secretly united—united with each other and against earlier and later ages—by a great mass of common assumptions. We may be sure that the characteristic blindness of the twentieth century—the blindness about which posterity will ask, "But how could they have thought that?"—lies where we have never suspected it, and concerns something about which there is untroubled agreement between Hitler and President Roosevelt or between Mr. H. G. Wells and Karl Barth. None of us can fully escape this blindness, but we shall certainly increase it, and weaken our guard against it, if we read only modern books. Where they are true they will give us truths which we half knew already. Where they are false they will aggravate the error with which we are already dangerously ill. The only palliative is to keep the clean sea breeze of the centuries blowing through our minds, and this can be done only by reading old books. Not, of course, that there is any magic about the past. People were no cleverer then than they are now; they made as many mistakes as we. But not the same mistakes. They will not flatter us in the errors we are already committing; and their own errors, being now open and palpable, will not endanger us. Two heads are better than one, not because either is infallible, but because they are unlikely to go wrong in the same direction. To be sure, the books of the future would be just as good a corrective as the books of the past, but unfortunately we cannot get at them.[43]

43. Lewis, introduction to Athanasius, *De incarnatione*, xx.

CHAPTER TWO

How to Read Plotinus

Plotinus might be "literally" and "factually" right. To suppose that only our own era and only our authorities are immune to the sort of complacent error that we identify in earlier eras and authorities is conceit. "After Aristotle and Ptolemy, the idea that the earth moves—that strange, ancient and 'entirely ridiculous,' Pythagorean view—was thrown on the rubbish heap of history, only to be revived by Copernicus and to be forged by him into a weapon for the defeat of its defeaters."[1] What other utterly ridiculous views will be reforged by our successors we cannot tell. But till that day, we may as well acknowledge that we shall not read Plotinus for any detailed medical or astronomical information—even when we partly agree with him. In his treatise "Against the Gnostics" Plotinus mocks sectarian attempts to cure disease by exorcising demons.[2]

They themselves most of all impair the inviolate purity of the higher powers. . . . For when they write magic chants, intending to address them to those powers, not only to the soul but to those above it as well, what are they doing except making the powers obey the word and follow the lead of people who say spells and charms and conjurations, any one of us who is well skilled in the art of saying precisely the right things in the right ways, songs and cries and aspirated and hissing sounds and everything else which their writings say has magic power in the higher

---

1. Feyerabend, *Against Method*, 49.
2. See Plutarch, "Table Talk" 7.706e (*Moralia*, vol. 9, 55): "sorcerers advise those possessed by demons to recite and name over to themselves the Ephesian letters." These magical charms are attested from at least the fourth century BC; they seem to be six seemingly unmeaning terms: *askion kataskion lix tetrax damnameneus aision* (Clement of Alexandria, *Stromata* 5.8), either recited or worn as amulets.

world? . . . When they say they free themselves from diseases, if they meant they did so by temperance and orderly living, they would speak well; but in fact they assume that the diseases are evil spirits, and claim to be able to drive them out by their word; by this claim they might make themselves more impressive in the eyes of the masses, who wonder at the power of magicians, but would not persuade sensible people that diseases do not have their origin in strain or excess or deficiency or decay, and in general in changes which have their origin outside or inside. The cures of diseases make this clear too. With a vigorous motion of the bowels or the giving of a drug the illness goes through the downward passage and out, and it goes out too with bloodletting; and fasting also heals. Does the evil spirit starve, and does the drug make it waste away? . . . If it came into the man without any cause of disease, why is he not always ill? But if there was a cause, what need is there of the spirit to produce the illness? For the cause is sufficient by itself to produce the fever. (II.9 [33].14)[3]

And when considering the stars, Plotinus rejected the Aristotelian notion that the heavens and their denizens were made of a different sort of stuff than terrestrial matter (II.1 [40].2, 14–7). They followed the tracks they did because that was how space was configured. Not till many centuries later did Nicolas of Cusa and his follower Copernicus perceive that Platonists should be more comfortable if the *sun* were the center round which the "planets," including this terrestrial globe, were orbiting, and if their "setting" were simply something that happened "from our point of view" (III.1 [3].6, 13–4). Giordano Bruno's further insight that the stars were suns, that there were no celestial spheres to hem us in, was also difficult for Hellenic thinkers to see—except that Plotinus had been much more at ease with the Infinite than any of his predecessors and most of his successors. The birth of modern science was from Platonic and Neoplatonic roots—and we have not yet fully internalized even its most robust conclusions (e.g., that the earth rotates and travels round the sun). We still speak of sunrise and sunset.

---

3. "Bloodletting," as advised by Galen, now seems to most of us a harmful superstition. But it is still the treatment of choice for victims of hemochromatosis, a genetic disease endemic in Europe that involves the abnormal retention of iron, and for some other conditions: for example, metabolic syndrome—"an increasingly prevalent but poorly understood clinical condition characterized by insulin resistance, glucose intolerance, dyslipidemia, hypertension, and obesity" (Michelson et al., "Effects of Phlebotomy-Induced Reduction"). But both bloodletting and enemas (which Plotinus himself declined: *Life* 2.1–3) perhaps seemed plausible treatments on the basis of a purgative model of healing not all that far removed from the exorcists' model!

Plotinus's detailed factual opinions were not absurd, even if he accepted what was then the commonsense opinion that there were demons, that the stars were living and immortal beings, that "magic," in some sense, "worked." But he was not writing astronomical or medical treatises, and the use he makes of commonsense opinion, and expert theory, was protreptic and allegorical more than "factual." He was writing chiefly, not about "the physical world," but about the world of our experience, the world we live, in which it is obviously true that there are differing modes of consciousness and symbol. It is that discourse, and how he manages it (including discourse about the world itself), that are my central concern in everything that follows. Phenomenology, not physics, is my goal. What would it be like to live Plotinus's world (i.e., the world that he proposes), and not ours?[4] How shall we awaken from the "dream and delirium" of ordinary waking life? What is it about that "ordinary life" that warrants the description that it is, as Marcus Aurelius said, delirium?[5]

Am I ignoring Hadot's warning?

> We run the constant risk of mistaking a schoolroom commonplace for a revelatory detail. A psychoanalyst may think to have discovered a symptom where, in fact, there is only an impersonal banality. For example, one could follow the methods so dear to modern literary criticism, and approach Plotinus by studying the fundamental images which dominate his work: the circle, the tree, the dance. But most of these images are not spontaneous: they are traditional and imposed by the texts to be commented on or the themes to be developed. No doubt, we could specify the transformations Plotinus makes them undergo; the fact remains that they do not emanate from the depths of his personality.[6]

This is not unlike Armstrong's contention that Plotinus was not concerned with the myths he inconsistently allegorizes. But my attention is indeed on the *tradition*, not primarily on Plotinus's own personality: what do these images convey, and what do the myths mean, at least as Plotinus and his contemporaries would have understood them? Nor is it absurd to think that the way he *plays* with or distorts the images tells us something of what

---

4. That it is important to *live* the world, not merely talk about it, is attested by Porphyry, *To Marcella*, 33–4 (§8): "For it is a man's actions that naturally afford demonstrations of his opinions, and whoever holds a belief must live in accordance with it, in order that he may himself be a faithful witness to the hearers of his words."

5. Aurelius, *Meditations* 2.17.1.

6. Hadot, *Plotinus; or, the Simplicity of Vision*, 18.

he himself was like and what he wished to tell us. As Ferwerda remarks, in his survey of the images and metaphors to be found in the texts, "[Plotin] s'est servi d'un vocabulaire existant, mais il l'a transformé en lui donant un sens à lui, afin de l'adapter aux exigencies de sa proper pensée."[7] At the very least, just saying that an image is a "commonplace," even a banal commonplace, risks losing something of significance. Plotinus would have had an education in rhetoric (it was part of the normal curriculum for the educated elite) and so would have been used to acknowledging and expanding literary and other allusions in the texts he studied.[8] Hadot's real quarrel was with those who sought to *psychoanalyze* Plotinus, mostly on the basis of misunderstood remarks of Porphyry's.[9] But Hadot too has his image of Plotinus, better grounded and more useful!

As many of Plotinus's recent commentators have suggested, the text is not to be read *simply* as the record of an argument. Plotinus does argue. That is, he offers solutions to intellectual problems, and often argues the case backward and forward till it isn't entirely clear what his conclusion is. He *argues*: it is certainly not true that he merely reports the results of mystical experience and expects us to believe his revelations. "Since he encouraged his students to ask questions," Porphyry tells us, "the course [that he offered in Rome] was lacking in order and there was a great deal of pointless chatter."[10] Porphyry felt differently about the habit when he was the one asking questions: to an auditor who complained that he had come to listen to *Plotinus's* exposition and that Porphyry was taking up too much time, Plotinus is said to have answered that until he had solved Porphyry's problems, there would be nothing to expound. But though Plotinus argued and counterargued, it was important to him that the conclusions were not merely, as we now misleadingly call it, "theoretical." The goal was not simply to decide that one proposition or another best fitted into a systematic science but rather to come to see the reality that such propositions might express— and still more, to be the sort of person who could see that reality. What was aimed at was a *real* assent, not merely a notional one.[11] It was not enough,

7. Ferwerda, *Signification des images*, 23. There is a more detailed and helpful discussion of many Plotinian images in P. Miller, *Biography*.

8. See E. Watts, *City and School*, 4–5.

9. Hadot, *Plotinus; or, the Simplicity of Vision*, 74–82.

10. Porphyry, *Life* 3.37–8. See Snyder, *Teachers and Texts*, 111–8, for a short comparison of Plotinus's reported techniques and those attributed to other ancient teachers.

11. See Newman, *Grammar of Assent*, 93–4: "[Some philosophers] sit at home, and reach forward to distances which astonish us; but they hit without grasping, and are sometimes as confident about shadows as about realities. They have worked out by a calculation the lie of a country which they never saw, and mapped it by means of a gazetteer; and, like blind men,

as it were, to "know the way to Larisa" and be able to repeat the directions: what mattered was getting to Larisa and knowing the way because we could see where it was and where we were at present in relation to Larisa.

Chittick, writing about Islamic thought, quotes one of his former professors at Tehran University to the effect that some of his young colleagues "know everything one can possibly know about a text, except what it says":[12] which is to say, what it *means* for their own lives and for others. That must be a warning to us all—not to mistake scholastic expertise for philosophical insight.

The illustration I have just offered (drawn rather from Plato's *Meno*[13] than from Plotinus) is both a reminder that Plotinus often employed metaphors and a further illustration of the way that simple metaphors can differ from the sort of images he often used. To find the way to Larisa we must go there—but the sort of alteration of consciousness that Plotinus has in mind is, notoriously, "not a journey for the feet" (I.6 [1].8, 23). He wishes to "change our minds" and offers, in effect, an unsystematic set of exercises to accomplish that. Changing the way we look at things, and so changing the premises and observations that we shall find plausible or obvious, involves more than argument.

> But how is the good man affected by magic and drugs? He is incapable of being affected in his soul by enchantment, and his rational part would not be affected, nor would he change his mind; but he would be affected in whatever part of the irrational in the All there is in him, or rather this part would be affected; but he will feel no passionate loves provoked by drugs, if falling in love happens when one soul assents to the affection of the other [i.e., to the life of the living body]. But just as the irrational part of him is affected by incantations so he himself by counter-chants and counter-incantations will dissolve the powers on the other side. (IV.4 [28].43)

Those counterchants and counterincantations are arguments (IV.4 [28].43, 19ff.) and not unmeaning strings of nonsense syllables.[14] As Arm-

though they can put a stranger on his way, they cannot walk straight themselves, and do not feel it quite their business to walk at all."

12. Chittick, *Science of the Cosmos*, 9. See also Kingsley, *Ancient Philosophy*, 369: "true esoteric teaching aims not at filling the disciple or pupil with mere fascinating theories but with opportunities for making these ideas and theories real in his own experience."

13. Plato, *Meno* 97a. Larisa was a city in Thessaly and Meno's birthplace—and so a journey there would, for Meno, be significantly a journey "home."

14. Though there is a case even for such spells: see P. Miller, "In Praise of Nonsense."

strong has written, "philosophical discussion and reflection are not simply means for solving intellectual problems (though they are and must be that). They are also charms for the deliverance of the soul."[15] But not all Plotinus's charms are simply argumentative: some require us instead to use our imagination. As Chittick also urges us:

> If the heart is to perceive the Word of God resounding in itself, and if it is to intensify its own spiritual instinct, it must open what Ibn 'Arabi calls its "two eyes"—the eye of reason and the eye of imagination, or discursive thought and mythic vision.[16]

At the least, they require us to read attentively—and sympathetically: "if there is no sympathy for a certain way of thinking, or at least for the human beings who thought so, there can be no proper understanding in philosophy."[17]

Dillon, commenting on the image in V.8 [31].9, to which I shall often return:

> Here we are being called upon to use our imagination creatively, to attain to a purely intellectual conception. It is worthwhile, perhaps, to try to perform the exercise as Plotinus prescribes. I have attempted it repeatedly, and the sticking point is always the instruction, once one has conjured up the universe (as a luminous, diaphanous globe, with all its parts distinct and functioning), then to think away the spatiality ("*aphelon ton onkon labe*")—and not just by shrinking it! It is in fact an excellent spiritual exercise. Calling upon God here is no empty formality. If it is done effectively, it has a quasi-theurgic result: "He may come, bringing his own cosmos, with all the gods that dwell in it—He who is the one God, and all the gods, where each is all, blending into a unity, distinct in powers, but all one god, in virtue of that divine power of many facets." In other words, if you perform the exercise correctly, you will achieve a mystical vision of the whole noetic cosmos. And Plotinus knew what he was talking about.[18]

---

15. Armstrong, "Plotinus," 260, after V.3 [49].17. See also Plato, *Laws* 2.659e: "that is why we have what we call songs, which are really charms for the soul. These are in fact deadly serious devices for producing this concord (*sumphonian*) we are talking about; but the souls of the young cannot bear to be serious, so we use the terms game and song for the charms, and practice them as such."

16. Chittick, *Science of the Cosmos*, 71.

17. Staal, *Advaita and Neoplatonism*, 7.

18. Dillon, "Plotinus and the Transcendental Imagination" (= Dillon, *Golden Chain*, 58–69).

Similar, though less detailed, comments, as I observed before, have been made by other commentators, including Hadot, Shaw, and Rappe. Are they right to suppose that this is how Plotinus intended to be read, and are they right to hint that reading the text like this can have the kind of consequences that he perhaps describes? What other writers of his day, or recognizably within his tradition, proposed similar devices? What did the myths and metaphors they employed *mean* to them and to their first readers? Can Plotinus's philosophy be understood without attention to these devices, or must understanding come only after the sort of transformation that perhaps they engineer?

One further warning is required. As Hall has pointed out, we cannot appreciate a play without experiencing it, exactly, as a *performance*—rather, as many performances, by many different actors and directors, on many different occasions.[19] Taking the bare text as the "real play" is like preferring a recipe to a finished dish, or a music score to a concert. Correspondingly, Plotinus's written text (especially, as Rappe has said, if it is more like a "meditation manual")[20] has to come alive for us in our response to it. This may also be assisted by our (necessarily partial) understanding of how the original audience could hear or read it, but there is little gain in aiming only at an "authentic" interpretation: we don't have the necessary information, and even if we did, we are ourselves quite different people than his original audience.[21] The contrary error, of reading whatever we please into an intrinsically unmeaningful row of symbols, is even less helpful. There are practical and hermeneutic problems here—not to be solved by dour refusal to speculate or engage—but there is also a theoretical issue: Platonists, it might seem, *did* prefer the score to the performance! The real thing, the form of beauty, is to be grasped noetically, and any attempt to realize it in the merely phenomenal world will be defeated by the recalcitrance of things. Even the attempt may be a sign of weakness. Is this an argument, after all, for abstracting formal arguments from the mere text and refusing all extraneous, accidental associations of the sort I shall be examining? What follows will be my answer.

---

19. P. Hall, *Exposed by the Mask*, 9–10, 13–4.

20. Rappe, *Reading Neoplatonism*, 3.

21. "Authenticity is a will-o'-the-wisp. . . . It changes from decade to decade" (P. Hall, *Exposed by the Mask*, 73).

CHAPTER THREE

Theories about Metaphor

By Aristotle's misleadingly straightforward account, "metaphor consists in applying to one thing a word that belongs to something else."[1] The simplest theory of metaphor is the Aristotelian: we use metaphors purely ornamentally to say things that should better be said in more appropriate ways. Or else perhaps we speak "metaphorically" when we do not yet have words that are fitted more exactly to the relevant realities. And it is then assumed, without much argument, that all words originally have purely corporeal referents and are thereafter used to speak of noncorporeal experience. All three assumptions are contentious, and the last especially so. Why, after all, should we suppose that our ancestors were first of all acquainted with merely corporeal realities, or even that they had any notion of the "merely corporeal"? Corporeality is a piece of theory: our first worlds are subjective, human, meaningful. We recognize smiles and faces long before we form any notion of merely corporeal things, existing in their sunny selfishness beyond our gaze or grasp. Waves of feeling are as real, as unavoidable, as particular things. Our first language is one of cries and laughter. Even our later language is not centered upon merely corporeal things. The things we live among and recognize are identified by their historical and personal associations, quite apart from any "merely material" properties. The land *we* live in may be a quite different land from others. "When Hindu and Muslim dispute over Ayodhya, or Hopi and Navaho over the Five Peaks, or Protestant and Catholic Irish over the lesser streets of Belfast, they are all contending for their own visions of Eden."[2] We mind about symbols and feel them

---

1. *Poetics* 1457b6f. Aristotle's Greek does not explicitly use the metaphor of "belonging": *metaphora estin onomatos allotriou epiphora.*
2. Citing my own *G. K. Chesterton*, 48.

more deeply than naïve materialists imagine. A broken and contrite heart is not "literally" in need of surgical intervention, but it is also not a merely ornamental image. To experience contrition is to ache.[3] It is the *phenomenal* heart that breaks, the originally experienced reality from which we abstract or create the image of a merely corporeal organ. A broken heart is not a metaphor, drawn from external observations of a defective organ, but an actual experience.[4] Similarly, the light that is identified with intellectual enlightenment in many human languages is not so called for its notional resemblance to the light of day: the light of the mind and the light of day are alike in bringing color, detail, and direction—not always in the same degree. So Maimonides (1135–1204):

> Sometimes Truth flashes up before us with daylight brightness, but soon it is obscured by the limitations of our material nature and social habits, and we fall back into a darkness almost as black as that in which we were before. We are thus like a person whose surroundings are from time to time lit up by lightning, while in the intervals he is plunged into pitch-dark night. Some of us experience such flashes of illumination frequently, until they are in almost perpetual brightness, so that the night turns for them into daylight. . . . Some see a single flash of light in their whole lives. . . . With others again there are long or short intermissions between the flashes of illumination and lastly there are those who are not granted that their darkness be illuminated by a flash of lightning, but only, as it were, by the gleam of some polished object or the like of it, such as the stones and suchlike substances which shine in the dark night.[5]

What now seems "metaphorical," in other words, may once have been simply descriptive: now reckoned metaphor because we have decided that the words somehow "belong" chiefly or entirely to some particular realities. As Harrison asks, "why should we suppose that the literal is located in pudding-talk rather than time-talk?"[6] An expression may *become* a metaphor when one particular meaning is more often remembered. Stanford, writing particularly on Greek metaphor, suggests, for example, that the

---

3. See J. Van den Berg, *Phenomenological Approach to Psychiatry*.

4. Crowley, *Love and Sleep*, 496. Cf. IV.3 [27].23, 44–6: the heart is the appropriate housing for the "seething of the spirited part."

5. Maimonides, *Guide of the Perplexed*, 44.

6. Harrison, "Metaphor," 232.

term "*anthos*," now routinely translated "blossom," may have as its core meaning merely "what rises to the top."[7] It can, after all, be applied as easily to scum, rashes, and beards as to flowers. By this account, "*oromen anthoun pelagos Aigaion nekrois*"[8] does not mean "we see the deep *aflower* with corpses." To which some readers might reply, of course, that the phrase still carries some such image along with it, even if the phrase did not "originally" mean "aflower." In the case of light, we now have the weird result that the light identified with electromagnetic radiation is supposed to be "real light," though most of it is invisible, "dark light." It would be more sensible to think that light as physicists intend the term is metaphorically so called, since most of us are helped to see by some of it. The first senses of "sight" and "light" are the subjective. The physical land we live on lies on the far side of many experienced landscapes—an issue to which I shall return in considering how we come to realize a shared, "objective" cosmos.

Distinctions matter, and what at first was classed together may turn out to be really different. In which case, the older terms now seem inappropriate, poetical, or ornamental—maybe even evoking inappropriate emotions. Stebbing's familiar complaint against the use of metaphors was that it was "largely emotive, when it is not merely the result of unclear thinking."[9] The catch, of course, is that this very claim itself embodies metaphors: "largely," "emotive," "result," "unclear," if any words are metaphorical, are metaphors (and emotive). A word's "belonging" rather to one reality than another requires an extension of the notion of "belonging." Samuel Parker, an early member of the Royal Society, denouncing the use of metaphor, managed an even wilder collection of metaphors himself: "wanton and luxurious fancies climbing up into the Bed of Reason, do not only defile it by unchaste and illegitimate Embraces, but instead of real conceptions and notices of Things impregnate the mind with nothing but Ayerie and Subventitious Phantasmes"![10] We cannot so easily be rid of them, nor should we wish to be. If metaphorical assertions are always or mostly "literally false," as Davidson seemed to propose,[11] then what are we to say of the very idea of "literal truth"? A statement is true if in some sense it "maps" reality—but statements only metaphorically "map" the world, and so (on

7. W. B. Stanford, *Greek Metaphor*, 111–2.

8. Aeschylus, *Agamemnon* 649.

9. Stebbing, *Introduction to Logic*, 18.

10. Samuel Parker, *Free and Impartial Censure of the Platonick Philosophy* (1666), cited by Draaisma, *Metaphors of Memory*, 55.

11. D. Davidson, "What Metaphors Mean." Davidson's conclusion is more nuanced: there can be no precise specifications for the "truth-conditions" of a metaphorical proposition.

that hypothesis) are false. If it can be really true that grass is green only if "grass is green" maps, mirrors, or corresponds to grass's greenness, and such claims about its mapping, mirroring, or corresponding to realities are *metaphors*, and false, then nothing that we ever say is true. It is easier to agree that even statements using clearly metaphorical terms may sometimes be entirely accurate, proved "true" in the telling.[12]

So the first thing to realize about Plotinus's use of metaphor is that sometimes no *metaphor* is intended. Plotinus means exactly, literally, what he says, and we are deceived because we have come to think that most words get their "real" sense chiefly from corporeal realities. "The light of the mind" is not a metaphor. His blunt instruction to "shut your eyes, and change to and wake another way of seeing, which everyone has but few use" (I.6 [1].8, 28),[13] may perhaps be obeyed—exactly—by shutting our eyes and attending to our immediate conscious experience! One way of evading the seemingly endless stream of remembered follies and anticipated dangers is simply—however paradoxically—to "feel the body from within" and so anchor ourselves to Now.[14]

There are also occasions when the metaphor is only a convenience: a whole class of entities is described by terms originally devised to mean only some subset of those entities, and the original sense has no real influence on the new. To put it another way: we come to see that there are analogous structures and use an old word to cover those analogies. Or rather, a real presence is intuited where it was not before. Sometimes that realization is a shock—and the old sense lingers. Once "apes" meant only what "chimpanzees" now means, and its extension to orangutans, gorillas, bonobos—the recognition of the very same form in these only slightly different shapes—made little difference. When we see *ourselves* as apes (even "naked apes"), our understanding of ourselves and of our cousins alters as much as when we came to call the earth "a planet." These shifts of meaning are a part of what we do in learning to "carve reality at the joints."[15] But there are other occasions when Plotinus would acknowledge that his terms are irreducibly "metaphorical," that they do not identify any wider class, and that most of

---

12. See my "Possible Truth of Metaphor."

13. It is worth noting that a "mystic," originally, is one who closes her *eyes*, so as to increase the chance of opening "the mind's eye" on a greater reality. *Mustes* and *epoptes* (one who sees) are a linked pair. See Montiglio, *Silence in the Land of Logos*, 25. Montiglio goes on to offer the tentative suggestion that "*muesis* is not only a silencing of mouth or eyes, but also a learning of a special way of speaking, listening and seeing" (32). See also V.5 [32].12.

14. Tolle, *Power of Now*, 78.

15. Plato, *Phaedrus* 265e; Plato, *Statesman* 287c.

their apparent associations don't fully apply to the cases he describes. "The philosophers, assuming that [an unhindered] state of intellect is most pleasing and acceptable, say that it is mixed with pleasure because they cannot find an appropriate way of speaking about it [*aporiai oikeias prosegorias*]; this is what the other words which we are fond of do metaphorically [when we carry them over, *metapherontes*], like 'drunk with the nectar' and 'to feast and entertainment,' and what the poets say, 'the father smiled,' and thousands and thousands of others" (VI.7 [38].30, 24–30).[16] Just in that such states of intellect, and still "higher" realities, are so unlike everything that we can ordinarily encounter, we have no recourse except to "inappropriate" or merely evocative language. Other philosophers have thought so too. "If anyone wants to teach it without the help of similes and riddles, his exposition of it will be so obscure and oracular that he will become even less intelligible than if he had used metaphors and riddles."[17] This is especially true, notoriously, of the One.

> It is therefore truly ineffable: for whatever you say about it you will always be speaking of a "something." But "beyond all things and beyond the supreme majesty of Intellect" is the only one of all the ways of speaking of it which is true; it is not its name, but says that it is not one of all things and "has no name," because we can say nothing of it: we can only try, as far as possible, to make signs to ourselves about it. (V.3 [49].13, 1–7)

"Making signs to ourselves" is maybe all we ever do, and even the most "literal" communication has its point only in settling our attention on some present or potential fact, experienced in some way partly related to the signs we make. The more "literal" our communication, perhaps, the easier it is to see what is implied by it; the more "metaphorical" or "allusive" or evocative, the more we can be puzzled about how far the resemblance stretches. It is, relatively, easy to see what a statement, "taken literally," contradicts (which was perhaps Davidson's real point); when it is "taken metaphorically," its apparent contrary may also be as true. Interestingly, it is a symptom of schizophrenia to take communications "literally" and be pedantically outraged by what then seems false[18] or else determined

---

16. See also VI.5 [23].9, 19, on not taking descriptions "literally" (*oukh hos toi rhemati legetai*).

17. Maimonides, *Guide of the Perplexed*, 45.

18. Benjamin, "Thinking Disorders in Schizophrenia."

to construct the claim as "true." "The psychotic means that he is 'really' and quite 'literally' dead, not merely symbolically or 'in a sense' or 'as it were,' and is seriously bent on communicating his truth."[19] In both cases, there is a failure to hear the words appropriately. Or as Augustine said: "this really is a terrible slavery of the soul—this taking of symbols for reality, this inability to raise the eyes of the mind beyond the physical creation and take in the eternal light."[20] We need to learn to read and listen to Plotinus, bearing in mind the goal of his endeavor. Not everything is to be taken "literally" (VI.5 [23].9, 19), but neither is much, if anything, to be taken merely, as it were, "musically," as if the content of the utterance had no importance, but only its sound or associated imagery.[21]

Often, we don't really understand even what a particular metaphor intends, especially when it is drawn from the radically *different* experience of third-century Rome—different, often enough, in ways that we have not noticed, since no contemporary writer ever bothered to mention the obvious. What is it to be "drunk" or "naked" or "alone"? What important conclusions or insights can be achieved by a "bastard" form of reasoning? Why and how is each soul (an) Aphrodite? Jonas, considering why *vision* is so often taken as the proper metaphor or analogue for intellectual insight (!), suggested that there are at least three reasons: in seeing we see things all together and at once (whereas our hearing is spread out over time); what we see is distant from our own emotion, so that we are at least partly detached from it; the visual field stretches out without any discernible limit.[22] But as Bartsch points out, this is not how the ancients thought about vision: "ancient models for the workings of vision were remarkably tactile, and, moreover, were implicated in the decidedly physical process of erotic arousal." Nor did it seem to them that they could see "forever," that there was no diminution over distance nor obstacles to further sight.[23] Nor is it true, in fact, that we see things altogether, without temporal succession: any genuinely fixed gaze, precisely, concentrates on one thing within a half-seen field, and we make our way through the world by constant sideways

19. Laing, *Divided Self*, 38.
20. Augustine, *On Christian Teaching* 3.9.
21. Cf. Shaw, *Theurgy and the Soul*, 109.
22. Jonas, *Phenomenon of Life*, 145.
23. Bartsch, *Mirror*, 45–6, 57–9. The dominant theory of vision was that our eyes emitted beams that bounced back to us: reifying, perhaps, the *attention* that we have to give to the world if we are to see (and even Aristotle, who distrusted that particular model, found some—faulty—empirical reason to adopt it on occasion; see ibid., 62–4). We build up our model of the local world from echoes.

glances. Seeing, quite as much as hearing, depends on memory. Nor is it only the peculiar ancients who have sometimes reckoned vision to be something close to copulation![24]

> Open to joy and to delight wherever beauty appears:
> If in the morning sun I find it, there my eyes are fix'd
> In happy copulation; if in evening mild, wearièd with work,
> Sit on a bank and draw the pleasures of this free-born joy.[25]

The neutral, distant, all-encompassing gaze may be what Jonas—and many other academics—wish, but it is not necessarily true even to common contemporary experience, let alone the ancient. Vision's priority over hearing, touching, smelling, tasting is probably due to the fact that most of us find it easier to make and convey distinctions within the visual rather than the other fields[26] (wine tasters or musicians may experience things differently). Disentangling our own immediate responses to these terms, and our theories about them, from anything Plotinus or another might intend requires more care than we mostly have time to give. That will often be the main task of this monograph.

Can we avoid the problem? Might metaphors, after all, be simply a sort of code, and readily decoded? Plotinus agreed with earlier philosophers that "the mysteries and myths about the gods" speak "riddlingly" and sometimes seem to offer merely allegorical interpretations—that Kronos, who ate his own offspring, really *stands for* Intellect, and that Zeus, who escaped being eaten, *stands for* Soul.[27] The same associations appear elsewhere in the *Enneads*, though inconsistently. His justification for thus reinterpreting the stories is that, in the standard historical perspective of his day and earlier days, civilization had long ago achieved a sounder knowledge of the cosmos, since preserved in popular stories which were remembered for other reasons than their cosmological truth. They are "the remnants of philosophy that perished in the great disasters that have befallen mankind, and

---

24. See ibid., 57–8, citing Achilles Tatius, *Clitophon and Leucippe* 1.9.4–5: "the outward emanation of beauty, which flows through the eyes into the soul, is a kind of copulation between separated bodies, and is not far from physical sex."

25. Blake, "Visions of the Daughters of Albion" (1793) 6.21–7.2 (Oothoon speaks) (*Writings*, 194).

26. See also Aristotle, *Metaphysics* 1.980I: "sight especially makes possible knowledge and clarifies many differences."

27. V.1 [10].4, 8–10; V.1 [10].7, 33–4. For the same association of *koros*, fullness, and *nous*, see also V.9 [5].8, 8; III.8 [30].11, 38–41. See Hadot, "Ouranos, Kronos and Zeus."

were recorded for their brevity and wit."[28] So dramatic, or even brutal, are those stories that we might well prefer *not* to infect our imaginations with them, and allegorizing them may seem like an evasion rather than an exercise. But the exaggerated horror of the stories may instead have the moral Proclus (AD 412–85) identified:

> It seems to me that the grim, monstrous, and unnatural character of poetic fictions moves the listener in every way to a search for the truth, and draws him towards the secret knowledge; it does not allow him, as would be the case with something that possessed a surface probability, to remain with the thoughts placed before him. It compels him instead to enter into the interior of the myths and to busy himself with the thought which has been concealed out of sight by the makers of myths and to ponder what kinds of natures and what great powers they introduced into the meaning of the myths and communicated to posterity by means of such symbols as these.[29]

Even the brutality of the stories may serve to fix them in the popular tradition and so make them available for their proper use by enthusiasts,[30] when they are read or enacted in the appropriate way. A passage of Plutarch seems to confirm that Platonists could ask us to be *doing* something with the stories, as also with the ritual acts.

Ancient natural philosophy among both Greeks and barbarians took the form of an account of nature hidden in mythology, veiled for the most part in riddles and hints, or of a theology such as is found in mystery ceremonies in which what is spoken is less clear to the masses than what is unsaid, and what is unsaid gives cause for more speculation than what is said. This is evident from the Orphic poems and the accounts given by the Phrygians and Egyptians. But nothing does more to reveal what was in the mind of the ancients than the rites of initiation and the

---

28. Aristotle, *On Philosophy* frag. 8 Rose (W. Ross, *Fragments*, 77 [frag. 10]). Aristotle even suggests that everything has already been discovered—and forgotten—an infinite (or at least an indefinite) number of times: *De caelo* 270b19–20; *Meteorologica* 339b27–8; *Politics* 7.1329b25–6. So also *Ecclesiastes* 1.10: "Is there anything of which one can say, 'Look this is new'? No, it has already existed, long ago before our time. The men of old are not remembered, and those who follow will not be remembered, by those who follow them."

29. Proclus, *Commentary on "Republic"* 1.85.16, as translated by Coulter, *Literary Microcosm*, 57. See also Lankila, "*Proclus, Erototokos and 'the Great Confusion.'*"

30. Of whom Euthyphro was one; see Plato, *Cratylus* 396d.

ritual acts that are performed in religious services and with symbolic intent.[31]

Rituals themselves embody stories, and in performing the rituals we invoke appropriate spirits, act out particular dreams, even raise ourselves to a higher, brighter life.

> Such invocation does not draw down beings that are impassive and pure, to that which is susceptible and impure. On the contrary, it makes us who had become impressionable through the generated life, pure and steadfast.[32]

Or as a much later writer said:

> Fairy tales are not responsible for producing in children fear, or any of the shapes of fear; fairy tales do not give the child the idea of the evil or the ugly; that is in the child already, because it is in the world already. Fairy tales do not give the child his first idea of bogey. What fairy tales give the child is his first clear idea of the possible defeat of bogey. The baby has known the dragon intimately ever since he had an imagination. What the fairy tale provides for him is a St. George to kill the dragon.[33]

It may be that Plotinus wished to "denature" the old stories, giving them a merely allegorical reading, in which the terms are only an arbitrary code that would not, should not, engage the imagination. It may also be—it is the hypothesis that I am trying out—that the engaged imagination is our best hope. What does it really mean to think of Intellect as Kronos (punningly, *nous en koroi* or *koros kai nous*)?[34] How do we fill up our souls? How do we retrieve, reincorporate, reenvision our own creations, the images we have projected on the outer world? What relevance to the Plotinian endeavor have the original, obvious readings of that story (in which a new life, promising justice, breaks away from merely amoral, all-consuming power—or in which filial distrust of fathers is given celestial sanction)?

Therapists who practice one variety or other of "talking cure" attempt

---

31. Plutarch, frag. 157.16–25 Sandbach, cited by Boys-Stones, *Post-Hellenistic Philosophy*, 108. See Van Nuffelen, "Words of Truth."

32. Iamblichus, *De mysteriis* 1.12, cited by Assmann, *Religio Duplex*, 19.

33. Chesterton, *Tremendous Trifles*, 102.

34. "Intellect in satiety" or "satiety and intellect." See also V.1 [10].4, 8, after Plato, *Cratylus* 396b.

to take on their patients' metaphors: "to do this you need to pay exquisite attention to the metaphoric nature of what is being said and done, and then to incorporate this information into your Clean Language."[35] So also Siegelmann: "much of psychotherapy consists in identifying previously unconscious metaphors and discovering how we unwittingly live by them."[36] Plotinus is not our patient—but the same advice applies and is as difficult to follow. Readers—including, of course, myself—ceaselessly intrude their own metaphors, their own readings of metaphors, into the text and cannot easily be checked by the author's inattention or aggrieved complaint (since the author of our text is long departed). The best we can manage is simply to try to attend to what is said and try to explore his metaphoric landscape (as Plotinus also explored Plato's). Maybe patience will, occasionally, be rewarded, as Julian insisted:

> The more paradoxical and prodigious the riddle is the more it seems to warn us not to believe simply the bare words but rather to study diligently the hidden truth, and not to relax our efforts until under the guidance of the gods those hidden things become plain, and so initiate or rather perfect our intelligence or whatever we possess that is more sublime than the intelligence, I mean that small particle of the One and the Good which controls the whole indivisibly.[37]

35. Lawley and Tompkins, *Metaphors in Mind*, 28.
36. Siegelmann, *Metaphor and Meaning*, 67.
37. Julian, *Oratio* 7.217c (*Works*, vol. 2, 105).

CHAPTER FOUR

Dialectic

Plotinus uses arguments. We may often find those arguments unpersua-
sive, since his conclusions are so distant from our ordinary opinions and
concerns—as when he seeks an answer to the question whether our souls,
if they survive at all, can remember being us or recognize themselves or
others. His answers to those particular questions do not rest on testimony or
anecdote: he does not, for example, mention that Empedocles remembered
being "a bush and a bird and a dumb fish in the sea," nor that Hermotimus
of Clazomenae offered evidence that he, his soul, had lived as a minor Homeric hero (by recognizing Menelaus's shield).[1] On the other hand, common
opinion had some authority: what everyone or almost everyone supposes
may perhaps be true (VI.5 [23].10).[2] And it was at least a widespread opinion,
in his day, that souls transmigrated—and must therefore somehow retain
their own identity through time and their distinctness from all other souls.[3]
There is more to be said about the significance of this doctrine; what matters here is his mode of argument, or its main source.

That mode is dialectical: "the valuable part of philosophy" (I.3 [20].5, 9).[4]
But what is dialectic? "It is the [hexis] which can speak about everything in
a reasoned and orderly way" (I.3 [20].4, 3).[5] Dialectic involves correct iden-

---

1. Diogenes, *Lives* 8.4. Hermotimus was also said to be an earlier incarnation of Pythagoras's soul.

2. See Owen, "Tithenai ta phainomena."

3. See Rich, "Reincarnation in Plotinus"; Stamatellos, "Plotinus on Transmigration."

4. Citing Plato, *Philebus* 58d6–7: "the purest part of intelligence and wisdom."

5. Armstrong (*Enneads*, vol. 1, 157) translates "*hexis*" as "science": this seems too strong.
The term more usually means "habit" or "disposition"—though it is of course crucial to dialectic that it is principled and systematic in the way that being "*episteme*" requires, and Plotinus
does refer to it as such a few lines later: I.3 [20].5, 1.

tifications and differentiations, evaluations and discriminations (and we get better at it by practice).

> Casting off falsehood and feeding the soul in what Plato calls "the plain of truth," using his method of division to distinguish the Forms, and to determine the essential nature of each thing, and to find the primary kinds, and weaving together by the intellect all that issues from these primary kinds, till it has traversed the whole intelligible world; then it resolves again the structure of that world into its parts, and comes back to its starting point; and then, keeping quiet (for it is quiet in so far as it is present There) it busies itself no more, but contemplates, having arrived at unity. (I.3 [20].4, 11–8)[6]

The study of logic or of the physical world, even the application of virtues and principles to practical dilemmas, are all inferior parts or aspects of philosophy: the real point is to "see" the truth, handing "petty precisions of speech" over to another discipline (I.3 [20].4, 11–8). Miller captures the thought precisely:

> Plotinus was not systematic: "he treats the same subjects in different ways in different places," as his student Amelius said (*Life* 17). . . . [He] suggests that the dialectic method, which is the interweaving activity of perfect mind, "knows the movements of soul" (I.3 [20].5). It is just at this point that Plotinus' style, his way of knowing, becomes one with the matrix of thought itself—soul—whose movement is a labyrinthine dance of "real beings" within. For Plotinus "every soul that knows its history" is aware that its true motion is a circling around its source; real knowing is a divine wandering within, not a straightforward march towards some external object.[7]

Dialectic gets its beginnings, its "clear principles," directly from intellect (*nous*) and then "combines and interweaves and distinguishes their consequences, till it arrives at perfect intelligence [*nous*]" (I.3 [20].5, 3–5).[8] This is not to deny any place to other forms of argument, but to insist on the

---

6. Quoting Plato, *Phaedrus* 248b6. The metaphor implicit in Plotinus's use of "There" to mean the real, intelligible world is not one that I shall be examining at length.

7. P. Miller, *Biography*, 104–5, drawing "divine wandering" (*ale theia* as the—implausible—root of *aletheia*, "truth") from Plato, *Cratylus* 421b.

8. Following the metaphors of Plato's *Sophist*.

preeminence of demonstrative deduction (but how exactly?) and its eventual completion. A fully purified intellect would not need to go through the dialectical processes of combination and differentiation: what it sees it sees completely and at once. We are not so pure, and must gradually uncover or discern what is already implicit in the very first principles of thought (whatever these may be). Those first principles are not *separate* from intellect, as though we only ever saw *images* of real things or an abstract propositional account of them, never the real things themselves. If that were all we could ever manage, Plotinus observes, we could never know how accurately those images matched the truth (V.5 [32]).[9] *Nous*, accordingly, must be the direct, unmediated grasp of real things, normally hidden from us by the mists of desire, anger, and stale opinion. Nor can it contain merely propositions, whose truth or otherwise depends on how things are.[10]

Sorting through implications is a process taking time and leading—it is to be hoped—to some resolution of the difficulties we face. Is it in practice intended to be straightforwardly a matter of identifying first principles and thence deducing necessary consequences, without regard to empirical observations or experimental tests? Must it then be incapable, as Augustine pointed out,[11] of discovering "the facts of zoology or history," which are subject to imponderable accidents of place, time, and person and so cannot be strictly deduced, at least from any principles available to mortal minds? The actual process and effect of dialectical reason may be rather different from this image: Plato proposes instead that we try to understand what follows from hypotheses and whether they conflict with our experience or with more firmly held convictions. Rather than conceive of dialectic as a simple progress from assumptions A and B to a conclusion Z, we may rather suppose that A, B, and the reverse of Z (not-Z) are presented as an "inconsistent triad": at least one, it turns out, must be false (assuming, as we must, that the truth cannot be in contradiction), and which ones we retain will be for further judgment. Nor is dialectical reasoning irrelevant to experience: it was, after all, such reasoning that Galileo used to demonstrate the error in a post-Aristotelian assumption (that heavy bodies fall faster than light bodies).[12] Dialectic is, in essence, the uncovering of error (and so gradually

9. See Armstrong, "Background of Doctrine 'That Intelligibles Are Not outside Intellect'"; and my own "Plotinian Account of Intellect."

10. See Rappe, *Reading Neoplatonism*, 23–90, for helpful discussion of the role of dialectic in Plotinian epistemology.

11. Augustine, *De Trinitate* 4.21; O'Daly, *Augustine's Philosophy of Mind*, 101.

12. "Suppose a large stone falls with a speed of, say, eight, and a smaller moves with a speed of four: it is clear that on uniting the two the more rapid one will be partly retarded by the

reveals the truth by elimination).[13] The detail of our lives together, we may agree, cannot be inferred—by us—from any clear first principle, but at least we can eliminate some seeming possibilities! And once again, though we now constantly fall back into imagining this as a journey through *propositions* and their merely *logical* implications, it may be better to think of it rather as a *narrative* journey, a way of wondering how the first principles relate to each other and to their images.

Those who have achieved their end no longer need those processes, any more than an experienced musician needs to think exactly how to pluck the strings (IV.4 [28].12). "What calculation [*logismos*] can there be or counting or memory when intelligence [*phronesis*] is present?"[14] The dialectical process, then, for the philosopher, is very much like the training that a musician must receive: beginning from the sounds and rhythms that excite him, the musician must be led toward an appreciation of universal principles and the beauty which is in them (I.3 [20].1, 28–34). Likewise, the lover must be led on from physical and social beauty, as well as from the beauty of arts, sciences, and virtues, to the higher way (I.3 [20].2, 10–5). Philosophers, so Plotinus thinks, are disposed in this direction by their nature but must also be trained in mathematics, to feel confident in "the existence of the immaterial," and then in dialectical discrimination. The starting point will often—and maybe always—be a puzzle. According to Heracleitos, "the lord whose oracle is in Delphi neither speaks nor suppresses, but indicates."[15] As Iamblichus also declared, Apollo (together with the eldest of the Muses, Calliope) is the inspiration of philosophers not because he speaks "rationally" and "clearly"[16] but because he poses riddles: dialectic is dealing with ambiguity and homonymy "and

---

slower and the slower will be somewhat hastened by the swifter. . . . But if this is true, the system will move with a speed less than eight; but the two stones when tied together make a stone larger than that which before moved with a speed of eight" (Galilei, *Dialogues*, 63–4).

13. The Holmesian rule (that once we have discarded the impossibilities, what remains, however improbable, must be true) is not in fact a reasonable forensic dictat (we can never know that we have thought of all the options), but it may serve as a guideline in metaphysics.

14. After IV.4 [28].11, 12–3. See also IV.3 [27].18, 6–8: "in the crafts reasoning [*logismos*] occurs when the craftsmen are in perplexity, but when there is no difficulty, the craft dominates and does its work."

15. Heracleitos 22B93DK; Waterfield, *First Philosophers*, 40.

16. According to Guthrie, *Greeks and Their Gods*, 73, Apollo "is the very embodiment of the Hellenic spirit. Everything that marks off the Greek outlook from that of other peoples, and in particular from the barbarians who surrounded them—beauty of every sort, whether of art, music, poetry or youth, sanity and moderation—are all summed up in Apollo." But this is a serious misunderstanding—of Apollo and of the philosophical mind. So far from being the god of an ethnocentric "sanity," Apollo deals through prophetic madness, dangerous riddles, plague,

the ferreting out of any double meaning."[17] It is conducted in disputatious dialogue[18]—which is why Hermes carries, so Iamblichus says in the letter just cited, a staff with two snakes looking toward each other, poised to test themselves against each other! But disputation itself, though valuable, is not of the essence: the eristical mode, though attractive especially (perhaps) to the young, is not dialectic.

> When he thinks that he is reasoning he is really disputing, just because he cannot define and divide, and so know that of which he is speaking; and he will pursue a merely verbal opposition in the spirit of contention and not of fair discussion.[19]

The goal is not winning arguments (or silencing opponents) but rather "the purification of the intellect through refutation," as I shall observe hereafter.[20] And perhaps our awakening is an effect of intellectual despair—the moment when we acknowledge that we cannot any longer cope.[21]

All three types of seeker may eventually need no further training or habituation. All may come to see and be the beautiful—and it seems that the philosopher eventually can have little more to *say* than can lover or musician, nor any need to "intellectualize."

> One must not then suppose that the gods and the "exceedingly blessed spectators" in the higher world contemplate propositions [*axiomata*], but all the Forms we speak about are beautiful images in that world, of the kind which someone imagined to exist in the soul of the wise man, images not painted but real. This is why the ancients said that

---

betrayal, and the very distant. Kingsley's judgment is more to the point: Apollo is "a god of impossible enigmas" (*Story Waiting to Pierce You*, 43), and perhaps of insoluble antinomies.

17. Iamblichus, *Letters*, 7–10 (letter 5, "On Dialectic"); see also Addey *Divination and Theurgy*, 273–4.

18. See Long, *Conversation and Self-Sufficiency*.

19. Plato, *Republic* 5.454a. See also Plato, *Meno* 75cd (trans. Jowett): "if he were a philosopher of the eristic and antagonistic sort, I should say to him: You have my answer, and if I am wrong, your business is to take up the argument and refute me. But if we were friends, and were talking as you and I are now, I should reply in a milder strain and more in the dialectician's vein; that is to say, I should not only speak the truth, but I should make use of premises which the person interrogated would be willing to admit."

20. Iamblichus, *Letters*, 15 (letter 5: Stobaeus, *Anthologia* 2.2.5). Dillon and Polleichtner remark (70) that Iamblichus seems to be unique in considering such riddles as a stimulant to dialectic, but he could fairly refer back to the way Herodotus also treats the Delphic and other oracles.

21. See Zimmer, *King and Corpse*, 202–38.

the Ideas were realities and substances. The wise men of Egypt, I think, also understood this, either by scientific [*akribes*] or innate [*sumphute*] knowledge, and when they wished to signify something wisely, did not use the forms of letters which follow the order of words and propositions [*logoi* and *protaseis*] and imitate sounds and the enunciations of philosophical statements [*prophoras axiomaton*], but by drawing images and inscribing in their temples one particular image of each particular thing, they manifested the non-discursiveness of the intelligible world, that is, that every image is a kind of knowledge and wisdom and is a subject of statements, all together in one, and not discourse [*dianoesis*] or deliberation [*bouleusis*]. (V.8 [31].5–6)[22]

Questions arise. If the goal is an unarticulated union with reality—and eventually with the One, the Good, itself—and merely verbal discriminations and calculations may entirely miss the point, what then *is* the point of "philosophizing," or even of "reasoning" in general? Might not lover and musician do as well, or better? Again: what reason is there to believe that "philosophers" are uniquely virtuous "by nature" and need only to perfect their ethical and intellectual virtues (I.3 [20].3, 8)? If we are eventually to put discrimination aside, how can exercises in analysis and synthesis assist us toward that goal? What can the first principles of demonstration be, especially if they are not propositions? What sort of union between subject and object is implied by the notion that the intelligibles must be within the intellect? How does an appeal to "reason," "rational insight," *nous*, differ from an appeal to faith (if it does)? And finally, why are we—even nascent philosophers—so lost to our original being as ever to need discipline or lengthy training? What has gone wrong? As Plotinus plaintively asks himself: "when I am come down from Intellect [*Nous*] to discursive reasoning [*logismos*], I am puzzled how I ever came down, and how my soul has come to be in the body when it is what it has shown itself to be by itself, even when it is in the body" (IV.8 [6].1, 8–11).

The answer to that last question may lie with metaphysics (and a theory about the Fall), but a gesture toward a phenomenological solution is still possible. We lose our grip on intelligible reality when we want to be independent and have all things *our* way.[23] In place of things as they are we see and feel them only as they are *for us*, in the light of our fears, desires, and stereotypical misjudgments. Quite what Plotinus himself meant by his experience

22. Citing Plato, *Symposium* 215b. See also IV.3 [27].11.
23. V.1 [10].1: "the beginning of evil for them was audacity [*tolma*]."

of Intellect we can only guess, but there are a sufficient number of other accounts that may serve as clues, such as Vaclav Havel's letters from prison:

> As I watched the imperceptible trembling of [the] leaves [of an enormous tree] against an endless sky, I was overcome by a sensation that is diffi-cult to describe: all at once, I seemed to rise above all the coordinates of my momentary existence in the world into a kind of state outside time in which all the beautiful things I had ever seen and experienced existed in a total "co-present"; I felt a sense of reconciliation, indeed of an al-most gentle consent to the inevitable course of things as revealed to me now, and this combined with a carefree determination to face what had to be faced. A profound amazement at the sovereignty of Being became a dizzying sensation of tumbling endlessly into the abyss of its mys-tery; an unbounded joy at being alive, at having been given the chance to live through all I have lived through, and at the fact that everything has a deep and obvious meaning—this joy formed a strange alliance in me with a vague horror at the inapprehensibility and unattainability of everything I was so close to in that moment, standing at the very "edge of the finite"; I was flooded with a sense of ultimate happiness and har-mony with the world and with myself, with that moment, with all the moments I could call up, and with everything invisible that lies behind it and has meaning. I would even say that I was somehow "struck by love," though I don't know precisely for whom or what.[24]

But might we not be justly skeptical? The rush of "oceanic feeling" (in Freud's vocabulary, after Romain Rolland)[25] may momentarily divert us from immediate practicalities by flooding us with sensations proper to our mammalian infancy. Would creatures of a different biological sort be likely ever to feel the world like that: creatures, for example, that must break out of their eggs and scurry down the sand to the sea, in the shadow of hun-gry seagulls? Their "oceanic feeling" might be rather different! Maybe only mammals (and a few other moderately nurturing sorts) have any experience of being sustained by, even united with, an unpredictable but "loving" pres-ence.[26] Do we have any good grounds to think that a much colder, less ac-

---

24. Havel, *Letters to Olga*, 331–2, cited by Bellah, *Religion in Human Evolution*, 6–7.

25. Freud, *Civilization and Its Discontents*, 11–3. See also Parsons, *Enigma of the Oceanic Feeling*.

26. Some critics might even think it significant that Plotinus apparently continued to breast-feed until he was eight (and was then shamed out of the practice by being told he was a pest) (Porphyry, *Life* 3.5). Why Plotinus shared this childhood memory, when he let so many

commodating cosmos may not be the truth? Isn't the very fact that we are
so often misled by our fears, desires, and stereotypical misjudgments good
reason to withhold our assent from such "oceanic" feelings? Isn't that what
"Reason" has come to mean for us, even if we don't always acknowledge it?
What we *feel* here and now should be contrasted, in imagination and careful reason, with how we would feel about more distant episodes, how we
are likely to feel ourselves "a twelvemonth hence,"[27] what advice we would
give *another* victim of adversity. Isn't the goal of "reason" to help us realize
that most things don't much matter, whether they are immediately good
or ill, as they will have been forgotten or neutralized from the more distant
point of view? What would it be like to be wholly persuaded by this colder
vision and to be united—in feeling and imagination—with "the view from
nowhere"?

The charge—of giving way to an agreeable emotion—can of course be
turned round against the accusers themselves! There is, after all, something
very agreeable in deconstructing other people's visions and proving oneself
more "realistic," more "courageously clear-sighted," than the norm. And
those for whom the colder vision is easiest are not usually people whose
judgment the rest of us respect: the sort of character I once mildly mocked
as a "prepubertal philistine with a block against tenderness and a gift for
mathematics."[28]

> Rosenstock-Huessy points out that Descartes's conceptual asceticism
> might have helped his studies, but "the truth is that the great Cartesius,
> when he obliterated the impressions of the child René, maimed himself
> for any social perception outside natural science."[29]

Are we to think that Plotinus and his peers preferred the *abstract* to the
concrete realities of ordinary life? Instead of assessing or measuring what
happens by reference only to our own state and feeling—thinking of things,
for example, as smaller or larger *than we are ourselves*—we should seek for

---

lapse, is unknown. Was he perhaps giving an example of how a sense of shame may help us to
overcome desire, as Plato proposed (or sometimes not: see *Republic* 4.439e)?

27. Johnson, commenting on Boswell's "serious distress" about some minor accident, according to Boswell, *Life of Johnson*, 224 (6 July 1763).

28. S. Clark, *Aristotle's Man*, 195.

29. Bellah, *Religion in Human Evolution*, 40, citing Rosenstock-Huessy, *Out of Revolution*, 756. The charge is unfair to Descartes, who had more social sense than this suggests, but
it may apply to those who refuse, for example, to trust even their own emotional response to
puppies or kittens in the absence of what they can regard as a purely formal "proof" that "animals have feelings."

some more universal measure,[30] without privileging any particular place or scale or moment. That might seem to be the implication also of the way they treat the love of visible and audible beauty in lover and musician: their discipline is gradually to grasp the common forms, the schemata and diagrams, rather than the rich particulars. Similarly in ethics: philosophers of this sort have tended to overlook such "thick" virtues as civility, courage, chivalry, modesty, and the like (all of which have definite, historically and culturally bounded descriptors) in favor of much "thinner" fare: "being good" or "right," which might (as so many have supposed) be applied to any character or action without overt contradiction. In all these cases there is something to be said in favor of the relatively "abstract" view: at the beginning of our musical or amatory career we may be individually moved by merely personal associations and only gradually come to see or hear those beauties that anyone can recognize and love. So also in ethical maturity: we may come to disown those merely tribal or superstitious values ("honor," as that is understood by ignorant and misogynistic patriarchs, for example) in favor of more universally acknowledged goods. But we cannot wholly dissociate ourselves from our particular physical and social context, nor do we greatly admire those who admit no value at all in personal associations, memories, and affections. "Platonists"—it is supposed—prefer bloodless ideals to real-life practicalities, while "Aristotelians" acknowledge the primary reality of individual, countable substances like our waking, bodily selves. In normal life we are likely to trust Aristotle's paradigmatic *phronimos* or *spoudaios*—with whatever personal and cultural variations.[31] Why should we trust some quite different character in matters metaphysical?

And why—if the universe were really as indifferent to anything we value as so many moderns say, and as uncomforting—should we set ourselves to realize that truth? There may be immediate practical reasons not to be deceived about some local matters and very great reason to be deceived about the greatest! As Plotinus pointed out, very many living creatures (both human and nonhuman) manage their local lives quite well without recourse to "reason" (I.4 [46].2, 35–43); the value of intellectual endeavor to uncover real relationships—real distinctions and implications—

---

30. See Plato, *Statesman* 284e, on the proper unit of measurement.

31. Aristotle, *Nicomachean Ethics* 3.1113a32: "what perhaps especially distinguishes the sound man [*spoudaios*] is his seeing the truth in every matter, as being their standard and measure." It is, for Aristotle, such a man who is "the measure of all things." Plato insisted, rather, that it was *God* who was the measure of all things (*Laws* 4.716c4). The positions are compatible as long as it can be agreed that this God may speak in all of us (see VI.5 [23].1, 3–4), and especially in his saints, the true *spoudaioi*.

rests on the value of reality itself, without regard to personal or practical advantage. Human beings, if they are to be reckoned something other than "animals," must have an eye to the whole truth, the cosmos as a living reality, rather than the simple local worlds, the *Umwelten*, of all other creatures. The World, our predecessors thought, was primarily for human beings and gods—because only human beings and gods are even acquainted with the World as such. "Animals know only one world, the one which they perceive by experience, internal as well as external. Men alone have the faculty of conceiving the ideal, of adding something to the real."[32] If all that is error, then what reason is there to suppose that we either should or could devote ourselves to the larger world rather than to the world of ordinarily human practicalities? In which case, the oceanic feeling, along with other fancies, has a part to play, precisely, in keeping us together. Either it is—as Havel and Plotinus thought—a glimpse of Truth (the truth that is also beauty) or it is only a particular *pathos*: but if it is the latter, we should enjoy and profit from it, since there is no value in any imagined "truth" that trumps it. Conversely, if reality is what moderns often claim, we have neither duty nor ability to find it out and may reasonably relapse to fictions![33]

But the questions remain. Even if—in some sense—we can see "the whole world" plain, or feel as if we can, why should we trust this vision or this feeling to be veridical? What should we have to say to some alien visitor who remarked that of course the World we imagine to be "real" is one that we can imagine ourselves to comprehend, but that the still wider World encountered by less bounded intelligences is "not only queerer than we suppose, but queerer than we *can* suppose"?[34] In which case, of course, our own "queerer" visions might be nearer to the truth than those we consider sensible! *Feeling* that one knows everything, or that at any rate one

---

32. Durkheim, *Elementary Forms*, 421. Durkheim, knowingly or not, is here repeating a common theme. See, e.g., Augustine, *City of God* 11.27 (as quoted by O'Daly, *Augustine's Philosophy of Mind*, 206): "man alone among living beings has this powerful and remarkable urge [sc. to know]; and even if some animals have a much keener sense of sight than we to look into this [sc. physical] light, they cannot attain to that incorporeal light by which our mind is somehow irradiated, so that we are able to judge all these matters rightly." The tradition may be mistaken. See further my "Does 'Made in the Image of God' Mean Humans Are More Special than Animals?"

33. The epistemological collapse of naturalism is acknowledged by Nagel, *Mind and Cosmos*, mostly on the basis of Plantinga's discussion (see, e.g., *Warrant and Proper Function*). I made this point independently in my Gifford and Stanton lectures: see *From Athens to Jerusalem*; *God's World and the Great Awakening*.

34. Haldane, *Possible Worlds*, 286.

did know everything in that forgotten timeless moment, is not necessarily to know anything at all. Hermes Trismegistus made an even larger claim than Plotinus:

> You must think of god in this way, as having everything—the cosmos, himself, <the> universe—like thoughts within himself. Thus, unless you make yourself equal to god, you cannot understand god; like is understood by like. Make yourself grow to immeasurable immensity, outleap all body, outstrip all time, become eternity and you will understand god. Having understood that nothing is impossible to you, consider yourself immortal and able to understand everything, all art, all learning, the temper of every living thing.[35]

The more plausible moral would be that the attempt will reveal exactly why we do *not* have the mind of God, rather than being a recipe for attaining it and its associated virtues. And even if we did succeed in the attempt, must it have a salutary effect? Why should philosophers (and especially dialectical philosophers) be thought more virtuous by nature, and with a better grasp of the eventual end, than lovers or musicians? Why should the practice of dialectical philosophy be thought likely to assist at all? Might it not rather—precisely by detaching people from traditional norms and personal intuitions—lead in a wholly amoral and very dangerous direction? That "dry light shed on things" may "wither up the moral mysteries as illusions."[36] A familiar thought might be that those with a "philosophical temperament" are perhaps a little more detached from ordinary life and time than lovers and musicians: and it is this natural detachment that gives them their start on the intellectualizing enterprise I gestured toward before. But this is not what Plotinus suggests elsewhere: our "journey home" is prompted by desire. Maybe nascent philosophers are just a little high! And in that case the analytic and synthetic discipline of dialectical philosophy is itself delightful rather than detached.

> The true spirit of delight, the exaltation, the sense of being more than Man, which is the touchstone of highest excellence, is to be found in mathematics as surely as in poetry.[37]

35. *Corpus Hermeticum* 11.20 (Copenhaver, *Hermetica*, 41).
36. Chesterton, *Poet and the Lunatics*, 70.
37. B. Russell, *Mysticism and Logic*, 62, cited by Bellah, *Religion in Human Evolution*, 42, after Polanyi, *Personal Knowledge*, 199.

Better to see how *ideas* and concepts fit together in beauty than merely to delight in physical representations of those principles: lovers and musicians run a greater risk of being diverted by sensation and by merely personal association. Insofar as ordinary virtue involves detachment from bodily sensation and parochial triumph, it is the "philosophical" who have the better part, but not because their vision is more abstract or less engaging. They may simply find the ordinary temptations a little less to their taste than other, "higher" distractions: they will be in the library reading rather than drinking in the bar or seeking to get laid. And even this claim is surely doubtful. In reckoning that those of the "philosophical" temperament have a little more of "natural virtue" and a slightly easier route up to enlightenment, Plotinus may himself be a little too parochial, a little too inclined to exaggerate the importance of being just like him. The problem for Clever People (and philosophers are supposed, even if only by themselves, to be quite clever), and especially Clever People who are persuaded that they are also Good, is that they can readily rationalize whatever they wish to do. They know that they are Good because they have managed some—probably fairly painless—sacrifice (of money or social position or even, maybe, diet) and can thence conclude that anything they really want to do must be something that a Good Person would want and do. Even or especially Clever People should not so readily trust in their own cleverness. "If we repose our trust in our own reasonings, we shall construct and build up the city of Mind that corrupts the truth."[38]

But leaving these warnings aside, it is still unclear what it is that an ideal dialectical philosophy discerns and trust. Clearly, this is not simply a set of supposedly self-evident propositions (since propositions, at best, are only images of the real). What are the realities, perceived as beauty,[39] that are contained in intellect? What is "the Mind of God," especially as it is embodied and particularized in human form? Only those can know the Mind of God who have it. Can the rest of us even begin to recognize its signs?

38. Philo, *Legum allegoriarum* 3.228 (Collected *Works*, vol. 1, 457).
39. "Beautifulness is reality" (I.6 [1].6, 21).

PART II

Metaphorically Speaking

CHAPTER FIVE

Naked and Alone

W here to begin?[1] We are perhaps least likely to be understanding Plotinus when we assume too rapidly that we have understood. The words and images that we read most easily may be exactly the ones that we have misinterpreted. It is wise to take things slowly, and to ask what it was that his first auditors and readers were likely to have understood (even if, in the end, we hope to understand rather more than they did).

The first metaphorical instruction to consider is the "gymnosophistical." It has had a long post-Plotinian history. So Edward Herbert, English Rationalist (1583–1648):

> Those who would enter the shrine of truth must leave their trinkets, in other words their opinions, at the entrance, or as one might say in the cloakroom. They will find that everything is open or revealed to perception as long as they do not approach it with prejudice.[2]

And John Colet (1466–1519):

> Would anyone see truth? Then he must wholly strip and lay bare himself, laying aside all the thoughts of his mind . . . by which he deemed that he had learnt something.[3]

---

1. Some of the following material was presented to a British Society for the History of Philosophy conference on Platonism and modernity, held in Cambridge in 2003, in the context of a study of Edward Herbert: "Going Naked into the Shrine."

2. Herbert, *De veritate*, 72. "Trinkets" echoes an ancient pun: "to take off one's ornaments (*kosmos*) is to take off the world (*kosmos*)," so Jonathan Smith observes in "Garments of Shame," 235. Smith also notes a parallel Coptic pun: being naked, and leaving the world.

3. L. Miles, *John Colet*, 128, citing Colet, *Exposition of St. Paul's Epistle to the Romans*, 45. Colet further associates this stripping with a spiritual circumcision; L. Miles, *John Colet*,

So also *Theologia Germanica* (late fourteenth century; first printed in 1513): whoever wishes to cast a glance into eternity must be quite pure and wholly stripped and bare of all images.[4] And Meister Eckhart: "into the Naked Godhead none may get unless himself be Naked."[5] Jan van Ruysbroeck (1293–1381) also offered an interpretation of the metaphor:

> The God-seeing man . . . can always enter, naked and unencumbered with images, into the inmost part of his spirit. There he finds revealed an Eternal Light. . . . It [his spirit] is undifferentiated and without distinction, and therefore it feels nothing but the unity.[6]

The association of nakedness and the sacred goes back at least to Philo of Alexandria's (f1. AD 40) allegory whereby the high priest must strip off the soul's tunic of opinion and imagery to enter the Holy of Holies. He must "enter naked with no coloured borders or sound of bells, to pour out as a libation the blood of the soul and to offer as incense the whole mind to God our Saviour and Benefactor."[7]

Plotinus picked up that association:

> The attainment [of the good] is for those who go up to that higher world and are converted and strip off what we put on in our descent; (just as for those who go up to the celebrations of sacred rites there are purifications and strippings off of the clothes they wore before, and going up naked) until passing in the ascent all that is alien to the God, one sees with one's self alone. (I.6 [1].7, 4–9)[8]

So also Porphyry: "Naked was [the wise man] sent into the world, and naked shall he call on Him that sent him. For God listens only to those

---

129, citing Colet, *Exposition of St. Paul's Epistle to the Romans*, 80. See also G. Clark, "In the Foreskin of Their Flesh."

4. L. Miles, *John Colet*, 141.

5. Jones, *Flowering of Mysticism*, 77. The slogan echoes Jerome's injunction "nudus nudum Jesum sequi": *Epistle* 52.5, cited by M. Miles, *Carnal Knowing*, 63.

6. Ruysbroeck, *Spiritual Marriage*, 185–6, cited by Stace, *Mysticism and Philosophy*, 94 (who misleadingly identifies that inner reality with "the pure self or ego").

7. Philo, *Legum allegoriarum* 2.56 (*Collected Works*, vol. 1, 259), after *Leviticus* 16.1ff. See also Philo, *De gigantibus* 12.53–4 (*Collected Works*, vol. 2, 470–3): "only those who, having disrobed themselves of all created things and of the innermost veil and wrapping of mere opinion, with mind unhampered and naked will come to God."

8. See also Proclus, *Elements*, 182–1, proposition 209: "[The soul] ascends by putting off all those faculties tending to temporal process with which it was invested in its descent, and becoming clean and bare (*kathara kai gumne*) of all such faculties as serve the uses of the process."

who are not weighed down by alien things, guarding those who are pure from corruption."⁹ Elsewhere Porphyry varied the destination: "Let us go stripped, without tunics, to the stadium, to compete in the Olympics of the soul. Stripping off is the starting point, without which the contest will not happen."¹⁰ Stripping off for effortful action is a metaphor that may make sense—except of course that contemplation does not require that sort of effort, or straining after effect. The shrine metaphor, on the other hand, picks up the soul's passivity before the unadorned truth—except that it is difficult at first to see how stripping might help the priest *see* clearly, and what needs to be stripped might more obviously be the *object*: as Socrates tells Alcibiades, with respect to the attractiveness of "the citizen body of great-hearted Erectheus," "you ought to see it undressed" (IV.4 [28].43, 22).¹¹ The Naked Truth is more often distinguished from the Elaborated Lie,¹² but in these passages it is the Lover that is naked.

Perhaps it is the Lover that is to be assessed? The people of the age of Kronos, according to Plato's *Statesman*, were not naked because they were destitute but because they had nothing that they needed to conceal.¹³ Consider also Plato's story of Glaucus, picked up by Berkeley in *Siris*:¹⁴ to see the soul we must knock off its encrustations. That is how we shall be judged by Minos (who is also naked and "with his naked soul shall pierce into the other naked souls"): stripped of the misleading evidence of health or wealth or bodily beauty.¹⁵ In that earlier age, or in that other realm, no one has any need of such disguises. "The nakedness of Dionysus," so Kofman paraphrases Nietzsche, "does not symbolize the very presence of Being

9. Porphyry, *To Marcella*, 501 (§33).

10. Porphyry, *Abstinence*, 43 (I.31). This metaphor was literally enacted when Christians were sent naked into the arena: so the martyr Febronia (in Diocletian's reign) accepted what was meant to be humiliation (which is the more common attitude to nakedness), saying, "What athlete entering the contest at Olympia engages in battle wrapped up in all his clothes? . . . Should I not meet torture with a naked body, until I have vanquished your father Satan?" (cited by M. Miles, *Carnal Knowing*, 58). The Romans did not approve of athletic nakedness, so Porphyry is speaking to a wider audience than Rome.

11. Citing Homer, *Iliad* 2.547, after Plato, *Alcibiades* 132a5. See also Plato, *Charmides* 153a–157c, where the obvious erotic charge is emphasized (and then diminished).

12. See Hadot, *Veil of Isis*, for a study of the image of nature's unveiling.

13. Note that here and elsewhere the "age of Kronos," as an age not of amoral power but of natural virtue, is reckoned superior to the present age of Zeus.

14. Berkeley, *Siris*, 313–2 (*Works*, vol. 5, 145), citing Proclus, *Alcibiades*, after Plato, *Republic* 10.611c. See also I.1 [53].12.

15. Plato, *Gorgias* 523c ff., after Empedocles 31DK126. See Rist, *Plotinus*, 188–98. See also Philo, *De Providentia* 2, 35 (*Collected Works*, vol. 9, 483). It may also be relevant that the boys and girls of Magnesia must dance together naked, "provided sufficient modesty and restraint are displayed by all concerned" (*Laws* 6.772).

in its truth, but the innocence of a life which has nothing to reproach itself for, which is strong enough not to be ashamed of its perspective and its evaluations, beautiful enough to accept and love itself without having to put on a mask."[16] Rohr associates that "nakedness" with intimacy:

> I wonder how a person who has never practiced risky self-disclosure with at least one other human being would know how to be intimate with God. I sincerely doubt the possibility. (Is this the real meaning of "nakedness"?)[17]

Alternatively—and this may be closer to the Neoplatonic usage—the people of Kronos's age were "naked" because they belong to the incorporeal realm, separate from this one not as an earlier aeon but as a different world.[18]

But the passages of Philo, Plotinus, Colet, and Herbert do not explicitly involve a judgment on the soul, nor even a recommendation to strip shame away, but rather advice to the soul on how to "see" its Beloved. One answer may be that the naked may not *see* more clearly but will certainly *feel* more accurately. The priest goes up into darkness and needs all his skin as a sensorium: maybe Plotinus's and others' continued use of "sight" as the crucial sense is inadvertent. We are instead to imagine that beauty is to be known, as it were, through touch and being touched. As Henry points out, Plotinus does use "expressions which are more appropriate to the sense of touch than to the sense of vision."[19] Even the other—and to us more natural—association with nakedness (erotic rather than athletic) may be intended: certainly Plotinus does occasionally speak, like other mystics, with distinctly erotic overtones. "The lover here below also has beauty in this way, not by receiving it, but by lying with it" (VI.5 [23].10, 6–7).[20]

But the erotic charge should be put aside (though in so doing, I am also putting aside important questions about the different valencies of naked-

---

16. Kofman, *Nietzsche and Metaphor*, 96, after Nietzsche, *Beyond Good and Evil*, 295.

17. Rohr, *Immortal Diamond*, 173–4; see also 164–5.

18. Dillon, "NeoPlatonic Exegesis of the Politicus Myth," observes that Proclus makes this symbolic use of the nakedness motif in his comments on the *Statesman* (*Platonic Theology* 5.7–8). God's provision of "garments of skin" after the Fall was similarly interpreted in some Hebrew and early Christian circles: Philo, *Quaestiones* 1.53 (*Supplementary Works*, vol. 1, 31); Clement, *Stromata* 3.14. See J. Harris, *Odes and Psalms of Solomon*, 67–8.

19. Henry, "Place of Plotinus in the History of Thought," lxviii: see esp. VI.9 [9].8ff. See also Wald, *Self-Intellection and Identity*, 146ff., after V.3 [49].10, 39ff.

20. See Mazur, "Having Sex with the One."

ness for male and female).[21] The object after all is to escape from our corporeal—and our social—entanglements: we need to stop "dressing the part," simultaneously disguising and actively *creating* ourselves, for the different roles and characters we play.[22]

> Our country from which we came is There, our Father is There. How shall we travel to it, where is our way of escape? We cannot get there on foot; for our feet only carry us everywhere in this world, from one country to another. You must not get ready a carriage, either, or a boat. Let all these things go, and do not look. Shut your eyes, and change to and wake another way of seeing, which everyone has but few use. (I.6 [1].8, 22–9)[23]

Shut your eyes, and notice where you are! Notice the reality that sustains you even in your least agreeable moments. The realization that I am Here is the beginning of understanding, a revelation that—in other traditions—is induced by silly questions (as it might be, "what is the sound of one hand clapping?").[24] Becoming present to oneself is also becoming aware that there is a real world, as it were, "behind" or "within" phenomena. What is it that is "behind the scenes"? We are.

Another, related reading is possible—though it does not seem likely that Plotinus himself intended this. Naked bodies are sometimes felt to be "objectified," to be the object of an interested, erotic, or dismissive gaze. This is now reckoned, at least in liberal circles, "a bad thing" and is the main principled argument against pornography (and much Western art). But part of the process of enlightenment is indeed the discovery that we are "objects," that there are other creatures in the world for whom our precious subjectiv-

21. Historically, as M. Miles, *Carnal Knowing*, shows, naked *men* are typically stripped for action, and naked *women* are to be enjoyed or else, perversely, humiliated.

22. Pallis, "Do Clothes Make the Man?" (reprinted in Lings and Minnaar, *Underlying Religion*, 266–82). Pallis repeats the story, without reference, that the high priest went naked into the Holy of Holies ("Do Clothes Make the Man?," 150) but also emphasizes the importance, for most of us, of Tradition and of the clothes that indicate our membership in whatever our tradition is.

23. See also IV.3 [27].24. "A tradition, at least as old as Proclus . . . made of Homer's blindness a metaphor for transcendent vision" (Lamberton, *Homer the Theologian*, 8, after Proclus, *In Republicam* 1.193–4). The passage is echoed in Augustine, *Confessions* 8.8.19: Augustine denies the need of ships, chariots, or even feet to enter into God's will and covenant ("not to go only, but to enter there, was naught else but to will to go").

24. I owe the initial insight to Sansonese, *Body of Myth*, a book worth reading despite its eventual descent into dubious etymologies. What *is* the sound of one hand clapping? Well, listen! Where are you at the moment? Here! See also Tolle, *New Earth*, 52–3, on this inner feeling; and S. Taylor, *Waking from Sleep*, 111, on the renewal of energy that may come from thus feeling our bodies "from within."

ity is less important than it is to us. "Going naked into the shrine" is being
exposed, and knowing that we are exposed, to judgment—and this knowledge is a recognition of the wider world and a truth that is not just what we
wish. Knowledge comes in the discovery that we can be mistaken—as we
never could be if our thoughts were all there were. To get there, to "sober
up," we "must rip off the tunic that [we] wear, the garment of ignorance, the
foundation of vice, the bonds of corruption, the dark cage, the living death,
the sentient corpse, the portable tomb, the resident thief, the one who hates
through what he loves and envies through what he hates."[25]

This last aspect of the metaphor is not unconnected with the issue I addressed in the previous chapter, under the heading of "Dialectic." One thing
that is often found enormously difficult—for all of us, and especially for
those not at all inclined toward "philosophy" in the sense that the ancients
meant it—is to put up with refutation or even with robust rebuttal. The challenge is to admit that we might be wrong! One's own thinking is of all things
the most dear to each of us, and being shown how flawed, parochial, and
disconnected even our most serious efforts are is correspondingly painful.

> Refutation is the greatest and chiefest of purifications, and he who has
> not been refuted, though he be the Great King himself, is in an awful
> state of impurity; he is uninstructed and deformed in those things in
> which he who would be truly blessed ought to be fairest and purest.[26]

The other odd feature of the metaphor about sacred nakedness is that it
seems to have no literal foundation. There seems to be no solid reference
to the custom in pagan circles, nor yet in Hebraic, despite some commentators' claims. Philo's explication of Leviticus is especially strange, in that the
Levitical Code requires the high priest to go *clothed* into the Holy of Holies,
even if the clothes are special ones, to be donned only for the occasion.[27]
And Philo himself elsewhere uses exactly this requirement as a metaphor
or symbol: the high priest puts on, symbolically, the world and carries
that into the Presence.[28] It is more usual (and probably more Hebraic in

---

25. *Hermetic Corpus* 7.1 (Copenhaver, *Hermetica,* 24).

26. Plato, *Sophist* 227c. On the further history of this trope, see Boyle, "Pure of Heart";
S. Ross, *Metaphysical Aporia.*

27. *Leviticus* 16.4 (see also 16.23, 16.32). *Exodus* 28.43 decrees that a priest who exposes
himself (i.e., his genitals) in the sanctuary is to be put to death.

28. Philo, *Life of Moses* 2.117–21 (*Collected Works,* vol. 6, 505). It is perhaps significant
that Plotinus makes no direct use of this metaphor of being clothed, as it were, in incorruption
(*1 Corinthians* 15.53–4; see also *2 Corinthians* 5.4, *Ephesians* 6.13ff.) or in new, white raiment

spirit)[29] for Philo to speak of the *wrong sort* of nakedness: Noah's nakedness when he has drunk wine.[30] A naked mind is one without perception, or without virtue,[31] and Philo expressly condemns those who ignore the *literal* significance of the Law: "as though they were living alone by themselves in a wilderness, or as though they had become disembodied souls, and knew neither city nor village nor household nor any company of human beings at all, overlooking all that the mass of men regard, they explore reality in its naked absoluteness."[32] So we *shouldn't* strip, either physically or intellectually, either ourselves or the world. No one familiar with Philo—an Alexandrian Jew intent on offering a Hellenic reading of the Hebraic texts—expects consistency, but it seems odd that he should simply contradict the text that he purports to allegorize. Perhaps he chose here to suggest that the priest *should* go naked, and that the bells and colored borders required by the text were unnecessary or offensive luxuries? Or perhaps there was a variant, Alexandrian ritual? Or perhaps—most probably—he merely chose to misinterpret the injunction that the high priest should take the clothes off again, and wash, before donning his ordinary clothes and leaving the Sanctuary.[33]

The situation is no clearer on the Greek side. There are rites in which one stripped before undergoing a transformation: but these seem to involve werewolves,[34] which could hardly appeal to either Philo or Plotinus! Rist

---

(*Revelation* 3.5). But cf. *Hermetic Corpus* 10.18: "when the mind has got free of the earthy body, it immediately puts on its own tunic, a tunic of fire, in which it could not stay when in the earthy body" (Copenhaver, *Hermetica*, 34). Is this "tunic of fire" the star-body that each Plotinian soul has been and is?

29. The Rabbinic tradition is insistent that males must not be naked in any sacred context, even while discussing the Torah (nor females anywhere, outside the home). See Satlow, "Jewish Constructions of Nakedness." Romans also reckoned that public nudity was shameful. Cicero, *Tusculan Disputations* 4.70, cites Ennius approvingly as claiming that "flagiti principium est nudare inter civis corpora" (see Craig Williams, *Roman Homosexuality*, 64, 292).

30. Philo, *Legum allegoriarum* 2.60 (*Collected Works*, vol. 1, 261), after *Genesis* 9.20ff. Philo was not alone in finding nakedness ambiguous: in the Christian West nakedness has variously signified purity, new birth, vulnerability, and carnal appetite. See M. Miles, *Carnal Knowing*, 35. The meaning of drunkenness and sobriety will concern me later.

31. Philo, *Legum allegoriarum* 3.16, 3.18 (*Collected Works*, vol. 1, 333, 337), after *Genesis* 3.9ff.

32. "*Ten aletheian gunmen*": Philo, *De migratione Abrahami* 16, 89–90 (*Collected Works*, vol. 4, 183); see Wolfson, *Philo*, 67.

33. *Leviticus* 16.23. Philo also speaks of Moses's "naked philosophy" (*Quod omnis probus liber sit* 43 [*Collected Works*, vol. 9, 35]): one possessed by love of the divine has become a god among men.

34. Pliny, *Natural History*, vol. 8, 81; Petronius, *Satyricon* 3.21, 24; cf. Augustine, *City of God* 18.17. I owe these references to Richard Buxton.

suggests that Plotinus might have the rites of Isis in mind, but gives no actual reference.[35] Witt agrees, bringing a mosaic from Antioch in evidence that initiates went naked into the shrine (but the scene is allegorical—and badly damaged).[36] Egyptian priests—according at least to Plutarch—did attempt to *purify* their bodies, "shaving and making the whole body evenly smooth" and wearing only *linen* clothes rather than anything that could be considered "surplus matter" (such as wool, fur, hair, or claws).[37] But this is not the same as literal nakedness. Both Jews and Christians practiced naked baptism, signifying that the "old man with his deeds" was stripped away, and the proselyte new-born,[38] and it has been suggested that nakedness was normal in ancient pagan initiation rites (indeed, that athletic nakedness is an effect of this),[39] but this is not the rite that either Philo or Plotinus mentions. Bremmer suggests that "Hellenistic and later mediums practiced their art naked or lightly clad," like shamans,[40] but the evidence for this

35. Rist, *Plotinus*, 191. Burkert, *Ancient Mystery Cults*, 39, observes that white linen was the usual costume for an Egyptianized sanctuary. Bonfante, "Nudity as a Costume," 546, cites Frankfort, *Art and Architecture*, 10, as suggesting that it was common practice in Predynastic and Early Dynastic Egypt to be naked before the gods, apparently on the evidence of vase paintings.

36. Witt, *Isis in the Graeco-Roman World*, 161–2. Witt also suggests that Plotinus "could hardly have failed to know" that Isis was commonly herself called "the only one" (307n46), and that this makes Isis equivalent to the One Itself. This speculation is not convincing: *Osiris* is the beauty that Isis "ever loves, and pursues it and unites with it, filling this our world with all the beautiful and good qualities which have a part in its creation" (Plutarch, *De Iside et Osiride*, 243–5 [382d, chap.78]). See also Plutarch, *De Iside et Osiride*, 203–5 (372d, chap. 53): "Isis is the female principle in nature and that which receives all procreation. . . . She has a love of the foremost and most sovereign thing of all, which is the same as the Good, and this she longs for and pursues. The lot which lies with evil she shuns and rejects; for both she is indeed a possible sphere and material, but she leans ever of herself to what is better, offering herself to it for reproduction and for the fructifying in herself of effluxes and likeness. In these she rejoices and she is glad when she is pregnant with them and teems with procreations. For procreation in matter is an image of being, and what comes into being is an imitation of what is." She might then stand, in Plotinian terms, for Matter, Soul, or *Nous* (all of which are variously pregnant with the offspring of a higher hypostasis), but certainly not for the One.

37. Plutarch, *De Iside et Osiride*, 123 (352e, chap. 3).

38. M. Miles, *Carnal Knowing*, 24ff. Cf. Conick and Fossum, "Stripped before God."

39. See Bonfante, "Nudity as a Costume," after Gennep, *Rites of Passage*, 65–115. Michael Chase reminds me that in Aristophanes's *Clouds* the would-be philosopher Strepsiades is told (lines 497–9) to strip off his cloak before entering Socrates's school "naked," *perhaps*—so a late-antique scholiast commented—in imitation of the mysteries. But what Aristophanes's audience would have understood by the joke is uncertain. Nor is it clear whether Strepsiades was wearing a tunic (or only—this being comedy—a codpiece). The assumption that he *must* have had a tunic (and, accordingly, that "*gumnos*" does not mean *really* naked) seems the product of late, un-Greek, embarrassment rather than clear historical evidence.

40. Bremmer, *Early Greek Concept*, 39, after M. Smith, *Clement of Alexandria*, 223.

is very weak. Most likely, the ritual that Plotinus relies upon is the one briefly—and very strangely—invented by Philo (and almost our only reason apart from the fragments of Numenius to suspect that Philo's works had any effect on pagan Alexandria).

So a literal reading of the metaphor raises at least two questions. Why should it be easier to see when naked? What sort of ritual did Philo, Plotinus, and the others have in mind? Nakedness may indeed make another kind of perception easier. And maybe Philo and the rest *imagined* a literal rite into existence because it suited them. Maybe they didn't think that the priest went *literally* naked, but used that phrase exaggeratedly to cover the sort of cleansing and reclothing rituals that were recommended in Leviticus or in pagan rites: the priest was *purified*, not nude, but ascribing nakedness fit better the conclusion, that we must leave our bodily opinions and affections far behind.[41] This may not be wholly possible till death (or even after): till then we must merely imagine that release. So Descartes:

> A mind newly united to an infant's body is wholly occupied in perceiving or feeling the ideas of pain, pleasure, heat, cold and other similar ideas which arise from its union and intermingling with the body. Nonetheless it has in itself the ideas of God, itself and all such truths as are called self-evident in the same way as adult humans have when they are not attending to them; it does not acquire these ideas later on, as it grows older. I have no doubt that if it were taken out of the prison of the body it would find them within itself.[42]

Or as Herbert put it: "here it behoves us to have a little patience for a while until we are freed of our body and the world."[43] But there is a problem here as well. It is not merely *difficult*, as Pyrrho said, to strip off human nature.[44] It may well seem counterproductive. It is true, as Berkeley said, that

41. The notion also occurs in the Hindu tradition, as in *Taittiriya Upanishad* 2.2–5. My thanks to Jonardon Ganeri for this and other Indian references.

42. Descartes, *Philosophical Letters*, 111: "Letter to Hyperaspistes."

43. Herbert, *De veritate*, 104. The Hindu tradition agrees with Plato that even this death may not conclude the problem. According to the *Bhagavad-gita* 2.22, "as a man casting off worn-out garments takes other new ones, so the dweller in the body casting off worn-out bodies takes others that are new." It is widely believed that Platonists considered the body as clothing for the soul. There is some truth in this, but it should also be noted that Plotinus reckoned that the soul was *not* "in the body" but rather the body "in the soul" (see IV.3 [27].20).

44. "Ekdunai ton anthropon"; Diogenes, *Lives* 9.66 (Long and Sedley, *Hellenistic Philosophers*, 1C).

> in our nonage while our minds are empty and unoccupied many notions
> easily find admittance, and as they grow with us and become familiar to
> our understandings we continue a fondness for them. . . . But we would
> do well to consider that other men have imbibed early notions, that they
> as well as we have a country, friends, and persons whom they esteem.
> These are pleas which may be made for any opinion, and are conse-
> quently good pleas for none.[45]

But without those implanted opinions, and without our bodily affections
and modes of perception, what shall we ever hope to find out for ourselves?
If we really attempted to put aside all "prejudice," all opinions taken upon
trust, we should find ourselves entirely destitute.

> The more we think, the more difficult shall we find it to conceive how
> mere man, grown up in the vulgar habits of life, and weighed down by
> sensuality, should ever be able to arrive at science without some tradi-
> tion or teaching, which might either sow the seeds of knowledge, or call
> forth and excite those latent seeds that were originally sown in the soul.[46]

Even if a few brilliant intelligences could cope with believing all and only
what they themselves have "proved" (on what basis, who knows?), that cannot be the normal condition of humanity. Why should we suppose that *all*
our opinions, affections, and perceptions are false or unreliable? And if they
were, how could we hope to correct them? And why should we suppose that
a purely intellectual approach will discover Truth? What is it *like* to leave
aside our bodies or our individual souls? What shall we know if we have no
senses and no particular location or boundary?

Herbert also acknowledged the importance of "common notions": "Reason is the process of applying common notions as far as it can, and has
nothing beyond them to which it can appeal. Common Notions, therefore,
are principles which it is not legitimate to dispute."[47] "Anyone who prefers
persistently and stubbornly to reject these principles might as well stop his
ears, shut his eyes and *strip himself of all humanity*."[48]

So if we are not to strip off all humanity but rather hang on to such
"common notions," it may be presumed that we should *not* after all go

---

45. Berkeley, *Sermon on Religious Zeal* (1709–12) (*Works*, vol. 7, 20).
46. Berkeley, *Siris*, 339 (*Works*, vol. 5, 154).
47. Herbert, *De veritate*, 120.
48. Ibid., 131 (my italics).

naked into the shrine. Maybe we should leave off *only* our "trinkets" and retain our clothes. According to Plotinus, "a general opinion affirms that what is one and the same in number is everywhere present as a whole, when all men are naturally and spontaneously moved to speak of the god who is in each one of us one and the same."[49] That is not a notion he would wish abandoned. Nor does he approve of those who imagine that they alone have insight and "have the insolence to pull to pieces what the godlike men of antiquity have said nobly and in accordance with the truth" (II.9 [33].9, 12–3). We are neither "naked apes" nor "naked angels" but clothed with tradition, symbol, and received opinion.

> How you ever noticed how true is that old phrase, "clothed and in his right mind"? Man is not in his right mind when he is not clothed with the symbols of his social dignity. Humanity is not even human when it is naked. But in a lower sense it is so of lesser things, even of lifeless things. A lot of nonsense is talked about auras; but this is the truth behind it. Everything has a halo. Everything has a sort of atmosphere of what it signifies, which makes it sacred.[50]

So what grounds the suggestion that we should strip, and what exactly is it that Plotinus means us to discard, and when?

Rist suggests that when Proclus speaks of stripping away our garments "and the advance of the naked soul," he is speaking "literally" of the physical accretions picked up in the soul's original descent into the corporeal, while Plotinus "speaks metaphorically and analogically."[51] This may be so, just as it may be that the Aztecs, being a literal-minded people, misread the spiritual metaphors of the Maya.[52] "A broken and a contrite heart, O God, thou wilt not despise!"[53] Is it enough to translate the remarks of Philo, Plotinus, or Herbert from their fanciful and ornamented language into explicit ethical or religious dictat? "Put aside all personal prejudices and corporeal desires; keep your attention fixed upon eternal and unchang-

---

49. Armstrong comments that this is "one of Plotinus' rare appeals to the common experience of mankind" (vol. 5, 326n). See also IV.4 [28].31, 30–2: "we grant that what is agreed by all, or by most people, is so, insofar as rational discussion will show it to be so."

50. Chesterton, *Poet and the Lunatics*, 68.

51. Rist, *Plotinus*, 191.

52. Séjourné, *Burning Water*. See also Hillman, *Dream*, 114–7, on taking images "literally"—a theme he associates with Heracles and the "heroic ego" (but Heracles has a different significance in Plotinian thought).

53. *Psalm* 51.17.

ing realities; see things as they are." No doubt that instruction too embodies metaphors, however moribund: can such things be literally "put aside"? What glue is appropriate to fix attention? But the essence of the instruction can—perhaps—be carefully conveyed in these less fanciful and ornamented terms.

Or perhaps it can't.

The advice is to "look inward," identify the garments, emotional baggage, and "trinkets," and put them aside "in imagination." "[Our] business, if [we] are to be beautiful again, is to wash and clean [ourselves] and so again be what [we were] before."[54] In one way, this is no more than any adult has long learned to do. We "put aside" such issues as can only interfere with the performance of a present duty. We may even "imagine" their being placed in a container, or folded neatly away, to make space for a more focused attention. We may imagine a candle flame and feed our present worries into it till our minds are, maybe, quiet. If we were not to do so, if we continued to be thinking and feeling about all the potential claims on that attention all the time, we should never accomplish anything. "Multitasking" is of course a fashionable nostrum: women, it is said, have always had to have an ear to the multiple requirements of an everyday household, and all of us may be similarly occupied. Heads of department, at any rate, can't afford entirely to forget about student progress cases, essay marking, staff promotion, research bids, and book-ordering policy even when they really want to be preparing tomorrow's lecture or doing their own research! And that research in turn can't always be exactly focused: perhaps a multitude of partly remembered texts and topics gradually coalesce, gradually reveal their unity. We should not always, and we cannot always, be doing One Thing Only. On the contrary, the intellect exists in looking *toward* an unimaginable One, and so being filled with a complexity whose unity is visible only in the light of that unseen (III.8 [30].8, 31ff.).[55] If the One, the Good, holds beauty (the beauty that is intelligible reality) before it as a bulwark or a veil (I.6 [1].9, 34ff.),[56] it is equally the case that the intellect is clothed in that bright raiment as it looks toward the One.

But if that cloak or clothing is, in its way, appropriate, it remains the case that even multitaskers do not literally do everything at once, nor attend

---

54. After I.6 [1].5, 47ff.

55. See also II.9 [33].9, 37, on the multiplicity of gods through which God is known.

56. See also *Isa Upanishad* 15: "The face of truth is covered with a golden dish. Uncover it, O Pusan, for me, a man faithful to the truth." So also according to Avicenna (Ibn Sina), God is "veiled in His own beauty" (Corbin, *Avicenna*, 149–50).

to everything. And multitasking is not always what is needed. Maybe there has been too much emphasis, historically, on the fully focused mind—a mind that only those who have no household or other administrative duties could even imagine—but there will still be times when focusing, washing, or stripping is required. There is also a perverse image of the multitasker's life: one madly divided between equally pressing needs and longings, without any sense of a coherent outcome.

> There was an old sailor my grandfather knew
> Who had so many things that he wanted to do
> That, whenever he thought it was time to begin,
> He couldn't because of the state he was in.

The sailor, to be sure, was a *failed* multitasker:

> He thought of his hut . . . and he thought of his boat,
> And his hat and his breeks, and his chickens and goat,
> And his hooks (for his food) and the spring (for his thirst) . . .
> But he *never* could think which he ought to do first.[57]

It is still, even for multitaskers, worth remembering "the one thing needful" rather than the "many things,"[58] and not allowing oneself to be distracted. Some things matter more than others, and—in the end—one thing matters more than anything else. "A man has not failed if he fails to win beauty of colours or bodies, or power or office or kingship even, but if he fails to win this and only this" (I.6 [1].7, 34–5)—though what "this" may be must wait for later exposition.

> You should collect and combine into one the thoughts implanted within you, endeavouring to isolate those that are confused, and to drag to light those that are enveloped in darkness. The divine Plato too made this his starting-point, summoning us away from the sensible to the intelligible. Also if you would remember, you would combine what you have heard, and recall it by memory, desiring to turn your mind to discourses of this kind as to excellent counsellors, and afterwards practising in action what you have learned, bearing it in mind in your labours.[59]

57. Milne, *Now We Are Six*, 36.
58. See *Luke* 10.41–2.
59. Porphyry, *To Marcella*, 35–6 (§10).

Art theorists have used the resources of the English language to distinguish "nakedness" and "nudity"—a distinction not made in Greek, Latin, or Hebrew.[60] The naked are the stripped, the unconcealed, visible in their plain, "natural" condition. The nude, on the other hand, have put on a particular form, as it were, of "unclothedness" as a garment: whether for aesthetic or pornographic reasons, the nude are posed, with stereotyped posture, facial expression, gesture. Nudity is an art form, whether this is approved (as it is by Kenneth Clark) or disapproved (as it is by many feminist critics).[61]

> For me the naked and the nude
> (By lexicographers construed
> As synonyms that should express
> The same deficiency of dress
> Or shelter) stand as far apart
> As love from lies, or truth from art.[62]

The distinction is not explicitly made in the Greek or other ancient texts, but it is still one that offers another point of entry to the metaphor. On the one hand, Plato's use of nakedness, as above, is to suggest that the naked are unconcealed: spots, scars, tags, and sagging flesh are all on view. On the other, the point of putting these on view is to encourage us to remedy our failings, and the statues that we may make of ourselves and others are idealized. The mortal man who served as template for Pheidias's Zeus might not recognize himself in the statue. The model for Praxiteles's Aphrodite[63] was also not represented, as we say, "photographically." Indeed, it may be—as later artists have testified[64]—that Pheidias and Praxiteles borrowed different body parts from different models and "airbrushed" the scars of individual life. "Underneath such descriptions is an idea of a singular, universal body, an idealized composite of the 'best' features of real bodies."[65]

---

60. "Nudity" comes into English centuries after "nakedness," being Latin in its origin rather than Teutonic—but it does not seem that the terms originally differed in meaning or affect. See Berger, *Ways of Seeing*, 54; Spivey, *Greek Sculpture*, 111–3. Spivey suggests (111, 115) that depicting characters in "the costume of nudity" elevates a scene "from the realistic to the supernatural."

61. On which see Barcan, *Nudity*, after K. Clark, *Nude*; Kuhn, *Power of the Image*. Barcan herself prefers not to distinguish nakedness and nudity.

62. Graves, *Poems*, 189.

63. Of which it was said that Aphrodite herself wondered when Praxiteles had seen her naked (Paton, *Greek Anthology* VI.160).

64. E.g., Raphael; see K. Clark, *Nude*, 109.

65. Barcan, *Nudity*, 34.

Feminist commentators, not unreasonably, have deplored the false image of particular—and often female—bodies that such art contrives, creating a standard against which all actual women must fall short. It is not clear that recent artistic efforts to portray *actual* bodies, unadorned and unairbrushed, avoid the problem: pornographic realism is just another artistic style, as much a pose as the most "tasteful" statue. Nor is it necessarily an error to look toward the "ideal form," echoed in mortal flesh: there is at any rate psychological evidence, as well as philosophical tradition, to suggest that we most admire "the norm," revealed in composite photographs as images of an unearthly beauty.[66] So it is also in more abstract matters: as Plotinus argued, in one of the few ancient testimonials to democracy, an assembly of variously mistaken mortals may produce a better and more accurate result than any individual—at any rate, we may add, as long as the members of that assembly are allowed their individual opinions and are not seduced by charismatic or expert leaders (VI.5 [23].10).[67]

Did Plotinus intend us to image a form of nakedness that lets us stand as individuals with our particular histories and failings, or did he intend a still stricter "stripping"—a stripping that brings us closer to the human norm by polishing away our difference? Is it nakedness or nudity in question? Our own untutored sensibility or "common notions"? It seems likely that he meant the latter.

> Let us take soul, not the soul in body which has acquired irrational desires and passions and admitted other affection[s], but the soul which has wiped these away and which, as far as possible, has no communion with the body. . . . Consider it by stripping, or rather let the man who has stripped look at himself and believe himself immortal, when he looks at himself as he has come to be in the intelligible and the pure. (IV.7 [2].10, 8–11, 30–3)[68]

66. Beauty can also be increased by accentuating particular features that are more or less typical (at least in the eye of the beholder) of feminine or masculine faces. In the process, "defects" are smoothed out.

67. See also Aristotle, *Politics* 3.1281a42–b2. The notion should not be taken too far (see IV.4 [28].17 for a more familiar judgment on the follies of an undisciplined assembly, whether in the soul or in the city): a massed choir of voices, variously out of tune and rhythm, does not necessarily sound good. And "though these *common notions* may be very busy sometimes in the vegetation of divine Knowledge; yet the corrupt vices of men may so clog, disturb and overrule them (as the Naturalists say this unruly and masterless *matter* doth [clog] the natural *forms* in the formation of living creatures) that they produce nothing but Monsters miserably distorted and misshapen"; John Smith (1660), in Patrides, *Cambridge Platonists*, 132.

68. He goes on to speak of cleaning up "self-control [better, "self-possession"] and justice" in ourselves, as one cleans ancient statues, "rusted with time" (IV.7 [2].10, 47), after Plato, *Phaedrus* 247d.

Stripping off in imagination, stripping off the imagined baggage, polishing ourselves into the ideal form, or knocking off the incrustations (I.1
[53].12, 14–5) may be no more than the necessary focus on some one significant task. According to one verse submitted in a contest for the post of
patriarch in the Ch'an school of Greater Vehicle Buddhism:

> The body is the Bodhi tree,
> The mind is like a clear mirror.
> At all times we must strive to polish it,
> And must not let the dust collect.[69]

But the successful candidate, an illiterate peasant named Hui Neng, later
responded:

> Bodhi originally has no tree,
> The mirror also has no stand.
> Buddha nature is always clean and pure;
> Where is there room for dust?[70]

The constant effort to clean, polish, strip, and the rest may prove ineffec-
tive, and even counterproductive. The true goal—according to Buddhist
speculation—is to recognize that there is nowhere we need to go. And perhaps this is closer to Plotinus's vision.

> Plotinus' philosophy can be understood as a bold attempt to train the
> mind to break the power of the image and to interrupt the perpetual di-
> version of our consciousness into a state of alienation from the soul.[71]

The object in Plotinus and the rest is to go up "into the shrine"—and where
shall we find that? It is not, after all, a "journey for the feet"! How shall
we enter the inner sanctuary, passing even the choir of the virtues, and the
temple images (VI.9 [9].11)?[72] Is there after all some proper way of "stripping off humanity" or acknowledging our underlying nakedness?
    "This is the intention of the command given in the mysteries here

---

69. Hui Neng, *Platform Sutra*, 130.
70. Ibid., 132.
71. Wildberg, "Dionysus in the Mirror of Philosophy," 231.
72. See also V.1 [10].6. This image too either is a Plotinian invention or borrowed from the
Hebraic tradition.

below not to disclose to the uninitiated; since that Good is not disclosable, it prohibits the disclosure of the divine to another who has not also himself had the good fortune to see" (VI.9 [9].11, 1–4). Even the initiate, most of the time, will see no more than images, and herself be clothed in virtue and (as Philo suggested)[73] the world. According to Herbert, "when we have thrown off our earthly chains, a new and more amenable matter, consisting of new elements, will be supplied, so that we shall appear clothed throughout in heavenly glory."[74] During our ascent, Plotinus hints or jests, we shall be stars (as indeed we—in our higher identity—already are).[75] But it seems likely that he envisages a final stripping—or rather a final recognition that we are already naked, empty, bright. There is neither dust nor mirror. If the One is to be apprehended, it can only (if at all) be by the One. "There was not even any reason or thought, and he himself was not there, if we must even say this; but he was as if carried away or possessed by a god, in a quiet solitude and a state of calm, altogether at rest and having become a kind of rest" (VI.9 [9].11, 11–6). What comes away from that interior temple carries an image of conversing "not with a statue or image, but with the Divine itself" (VI.9 [9].11, 21–2).[76]

So Damascius on *Phaedo* 66d: "the last garment and the one most difficult to cast off is, on the appetitive level, ambition, and on the cognitive level, *phantasia*. Hence even the majority of philosophers are hampered by these, and especially by *phantasia*. Therefore Plato here bids the philosopher to strip himself even of this last garment."[77]

It is at this point, perhaps, that my earlier remark—that it is more often the Truth that we imagine naked rather than the one who sees that Truth— can be turned round. To "see" the naked Truth one must be naked, since none but that Truth can see.[78] Nor is its "seeing" any sort of intellection, but the final absence of distracting thought. These distractions, it may be, are not simply our "opinions" but our consciousness of status and reputa-

73. Philo, *Life of Moses* 2.117–21 (*Collected Works*, vol. 6, 505).

74. Herbert, *De veritate*, 172. See Ricks, "Garment of Adam," on the tradition that Adam and Eve were first clothed in "garments of glory" before the Fall and in "garments of skin" (variously interpreted) afterward.

75. See IV.3 [27].17 for our souls' descent into the stars, and IV.4 [28].5 for the ascent. It was an Egyptian opinion that the stars embodied the souls of the dead (Hornung, *Conceptions of God*, 81).

76. On the ambiguous nature of "nympholepsy," whether inspirational or delusive, see further Connor, "Seized by the Nymphs."

77. Cited by G. Watson, *Phantasia*, 125.

78. See also I.6 [1].9, 30–1: "no eye ever saw the sun without becoming sun-like."

tion: "going naked" is to be "open," "empty," "unashamed," and only those able to risk that loss can really expect to "see."

And might this intellectual exercise be ritually enacted? Might we be expected not only to *imagine* ourselves casting off the works of darkness but to go through an actual, bodily ritual, in which the garments we lay aside are, imaginatively, imbued with symbols, and we become, for a moment, pure, alone, in touch? The tradition of modern witchcraft, Wicca, does include ritual nakedness, perhaps as an *effect* of these very metaphors, or perhaps to mean something else entirely.[79] There have also been some odd associations for high-principled naturism or even more high-principled ecomysticism. Plotinus cannot easily be blamed for these: someone who boycotted the baths and—by Porphyry's account—was "ashamed to be in a body" presumably preferred to be, literally speaking, clothed. *Public* ceremonial—by Porphyry's account at least—was no part of Plotinus's way, though he and his friends did celebrate the birthdays (or the death days) of Socrates and Plato. Since public ceremonial would usually have involved animal sacrifice or gladiatorial games, his abstinence in this is not surprising.

On the other hand, though "literal" public nakedness was probably not what he had in mind, he seems to have had no personal possessions, nothing to hold his attention to corporeal needs. Perhaps there is another implication of the gymnosophistical instruction, one missed by the merely intellectual interpretation. When Saint Francis of Assisi, not yet sanctified, gave up his clothes (except a hair shirt or an old tunic begged from a farmer), he was making a serious and symbolic point: he was abandoning the wealth and station of his father, in favor of "holy poverty."[80] Naturism makes much of "healthy," "natural" values and is indulged on beaches, in the sun—and mostly on beaches kept from public view, by relatively wealthy patrons. Franciscan nakedness is closer to what Plotinus meant, founded not in the pleasure of naked skin but in rejection of everything not needed, including the distinctions of wealth and status. So if there is a public ritual associated with the gymnosophistical instruction, it is a vow of poverty. Thus, Heraclas, a Christian pupil of Ammonius Saccas and later bishop of Alexandria, "stripped off" (*apodusamenos*) his common clothing to adopt a "philosopher's garb."[81]

Perhaps Plotinus himself did not go so far. He cared for the property of the orphans entrusted to his charge (in case they turned out *not* to be phi-

79. See Luhrmann, *Persuasions of the Witch's Craft*; Hutton, *Pagan Religions*.
80. See Chesterton, *St. Francis*, 51.
81. According to a letter of Origen, cited by Eusebius, *History*, 19 (6.19, 13–4).

losophers, and so to need that property),[82] but by the standards of his day
he lived in comfort, nor did he explicitly require his followers to abandon
anything—though if their property *were* taken away, "they may recognize
that it was not theirs before either, and that its possession is a mockery to
the robbers themselves when others take it away from them; for even to
those who do not have it taken away, to have it is worse than being deprived
of it" (III.2 [47].15, 40–1).[83] One senator, Rogatianus, did abandon wealth
and status to live the philosophic life on Plotinus's advice or inspiration, but
this was exceptional enough to be noticed and was held up by Plotinus as
an example of philosophical devotion (and even he probably kept enough for
comfort).[84] Others—like Serapion, "unable to free himself from the degradation of finance and money-lending"[85]—did not.

82. Porphyry, *Life* 9.14. A similar story is told of other philosophers—for example, of Crates
the Cynic (see Diogenes, *Lives* 5.88). It does not follow that Plotinus didn't say it.

83. See also III.2 [47].5, 15: "some troubles are profitable to the sufferers themselves,
poverty and sickness for example." The robbers, we should note, might well be imperial agents,
expropriating funds to maintain the army and bureaucracy.

84. Porphyry, *Life* 7.40. Rogatianus ate only every other day: is it entirely irrelevant that
Plotinus remarks (IV.4 [28].28, 38) that people get bad-tempered when they haven't eaten?

85. Porphyry, *Life* 7.47–50.

CHAPTER SIX

On Becoming Love

I have spoken repeatedly of "love."[1] But what exactly is meant by this? Need we distinguish *eros, agape, philia*, and *storge*[2] or insist that "Christian *agape*" is different from the dangerous delusions of friendship or erotic fancy?[3] Even within the pagan tradition it is possible to distinguish the Orphic and Hesiodic Eros, First Begotten, also known as Phanes; the Empedoclean Eros, in permanent tension with Eris, Strife; Eros, the child of Ares and Aphrodite; and the child of Poros and Penia, in Plato's allegory.[4] The notion, still common among commentators, that there is a simple contrast to be made between pagan *eros* and Christian *agape* is at least unhelpful. So is the underlying notion, misread from Plato, that we can only be said to "love" things that we do not "have."

> Dionysius speaks Proclus' language when distinguishing four kinds of Love, (1) the *eros epistreptikos*, of lower things for higher ones and ultimately for the absolute and transcendent Good, (2) the *eros koinonikos*, of equal things for one another, (3) the *eros pronoetikos*, of higher beings for lower ones, (4) the *eros sunektikos*, of things for themselves.[5]

---

1. Earlier versions of this chapter were presented at Leuven in 2000 and in Manchester and Oxford in 2006.

2. See Lewis, *Four Loves*. Lewis employs these terms to make significant distinctions, but he does not make the mistake of thinking that such distinctions are easily found in the Greek texts.

3. Nygren, *Agape and Eros*; D'Arcy, *Mind and Heart of Love*.

4. See M. Edwards, "Gnostic Eros and Orphic Themes."

5. Vogel, "Greek Cosmic Love," 59, after Pseudo-Dionysius, *Divine Names* 4.11.5 (708c–713d) (*Works*, 80–3). Vogel (62) is too harsh in remarking of Nygren that "obviously the Swedish theologian had not the faintest idea of what the spirit of Platonism was"—but she was right that Nygren's belief that "Platonic Eros" must be self-serving is, for the reasons she outlines, false.

The title of my chapter—"On Becoming Love"—is drawn from the twenty-second section of VI.7 [38], "On the Forms and the Good," which Armstrong reckoned "perhaps the greatest of the single works of Plotinus."[6] Here Plotinus describes the soul's attraction to the forms—that is, to reality—as they are colored by light from the Good: "the soul, receiving into itself an outflow from thence, is moved and dances wildly and is all stung with longing and becomes love."[7] The description echoes what he had said much earlier, in I.6 [1], "On Beauty": "these experiences must occur whenever there is contact with any sort of beautiful thing, wonder and a shock of delight and longing and passion and a happy excitement. One can have these experiences by contact with invisible beauties, and souls do have them, practically all, but particularly those who are more passionately in love with the invisible, just as with bodies all see them, but all are not stung as sharply, but some, who are called lovers, are most of all" (I.6 [1].4, 16–7).

Properly understood, to be is to be beautiful. The beauty of things rests in their reality. But even those beauties excite us only when they are, as it were, illuminated. Without that, it is as if we were "in the presence of a face which is certainly beautiful, but cannot catch the eye because it has no grace playing upon its beauty. So here below beauty is what illuminates good proportions rather than the good proportions themselves, and this is what is lovable. For why is there more light of beauty on a living face, but only a trace of it on a dead one even if its flesh and its proportions are not yet wasted away? And are not the more lifelike statues the more beautiful ones, even if others are better proportioned? And is not an uglier living man more beautiful than the beautiful man in a statue?" (VI.7 [38].22, 27–32). What illumines them is the source of their being—namely, the Good, the One—or just occasionally to *hyperkalon*, whether that is the supremely beautiful or what lies beyond beauty. In both passages, however the thing is phrased, the excitement is real, and to be welcomed. Becoming love, or falling in love with beauty, is apparently a Good Thing.

This is not as obviously true as we might wish. We are very easily deluded, and might expect philosophers to warn us of that peril and busily unweave our rainbows and "the tender-person'd Lamia."[8] Plotinus certainly

---

6. Armstrong, *Enneads*, vol. 7, 78.

7. Ferwerda, *Signification des images*, 99–100, connects this "sting" with III.5 [50].7, 19 (on love) and also with III.2 [47].9, 33, where Plotinus employs the Stoical notion that bedbugs serve to stop us sleeping late (cf. chap. 18 below). The connection with being startled awake is not inappropriate, though Plotinus may not have felt this particular association. Evils in general keep us from slumber: II.3 [52].18, 8.

8. Keats, "Lamia," pt. 2, line 238 (*Works*, 177).

wishes us free from all enchantments, especially the "magic of nature" (*he tes phuseos goeteia*).

> This is what the magic of nature does; for to pursue what is not good as if it was good, drawn by the appearance of good by irrational impulses, belongs to one who is being ignorantly led where he does not want to go. And what would anyone call this other than magical enchantment? The man then alone is free from enchantment who when his other parts are trying to draw him says that none of the things are good which they declare to be so, but only that which he knows himself, not deluded or pursuing but possessing it. (IV.4 [28].44, 30–7)

Falling in love happens when a soul assents to the affection of the other (IV.4 [28].43)—that is, to the passions of the alien soul that is wrapped round our real self (VI.4 [22].14), the self each of us was before we were born.

> Even before this coming to be we were there, men who were different, and some of us even gods, pure souls and intellect united with the whole of reality; we were parts of the intelligible, not marked off or cut off but belonging to the whole; and we are not cut off even now. (VI.4 [22].14, 18–22)[9]

To recall ourselves is to cast off that "other man," who has "wound himself round us," so that we here-now have come to be double. Moralists in a related tradition may note the obvious parallel.

> It is time for you to wake out of sleep, for deliverance is nearer to us now than it was when first we believed. It is far in the night; day is near. Let us therefore throw off the deeds of darkness and put on our armour as soldiers of the light.[10]

The countercharms that are needed will remind the lover that the beauty he desires is not exclusively possessed by his beloved and is not identical with the underlying body. "He must be taught not to cling around one body and be excited by that, but must be led by the course of reasoning to consider all bodies and shown the beauty that is the same in all of them" (I.3 [20].2, 5–8). He is then to follow the route laid out by Plato, till "from

---

9. Note that "men" here translates *anthropoi* (i.e., human beings), but that, like almost all well-known philosophers till very recently, Plotinus is thinking primarily of the male.

10. Paul, *Romans* 12.11–2 (New English Bible).

virtues he can ascend to intellect, to being; and There he must go the higher way" (I.3 [20].2, 13–5).

Bishop Nonnus of Edessa, in contemplating the beauty of a dancer (the future St. Pelagia), "took it as a subject for glorifying the sovereign beauty, of which her beauty was only the reflection, and feeling himself transported by the fire of divine love, shed tears of joy. . . . He was raised," continues St. John Climacus, "to a wholly incorruptible state before the universal resurrection."[11]

It is not unduly cynical to wonder a little about Bishop Nonnus's emotions! Certainly we might wonder about our own.

I think [so Seneca wrote] Panaetius gave a charming answer to the youth who asked whether the wise man would fall in love: "As to the wise man, we shall see. What concerns you and me, who are still a great distance from the wise man, is to ensure that we do not fall into a state of affairs which is disturbed, powerless, subservient to another and worthless to oneself."[12]

All too easily "the soul becomes ugly by mixture and dilution and inclination toward the body and matter" (I.6 [1].5, 48–50). In consenting to that "other soul's affections," the individual soul loses its freedom. "When the soul is altered by the external causes, and so does something and drives on in a sort of blind rush [tuphlei tei phorai], neither its action nor its disposition is to be called free. . . . When in its impulse it has as director its own pure and untroubled reason [logon], then this impulse alone is said to be in our own power and free" (III.1 [3].9, 5–12).[13] That alone expresses the thing, the self, we were.

So also Philo of Alexandria:

One thing reinforced by drunkenness is that gluttony whose great power for mischief is so widespread and constant, which leaves those who in-

---

11. Evdokimov, *Ages of the Spiritual Life*, 150, after Migne, *Patrologia Graeca* 88.893.

12. Seneca, *Letters* 116.5 (Long and Sedley, *Hellenistic Philosophers*, vol. 1, 423 [66C]).

13. This is not to engage with arguments about "free will" and "determinism." Plotinus insisted that we were ourselves real causes, whose acts weren't simply and uncontroversially what the world demands, as the Stoics thought (see III.1 [3].4, 25–9), but "freedom" in this context is simply not being forced into an unnatural or inauthentic form. Acting according to our deepest nature is freedom, whether or not that nature arises from causes outside our control.

dulge in it, as we may see, with a void in their desires even though they
have every vacant place in their bodies filled.[14]

So falling in love is a dangerous sort of drunkenness, and we should expect the philosopher to withdraw from it, to "keep his head" (or hers). It is
not only the corporeal that may prove distracting. Beauty itself, even the
higher beauty of the intellect, the forms whether taken singly or as aspects
of the whole intelligible reality, is something less than the Good. "Beauty
brings wonder and shock and pleasure mingled with pain" (V.5 [32].12, 35–6)[15]
and may draw the soul *away* from the Good, "as the beloved draws a child
away from its father" (V.5 [32].12, 35–6). Though Plotinus does not quite say
so, we may begin to suspect that falling in love with laws and institutions
may be yet *more* dangerous than more familiar appetites![16] Philosophy itself
may often be a distraction.

> It is important to realise that, as the whole context makes clear, it is in-
> telligible beauty, the beauty of the World of Forms, which is in question
> here: the passage cannot possibly mean that we are liable to be distracted
> from our spiritual quest by the beauties of the sense-world, which would
> be commonplace Platonism enough. It is Platonic metaphysics at what
> most people before, and a great many after, Plotinus would have thought
> was its highest, which may get in the way. It is the *eros* of the philoso-
> pher as Plato understood it which may seduce us from reunion with our
> father, waiting quietly for us, always available. Philosophy may provide
> the philosopher with the ultimate temptation which will lead him away
> from what he really desires and needs.[17]

On the other hand, Plotinus regularly uses bodily love as his best image
for our association with the Good. "If anyone does not know this experience
[i.e., to return to the father] let him think of it in terms of our lives here, and
what it is like to attain what one is most in love with" (VI.9 [9].9, 38–41). It

---

14. Philo, *De ebrietate* 50.206 (*Collected Works*, vol. 3, 425). See also Cicero, *Tusculan
Disputations* 4.36: "the man thus afflicted should be advised what madness love is: for of all the
perturbations of the mind, there is not one which is more vehement; for (without charging it
with rapes, debaucheries, adultery, or even incest, the baseness of any of these being very blame-
able; not, I say, to mention these) the very perturbation of the mind in love is base of itself, for,
to pass over all its acts of downright madness, what weakness do not those very things which
are looked upon as indifferent argue?"
15. See also V.5 [32].12, 37.
16. See IV.4 [28].44, 11–2.
17. Armstrong, "Elements," 21.

is a "passionate experience like that of a lover resting in the beloved" (VI.9 [9].4, 18–9). "The lover here below has beauty in this way, not by receiving it but by lying with it" (VI.5 [23].10, 6–7). "Lovers and their beloveds here below imitate this in their will to be united" (VI.7 [38].34, 14–6). Nor are these experiences to be rejected absolutely: after all, "how could there be a musician who sees the melody in the intelligible world and will not be stirred when he hears the melody in sensible sounds?" (II.9 [33].16, 39–41). We *ought* to be "in love" and *ought* to look on all the things around us with affection and delight.

> Intellect . . . has one power for thinking, by which it looks at the things in itself, and one by which it looks at what transcends it by a direct awareness and reception, by which also before it saw only, and by seeing acquired intellect and is one. And that first one is the contemplation of Intellect in its right mind, and the other is Intellect in love, when it goes out of its mind "drunk with the nectar"; then it falls in love, simplified into happiness [*haplotheis eis eupatheian*] by having its fill, and it is better for it to be drunk with a drunkenness like this than to be more respectably sober. (VI.7 [38].35, 20–8)

But how is this to be? Why should we not insist instead that *sober* reason is right reason (a topic I shall also address below, in considering the meaning and role of drunkenness)? After all, Plotinus's barbed complaint against the Gnostics has a point: "to set oneself above intellect is immediately to fall outside it" (II.9 [33].9, 52). "The desire of good often involves the fall into evil" (III.5 [50].1, 64–5). Taking things philosophically, it has often been supposed, is to try to see them *without* personal attachment, as one might consider the affairs of strangers.

> In the case of particular things that delight you, or benefit you, or to which you have grown attached, remind yourself of what they are. Start with things of little value. If it is china you like, for instance, say, "I am fond of a piece of china." When it breaks, then you won't be as disconcerted. When giving your wife or child a kiss, repeat to yourself, "I am kissing a mortal." Then you won't be so distraught if they are taken from you.[18]

---

18. Epictetus, *Discourses*, 222 (*Encheiridion* 3). This was also Anaxagoras's response to the news that his sons were dead: that he already knew they were mortal (Diogenes, *Lives* 2.13). Nevertheless, it is also said that he killed himself in despair.

And again:

> We can familiarize ourselves with the will of nature by calling to mind
> our common experiences. When a friend breaks a [clay cup], we are quick
> to say, "Oh, bad luck." It's only reasonable, then, that when a [cup] of
> your own breaks, you accept it in the same patient spirit. Moving on
> to graver things: when somebody's wife or child dies, to a man we all
> routinely say, "Well, that's part of life." But if one of our own family is
> involved, then right away it's "Poor, poor me!" We would do better to
> remember how we react when a similar loss afflicts.[19]

This sort of advice may sometimes be helpful, but it is hard to believe that
many of us can entirely follow it, or even believe that we should. There is
something that we value, exactly, in personal attachment, and in finding
something (a cup, a tree, a child) entirely precious (nor do we forget that
others feel that way about their own beloveds). Is there perhaps a different
way to cope with losses and departures, a way that does not denigrate or
diminish what we—and others—value?

To begin to answer that I must refer briefly to Plotinus's metaphysical
theories and try to show their phenomenological relevance. Intellect is generated, so Plotinus says, in its own turn toward the One. In turning it is
filled with the multiple forms that are the only way that the One can be
conceptualized.[20] But the One itself is beyond all form (as being the cause
of form). Intellect, it can then be said, exists both as a bare recognition of,
and delight in, the transcendent and as the active intellect conjoined with
the intelligibles, as intelligible reality. Epistemologically, we see the *form*
of things, we grasp them intellectually, when we see how different parts
and elements cohere in a single purpose. Ontologically, intelligible reality
is unified because it has, in all its parts, a single point and origin. Even in
its, as it were, *intellectual* phase the intellect is superior to soul, since soul
can apprehend things only from particular points of view, in linear fashion,
whereas intellect holds every truth together as a theorem of a united science.[21] From our point of view, awakening to that intellectual whole, and
realizing that we ourselves are points or perspectives, that there—crudely—

---

19. Epictetus, *Discourses*, 232 (*Encheiridion* 26).

20. Plato uses the same metaphor of turning, or being turned, away from darkness to the
light: *Republic* 7.518cd.

21. This is only an analogy: strictly, the divine intellect contemplates, not *propositions*, but
the real things that our propositions are about (V.8 [31].5–6).

really *is* a world of which our sensory experiences are only copies, shadows, or reflections, is waking up from a drunken stupor. My present *feeling* is that I am here, and you (as it were) are over there, and that if you suddenly fall over, it doesn't hurt (me) a bit. Sympathy (and mirror neurons) may partly unite us, but any pain *you* feel is still not *mine*.[22] This world, the world we usually inhabit, is, as Marcus Aurelius said, a dream and a delirium,[23] structured by fears and fantasies. The moment of discovering that our child, our spouse, our colleague, our dog, or the birds of the air are separate existents, with their own perspective—a perspective within which we ourselves may play a smaller part than we had casually assumed—will always be a shock.[24] And one that we habitually forget as soon as possible: "It is as if people who slept through their life thought the things in their dreams were reliable and obvious, but, if someone woke them up, disbelieved in what they saw with their eyes open and went to sleep again" (V.5 [32].11, 19-23).

By this standard it is not only the world we seem to see that is a shadow: we are shadows ourselves—or at least the selves we know are shadows:

We are unsubstantiated dreams, impalpable visions, like the flight of a passing bird, like a ship leaving no track upon the sea, a speck of dust, a vapour, an early dew, a flower that quickly blooms and quickly fades.[25]

Or as Pindar put it: "man is a shadow's dream [*skias onar*], but when (a) god sheds a brightness then shining light is on earth, and life is as sweet as honey."[26]

This much, this "objective" gaze, is something that even materialists can agree with (as the Stoics did), though they may not realize—almost certainly do not realize—its potential. The "real world," they thought, is

22. See my "Plotinian Dualisms and the 'Greek' Ideas of Self." To avoid misunderstanding: when I offered this thought at an Anglo-Chinese convivium in 2006, I was disturbed to discover that some auditors imagined that I was endorsing a purely egoistical doctrine, that no one else's suffering could ever matter much to us. My point was entirely opposite: that this suffering, even if it is born of ignorance, matters immensely, and that our acknowledgment of this depends on our opening the eye of "intellect," not as the conclusion of an abstract (and somewhat inconclusive) argument, but as a real discovery, a revelation.

23. Aurelius, *Meditations* 2.17.1.

24. See Blake, *Marriage of Heaven and Hell*, pls. 6–7 (*Writings*, 150): "How do you know but every bird that cuts the airy way, is an immense world of delight, closed by your senses five?"

25. Gregory Nazianzen, *Orationes* 7.19 (AD 369); cited by Rahner, *Man at Play*, 235.

26. Pindar, *Pythian* 8.95–7. The phrase is remembered by Thomas, *Neb*, 78. See Morgan, *R. S. Thomas*, 27–8.

one without privileged times, scales, or locations, and arguably without real identities or explanations (V.1 [10].4).[27] But for Plotinus materialists were still asleep (III.6 [26].6, 65–6).[28] Even modern physicists, who have followed the Platonic or Pythagorean line by seeing the world, the real world, as mathematics, fail, in his eyes, to understand what must "breathe fire into the equations."[29] Even they, though liberated from a merely mechanical determinism, suppose too easily that the cosmos is a closed, repetitive system. Even they miss the splendor that, like Havel and Thomas, Colin Wilson saw in the revelation. The hero of one (flawed) work by Wilson delineates Wilson's own response. In his youth, while staying at a farm, Wilson's protagonist had been reading about Nineveh when it occurred to him to bring in some clothes drying on a line:

> Just inside the farmyard there was a large pool of grey water, rather muddy. As I was taking the clothes from the line, my mind still in Nineveh, I happened to notice this pool, and forgot for a moment where I was or what I was doing there. As I looked at it, the puddle lost all familiarity and became as alien as a sea on Mars. I stood staring at it, and the first drops of rain fell from the sky, and wrinkled its surface. At that moment I experienced a sensation of happiness and insight such as I had never known before. Nineveh and all history suddenly became as real and as alien as that pool. History became such a *reality* that I felt a kind of contempt for my own existence, standing there with my arms full of clothes.[30]

Intellect looks toward what lies beyond being (*to epekeina tou ontos*) (I.3 [20].5, 8), and in being filled with intellect, the soul is drunk with the nectar, *risen* in love in ways that transcend ordinary reasoning. Proclus

---

27. How can there be real boundaries in a merely material world, and what can be the *laws* that govern it? "Laws" that merely describe what happens (i.e., are merely our descriptions of what happens), it should be obvious, neither *explain* what has happened already nor license any guess as to what will happen next.

28. See also V.9 [5].1, where he likens them to flightless birds.

29. "Even if there is only one possible unified theory, it is just a set of rules and equations. What is it that breathes fire into the equations and makes a universe for them to describe?" (Hawking, *Brief History of Time*, 174). Plotinus's answer, on this reading at least, is that the world (and everything in it) exists because it wants to (the paradox is obvious). Very strangely, Hawking and other determinedly atheistic physicists sometimes seem to want the same conclusion—that reality hauls itself into existence "by its bootstraps" (a doctrine well mocked by K. Ward, *God, Chance and Necessity*, 49). At least, Plotinus did not suppose that this endeavor had a temporal beginning.

30. Wilson, *Mind Parasites*, 18. See my essay *"Mind Parasites"* for further analysis of Wilson's fiction.

was of the same opinion, declaring that our union with the One is by a kind of "bastard belief" (*nothe doxa*) like that which uncovers matter[31] (not that either intuition is entirely "illegitimate" or to be "disowned"). Matter itself can never be encountered but is present everywhere in "golden chains" (I.8 [51].15). Just so the One holds a golden veil or barrier before itself (I.6 [1].9). And what is the difference between Matter and the One, if neither can be described? They differ only, so it seems, in the attitude we bring to them. Looking one way, the world dissolves into disconnected bits having no shape or pattern. Looking the other is to see a world "full of signs" (II.3 [52].7, 13) and to rise in love. Balthasar, a modern Catholic theologian, writes:

> The whole world of images that surrounds us is a single field of significations. Every flower we see is an expression, every landscape has its significance, every human or animal face speaks its wordless language. It would be utterly futile to attempt a transposition of this language into concepts. . . . This expressive language is addressed primarily, not to conceptual thought, but to the kind of intelligence that perceptively reads the gestalt of things.[32]

Falling in love is giving in to sensation, seeking to possess without sharing. Becoming love is awakening to joy.

A passage from Frye, describing how one might feel if shipwrecked like Crusoe on a deserted island, is enlightening:

> Looking at the world as something set over against you splits your mind in two. You have an intellect that feels curious about it and wants to

---

31. Proclus, *Commentary on Timaeus* 1.216, cited by Rosan, *Philosophy of Proclus*, 215, after Plato, *Timaeus* 52b2, referring to the reasoning that results in the notion of *chora*, "space"; see II.4 [12].10. Democritus seems to have been the first to distinguish "legitimate" and "bastard" conclusions, born of "reason" and "sense perception" respectively. See Sextus Empiricus, *Against the Mathematicians* 7.135.1–139.4; Waterfield, *First Philosophers*, 176. We ought, he supposed, to be wed to Reason. But what did Plato, Plotinus, and Proclus intend by the metaphor? Is it "reason" or "sense perception" that should count (obviously, for the *male* philosopher) as bride rather than mistress? In general, like Galileo's Aristarchus and Copernicus, "they were able to make reason so conquer sense that, in defiance of the latter, the former became mistress of their belief" (Galilei, *Dialogues*, 381). But it does not seem that it is *sense perception* that leads us to posit Matter or the One: is it rather, in these cases, that there is some suspicion that "reason"—for good or ill—is enticing us away from "common sense," and that its products will not be received in polite society? "Reason" is not in ordinary fact our bride, but something stranger and more alluring.

32. Balthasar, *Theo-Logic I*, 140, quoted by Caldecott, "Liturgy and Trinity."

study it, and you have feelings or emotions that see it as beautiful or austere or terrible. You know that both these attitudes have some reality, at
least for you. If the ship you were wrecked in was a Western ship, you'd
probably feel that your intellect tells you more about what's really there
in the outer world, and that your emotions tell you more about what's
going on inside you. If your background were Oriental, you'd be more
likely to reverse this and say that the beauty or terror was what was
really there, and that your instinct to count and classify and measure and
pull to pieces was what was inside your mind.[33]

In even momentarily accepting that division between Oriental and Oc-
cidental minds, Frye erred: Plotinus offered a better version. Both attitudes,
"intellect" and "emotion," so called here, are intellectual. And Plotinus,
by this account, was "Oriental." The better way of approaching reality is
in awe, in trembling delight, in a fall of barriers, in forgetfulness of self.
In everyday life, indeed, it may be dangerous to forget our limits or to allow just any images to rampage through our mental landscape. We should
certainly not forget the influence of bodily fluids on our imagination (VI.8
[39].3, 1–26)! But it is just as dangerous to evacuate the world, the world
of our experience, of any "meaning." We must not guard ourselves against
treating others, for example, as "sexual objects" by thinking of them just
as "objects"!

If the Intellect is *not* to be weighed down by multiplicity, then "it must
return, so to speak, backwards, and give itself up, in a way, to what lies
behind it (for it faces in both directions); and there, if it wishes to see that
First Principle, it must not altogether be intellect" (III.8 [30].9, 30–1). To see
things simply "as they are," without the feeling that Plotinus describes, is
to lose one's grip on Good. Ontologically, why is there anything? Epistemologically, why exactly should we care?

So intellect must somehow "not be intellect," must look beyond both
the forms and the formulae. There are two ways in which intellect can "not
be intellect." The first, and the more familiar, involves that drift down into
drunkenness, into the self-validating delusion that there are separate, rival
selves, or that there is no other self of any importance but "my own." The
second is another sort of inebriation, "drunk with the nectar" that preceded
the invention of wine, in which the soul, in its highest aspect, turns toward
the One. This seems to be the very same condition that is identified as "intellect out of its mind," or "intellect in love" (on which I shall have more to

33. Frye, *Educated Imagination,* 17.

say). But how do we tell the one from the other? Each side, perhaps, considers the *other* drunk (i.e., unreliable)!

There is a passage from a later, neglected philosopher that may make the point and suggest an answer.

> In his *Metaphysics of Sexual Love* Schopenhauer brilliantly develops the idea that love is only a fleeting illusion. The "will" desires to realize itself once more in an individual, and so it suggests to John that Mary is a rare beauty and to Mary that John is a great hero. As soon as the goal of the "will" is achieved, as soon as the birth of a new being is assured, the will abandons the lovers to themselves and they then discover with horror that they have been the victims of a dreadful mistake. John sees the "real" Mary—that is, a dense, stupid, and ill-natured woman; Mary, on her side, discovers the real John—a dull, banal, and cowardly fellow. And now, after the delusions of love have been dissipated, the judgments Mary and John pronounce on each other agree perfectly with the judgments of all, with what *semper ubique et ab omnibus creditum est*. For everyone always thought that Mary was ugly and stupid and John cowardly and foolish. Schopenhauer does not doubt in the least that Mary and John saw true reality precisely when they saw what everyone else saw. And not only Schopenhauer thinks so. This is again *quod semper ubique et ab omnibus creditum est*. But it is precisely because this truth appears so unquestionable that there is good reason to raise the question of the legitimacy of its pretensions. Did John and Mary really deceive themselves during the short time when, the "will" having kindled its magic flame in them, they abandoned themselves to the mysterious passion that drew them together and they saw each other as so beautiful? May it not be that they were right precisely when they were alone in their opinion and appeared to all others as poor idiots? May it not be that at that time they were in communion with true reality and that what their social natures oblige them to believe is only error and falsehood? Who knows![34]

Plotinus does of course himself insist that the judgments of an assembly are likely to iron out individuals' errors (VI.5 [23].10, 18–9), and so might be expected to accept the common judgment (IV.4 [28].31, 30). On the other hand, most people are asleep! And are we entirely sure, in any case, that

---

34. Shestov, *Potestas Clavium*, pt.1, chap. 6. The point is dramatized by Charles Williams in several of his writings: see, e.g., *Shadows of Ecstasy*.

common people think the world banal? Maybe that is itself an illusion of the chattering classes.

> The perplexity arises especially because our awareness of the One is not by way of reasoned knowledge [*episteme*] or of intellectual perception [*noesis*] as with other intelligible things, but by way of a presence superior to knowledge. The soul experiences its falling away from being one and is not altogether one when it has reasoned knowledge of anything; for reasoned knowledge is a rational process [*logos*], and a rational process is many. The soul therefore goes past the One and falls into number and multiplicity. One must therefore run up above knowledge and in no way depart from being one, but one must depart from knowledge and things known, and from every other, even beautiful, object of vision. . . . Therefore, Plato says, "it cannot be spoken or written," but we speak and write impelling towards it and wakening from reasonings to the vision of it, as if showing the way to one who wants to have a view of something. (VI.9 [9].4, 1–14)[35]

As we get "closer" in imagination to that One, we may conceive of it as "lovable and love and love of himself" (*erasmion kai eros ho autos kai autou eros*; VI.8 [39].15, 1). The trio is matched elsewhere as "intellect, object and thinking" (and I suspect that the same pattern is intended here: the lover, the beloved, and loving), with the note that when these are the same, all disappear (VI.7 [38].41)—into the One.[36] "Intellect drunk with the nectar" amounts to the same thing as Soul wordlessly at one with her beloved: the moment when the beloved is not seen as any sort of exterior form, even of the finest sort, but felt as actual presence, without any room for words. "If [the Soul] remains in Intellect it sees fair and noble things, but has not yet quite grasped what it is seeking" (VI.7 [38].22, 21–2). And in becoming love it ceases merely to admire *form*, as though anything that looked "just like" the beloved would do just as well.[37] It "becomes love" (VI.7 [38].22, 8–9), by grace. But there may also be some advice on how—maybe—to achieve it.

> Those who are altogether, we may say, drunk and filled with the nectar, since the beauty has penetrated through the whole of their soul, are not

---

35. After Plato, *Letter* 7.241c5.

36. See also V.1 [10].4. 38: "if you take away otherness, it will become one and remain silent."

37. VI.7 [38].26, 21–2: "one would not delight in a boy because he was present when he was not present."

simply spectators. For there is no longer one thing outside and another outside which is looking at it, but the keen sighted has what is seen within. . . . One must transport what one sees into oneself, as if someone possessed by a god, taken over by Phoebus or one of the Muses, could bring about the vision of the god in himself, if he had the power to look at the god in himself. (V.8 [31].10, 32–45)[38]

That god will come when called for—but we must prepare the way (V.8 [31].9).

Is all this "merely" metaphor, merely a way of giving us novices some slight echo of a mystical path beyond us? Coming close to the One is a bit like being drunk or falling in love or being in bed together or talking happy nonsense, but of course those actual experiences are ones often to be avoided and exemplify, in other contexts, the madness and delirium of fallen life. Or are these lesser experiences to be valued after all as intimations, even versions, of the *risen* life? Falling in love, drunkenness, or other spiritual experiences are valued because they really raise us from our ordinary sloth. In which case, they are not to be disowned but practiced. They tell us more of the truth than the merely "objective" eye, valuable though that latter is.

How are we to ascend?

It does no good at all to say "Look to God," unless one also teaches how one is to look. . . . In reality it is virtue which goes before us to the goal and, when it comes to exist in the soul along with wisdom, shows God; but God, if you talk about him without true virtue, is only a name. Again, despising the universe and the gods in it and the other noble things is certainly not becoming good. . . . For anyone who feels affection for anything at all shows kindness to all that is akin to the object of his affection, and to the children of the father that he loves. But every soul is a child of That Father. (II.9 [33].15, 33–II.9 [33].16, 10)

And again:

When [the soul] is there [i.e., in the intelligible realm] [she] has the heavenly love, but here love becomes vulgar; for the soul there is the heavenly Aphrodite, but here becomes the vulgar Aphrodite, a kind of whore. And every soul is Aphrodite. . . . The soul then in her natural state is in

38. See also VI.7 [38].15; V.3 [49].14.

love with God and wants to be united with him; it is like the noble love
of a girl for her noble father. (VI.9 [9].9, 28–35)[39]

So what is it to become love? And how are we to do it? Many of us—
and I include myself—would like to imagine that he would, like some other
mystics, recommend literal "tantric" sex, but I must decline that option.
Literal sex involves the actors far too deeply in corporeal sensation, even if
it also—sometimes—opens our eyes to beauty. Those who consent to the
"other soul," to nature, give up their freedom and are closed off from other
souls in the very act of intercourse. The point is not, as many commentators have supposed, that Plotinus "despised the body": on the contrary, he
argued against those who did, and who imagined themselves "superior" to
nature. And he refers to sexual intercourse, *mixis*, often enough to suggest
that he acknowledged the general, perhaps even his own personal, desire
for it. But his advice to lovers is Platonic: "if they remain chaste there is
no error in their intimacy with the beauty here below, but it is error to fall
away into sexual intercourse" (III.5 [50].1, 36–7). Quite what the error is,
needs further inquiry. Even a chaster version of romantic love, in which the
lovers enjoy their beloveds' beauty without requiring sex, is dangerous—as
it hardly needs ascetics, puritans, or "killjoys" to remind us. It may even
be *more* dangerous, more complacent and divisive, than a briskly pleasurable sharing of bodily fluids! All such rash strategies too easily become
that wanting to have things "our way" that was the beginning of the Fall,
wanting only what is "like" (VI.7 [38].27). "As if they were tired of being
together, they each go to their own" (IV.8 [6].4, 11–2), deserting the community to which they should be equally attached. On the other hand, the
fact that it's dangerous doesn't make it bad. And it would be just as misleading, and perhaps as dangerous, to ignore the emotional energies involved
in love. He is not recommending courtesy, neighborliness, or even mild
affection, valuable though all these may be. Becoming Love is more than
being kind, just as obedience to intellect is more than being clever. Maybe
love is altogether different from kindness or compassion, and "to be clever
is not wise."[40] Romantic, even thoroughly erotic, love perhaps creates divisions where none should be—but for most of us, already so far fallen, it is

39. The more usual archetype of that particular filial love is the virginal Athena (or, still
more alarmingly, Electra!). It is odd at least that Plotinus here prefers to evoke Aphrodite. In his
elaboration of Plato's *Symposium* myth he both invents and allegorizes a story that "since Aphrodite follows upon Kronos—or, if you like, the father of Kronos, Heaven—she directed her activity towards him and filled with passionate love for him brought forth Love" (III.5 [50].2, 33–5).

40. Euripides, *Bacchae* 395: "*to sophon ou sophia.*"

a reminder of "the dance of immortal love."⁴¹ And perhaps the fact that as individuals we direct that love at individuals is also not surprising, and not wrong. It isn't up to me to see the immortal beauty of just everyone I meet and be aroused by it,⁴² so long as I recall that each mortal thing is beautiful, and loved, by someone or some One.

It is up to me—in a way—to be aroused by something or somebody, to look toward the beauty of *this* individual someone, and to begin to recognize the illuminating grace that the Good sheds upon all its creatures. "Up to me," in a way: it is up to me simply to put myself in a position where that grace may also be shed on me. It is for the gods, after all, to come to us, and not for us to harass them! So the route to becoming love is to wait upon the gods or God.

> When we look outside that on which we depend we do not know that we are one, like faces which are many on the outside but have one head inside. But if someone is able to turn around, either by himself or having the good luck to have his hair pulled by Athena herself, he will see God and himself and the all. . . . He will stop marking himself off from all being and will come to all the All without going out anywhere. (VI.5 [23].7, 9–10)⁴³

We begin to "become love" when someone is suddenly real to us, as a living beauty, in the presence of the One. Becoming love is to realize that presence, a realization constantly challenged by our current situation, out here in the material, among things that often seem, to us, to be very far from beautiful. Love here, even at its best, is only "an imitation, since it is a loving of things which are separate; but the true love is all things being one and never separated" in the life of God (VI.7 [38].14, 21–4). The Delphic Oracle

---

41. This was not only Plotinus's idea. See Epicurus, *Vatican Fragment* 52: "love dances in a circle around the world, calling upon us all to awaken to the praises of the happy life" (cited by J. Miller, *Measures of Wisdom*, 152).

42. "For everything does not always produce the same effect when it encounters everything else. . . . as for instance, the beauty of Helen produced one effect on Paris, but Idomeneus was not affected in the same way" (III.3 [48].5, 40–3, after *Iliad* 3.230–3)!

43. The reference is to Homer's *Iliad* (I.197–8), where Athena (the goddess of good sense) recalls Achilles from a murderous rage. The phrase "without going out anywhere" is matched in a Buddhist exegesis (by Tu-shun, AD 557–640) of Indra's Net, wherein each jewel reflects and contains all others (on which see below): "it is precisely by not leaving this one jewel that you can enter all the jewels. If you left this one jewel to enter all the jewels, you couldn't enter all the jewels. . . . Because outside this jewel there are no separate jewels" (Kaza and Kraft, *Dharma Rain*, 59).

and Porphyry conclude their account of Plotinus's life with the expectation that he has gone to be a companion of those who "set the dance of immortal love."[44] "There the most blessed spirits have their birth and live a life filled full of festivity and joy; and this life lasts for ever, made blessed by the gods."[45] Our task here-now, he thought, was to present at least an image of that dance. Even a tortoise, he jokingly remarks, could avoid being trampled if it only managed to align itself with the movement of the dance (II.9 [33].7, 36–7). And that we can manage only if we look toward the leader of the chorus (VI.9 [9].8, 38ff.). In Carroll's brilliant line: "Turn not pale, beloved snail, but come and join the dance."[46]

And yet, how is it possible for us to "love" God or the gods in anything like the sense that we may love our earthly companions? Our delight in the latter seems not to be genuine love if it does not involve us in wishing our companions well, wishing to be of service to them, wishing for their company. But we can hardly wish *God* or even the gods "well" or aim to help them. To *serve* the gods, *therapeuein*, is not to help them but only to *please* them, as Socrates suggested.[47] We serve them by doing as they would wish us to—that is, to share in the making of many beautiful things, to live in beauty. We love God by loving our neighbors.[48] We enjoy God's company by enjoying theirs.

But there is one more gloss on Plotinus's remarks that I have been consciously evading. The erotic disposition of many (most?) males is heterosexual, and their images of delight are therefore—mostly—female. Plotinus's, like Plato's, seem mostly to be boys. This is not to say that he was himself a pederast in the notorious Greek style: there is no reason at all to think so. He was, we are told, outraged when the rhetorician Diophanes, a participant in his seminar, elected to compose and deliver a defense of Alcibiades's declaration that disciples should lie with their teachers.[49] And he reckoned, as above, that lovers made a mistake if they "descended" to actual intercourse. This would be to bind them to the realm of physical sensation, distracting them from higher beauties—and, incidentally, though he does not

---

44. *"Khoron sterixan erotos athanatou"* (Porphyry, *Life* 23.36–7, after 22.54–63). The words are not Plotinus's but still Plotinian: *sterizein* means "to establish, or set firm," but what is thus established is a *dance*.

45. Porphyry, *Life* 23.38–40.

46. Carroll, *Alice's Adventures in Wonderland* (1865), chap. 10, cited by Verney, *Dance of Love*, 20.

47. Plato, *Euthyphro* 13b–14b.

48. *1 John* 2.9–11.

49. Porphyry, *Life* 15.7–17, after Plato, *Symposium* 218d.

say so, confirming the Romans' poor opinion of philosophers.[50] Pederasty, though it was a social form of some importance in some Greek cities, was not something of which non-Greeks approved. Nor, of course, was it just the same as modern homosexual practice between consenting adults. Sodomizing slaves was not condemned; sodomizing the freeborn was—especially if the freeborn boy appeared to enjoy it and thus was at risk of retaining those desires in adulthood.

But what aspect of erotic love is emphasized in the working assumption that it is boys who are chiefly expected to be beautiful and the objects even of chaste desire?[51] Can we safely or helpfully ignore the context and connotations of pederastic love in examining and following the Plotinian or Platonic way? Or was Plotinus himself hampered by a cultural and literary tradition that was not wholly true to his better insights? *Marital* love embodies an intention to create and maintain a household, even to beget children.[52] *Pederastic* love is limited in its nature, by the passage of time and puberty. And it was assumed that the beloved boy, though he might admire his lover and wish to please him, was not himself excited by the act (or would be an object of some contempt if he too obviously were).[53] In this, it has been supposed, the beloved is like the ideal object of erotic love, the One, which is itself unaffected by any passion. Or are we reading the story the wrong way round? The other hypostases may yearn toward their origin and superior, but it is they who are more firmly penetrated—and in some sense impregnated—by their superior (VI.7 [38].15, 18–20; VI.7 [38].16, 32–3). "Our hearts are a virgin that God's truth alone opens."[54]

50. See Bartsch, *Mirror of the Self*, 164–82: a still worse suspicion was that the "philosophers" preferred the passive role.

51. Not *only* boys, of course: it would be as well for those Gnostics he criticizes in II.9 [33], Plotinus says, to "despise" the beauty in boys *and women*, "to avoid being overcome to the point of abandoned wickedness" (see II.9 [33].17, 27–32). It would be better still simply not to cling to those beauties, without insulting them (37–9).

52. Musonius Rufus (a first-century Stoic and teacher of Epictetus) insisted that the only "natural" and decent form of sexual intercourse was for procreation, thus ruling out courtesans, casual affairs—*and even one's own slave* (Musonius Rufus, 86.4–14, cited by Craig Williams, *Roman Homosexuality*, 239–40). See also King, *Musonius Rufus*, 55 (lecture 12); Lutz, *Musonius Rufus*. Plato proposed similar rules in *Laws* 8.838e–839a. Other Romans took it for granted that such intercourse was for the relief of sexual tension with any easily available object (see Horace, *Satires* 1.2.1149, cited by Craig Williams, *Roman Homosexuality*, 32) and insisted only that males should be properly "masculine" in their tastes (i.e., that they should be the penetrators, not the penetrated, and should—if sensible—steer clear of freeborn boys and women).

53. See Craig Williams, *Roman Homosexuality*, 183–8.

54. Mansur al-Hallaj (AD 858–922), cited by Ware, "How Do We Enter the Heart?," after Merton, *Conjectures*, 142.

Matter yearns to be formed into a likeness of intelligible being, and everything is both bound in sympathy with every other thing and "looking toward" the One beyond all being. The superior also cares for the inferior, proleptically imagining (perhaps) its growth in beauty. "Such a love is provident and preservative of the beloved, able to perfect and maintain them."[55] All these loves are, in different ways, "erotic." That pattern is also to be found—where else could it originate?—in the Divine itself: "so too gods love gods, the superior their inferiors providentially, and the inferior their superiors reflexively."[56] It is because the Divine is generous, not miserly, that there is anything else at all. Things exist as an effect of that eternal play—or at any rate this is how we might begin to see them straight.

> Picasso was right when he said that we do not know what a tree or a window is. All things are very mysterious and strange and we only overlook their strangeness and their mystery because we are so used to them. We only understand things very obscurely. But what are things? Things are God's love become things.[57]

---

55. Proclus, *Alcibiades*, 37 (55).
56. Ibid. See also *1 John* 4.19: "we love Him because He first loved us."
57. Cardenal, *Love*, 43.

CHAPTER SEVEN

Shadow Plays and Mirrors

Plato's most famous image, not much discussed by Plotinus, is the Cave of *The Republic*:[1] prisoners in a cave, chained from their beginnings, see only shadows cast on the wall in front of them from the puppets walked along a parapet behind them. The most respected of the prisoners are those who can guess what pattern the passing shadows make, and so predict their future shapes, without ever knowing *why* this is the pattern. In the story, real causes lie outside the prisoners' view, and if one of them were released from chains and led up past the puppeteers and into the open air, she would be dazzled and distraught. If she were to grow used to the real, outside world and go back down into the cave to advise her fellows of the truth, they would disbelieve and mock her (and the puppeteers, no doubt, would silence her).

Plotinus does not explicitly use *shadows* as his image for the world we dream we live in, but reflections (though the cases are less different than nowadays we think).[2] Plato had played with that metaphor as well; a little later in *The Republic* he had suggested that it was easy to make convincing copies of our visible reality, and that painters—especially those contemporary painters who specialized in trompe l'oeil[3]—were doing no more than

---

1. Plato, *Republic* 7.541a–517c; see IV.8 [6].2 and IV.8 [6].4, 28–31.
2. *Skia* may cover reflections, images, and phantoms as well as "literal" shadows: see Barber and Barber, *When They Severed Earth from Sky*, 166. The Barbers point out that the spirit world often presents, precisely, the *mirror image* of the world of everyday (168–9), after Eliade, *Shamanism*, 205.
3. See the story of Parrhasius and Zeuxis, rival painters: Zeuxis painted some grain on the floor so well that birds came down to peck; exalted by his success he asked Parrhasius to draw back the curtains to show off *his* painting. It was agreed that Parrhasius had won, having deceived a fellow painter rather than mere birds. Pliny, *Natural History*, vol. 9, 309 (35.36).

"holding a mirror up" to what was already an inferior copy of the real world, copying only what it variously *looked* like.[4] Mirrors were not necessarily unhelpful: a lover sees his own ideal nature—and his own faults—much more easily by seeing them mirrored in his beloved's eyes and character.[5] But there is a peril attached to such mirrors. We are easily tricked into supposing that what can be mirrored is all that really matters: so "some story said riddlingly a man wanted to catch [the beautiful reflection] and sank down into a stream and disappeared" (I.6 [1].8),[6] and the young Dionysus's wicked great-uncles used a mirror to lure him to his death (IV.3 [27].12).[7] I shall have more to say below on both of these images.

But first of all: what were the "mirrors" that Plato and Plotinus had in mind? What did they show that was very different from shadows? Ibn 'Arabi (d. AD 1240) could think in terms of *polished* mirrors, without smudges or refracted lights.[8] But there were no such *accurate* mirrors in Plotinus's day. Mirror images were variously distorted shadows.

Ingenuity even devises vessels that do conjuring tricks [*mirifica*], for instance those deposited as votive offerings in the temple at Smyrna: this is brought about by the shape of the material, and it makes a very great difference whether the vessels are concave and shaped like a bowl or convex like a Thracian shield, whether the centre is recessed or projecting, whether the oval is horizontal or oblique, laid flat or placed upright, as the quality of the shape receiving the shadows twists them as they come: for in fact the image in a mirror is merely the shadow arranged by the brilliance of the material receiving it.[9]

These mirrors were obsidian (which is volcanic glass), bronze, or silver. The first and obvious reflective surfaces are pools—or more conveniently

4. Plato, *Republic* 10.596de.

5. Plato, *Alcibiades* 132de; Aristotle, *Nicomachean Ethics* 9.1169b. See Bartsch, *Mirror of the Self*, 50–3.

6. This story is routinely—but inaccurately—identified with the tale of Narcissus (on which see Bartsch, *Mirror of the Self*, 84–102, who observes that the best-known version of that story, in Ovid's *Metamorphoses* 3.339–510, is atypical in blaming the event on Narcissus's disdain for the nymph Echo).

7. Clement, *Protrepticus* 2.18. See West, *Orphic Poems*, 155–7. Other toys or ritual objects were also used to entice him (knucklebone, ball, spinning-top, bull-roarer, apple, and wool), but the mirror always seems especially significant. See Pépin, "Plotin et le miroir de Dionyse."

8. See Sells, *Mystical Languages*, 63: "if the glass is polished," it "becomes invisible, with only the viewer's image reflected."

9. Pliny, *Natural History*, vol. 9, 97 (33.45).

bowls—of water. We look *down* into them and find our faces framed by the sky, the sun, and other stars, or merely waving branches.[10] Standing upright we observe that underneath "is a people that walk with their feet against ours."[11] Self-awareness is like "mirror-reflection when there is a smooth, bright, untroubled surface" (I.4 [46].10, 7–22). Seeking to touch our reflections breaks them up, and there is a real (or half-real) world beneath the surface in which perhaps we can drown (as Heracles's young friend Hylas drowned).[12] A less exact reflection can be found in polished-metal mirrors: surviving examples are almost all disk shaped, designed to be held in the hand or set upon a table—or hidden away in a small box, which (as it were) traps the reflection inside it when the lid is closed.[13] "Even more than this—drinking-cups are now made in such a manner, as to be filled inside with numerous concave facets, like so many mirrors; so that if but one person looks into the interior, he sees reflected a whole multitude of persons."[14] This could no doubt confirm the suspicion that we are mostly legion (VI.7 [38].41, 22–6).[15] Blown glass was apparently invented in Syria sometime in the first century BC, enabling glass windows as well as crock-

10. Plato, *Cratylus* 414c, suggests that "*katoptron*" has an intrusive *rho*: the word should be *katopton*, with its suggestion that we look *downward* into the reflective surface (a later generation might suspect instead that the mirror is "looking down" or "spying" on us).

11. Uno Harva recorded this remark from a Lapp shaman. Uno Harva, *Die religiösen Vorstellungen der altäischen Völker* (Helsinki: Suomaleinan Tiedeakatemia, 1938), 349, cited by Barber and Barber, *When They Severed Earth from Sky*, 165.

12. See I.6 [1].8, 9: we might thereby sink down into Hades and consort with shadows. See also III.6 [26].7, 41–2, on "falling into falsity, like things in a dream or water or a mirror." Hylas was pulled into the water by nymphs (i.e., he was literally "*nympholept*"), who left only an echo for Heracles as he tried to find his ward (or his beloved). See Apollonius Rhodius, *Argonautica* 1.1172–1272; Theocritus, *Idyll* 13; Virgil, *Eclogues* 6.41–2; Propertius, *Elegies* 1.20. Neither poets nor philosophers seem to have elaborated the allegory explicitly to suggest our seduction by watery images. One lengthy analysis of the myth, by Heerink, "Echoing Hylas," suggests that the poets used it "to express their poetics allegorically."

13. See Congdon, *Caryatid Mirrors*.

14. Pliny, *Natural History*, vol. 9, 95. Heron of Alexandria is credited with the invention of "*polytheoron*" mirrors, reflecting the same image multiple times (a device, so Seneca says, that a rich Roman, Hostius Quadra, employed to allow himself multiple images of his various copulations; *Naturales quaestiones* 1.16.3–5, discussed by Bartsch, *Mirror of the Self*, 103–14). That effect was used in China as well as classical antiquity to represent the thought that every real thing reflects all others: "each there has everything in itself and sees all things in every other, so that all are everywhere and each and every one is all and the glory is unbounded; for each of them is great, because even the small is great; the sun there is all the stars, and each star is the sun and all the others" (V.8 [31].4, 5–12; see also Numenius T33: Dodds, "Numenius," 23). See Pendergrast, *Mirror Mirror*, 31.

15. Gregory, *Mirrors in Mind*, 4, cites Cohen and Cox, *Telling without Talking*, suggesting that sufferers from multiple personality disorder (now professionally labeled as a form of dissociative identity disorder) do literally see many faces in mirrors (more probably, this is how

ery.[16] Thus, in late antiquity began the process that has resulted in our being surrounded everywhere by faint and fleeting images of ourselves in motion, but for the most part *mirrors*, then, were small devices showing us our own fixed gaze (we never ourselves *saw* the way our own eyes dart around and blink until the invention of film). Obsidian, bronze, and silver, however well they are polished, don't provide the seemingly lifelike images we now assume (though they seemed accurate enough to our forebears).[17] The reflected images of such mirrors are sparklier and vaguer than those of silvered glass and, so, that much more enticing:[18] producing shadows, even if colored shadows. What lies "behind" or "within" the reflective surface is not physically accessible (as it is in water), but may be the more attractive for that reason. If only we could step into that "Other World"—except that we suspect it might really be a trap, or at least a difficult reversal of our usual ways. And maybe the mirror-creatures could step *out* of the mirror into our familiar world. Which, indeed, is the mirror? Maybe both.

Another use of polished surfaces was as "burning glasses"—an invention sometimes credited to Archimedes, and later to Diocles.[19] Plotinus mentions this use only once (III.6 [26].14, 32–III.6 [26].15, 16), as a strange metaphor—the light and heat are gathered *away* from the reflective surface—for the way that matter is itself unaffected by the forms that play across it ("like an echo from smooth, flat surfaces"). This indeed seems to be the main moral Plotinus is making in his account of matter as, in some way, "mirroring" the

---

they choose to give artistic expression to their condition—or their iatrogenic delusion). See my "Personal Identity and Identity Disorders."

16. See Frank, *Glass and Archaeology*.

17. Bartsch, *Mirror of the Self*, 35–6, citing Apuleius, *Apologia* 14.8: it is especially emphasized that mirrors, unlike clay, stone, or painted images, reflect things—other than our eyes—*in motion* (something a little more, that is, than one segment of the real).

18. Some have interpreted Pliny (*Natural History*, vol. 9, 99 [33.45]) as claiming the invention of such glass mirrors when he reports that "a notion has arisen that the object is reflected with greater distinctness, by the application . . . of a layer of gold." This has been interpreted to mean "adding gold to the back [of glass]" but without clear warrant. All that Pliny suggests is a rumor that adding gold to the silver (*auro opposito*: in front rather than on the back) produces a better image. He also (36.67) mentions the use of "obsian glass" (much like obsidian) as a wall mirror, reflecting shadows rather than images. Octagonal shards of blown glass, lined with lead, were in use a few centuries later—but there is no need to suppose that Plotinus had these in mind.

19. Heath, *Greek Mathematics*, vol. 2, 18: "The story that Archimedes set the Roman ships on fire by an arrangement of burning-glasses or concave mirrors is not found in any authority earlier than Lucian; but it is quite likely that he discovered some form of burning-mirror." "Moslem writers regarded Diocles (240–180 BC) as the discoverer of the parabolic burning-mirror" (201). See also Pliny, *Natural History*, vol. 9, 33.66, for glass spheres filled with water acting as burning glasses.

real world. Reflections last in or on a reflective surface only while the thing itself is near enough to that surface to be reflected and have no further effect on water or on metal.[20] If it were otherwise, mirrors would be filling up with past reflections, and mere matter would begin to block the emergence of new forms in it. But as things are, mere matter is continually stripped back to its beginnings to remain available for whatever real things are to be represented, or presented, there. On the other hand, it is—somehow—thanks to matter that there are these images at all (III.6 [26].14).

Plotinus also imagines our souls as mirrors. *Nous* offers images to something in our souls via their verbal expression, and it is through these images—as long as the surface of our souls is undisturbed—that we normally manage what semblance of thought we can.[21] Reflections indeed appear at all levels of the Plotinian cosmos: the One, Intellect, and Soul all generate images in their subordinate (V.2 [11].1). The whole material or phenomenal cosmos is, as it were, an image (II.3 [52].18, 17),[22] and Soul is scattered through it so as to make many other little *cosmoi* within the single greater (I.1 [53].8, 17), as in a hall of mirrors. On the one hand, there would be no phenomenal world if Soul had not thus divided Herself; on the other, this event is a sort of accidental suicide.

So what is it that we see in mirrors and in still waters? The story of Narcissus, especially as it is told in Ovid's *Metamorphoses*, depends on his seeing his *own* image and eventually realizing that he is looking at himself. So also in the *Hermetic Corpus* the eternal Mind sees his own image reflected in Earth and falls in love.[23] And human lovers, according to Plato, see their own images reflected in their beloved's eyes.[24] But *Plotinus* does not suggest—as many modern discussions assume—that this is a route to self-understanding or even to self-awareness.[25] The man is attracted by what he sees, mistakes it for something to be grasped, and drowns—rather more as the dog of Aesop's fable lunges after the bone he sees in the water,[26] or

---

20. VI.4 [22].10; VI.5 [23].8, 17; III.6 [26].7, 25; III.6 [26].13, 35; IV.5 [29].7, 44; VI.2 [43].22, 34. Cf. Plato, *Timaeus* 50c4–5.

21. I.4 [46].10, 9; IV.3 [27].30, 10.

22. So also later Christian writers: according to Maximus the Confessor, the world is "an image and appearing of the invisible light, a very pure mirror, clear, showing a true reflection, immaculate, undarkened, welcoming, if it is proper to speak so: all the splendour of the primal beauty"; *Mystagogy* 23, cited by Evdokimov, *Art of the Icon*, 14.

23. *Poimandres* 1.14 (Copenhaver, *Hermetica*, 3).

24. "Self-knowledge," remarks Wohl acerbically, "becomes not only solipsistic but even onanistic" ("Eye of the Beloved," 47).

25. See Wildberg, "Dionysus in the Mirror of Philosophy."

26. Aesop, *Complete Fables*, 137.

as Hylas is entrapped by water nymphs. The peril of gazing into fountains, Varro reported, was that one might see the image of a nymph and be pulled down into madness:

> vulgo memoriae proditum est, quicunque speciem quandam e fonte, id est effigiem nymphae viderint, furendi non fecisse finem: quos Gracei *"nympholeptoi"* appellant.[27]

The sight may not always have such bad effects. Paul famously told the Corinthian Christians that "now we see through a glass, darkly, but afterwards face to face."[28] "Through a glass" does not mean through a transparent or clouded windowpane, but via a reflective surface, *eisoptron*, and what we see, *en ainigmati* ("riddlingly"), is not ourselves but—so Paul suggests—the reality that is Christ. Quite what theory of vision either Paul or Plotinus was assuming is unclear: the then-dominant theory—oddly to our tastes—spoke of visual rays (a reification of the *attention* we must give to things to see them) sent out from our eyes, which were diverted by reflective surfaces to some nearby object and then bounced back to us. What we see in such mirrors are the things themselves, at one or more removes, not distinct and lasting entities created on the mirroring surface by the action of the things. And what is seen may not be simply our own bodily forms but the things around us. These may at some times be seen more clearly than ourselves. So in the temple of Despoina in Arcadia, Pausanias tells us:

> On the right as you go out of the temple there is a mirror fitted into the wall. If anyone looks into this mirror, he will see himself very dimly indeed or not at all, but the actual images of the gods and the throne can be seen quite clearly.[29]

There need be nothing spooky about this effect: the statues would be in sunlight and the exiting observer in shade. The moral effect, of course, would be to emphasize the superior reality of the gods or at least their images. So what Plotinus might suppose that Hylas and the young Dionysus were

---

27. Varro, *De Latina lingua* 7.87, cited by Connor, "Seized by the Nymphs," 183–4.

28. Paul, *1 Corinthians* 13.12. See Kauntze, "Seeing through a Glass Darkly." Kauntze points out that Augustine (*De Trinitate* XV.8.14) suggests that in seeing ourselves in the mirror, we see an image of the Trinity, represented as memory, intellect, and will. This does not seem to be what Paul had in mind, but it is reminiscent of Plotinus's program elsewhere.

29. Pausanias, *Description of Greece* 8.37.7–8, cited by Addey, "Mirrors and Divination," 36. The mirror is probably dark glass ("obsian" glass; see above).

seeing in reflection was not *themselves*, nor did they mistake their own images.[30] Their error was simply not to turn around and see what was behind them—a reversal that we can only hope some god, like Athena, will compel. "It is the function of Athena to preserve life undivided, 'for which reason Pallas Athena is called Saviour'; but of the Titans to divide it and to entice it to the process of coming-to-be."[31] What does it mean "to try and grasp the shadows"? And what does it mean "to turn around"? That is another story.

Both Proclus and Plotinus are describing how the soul is trapped into Becoming, as a cosmological question, but the story has some significance also for our ordinary lives, whatever the cosmos itself turns out to be. Perhaps—if what we see is our own image—we must beware of being diverted from "real life" and a realistic engagement with genuinely "other" beings by the thought of our own magnificence.[32] Or perhaps we should acknowledge how much of what we love in others is only an affirmation of our own identity, a veil disguising what the "other" really is and also a revelation of what—for better or worse—we are. In the Plotinian context it seems rather that he is warning against a concentration on how things *seem* to us to be and against an assumption that it is sensations—the mere effects of whatever is really real—that are solid. The moral is much like that of Plato's Cave, where the prisoners are seduced, not by their *own* shadows, but by the shadows of real things (or, rather, in that more complex story, of the images of real things manipulated by the puppeteers) and dazzled when they are made to look away. Whatever of beauty or profit we see in the phenomena is only a dream, whether or not there is an eventual final, literal awakening. Almost all of us give notional assent—not always real assent—to the thought that there is a real world apart from our own perceptions which is the principal cause of those perceptions, and that enlightenment depends on our recovery of that insight. What I love or even acknowledge in others is not, after all, my own possession, nor even my own reflection, but rather those real Others, existing beyond my own immediate vision. And what are those Others? Merely other earthly organisms like myself, or are these too mere shadows, images, of eternal beings? That is a larger question, to which Plotinus has a firm reply:

---

30. Propertius, *Elegies* 1.20, 41–2: "et modo formosis incumbens nescius undis / errorem blandis tardat imaginibus." Heerink, "Going a Step Further," interprets this, wrongly, as Hylas's "narcissistic" admiration of his own reflection, but the reflections are plural—and turn out to be deadly.

31. Proclus, *Alcibiades*, 27 (43–4).

32. On which issue, see M. Harris, *Cows, Pigs, Wars, and Witches*, 266.

All our toil and trouble is for this, not to be left without a share in the best of visions. . . . A man has not failed if he fails to win beauty of colours or bodies, or power or office or kingship even, but if he fails to win this and only this. (I.6 [1].7, 34–5)

We need to win our way back to the truth, to turn from how things "seem" to how they are.

CHAPTER EIGHT

Reason Drunk and Sober

And what is this "best of visions"?[1] Plotinus's admirers and critics are alike divided into those who think of him as a "mystic" and those who reckon him opposed to the wilder movements of late-antique theosophy. My judgment is that he knew the worth of argument, and also that there was something better than that sort of reason. To understand him it is necessary to put aside preconceptions and try to listen to what he means, and not just what he seems to say. "Let [one who wishes to understand] abandon the verbal signification and grasp the meaning of what is being said" (VI.4 [22].2, 12–3; see also IV.8 [6].9).

He writes, remember, as follows:

> Intellect also, then, has one power for thinking, by which it looks at the things in itself, and one by which it looks at what transcends it by a direct awareness and reception, by which also before it saw only, and by seeing acquired intellect and is one. And that first one is the contemplation of Intellect in its right mind, and the other is Intellect in love, when it goes out of its mind "drunk with the nectar"; then it falls in love, simplified into happiness [haplotheis eis eupatheian] by having its fill, and it is better for it to be drunk with a drunkenness like this than to be more respectably sober. (VI.7 [38].35, 20–8)

---

1. An earlier version of this chapter was presented at the International Society for Neoplatonic Studies conference in Liverpool in 2004; some material appeared in the conclusion to Vassilopoulou and Clark, *Late Antique Epistemology*, 289–301.

Intellect in love, out of its mind and "drunk with the nectar," is, so
Plotinus tells us, better than intellect "in its right mind."[2] Thomas Taylor
perhaps made a similar point in commenting on Porphyry's interpretation
of the Cave of the Nymphs: "when Saturn is said by Orpheus to have been
intoxicated with honey or nectar, the meaning is that he then energized
providentially, in a deific and super-intellectual manner."[3] What does that
mean? What more can be said about "reason drunk and sober"? The question is threefold: how "metaphorical" is he being; what ordinary state does
he expect us to associate with his description; what reason can there be to
demote right reason and prefer, as it were, tight reason? More is involved
in understanding this even than the personal attachment and passionate
delight involved in "love."

That these phrases are intended "metaphorically" seems obvious: more
of us, at least, have more experience of falling in love, going mad, and getting drunk than we have of any sort of intellectual ecstasy, whatever that
may amount to. It seems clear that we are expected to get some sort of idea
of "intellectual ecstasy" from those more usual happenings. Nor is it an unfamiliar image. Leaving aside Plato's own occasional words in praise of *ma-
nia*, the Platonizing tradition had other authorities. According to the *Chaldaean Oracles*, for example, the soul once freed from the body and filled
with noetic light "glories in the harmony with which it is drunken."[4] Interestingly, Dillon has suggested that Plotinus's use of the phrase *anthos
nou*, in this very treatise, is a Chaldaean reminiscence.[5] Philo also speaks
approvingly of the "sober intoxication" or "Corybantic frenzy" that seizes
the mind "whirled round with the dances of planets and fixed stars, in accordance with the laws of perfect music," and so at last "descrying in [the
intelligible] world sights of surpassing loveliness, even the patterns and
originals of the things of sense which it saw here."[6]

---

2. This may also be what he intends at VI.7 [38].22, 11–4: "the beauty of Intellect is inactive till it catches a light from the Good, and the soul by itself 'falls flat on its back' and is
completely inactive and, though Intellect is present, is unenthusiastic about it."

3. T. Taylor, *Selected Works*, 183n.

4. Lewy, *Chaldaean Oracles*, 420.

5. Dillon, "Plotinus and Chaldaean Oracles," 135, with reference to VI.7 [38].35, 25.

6. Philo, *De opificio mundi* 70–1 (*Collected Works*, vol. 1, 55–7). See further Lewy, *Sobria
Ebrietas*. This may be one further slight reason, alongside the remark about sacred nakedness
which I discussed earlier, to suspect that Philo's works had some effect in Ammonius's circle.
The suggestion that Plotinus had some substantial contact with Jewish thought and practice is
rebutted by Merlan, "Religion and Philosophy," but it remains a bare possibility.

Therefore, my soul, if thou feelest any yearning to inherit the good things of God, leave not only thy land, that is the body, thy kinsfolk, that is the senses, thy father's house (*Genesis* 12.1), that is speech, but be a fugitive from thyself also and issue forth from thyself. Like persons possessed and Corybants, be filled with inspired frenzy [*baccheutheisa kai theophoretheisa*], even as the prophets are inspired. For it is the mind which is under the divine afflatus, and no longer in its own keeping, but is stirred to its depths and maddened by heavenward yearning [*eroti ouranioi*], drawn by the truly existent and pulled upward thereto, with truth to lead the way and remove all obstacles before its feet, that its path may be smooth to tread—such is the mind, which has this inheritance.[7]

This is of course not something that we do for ourselves: "while the radiance of the mind is still all around us, when it pours as it were a noonday beam into the whole soul, we are self-contained, not possessed. But when it comes to its setting, naturally ecstasy and divine possession and madness fall upon us. For when the light of God shines, the human light sets; when the divine light sets, the human dawns and rises."[8] The complete displacement that Philo describes is not what other sources suggest. According to *The Odes of Solomon*, "from the Lord's spring came speaking water in abundance to my lips, I drank and was drunken with the water of everlasting life, yet my drunkenness was not that of ignorance, but I turned away from vanity."[9] Perhaps there is less difference than we might suppose: in any case our *ordinary* thinking is displaced, and we cannot easily say, afterward, what it was we felt while "absent from ourselves."

What is it, after all, even to be ordinarily "drunk," whether with love, liquor, or sudden madness? "Drunkenness," according to the anthropologist, "also expresses culture in so far as it always takes one form of a highly patterned, learned comportment which varies from one culture to another:

---

7. Philo, *Quis rerum divinarum heres sit* 68–70 (*Collected Works*, vol. 4, 317). So also at the feast days of those dedicated to knowledge and contemplation, separate choirs of men and women first sing and dance, then "having drunk as in the Bacchic rites of the strong wine of God's love (*akratou spasantes tou theophilous*)," they unite into a single choir celebrating like those saved from the Red Sea (Philo, *De vita contemplativa* 11.83–7; *Collected Works*, vol. 9, 165). No *literal* wine was served at these feasts, nor meat, for "wine acts like a drug producing folly, and costly dishes stir up that most insatiable of animals, desire" (*De vita contemplativa* 9.74; *Collected Works*, vol. 9, 159).

8. Philo, *Quis rerum divinarum heres sit* 264 (*Collected Works*, vol. 4, 419). See also Iamblichus, *De mysteriis* 3.11.125 et al. (E. Clarke, *Iamblichus' "De mysteriis,"* 70–5).

9. Jonas, *Gnostic Religion*, 71, citing *Odes* 11.6–8.

pink elephants in one region, green snakes in another. . . . Drinking is essentially a social act, performed in a recognized social context."[10] Even within
a single culture, there are gloomy drunks and sleepy ones and violent ones;
drunks who dance and sing, drunks who forget their names and occupa-
tions, drunks who tell secrets to passing strangers—and especially drunks
who cannot tell, once sober, what it was they felt and did. There may be
common physical symptoms. Jeremiah gloomily declared, "all my bones
shake; I am like a drunken man, and like a man whom wine hath overcome, because of the Lord"[11]—though he is recording the depths of post-
prophetic misery rather than exalted inspiration. Plotinus himself records
"trembling" as one symptom of being "in love," though he makes clear
that this is less traumatic—it is "a trembling that is all delight" (MacKenna's translation; perhaps "fluttering" would be better) (I.6 [1].4, 17: *ptoesis
meth'hedones*). But such "trembling and shaking of the body and the pallor
and the inability to speak" (in this case consequent upon fear) are only corporeal (III.6 [26].4, 25).

And how can being drunk be a good thing, any more than falling in love
or being naked? The much more usual philosophical aphorism is that being
drunk is to have surrendered reason and self-possession, and any praise of
drunkenness has to be a deliberate reversal of that view. So also Philo's use
of this metaphor must be read in the context of his more usual attitudes.
The wages of "untimely candour" in the face of tyrants are for the speaker to
be subjected to pitiless cruelty: "not candour at all, rather are they the gifts
of foolishness, folly, and incurable melancholia." Telling truth to power is
rash, even if it is also something that we must honor.[12] Such behavior is
like putting to sea when a storm is at its height, in a fit of drunkenness:
that is, without considering consequences.[13] Intoxication, in Philo's usual
judgment, is a failure of common sense: foolishness, folly, *and melancholia.*
It is the same pattern that is seen in those who disobey rightful authority.

It is with good reason that the disobedient and contentious man who
"brings contributions," that is contributes and adds sins to sins, great

10. Douglas, "A Distinctive Anthropological Perspective," 4.
11. *Jeremiah* 23.9; see Stock, *Flutes of Dionysus,* 47.
12. Cf. the story of Zerubbabel and King Darius in *1 Esdras* 4. See Gruen, *Heritage and
Hellenism,* 162–7.
13. Philo, *De somniis* 2.83 (*Collected Works,* vol. 5, 479). Philo spoke from experience:
he was leader of a delegation of Alexandrian Jews to the mad emperor Caligula. See *Collected
Works,* vol. 10.

to small, new to old, voluntary to involuntary, as though inflamed by wine drowns the whole of life in ceaseless and unending drunkenness, sodden with drinking deep of the unmixed cup of folly, is judged by the holy word to be worthy of stoning. Yes, for he has made away with the commands of right reason, his father, and the observances enjoined by instruction, his mother.[14]

What is it to be like that? Why would anyone risk such calamity, whether at the hands of tyrants or of Philo's lawful authority? "We say that the lover of ill-considered aims, irrational contentions and vainglory is always puffed up by folly and claims to exalt himself not only above men but above the world of nature, and thinks that all things have come into being for his sake, and that they must each of them, earth, water, air, heaven, pay their tribute to him as king. . . . Some people are so brimful of folly that they are aggrieved if the whole world does not follow their wishes."[15] They have lost—as popular accounts of drunkenness in classical Athens also suggest— all sense of limits, all respect.

Is this a failure of ordinary reason? Or is "reason," especially as those of an academic temperament imagine it, itself part of the problem? Melancholia is like being drunk. "Wine in large quantity produces in men much the same characteristics which we attribute to the melancholic, and as it is being drunk it fashions various characters, for instance irritable, benevolent, compassionate or reckless ones. . . . We are often in a state of grieving, but could not say why, while at other times we feel cheerful without apparent reason."[16] Aristotle adds that wine is also aphrodisiac and can sometimes improve a poet (unless the remark is ironical): "Maracus the Syracusan was a better poet when he was out of his mind." Ficino was perhaps the first explicitly to identify Aristotle's melancholia with Plato's divine frenzy,[17] but the association seems natural. According to Plato, "when a man drinks wine he begins to be better pleased with himself, and the more he drinks the more he is filled full of brave hopes, and conceit of his power, and at last the string of his tongue is loosened, and fancying himself wise, he is brimming over with lawlessness, and has no more fear or respect, and is ready

14. Philo, *De ebrietate* 24.95 (*Collected Works*, vol. 3, 367).

15. Philo, *De somniis* 2.115 (*Collected Works*, vol. 5, 495). The same might be said of the Gnostics whom Plotinus deplored.

16. Aristotle, *Problemata* 30.

17. Marsilius Ficino, *De vita triplici* I 5 (*Works*, 497), cited by Klibansky, Panofsky, and Saxl, *Saturn and Melancholy*, 259.

to do or say anything."[18] Wine and the melancholic temperament both lead
to a neglect of ordinary concerns, a conviction that the world, somehow, is
ours, and that we—being clever people—know how to deal with it (until,
that is, we don't). When Porphyry was suffering from melancholia, Plotinus
prescribed travel—a normal remedy:[19] at least it is not clear that mere *arguments* against self-harming were much help!

It is in this context also that Philo, as I remarked earlier, warns against
conceit: "if we repose our trust in our own reasonings we shall construct
and build up the city of Mind that corrupts the truth. . . . Accordingly, the
dreamer finds on rising up that all the movements and exertions of the
foolish man are dreams void of reality. Yea Mind itself turned out to be a
dream."[20] Allegorizing the story of Lot's daughters, he suggests that "they
made their father drink Wine" means the "complete insensibility that the
mind should think itself competent to deliberate by itself on what is to its
interests."[21] He goes on to mock philosophical pretensions, pointing out
that "the multitude of so-called philosophers are divided into troops and
companies and propound dogmatic conclusions widely different and often
diametrically opposite not on some single chance point, but on practically
all points great and small, which constitute the problems which they seek
to solve!"[22]

Philo elsewhere contrasts drunkenness with the proper contemplative
spirit, typified—he suggests—in Aaron: "He is the reason whose thoughts
are lofty and sublime [*meteora kai hupsela phronon*], not with the empty
inflated bigness of mere vaunting, but with the greatness of virtue, which
lifts his thinking above the heaven and will not let him cherish any reasoning that mean and low. And being so minded he will never willingly
allow strong [*akraton*] wine or any potion which breeds folly to approach
him."[23]

In all these cases, whether the drunken are ordinarily greedy and forgetful or pretentiously depressed, it is "unmixed wine" that does the damage.
The popular view of drunkenness in classical Athens seems to have been

18. Plato, *Laws* 1.649. But cf. *Laws* 2.666: "The other story implied that wine was given
man out of revenge, and in order to make him mad; but our present doctrine, on the contrary, is,
that wine was given him as a balm, and in order to implant modesty in the soul, and health and
strength in the body."

19. Porphyry, *Life* 11.5 (*melancholikes tinos nosou*).

20. Philo, *Legum allegoriarum* 3.228–9 (*Collected Works*, vol. 1, 457). I shall return to this
image, of awakening from dreams.

21. Philo, *De ebrietate* 41.166 (*Collected Works*, vol. 3, 405), citing *Genesis* 19.33.

22. Philo, *De ebrietate* 48.198 (*Collected Works*, vol. 3, 421).

23. Philo, *De ebrietate* 31.123–32.124 (*Collected Works*, vol. 3, 387), citing *Leviticus* 10.8.

that it involves a loss of self-control—though Athenians were readier to disapprove of the *opsophagos*, the ravenous fish-eater, than of the drinker![24] Just possibly, there is a more civilized use of liquor (and the Athenians were also deeply suspicious of teetotalers, as being afraid to let down social barriers and reveal anything of their real motives: afraid, that is, of getting naked in case their ugliness were obvious to all).[25] There was at any rate some attempt to allegorize the worship of Dionysus Orthos at Athens (even if it seems likely that the Upright Dionysus was originally and simply phallic). Philochorus declares that "it was by drinking properly *mixed* wine that men ceased to stand in a bent posture as they were compelled to do by neat wine."[26] And Plotinus, we should note, insists that the intellect be drunk *with nectar*, the drink of the immortals—wine not having been invented, as he says in his development of Plato's *Symposium* fable (III.5 [50].7).[27] This theme is picked up in a Sufi poem by 'Umar Ibn al-Fārid:

> Rememb'ring the Belovèd, Wine we drink
> Which drunk had made us ere the vine's creation.[28]

Plotinus does, in his development of Plato's *Phaedrus* myth, appear to equate "being drunk with wine and filled with the nectar" (*oinotheis kai plerotheis tou nektaros*), but it may be that the word for "being drunk" does not strictly commit him to their being drunk with *wine* (*oinos*). Wine, after all, did not "then" exist.[29] The nectar that existed, that exists, before the world of sense comes into being is more to the point. The beauty that such drunken lovers see has "penetrated through the whole of their soul," and they are not simply spectators—"as if someone possessed by a god, taken over by Phoebus or one of the Muses, could bring about the vision of the god

---

24. See J. Davidson, *Courtesans and Fishcakes*, 143–7.

25. Ibid., 155–6.

26. Detienne, *Dionysos at Large*, 37. The joke in Homer's *Odyssey* is that the barbaric Cyclops drinks unmixed *milk* (*akraton gala pinon*, where the usual tag is *akraton methu pinon*).

27. Gregory the Great made use of a similar contrast, between wine as knowledge of the Law and the Prophets, and the *milk* of the gospel. See D. Turner, *Eros and Allegory*, 226 (see also 261 [Alcuin], 324 [Gallus]). This contrast does not have the right effect in a population lacking an adult capacity to digest milk (i.e., most of non-Caucasian humanity).

28. Ibn al-Fārid, "The Wine Song," cited in Lings and Minnaar, *Underlying Religion*, ix. That "Wine" has to be distinct from ordinary wine. See also Chittick, "Jami on Divine Love."

29. We can guess that this nectar was, literally, *mead*, a honey-derived drink long associated with poetic inspiration in India and the north as well as in Greece. See Scheinberg, "Bee Maidens." According to Porphyry, *De antro nympharum* 16, honey is the food of the gods. See also Ustinova, *Caves and the Ancient Mind*, 60.

in himself, if he had the power to look at the god in himself" (V.8 [31].10, 42–5).[30]

The two sorts or phases or activities of intellect also turn up elsewhere:

> If one likens it to a living richly varied sphere, or imagines it as a thing all faces, shining with living faces, or as all the pure souls running together into the same place, with no deficiencies but having all that is their own, and universal Intellect seated on their summits so that the region is illuminated by intellectual light—if one imagined it like this one would be seeing it somehow as one sees another from outside; *but one must become that, and make oneself the contemplation.* (VI.7 [38].15, 25–VI.7 [38].16, 3; my italics)

The distinction here is between knowing something "from outside" and "from within": in the vocabulary Lewis borrowed from Samuel Alexander, between "contemplation" ("abstract, external, impersonal, uninvolved") and "enjoyment" ("participant, inhabited, personal, committed").[31] It is notable that Lewis mentions in this context the supposed Persian custom of debating matters of decision both drunk and sober! Both forms of intellectual acquaintance have their place—but it is indeed *enjoyment* that should take precedence. So also Feynman, first citing an unnamed poet as saying that "the whole universe is in a glass of wine":

> If our small minds, for some convenience, divide this glass of wine, this universe, into parts—physics, biology, geology, astronomy, psychology and so forth—remember that nature does not know it! So let us put it all back together, remembering ultimately what it is for. Let it give us one more final pleasure: drink it, and forget it all![32]

---

30. After Plato, *Phaedrus* 246e ff.—a form of divine possession that does not wholly evict the human person, though it may silence the human mind.

31. Lewis, "Meditations in a Toolshed," 607, cited by M. Ward, *Planet Narnia*, 17. Lewis drew his *terminology* from S. Alexander, *Space, Time and Deity*, vol. 1, 12, who was addressing the difference between different objects of experience, in line with a difference between "cognate" ("I strike a stroke or wave a farewell") and "objective" ("I strike a man or wave a flag") accusatives. But Lewis seems rather to be employing Newman's distinction between real and notional assent and the different sorts of philosopher described earlier in this volume (see Newman, *Grammar of Assent*, 93–4).

32. Feynman, *Feynman Lectures*, vol. 1, 32 (chap. 3.7), cited by Midgley, *Science and Poetry*, 64. Reality, that is, is the whole, not forever to be broken down into its parts or aspects, and our best engagement with it is—exactly—to experience our own involvement in it and to forget our normal concerns ("take away everything!," *aphele panta*; V.3 [49].17, 39). I do not

The higher condition, Plotinus says elsewhere, is "as if carried away or possessed by a god, in a quiet solitude and a state of calm, not turning away anywhere in his being and not busy about himself, altogether at rest and having become a kind of rest. He had no thought of beauties but had already run up beyond beauty and gone beyond the choir of virtues, like a man who enters into the sanctuary and leaves behind the statues in the outer shrine. . . . They are secondary objects of contemplation. But that other, perhaps, was not a contemplation but another kind of seeing, a being out of oneself [ekstasis] and simplifying and giving oneself over and pressing towards contact and rest and a sustained thought leading to adaptation [perinoesis pros epharmogen], if one is going to contemplate what is in the sanctuary" (VI.9 [9].11, 12–25). Armstrong, in his note on this last passage, objected to the term "ecstasy," as giving a "very misleading impression of this austere and quiet mysticism."[33] But perhaps Plotinus was not always so austere. The condition he craves is that of "the self glorified, full of intelligible light—but rather itself pure light—weightless, floating free, having become—but rather being—a god; set on fire then, but the fire seems to go out, if one is weighed down again" (ei de palin barunoito; VI.9 [9].9, 59–60). "One aspect of Dionysus is his ability to make sorrows be forgotten"[34]— and such forgetfulness may be either bad or good.

The drunkenness of greed, conceit, sloth, and melancholia is an echo or perversion of a better state. Before Adam fell, "what is now gall in him sparkled like crystal, and bore the taste of good works, and what is now melancholy in man shone in him like the dawn and contained in itself the wisdom and perfection of good works; but when Adam broke the law, the sparkle of innocence was dulled in him, and his eyes, which had formerly beheld heaven, were blinded, and his gall was changed to bitterness, and his melancholy to blackness."[35] Just so, we may conclude, Plotinus's "flight of the alone to the Alone" (VI.9 [9].11, 51)[36] may be perverted into the state he

---

know how seriously Feynman intended this, nor whether he was aware of the Neoplatonic background.

33. Armstrong, Enneads, vol. 7, 342n1. Dionysius may have found it necessary to abandon these metaphors precisely to avoid confusion. See Harrington, "Drunken Epibole," 117: "Dionysius does not simply import the Plotinian theory; he removes from it the language of drunkenness and erotic love, which rarefies it considerably and, more importantly, changes the character of divine union to eliminate its generative capacity."

34. Detienne, Dionysos at Large, 180n105, after Euripides, Bacchae 380ff.

35. Klibansky, Panofsky, and Saxl, Saturn and Melancholy, 80, citing Hildegard of Bingen from Paulus Kaiser, ed., Hildegardis causae et curae (Leipzig: Teubner, 1903), 43.

36. But note that this translation (MacKenna's) is misleading: Jerome's tag better represents the goal—"nudus nudum Jesum sequi" (Epistle 52.5).

attributes to his Gnostic opponents, an obsession with the corporeal things they despise, a drunken self-contempt that cannot shake off the enchantment. The very imagination that Plotinus seeks to direct away from corporeal affairs may prove our undoing. And since we are all influenced by merely romantic, countercultural exaggerations of the value of intoxication, it is worth remembering the following barbed and accurate comment from a modern anthropologist:

> The moral collapse of Vietnam was scarcely caused by an overdose of objective consciousness about what we were doing. It consisted of the failure to expand consciousness beyond mere instrumental tasks to the practical and banal significance of our national goals and policies. We kept the war going in Vietnam because our consciousness was mystified by symbols of patriotism, dreams of glory, unyielding pride, and visions of empire. In mood we were exactly what the counter-culture people want us to become. We imagined we were menaced by slant-eyed devils and worthless little yellow men; we enthralled ourselves with visions of our own ineffable majesty. In short, we were stoned.[37]

It is open to Plotinus to suggest that "intellect in love," "drunk with the nectar," is the original inebriation, "before" wine and the sensible world existed. Losing our hold on that original we may be enticed instead by its reflection and deeply involved in sentimental melancholia, trivial passion, greed, and "visions of our own ineffable majesty"—all the things from which sober reason seeks to rescue us. Plato's suggestion that drunkenness is associated with matter[38] was picked up by Proclus.[39] Drunkenness is used in the Gnostic tradition as a metaphor for our seduction by the world. Our escape is like "a person who, having been intoxicated, becomes sober and having come to himself reaffirms that which is essentially his own."[40] Armstrong translates one passage of Plotinus in that light: "beginning as one it [i.e., Intellect] did not stay as it began, but, without noticing it, became many, as if heavy [with drunken sleep], and unrolled itself because it wanted to possess everything" (III.8 [30].8, 32–3). This is the unusual suggestion that Intellect itself is fallen into "a drunken sleep," with much the same motive as our souls' wish not to be all together, but for each to have

37. M. Harris, *Cows, Pigs, Wars, and Witches*, 266.
38. Plato, *Phaedo* 79c.
39. Proclus, *In remp* II, 129.12 (Ley, *Macrobius and Numenius*, 9, after E. A. Leemans).
40. *Gospel of Truth* 22.13–20 (Jonas, *Gnostic Religion*, 71).

her own.[41] The drunkenness that is here a "bad" thing, weighing down the intellect, may equally be a good thing, if we pass through it on the upward, rather than the downward, track (though here drunkenness makes intellect plural, and in the original passage makes it one). This may be so, though Armstrong perhaps reads too much into the phrase "*hoion bebaremenos*," which MacKenna prefers to translate as "it grew, as it were, pregnant" (invoking a different range of Plotinian metaphor; VI.7 [38].15). In the actual passage, all that is said is that intellect is, "as it were, weighed down" as it ceases to be single. What nuance Plotinus intended is unclear. That we are all asleep and dreaming may be something with which he would agree. That the sleep is drunken is not exactly what he says, though it can be admitted that it is the drunken Plenty that is "weighed down" (*bebaremenos*) by the principles with which he was filled, in the allegorical garden of the *Symposium* (III.5 [50].9, 38).

The two passages, from VI.7 [38] and III.5 [50], may indeed seem strangely at odds. If "drunk intellect" is better than "sober intellect," how is it that "intellect possesses itself in satiety and is *not* drunk with the possession" (III.5 [50].9, 18–9), by contrast with the drunken state, the stupor, of Plenty, Poros, in the garden of Zeus? And if "intellect out of its mind" is good, how is that different from "intellect which is not intellect, since it presumes to see [*tolmesas idein*] what is not its own" (i.e., Matter) (I.8 [51].9, 18–9)? One answer might be that all these terms are, after all, "metaphorical," merely "codes," and so need not be consistent. Notoriously, in the treatise on Love, Plotinus gets entangled in the different allegorical significance of Aphrodite, Zeus, and Kronos: Aphrodite is, varyingly, the daughter of Ouranos, Kronos, and Zeus, and both Zeus and Aphrodite seem to stand for Soul. Armstrong, typically, suggests that this shows "how little real importance Plotinus attached to myths and their allegorical interpretation."[42] Even if (as I suppose) he took them more seriously, metaphors live more easily with seeming contradiction. But there is a way of resolving the contradiction, in both the literal and the metaphorical. Being "drunk with the nectar" just is being taken out of oneself, elevated by a higher presence: "what is nectar for the gods but that which the divinity acquires?," in Armstrong's translation—or, as I would prefer, "what is nectar for the gods but that which supplies the di-

---

41. "As if they were tired of being together, they each go to their own" (IV.8 [6].4, 11–2; see also V.1 [10].1). Philo in several places suggested that souls fell when they were "sated" with contemplation, and he is followed in this by Origen, *De principiis* 2.8.3 (Chadwick, *Early Christian Thought*, 84–5, 151–2).

42. Armstrong, *Enneads*, vol. 3, 176n1.

vinity?" (*ho to theion komizetai*), except that the following sentence seems to support Armstrong! Plenty is "the plenitude and wealth of beauties" received into the Soul from Intellect, and "this is the being drunk with nectar." Similarly, intellect itself may be elevated into the One and is likewise "drunk with nectar." Being drunk with *wine* is to be weighed down; with *nectar*, to be elevated. But Plenty may, depending on the direction of our attention, be reckoned to be both: intellect "weighed down" because no longer in full, sober enjoyment of its own being; soul elevated because filled up with intellectual beauty. "Being drunk with wine and filled with the nectar" is not after all a hendiadys: these are two alternative possibilities. The better way of approaching reality is in awe, in trembling delight, in a fall of barriers, in forgetfulness of self, and at the same time a realization of that presence that indeed "owns" all things.[43] We may be "simplified into happiness" (VI.7 [38].35): enjoying the life that is the One. In everyday life, indeed, it may be dangerous to forget our limits or to allow just any images to rampage through our mental landscape. But it is just as dangerous to evacuate the world, the world of our experience, of any "meaning." There is a better way:

> Whatever name we give it ("intellect," "imagination" or "heart"), what Balthasar has in mind here is a faculty that transcends yet at the same time unifies feeling and thought, body and soul, sensation and rationality. It is the kind of intelligence that sees the meaning in things, that reads them as symbols—symbols, not of something else, *but of themselves as they stand in God.* Thus in the spiritual intelligence of man, being is unveiled in its true nature as a gift bearing within it the love of the Giver. Ultimately things—just as truly as persons—can be truly known only through love. In other words, a thing can be known only when it draws us out of ourselves, when we grasp it in its otherness from ourselves, in the meaning which it possesses as beauty, uniting truth and goodness. This kind of knowledge is justly called *sobria ebrietas* ("drunken" sobriety) because it is ecstatic, rapturous, although at the same time measured, ordered, dignified. It is an encounter with the Other which takes the heart out of itself and places it in another cen-

---

43. Cf. Traherne, *Centuries,* 177 (1.29): "You never enjoy the world aright, till the Sea itself floweth in your veins, till you are clothed with the heavens, and crowned with the stars: and perceive yourself to be the sole heir of the whole world, and more than so, because men are in it who are every one sole heirs as well as you. Till you can sing and rejoice and delight in God, as misers do in gold, and Kings in scepters, you never enjoy the world."

tre, which is ultimately the very centre of being, where all things are received from God.[44]

Though perhaps Plotinus was not quite so serious. He may recall that Plato recommended that older people use wine as a medicine to help themselves sing and dance to Dionysus, overcoming their diffidence and "the crabbedness of old age":[45] better, sometimes, to be drunk than dignified!

One further way of reading "drunkenness," to match the Franciscan reading of "nakedness" or holy poverty: if those who are "drunk" are careless of the consequences of their actions, may they not also be unconcerned for tomorrow? Sober reason, as we ordinarily conceive it, takes thought for tomorrow, what we shall eat, what we shall drink, and how large a debt we should incur for the purchase of housing, clothing, and computers. But we are sternly warned against all these preoccupations:[46] at the very least, we should not give so much attention to them as to ignore the present, where alone we encounter eternity.

There is also a modern reading of the two conditions, employing the language of neurology: left- and right-brain functions are distinct. The left hemisphere of the human brain appears to be chiefly responsible for analytical reasoning; the right, for a more "synthetic" or contemplative way of thinking—a distinction experienced by a neurologist, Jill Bolte Taylor, after suffering a stroke in her left hemisphere.[47] Left-brain reasoning, obedient to the standard "laws of logic" (noncontradiction, excluded middle, and identity), is a necessary corrective in our disorganized lives, but we can also see that "the real wiggly world slips like water through our imaginary nets. However much we divide, count, sort, or classify this wiggling into particular things and events, this is no more than a way of thinking about the world: it is never *actually* divided."[48] We can also experience the whole and understand that the divisions we impose between this and that, our insistence that *every* statement must be either true or false, are only convenient fictions. Drunkards know better, even if they also fail to grasp significant connections between this and that. Progress is not made exclusively by intellectual, argumentative means—indeed, such arguments depend upon the real existence of an intellectual, nondiscursive grasp of

44. Caldecott, "Liturgy and Trinity," citing Hans Urs von Balthasar.
45. Plato, *Laws* 2.666b.
46. *Matthew* 6.34.
47. J. Taylor, *Stroke of Insight*. See also McGilchrist, *Master and His Emissary*.
48. A. Watts, *Taboo against Knowing*, 59. See also my "Deconstructing the Laws of Logic."

"immutable justice and beauty" (V.1 [10].11), for which we can have no *argument* if we are not already *moved* by it. Plotinus finds nothing odd in appealing to tradition, nor yet to oracles about honoring the dead—or to the heroic dead themselves (IV.7 [2].15). Even the star-gods, though they do not determine what we shall do, may serve as examples, and we may request their aid (IV.4 [28].30). And the mysteries are constantly invoked as meaning what Plotinus himself has come to see, with Plato's help, as true (I.6 [1].6, VI.9 [9].11). So it is not at all obvious that Dodds, for example, was correct in his assertion that "Plotinus will have ignored the [Chaldaean] Oracles, recognizing them for the theosophical rubbish that they are":[49] the assumption that, because Plotinus was *rational*, he must therefore have disbelieved exactly what Dodds disbelieved, is a failure of historical imagination, and perhaps of philosophical good sense.

As we switch back and forth between our different states, each one may claim the title of sobriety. "It is as if people who slept through their life thought the things in their dreams were reliable and obvious, but, if someone woke them up, disbelieved in what they saw with their eyes open and went to sleep again" (V.5 [32].11, 19–23). To secure our real awakening, to "sober up" (according to one metaphor) or "drink up" (by another), we should drink nectar and not wine, remembering the old story that those who eat or drink the fruit of fairyland remain there (like Persephone). The question is, of course, how do we get that nectar (and how are we to be sure it's not illusion)? And is it, maybe, Lethe (which is Forgetfulness)? Or Nepenthe, chasing away sorrow?[50]

49. Dodds, "Numenius," 11. Dodds goes on to attack Numenius as one who "welcomed all the superstitions of his time, whatever their origin, and thereby contributed to the eventual degradation of Greek philosophical thought." Most recently on Numenius, see Van Nuffelen, *Rethinking the Gods*, 72–83.

50. *Odyssey* 4.219–21: "Helen, daughter of Zeus, took other counsel. Straightway she cast into the wine of which they were drinking a drug to quiet all pain and strife, and bring forgetfulness of every ill."

CHAPTER NINE

Dancing

What is the right way of living? Life must be lived as play. Playing certain games, making sacrifices, singing and dancing, and then a man will be able to propitiate the gods, and defend himself against his enemies and win in the contest.[1]

This declaration, by "the Athenian Stranger" in Plato's *Laws*, probably lies behind Plotinus's own occasional "playfulness" (III.8 [30].1)[2] and his constant use of "dancing" as an image of the better life. "We have the gods as fellow-dancers," and it is from the joy (*chara*) that is natural to the dance that we get the name "choruses."[3]

So what sort of dances are these? Unfortunately, we cannot tell in detail what ancient Greek or Roman dances were. Naerebout provides a summary of evidence drawn from Greek and Latin vocabulary, ancient texts, sculptures, and pictures on pottery and observes that even if we can iden-

---

1. Plato, *Laws* 7.796; see Huizinga, *Homo Ludens*, 18–9; Bellah, *Religion in Human Evolution*, 110.

2. See also Peirce, "Neglected Argument," 92 (6.458): "There is a certain agreeable occupation of mind which, from its having no distinctive name, I infer is not as commonly practised as it deserves to be; for indulged in moderately—say through some five to six per cent of one's waking time, perhaps during a stroll—it is refreshing enough more than to repay the expenditure. Because it involves no purpose save that of casting aside all serious purpose, I have sometimes been half-inclined to call it reverie, with some qualification; but for a frame of mind so antipodal to vacancy and dreaminess such a designation would be too excruciating a misfit. In fact, it is Pure Play. Now, Play, we all know, is a lively exercise of one's powers. Pure Play has no rules, except this very law of liberty. It bloweth where it listeth. It has no purpose, unless recreation."

3. Plato, *Laws* 2.653, cited by Bellah, *Religion in Human Evolution*, 110. This is a false etymology, however. *Choros* is more likely to be derived from *chora*, "place" (Naerebout, *Attractive Performances*, 178).

tify a given image as indicating *dancing* rather than running, stretching, posing, or whatever, we have no idea how one position flowed into another. Dances were passed on by word of mouth and example, not by written, formulaic description (or at any rate we have no such detailed description beyond remarks about jumping, stamping, and shouting).[4] Our principal textual evidence consists of Lucian's defense chiefly of the solitary pantomime and Libanius's defense of dancing in general. Lucian of Samosata (AD 125–80) lived a century earlier than Plotinus, and Libanius of Antioch (AD 314–94) a century later, but we can reasonably suppose that cultural conditions were not very different. The dances most familiar to the ancients—the ones they thought about in thinking about dance—were performed by groups (almost all single-sex) moving rhythmically together in a circular space, accompanied by musicians and singers. One common form had the dancers dancing and singing around their lyre player.[5] Another form of dance entirely, the mime or pantomime, was performed by a solitary dancer representing different characters and actions through well-rehearsed gestures like the gestures of Indian dancers.[6] Both sorts of dance were also visible in nature: the dance of the fixed stars and planets, on the one hand, and the manifold shapes which Soul animates, on the other. Dance forms were analyzed under three heads: *phorai*, *schemata*, and *deixeis* (i.e., movements, poses, and indicative gestures).[7] Some were noisier: "the dancing [of the Corybantes in Phrygia and the Curetes in Crete] was performed in full armour; sword clashed against shield, and inspired heels beat martial time upon the ground."[8] These were probably the war dances that Plotinus had in mind in his commentary on specifically human troubles (III.2 [47].15, 33–6), but they may also remind us of his more general view of Providence:

> In the universe the battle of conflicting elements springs from a single rational principle; so that it would be better for one to compare it to the

4. Naerebout, *Attractive Performances*, 262.

5. Lawler, *Dance in Ancient Greece*, 45, citing *Iliad* 18.567–72: "Young maidens and youths, gay of spirit, were carrying the fruit, sweet as honey, in woven baskets. And in their midst a boy played charmingly upon a clear-toned lyre, and sang sweetly in accompaniment, with delicate voice; and dancers followed along with him, leaping, with songs and shouts of joy."

6. See Lada-Richards, *Silent Eloquence*, chap. 3.

7. Plutarch, "Table Talk" 9.747bc (*Moralia*, vol. 9, 289–91). See Webb, *Demons and Dancers*, 74.

8. Lucian, "On Pantomime," 241–2. Corybantes also feature in Plato's *Ion* and *Euthydemus*. See Levenson, *Socrates among the Corybantes*. Plato associated Athena with such dancing: *Laws* 7.796b. See West, *Orphic Poems*, 137–8.

melody [*harmonia*] which results from conflicting sounds, and one will then enquire why there are the conflicting sounds in the rational proportions [of musical scales]. (III.2 [47].16, 39–40)

Armstrong's translation of this passage is misleading. High and low notes, Plotinus says, according to Armstrong, "come together into a unity— being the proportional laws of melody [*harmonias logoi*] they come together into the melody itself, which is another greater law of proportion [*logon meizona*]" (III.2 [47].16, 42–3).[9] But "*harmonia*" does not mean melody. The *logoi* are the ratios between different notes, and there is no need to suppose he is speaking of *several* "greater laws," but only of the one, greater, ratio, of 2:1 (which bridges the octave). Plotinus is not imagining—as we might suppose—discordant notes resolved into a unity,[10] nor even a melody composed of relatively high and low notes (what else?) which might each, singly, be imperfect (but why should they be?). Ancient musical theory did allow for the occasional sounding of two notes together ("concordance is the coincidence and blending of two notes that differ in height and depth of pitch"), and so producing "another species of note,"[11] but that too is not what is represented here. The *harmonia* Plotinus means is that proposed in music theory:[12] the potential in the well-tuned instrument for distinguishable notes, separated by tones or semitones. The ratio of one note to the equivalent in a lower octave is 2:1; the ratio between one note and one that is four notes lower is 4:3; the ratio between one note and another that is five notes lower is 3:2.[13] These are the recognized "concordant" intervals. Different *harmoniai*, such as the Dorian, Lydian, Mixolydian, and so forth, arrange the intervals (tone and semitone) between successive notes of the octave differently, and a total, systematizing account was offered by Aris-

9. Armstrong, *Enneads*, vol. 3, 97–9. My thanks to Andrew Barker for helping to clarify this passage.

10. This metaphor might be more popular among Christian Platonists, dissatisfied with the *current* state of things and hoping for a world-transforming change (not merely a change in our outlook). Pagan Platonists usually prefer, like Plotinus, to suppose that the current state of things already represents the best that—materially—there can be: II.9 [33].5, 24–32.

11. Aelianus the Platonist (late second century AD), quoted by Porphyry, *Commentary on Ptolemy's Harmonics* 33.20 (Barker, *Harmonic and Acoustic Theory*, 231, 233).

12. With which Plotinus was, so Porphyry says, very well acquainted, though Plotinus did not write directly on the subject (*Life* 14.7–10). Porphyry himself wrote a commentary on Ptolemy's *Harmonics*. See Barker, *Harmonic and Acoustic Theory*, 229–44.

13. A lucid account is given in West, *Ancient Greek Music*, 8–10, 160–4. The ratios are represented in the Pythagorean *tetraktys*: West, *Ancient Greek Music*, 275; see Burkert, *Lore and Science*, 72, 186–8.

tides Quintilianus (himself very likely a follower of Plotinian Platonism),[14] in which those differing *harmoniai* can be conceived as a single cycle.[15] The "fight" between the notes is that of the opposing values, "high" and "low."[16] This is, Plotinus proposes, a better analogy for the cosmic drama than a single play, "composing the complete story of the persons in conflict" (III.2 [47].16, 37–9). He may be nodding to a principle of plenitude: the point is not that tensions between elements of the cosmos are resolved in performance but that all these elements, though seemingly distinct, are eternally derived from a single principle, the "greater ratio," which contains the lesser ratios between these notes. The focus of ancient musical appreciation seems to be rather in the intelligible world (a sort of higher mathematics) than in any ordinary performance—though Plotinus also asks, "how could there be a musician who sees the [*harmonia*] in the intelligible world and will not be stirred when he hears [it] in sensible sounds?" (II.9 [33].16, 39–41).[17] All the elements of the *harmonia* are necessary for the life of the whole, even if that is not—in the modern senses—either "harmonious" or "melodious."

> If the parts are struck in a particular way, the speaking parts give out a corresponding sound, and others receive the blow in silence and make the movements which result from it; and from all the sounds and passive experiences and activities come a kind of single voice of the living creature, a single life and way of living. (III.3 [48].5, 8–13)[18]

14. See Mathiesen, *Apollo's Lyre*, 521–82, who identifies passages that seem to depend on Porphyry's commentary on Ptolemy; Barker, *Harmonic and Acoustic Theory*, 392–535.

15. See Barker, *Musician and His Art*, 166: "the interval structure of any *harmonia* can be converted into that of its successor simply by removing the interval at the bottom of its series and replacing it at the top. . . . The sequence of *harmoniai* is cyclic."

16. This sort of opposition, expressed—as Andrew Barker reminds me—in Eryximachus's speech in Plato's *Symposium* 187ff., goes back at least to the standard "Pythagorean" Table of Opposites (see Aristotle, *Metaphysics* 1.986a22–5): whereas we automatically think of high/low, hot/cold, wet/dry, and the rest as merely relative values within a continuum, there was a strong sense among "the ancients" that—like odd/even or male/female—they labeled distinct entities whose conversation *generated* the spectra that we encounter, and which might be grasped, intellectually, over against each other. At least some modern physical theory (incorporating opposing electrical and other charges) might suggest a similar fundamental polarity.

17. Armstrong again, mistakenly, takes *harmonia* as "melody." Plotinus here seems closer to the thought of Ptolemais (see Barker, *Harmonic and Acoustic Theory*, 239–42) than of Porphyry, who believed that musical performances were too distracting (*Abstinence*, 44 [1.34]). The latter opinion seems indeed to have been more common, and Plotinus here, as often elsewhere, deliberately subverts the consensus. See Quasten, *Music and Worship*.

18. See M. Miles, *Plotinus on Body and Beauty*, 117.

In these sounds we catch a glimpse of the underlying, diverse order, and of the hidden cosmic unity, rather than ordinarily *hearing* a resolution of discordant notes. The performance expresses, piecemeal, all the possible values of the intelligible whole.

But it is the single dancer, the pantomime, that Plotinus more often chooses as his image of the work of nature, on Earth and in the heavens.

> The activity of life is an artistic activity, like the way in which one who is dancing is moving; for the dancer himself is like the life which is artistic in this way and his art moves him. (III.2 [47].16, 23–7)[19]

Nature is like Proteus, taking on many different shapes and sizes as we seek to hold her. Conversely, "every dancer is almost an Egyptian Proteus."[20] In the dance or play of Nature differing, apparently opposed movements all have a place.

> So, then, there are good men and wicked men, like the opposed movements of a dancer inspired by one and the same art; and we shall call one part of his performance "good" and another "wicked," and in this way it is a good performance [*kalōs echei*]. But, then [so some will say], the wicked are no longer wicked. No, their being wicked is not done away with, only their being like that does not originate with themselves. . . . There is a place for every man, one to fit the good and one to fit the bad. (III.2 [47].17, 9–14, 22–4)

Neither Nature nor the human dancer need be thinking about what she is doing.

> The parts of the dancer's body cannot possibly keep the same position in every figure: as his body follows the pattern of the dance and bends with it, one of his limbs is pressed hard down, another relaxed, one works hard and painfully, another is given a rest as the figuring changes. The dancer's intention looks elsewhere; his limbs are affected in accordance

---

19. See also VI.1 [42].27, 20, where a more active Matter than usual, capable of becoming everything, is "like the dancer who in his dance makes himself everything."

20. Libanius, *Reply to Aristides on Behalf of the Dancers* (*Orations* 64), 117, cited by Lawler, "Proteus Is a Dancer" (translating *mikrou* as "on a smaller scale" rather than "almost"). See also Molloy, *Libanius*. Compare Theophrastus, who proposed that the universe adjusted its own parts to suit the whole, rather than agreeing with Aristotle's suggestion that there is a "natural resting place" for each sort of matter (Sorabji, *Matter, Space and Motion*, 202–4).

with the dance and serve the dance, and help to make it perfect and complete. (IV.4 [28].33, 12–9)[21]

Plotinus's use of the image relies on contemporary understanding of what such dancers did (and might easily be attacked for doing).[22]

> It is his profession to show forth human character and passion in all their variety; to depict love and anger, frenzy and grief, each in its due measure. Wondrous art!—on the same day, he is mad Athamas and shrinking Ino; he is Atreus, and again he is Thyestes, and next Aegisthus or Aerope; all one man's work.[23]

By doing this the dancer helped his audience understand their own possibilities and the history—as it was then understood—of humankind. It may even be that more was intended by these impersonations than was usually admitted: according to Libanius, "the dancer does not imitate [*mimeomai*] but makes present [*paristemi*] in himself the divinities he plays."[24] This is not an uncommon belief: consider, for example, an Indian case. For nine months in the year Hari Das is a manual laborer and prison guard. In the remaining three months he is the medium of a Hindu god:

21. See also Socrates's comment on a boy dancer: "no part of his body was idle during the dance, but neck, legs, and hands were all active together. And that is the way a person must dance who intends to increase the suppleness of his body" (Xenophon, *Symposium* 2.17, in *Memorabilia*, 551).

22. After all, by taking on the overt characters of the madman, fool, or woman, they were at odds with Plato's warning against actors' portrayal of characters one ought *not* to imitate (*Republic* 10.605). See also the characterization of the Homeric rhapsode Ion, in Plato, *Ion* 541e: "you have literally as many forms as Proteus; and now you go all manner of ways, twisting and turning, and, like Proteus, become all manner of people at once." And see also the appraisal of the two Sophists in Plato's *Euthydemus* 288b: "like the Egyptian wizard, Proteus, they take different forms and deceive us by their enchantments: and let us, like Menelaus, refuse to let them go until they show themselves to us in earnest."

23. Lucian, "On Pantomime" (*Works*, vol. 2, 258). Lucian wrote a century earlier than Plotinus, but it seems likely both that performances grew more professional over the years, and that the public continued to admire the skill and censure the presumed morals of performers. Some critics, perhaps correctly, have suspected satire—or at least wild exaggeration—in Lucian's account: see Nye, *Mime, Music and Drama*, 40–1. According to Zosimus (*New History*, 3 [1.6]) the pantomime dance was introduced to Rome in the time of Augustus, "as well as other things which remain to this day the cause of many evils."

24. Libanius, *Reply to Aristides on Behalf of the Dancers* (*Orations* 64), 116; Webb, *Demons and Dancers*, 77. Webb's interpretation could be challenged: the contrast might rather be between the sculptor, who imitates [beauty] in stone, and the dancer, who is himself present and so does a better job of making people *sophronesterous* by the sight. But the idea that the god is somehow present in the dancer is not unfamiliar.

"you become the deity. You lose all fear. Even your voice changes. The god comes alive and takes over. You are just the vehicle, the medium. In the trance it is God who speaks, and all the acts are the acts of the god—feeling, thinking, speaking."[25] The interpretation easier for modern Western common sense is that this is simply a form of theater (which we take for granted), but this is not how it seems to the participants. There may be moments even in the modern theater when a great actor does manage to incarnate a spirit. But the participants in such rituals do not consider themselves great actors, nor do they remember any details of what "they" do while possessed (a feature not mentioned for the classical pantomime). Nor do they suppose merely that the gods are their own hidden selves, as though Hari Das's evocation of the god Vishnu were evoking only Hari Das's Vishnu. It is thought to be possible instead for someone else to take on the role, the god, when Hari Das has to retire. Nor do the dancers seem to be damaged.

But invoking spirits—demons—may indeed have its downside. Christian commentators often condemned these dances precisely for this reason.

> Demons . . . are said to dance because dance is a constantly changing movement of the limbs. As the dancers come on stage with different masks (or characters) at different times, so demons, *using us like masks*, sometimes dance [the role of] the angry man, sometimes [the role of] the man full of desire and obsessed with the joys of the flesh, sometimes the liar. And this is what happens to us as we receive within ourselves the multifarious workings of demons and bend our hearts and our limbs in accordance with their will.[26]

Nor was it only Christians who had these concerns. Plato himself had insisted that such dancing, such impersonation, was improper, because it was likely to damage both dancers and their audience.

> And therefore when any one of these pantomimic gentlemen, who are so clever that they can imitate anything, comes to us, and makes a proposal to exhibit himself and his poetry, we will fall down and worship him as a sweet and holy and wonderful being; but we must also inform him that

---

25. Dalrymple, *Nine Lives*, 31; see further my "Personal Identity and Identity Disorders."

26. Pseudo-Basil of Caesarea (fourth century AD), *Commentary on Isaiah* 13.276, cited by Webb, *Demons and Dancers*, 163–4 (my italics). I address the issue of demons in more detail in chapter 15.

in our State such as he are not permitted to exist; the law will not allow them. And so when we have anointed him with myrrh, and set a garland of wool upon his head, we shall send him away to another city.[27]

Even Celsus, though seeking to persuade Christians to acknowledge demons with respect, agreed that "perhaps we ought not to disbelieve wise men who say that most of the earthly daemons are absorbed with created things, and are riveted to blood and burnt-offering and magical enchantments, and are bound to other things of this sort."[28] The risks are real—but the defenders of dance, and of music in general, might retort that the dance is designed to control as well as comprehend the demons. Sometimes dancers fail, precisely by the standards of good dancing.

> In Pantomime, as in rhetoric, there can be (to use a popular phrase) too much of a good thing; a man may exceed the proper bounds of imitation; what should be great may become monstrous, softness may be exaggerated into effeminacy, and the courage of a man into the ferocity of a beast.[29]

Lucian records an episode where one pantomime was so involved in his characterization of Ajax that he struck the dancer portraying Odysseus with a flute snatched from the musician. This did not please those who understood the nature of pantomime.[30] Hall remarks that the mask—and the whole artificiality of the theatrical performance—is a way of containing and expressing emotion that would otherwise be unbearable.[31]

This way of seeing the case is not so far removed from Plotinus's imagining internal statues, which he might hope to be animated once they were scrubbed clean, but the classical commentators generally supposed that the pantomime was rather practicing an art, as Lucian says, that required

---

27. Plato, *Republic* 3.398ab.

28. As quoted by Origen, *Contra Celsum,* 497 (8.60); see also Quasten, *Music and Worship,* 54.

29. Lucian, "On Pantomime," 263.

30. See Webb, *Demons and Dancers,* 76, 87–9. Lucian ("On Pantomime," 262) adds that "the illiterate riffraff, who knew not good from bad, and had no idea of decency, regarded it as a supreme piece of acting; and the more intelligent part of the audience, realizing how things stood, concealed their disgust, and instead of reproaching the actor's folly by silence, smothered it under their plaudits; they saw only too clearly that it was not Ajax but the pantomime who was mad." As William Hurt remarks, "there is a big difference between acting and acting out" (quoted by Bates, *Way of the Actor,* 61, from Norman, "Hurt: The Actor with the Atom Brain," 23)!

31. P. Hall, *Exposed by the Mask,* 24–5.

the highest standard of culture in all its branches, and involving a knowledge not of music only, but of rhythm and metre, and above all of your beloved philosophy, both natural and moral, the subtleties of dialectic alone being rejected as serving no useful purpose. Rhetoric, too, in so far as that art is concerned with the exposition of human character and human passions, claims a share of its attention. Nor can it dispense with the painter's and the sculptor's arts; in its close observance of the harmonious proportions that these teach, it is the equal of an Apelles or a Phidias. But above all Mnemosyne [Memory], and her daughter Polyhymnia [the Muse of Dance], must be propitiated by an art that would remember all things. Like Calchas in Homer, the pantomime must know all "that is, that was, that shall be"; nothing must escape his ever ready memory. Faithfully to represent his subject, adequately to express his own conceptions, to make plain all that might be obscure;—these are the first essentials for the pantomime, to whom no higher compliment could be paid than Thucydides's tribute to Pericles, who, he says, "could not only conceive a wise policy, but render it intelligible to his hearers"; the intelligibility, in the present case, depending on clearness of gesticulation. For his materials, he must draw continually, as I have said, upon his unfailing memory of ancient story; and memory must be backed by taste and judgement. He must know the history of the world, from the time when it first emerged from Chaos down to the days of Egyptian Cleopatra.[32]

Pantomimes, in brief, were supposed—by their supporters at least—to provide a route to understanding and to calm of the sort that philosophers typically professed: one relying on learning and practice rather than direct inspiration. Could Plotinus have agreed?

Lesbonax of Mytilene [a first-century rhetorician] called pantomimes "manual philosophers," and used to frequent the theatre, in the conviction that he came out of it a better man than he went in. And Timocrates, his teacher, after accidentally witnessing a pantomimic performance, exclaimed: "How much have I lost by my scrupulous devotion to philosophy!" I know not what truth there may be in Plato's analysis of the soul into the three elements of spirit, appetite, and reason: but each of the three is admirably illustrated by the pantomime; he shows us the angry man, he shows us the lover, and he shows us every passion under the control of reason; this last—like touch among the senses—is all-pervading.

32. Lucian, "On Pantomime," 251.

Again, in his care for beauty and grace of movement, have we not an illustration of the Aristotelian principle, which makes beauty a third part
of Good? Nay, I once heard some one hazard a remark, to the effect that
the philosophy of Pantomime went still further, and that in the *silence* of
the characters a Pythagorean doctrine was shadowed forth.[33]

Silence, after all, is how Nature works, being the barest trace of soul
(IV.4 [28].18) in the material, temporal world: "what comes into being is
what [she] sees in [her] silence" (III.8 [30].4, 5–6). And in the real, intelligible
world Spirit speaks only the truth, and "speaks it in silence" (VI.7 [38].34).
Plotinus, of course, could not approve Lucian's implied neglect of dialectic,
but there is still some congruence in the goals of the "manual philosopher"
and the Plotinian: by putting life on display they both awaken a right spirit.
"Such is the potency of his art, that the amorous spectator is cured of his
infirmity by perceiving the evil effects of passion, and he who enters the
theatre under a load of sorrow departs from it with a serene countenance,
as though he had drunk of that draught of forgetfulness 'that lulls all pain
and wrath.'"[34]

The pantomime, and theatrical choruses, wore masks, and this too may
be relevant to an understanding of the Plotinian stance: "Being in a mask
is a very lonely experience. It just feels as if you are a pair of eyes on legs,
because you can't see your limbs."[35] It may be a way of awakening something like that "other way of seeing" that Plotinus advocates (I.6 [1].8, 16–
28). And perhaps it is a *mask*, rather than a veil, that lies between the One
and us (I.6 [1].9, 37–9). The pantomime presents many characters, himself
resides behind them, and somehow conveys something of the peace lying
deep within reality (but may also, perhaps, be too far identified with those
same masks).

Did Plotinus dance himself or advise his followers to dance? Porphyry does not say so—but perhaps he wouldn't. Socrates—according to
Xenophon—danced alone at dawn (by implication, naked) and this amazed

33. Ibid., 258–9.
34. Ibid., 260. There may be a reminiscence here of a story that Empedocles calmed the
murderous rage of a dinner guest by uttering or singing a line of Homer (*Odyssey* 4.221) about
Nepenthe, "soother of grief and wrath, oblivion of all evils." See Iamblichus, *On the Pythagorean Life*, 50 (25 [113]). See Kingsley, *Ancient Philosophy*, 247. Iamblichus discusses the
therapeutic effects of music and ecstatic ritual further in *De mysteriis* 1.11, 3.9. See E. Clarke,
Iamblichus' "De mysteriis," 78–9.
35. Webb, *Demons and Dancers*, 92, citing Lee Haven-Jones from Croall, *Peter Hall's "Bacchae,"* 28.

and embarrassed his acquaintance.[36] He was also, Plutarch says, able to control his temper by controlling his outward physical reactions ("lowering his voice, adopting a smile, and softening his expression").[37] Plato's program of education required gymnastic, as well as "cultural," training, and not merely for its *physical* results.[38] The body was not, for any Platonist, simply an appendage nor merely a prison.

> Control of both the shape and the movements of the body, through a lengthy process of modelling first by nursemaids and mothers, then by the young man himself, was an essential part of the acquisitions of manhood.[39]

Just possibly Plotinus, who remarked that "we" worship the sun (IV.4 [28].30),[40] did so in the style of the Indians Lucian mentions:

> The Indians, when they rise to offer their morning salutation to the Sun, do not consider it enough to kiss their hands after the Greek fashion; turning to the East, they silently greet the God with movements that are designed to represent his own course through the heavens; and with this substitute for our prayers and sacrifices and choral celebrations they seek his favour at the beginning of every day and at its close.[41]

36. Xenophon, *Symposium* 2.12–20 (*Memorabilia*, 553); Athenaeus, *Deipnosophistae* 1.20e–21b. See Lawler, *Dance in Ancient Greece*, 125. Socrates offers the banal excuse that he wished to improve his health by an exercise that did not emphasize any one bodily part at the expense of others. Charmides, having spotted him and been persuaded that exercise was good, goes home and instead of dancing ("because he had never learned how"), practices shadow-boxing (or possibly the sort of *pyrrhic* dance that Plato recommended in *Laws* 8.815). There may have been more to Socrates's behavior—and Charmides's failure—than Xenophon could acknowledge. See also Bussanich, "Socrates the Mystic."

37. Plutarch, "On the Control of Anger" 455a–b (*Moralia*, vol. 6, 105); Webb, *Demons and Dancers*, 154; Sorabji, *Emotion and Peace of Mind*, 272. Seneca also advised the use of mirrors to discover how rage, for example, distorted one's face: *De ira* 2.36.1–2, cited by Bartsch, *Mirror of the Self*, 22.

38. See *Laws* 7.795d: "Pantomime dancing imitates poetic expression and it tries to portray precisely whatever is grand and liberal within them. The other kind, the war dance, seeks to preserve the courage, the flexibility and the beauty of the parts of the body."

39. Webb, *Demons and Dancers*, 154.

40. Proclus, nearly two centuries later, made "obeisance to the rising, midday and setting sun" (Marinus, *Life of Proclus* 22; M. Edwards, *Neoplatonic Saints*, 93). Whether Plotinus had a similar practice we cannot tell (*pace* Ferwerda's denial that the physical sun had any more than symbolic significance for Plotinus; Ferwerda, *Signification des images*, 59). See also Wakoff, "Awaiting the Sun."

41. Lucian, "On Pantomime," 245. The movements now known as "Salutation to the Sun" (*Surya Namaskara*) in hatha yoga are relatively modern, first publicized in Krishnam-

Respectable opinion, however, might not approve of such extravagances, rather agreeing with Aristotle: "professional musicians we speak of as vulgar people, and indeed we think it not manly to perform music, except when drunk or for fun."[42] Aristotle allowed that the young might be taught to sing and to play some simple stringed instruments, but not to professional standards. Better in general to listen and to watch. Professional dancers, like actors and musicians, stood outside the normal order of society and suffered accordingly. The symposiasts of Macrobius's *Saturnalia* in the early fifth century deplore the acceptance of dancing as a respectable occupation in the days of the Republic—and especially citizens' willingness to teach their children dancing.[43]

Would Plotinus have agreed? Or is it rather that dancing should join nakedness, drunkenness, and the insanity of love in his transvaluation of respected values? According to Cicero, "hardly anyone dances, unless he is drunk, or perhaps not quite right in the head."[44] If Plotinus did dance, Porphyry might well not have mentioned it, whether because he didn't think it significant or because he thought the information would damage his master's reputation—though Porphyry acknowledged, and even praised, the use of *music* as a guide to the divine, praise that Iamblichus thought misplaced.[45] Or else perhaps Plotinus didn't dance by himself at all.

The other form of dance was the circling chorus, and it is mainly this form that Plotinus uses to describe how best to live. By participating in the circling chorus, we imitate the motion of the heavens.[46] Lucian reck-

---

acharya, *Yoga Makaranda*; an English translation of the Tamil version (1938) by Lakshmi and Nandini Ranganathan is available at http://dailycupofyoga.files.wordpress.com/2011/04/yoga_makaranda.pdf. But salutations of some sort "to the sun" date from much earlier. There is nowadays a tendency analogous to the rationalizations of Xenophon's Socrates to suggest that the reason for the Salutation is merely to improve bodily health and well-being, but some practitioners acknowledge the devotional aspect. Further on Krishnamacharya, see Mohan and Mohan, *Krishnamacharya*; and on the development of modern yoga, see Singleton, *Yoga Body*, who brings out the conflict between early Western loathing of *hatha yoga* (as the province of contortionists, fakirs, and mountebanks) and present-day acceptance of—admittedly rather less extreme—contortions in the name of "health."

42. Aristotle, *Politics* 8.1339b.

43. Macrobius, *Saturnalia*, 231–4 (3.14).

44. Cicero, *Pro Murena* 6.13, cited in Macrobius, *Saturnalia*, 232n. Worse still, the term for someone who willingly submits to anal intercourse, *cinaedus*, was originally used for a "buttock-wiggling" dancer (Craig Williams, *Roman Homosexuality*, 177–8). By association, for Romans, dancers and "pathics" were alike despised.

45. See Iamblichus, *De mysteriis* 3.9: music may have natural effects, but it is the gods themselves that do the work, if so they please.

46. See IV.4 [28].8. The circular motion of the stars that Plotinus has in mind may be their visible motion nightly around the North Pole rather than their inferred motion around the

oned that the art of dance preexisted human culture, reaching its culmination in contemporary pantomime (the term is *orchesis*, which would also cover choral dancing, but Lucian chooses to concentrate on the single professional).

> In the dance of the heavenly bodies, in the complex involutions whereby the planets are brought into harmonious intercourse with the fixed stars, you have an example of that art in its infancy, which, by gradual development, by continual improvements and additions, seems at length to have reached its climax in the subtle harmonious versatility of modern Pantomime.[47]

The choral metaphor seems more appropriate for what we all do together, as well as for what the world does. In the words of a later poet, drawing on this tradition:

> Dancing, bright lady, then began to be,
> When the first seeds whereof the world did spring,
> The fire, air, earth, and water, did agree
> By Love's persuasion, nature's mighty king,
> To leave their first discorded combating,
> And in a dance such measure to observe,
> As all the world their motion should preserve.

---

earth. Nowadays the "North Star," Polaris, sits roughly at that pole; in Plotinus's day there was an empty space in heaven, and the fainter stars of Ursa Minor (Kochab and Pherkad; i.e., *Beta* and *Gamma Ursae Minoris*) were the visible stars closest to the pole. According to Manilius, *Astronomica* 1.275–93, it is the two bears that pull the heavens around the invisible, unmoving axis of the world "drawn through the empty spaces of the sky." In a still earlier age the Pole Star was Thuban in the constellation *Draco*—and perhaps this was the dragon that Apollo defeated at the navel of the world (see Barber and Barber, *When They Severed Earth from Sky*, 208, 240)! Whether this was significant for contemporary Mediterranean observers I do not know. Santillana and Dechend, *Hamlet's Mill*, suggested that astronomical observations lie behind much European mythology—in particular, that stories of past and predicted "disasters" have mostly referred to the precession of the equinoxes and the periodic "drowning" of constellations as the perceived axis of rotation shifts. They may be right despite being heavily and reasonably criticized by historians (though cf. Feyerabend, *Against Method*, 35–5), but they have little textual evidence for their strangely attractive theory. Ptolemy attributed the discovery or the plausible hypothesis of the precession (extrapolating from a tiny observable change) to Hipparchus of Rhodes in about 140 BC (Ptolemy, *Almagest* 3.1, 7.1–3). Proclus reckoned that the Egyptians and Chaldaeans ("who even before their observations were instructed by the gods") had reached the same conclusion—though he himself (like Manilius, *Astronomica* 1.521–3) found it incredible that the stars should ever change (Proclus, *In Timaeum* 40AB; cited by Kidd, *Poseidonius*, 269).

47. Lucian, "On Pantomime," 241.

Since when they still are carried in a round,
And changing come one in another's place;
Yet do they neither mingle nor confound,
But every one doth keep the bounded space
Wherein the dance doth bid it turn or trace.
This wondrous miracle did Love devise,
For dancing is love's proper exercise.[48]

We are all kept in order by the attraction of the One, whether or not we are aware of it, but that order is improved and beautified, for us, when we direct our attention "back" toward our center. Consider a passage that I mentioned earlier:

It is like a choral dance: in the order of its singing the choir keeps round its [*koruphaion*] but may sometimes turn away so that he is out of their sight, but when it turns back to him it sings beautifully and is truly with him; so we are always around him—and if we were not, we should be totally dissolved and no longer exist—but not always turned towards him; but when we do look to him, then we are at our goal and at rest and do not sing out of tune as we truly dance our god-inspired dance around him. (VI.9 [9].8, 38–45)[49]

Armstrong takes *koruphaion* as the chorus's "conductor," but this has the wrong connotations: the head or leader of the chorus is not standing on a rostrum at the front of the stage. Most likely he is simply the leader of the dance and of the chorus's singing. "If one takes away the leader," according to Demosthenes in an earlier century, "the rest of the chorus is done for."[50] Just possibly we are to think instead of the musician sitting at the center, in

48. John Davies (1569–1626), "The Praise of Dancing" (Gardner, *New Oxford Book of English Verse*, 175). "The Praise of Dancing" is an extract from "Orchestra, or a Poeme of Dancing" (Davies, *Poems*), in which one of Penelope's suitors, Antinous (soon to die at Odysseus's hands), seeks to persuade Penelope to dance with him. Penelope at last responds by declaring the love of which Antinous speaks to be "of every ill the hateful father vile / That doth the world with sorceries beguile, / Cunningly mad, religiously profane, / Wit's monster, reason's canker, sense's bane." What irony Davies intended, in a poem culminating in extravagant praise of Queen Elizabeth of England, is unclear. Antinous's view of dancing, at least, is traditional, even if he hopes to put it to nefarious ends.

49. See also III.6 [26].2, 8–17: "each one, as they sing together, must also sing his own part beautifully by his own personal art of music."

50. Demosthenes, *Against Meidias* 60, cited by West, *Ancient Greek Music*, 46. West goes on to report from other ancient sources that "he gave the lead and did his best to keep his fellows to the proper rhythm, which they managed better when there were more of them. . . . [His]

the place of Apollo (who is the god "who sits in the centre, on the navel of the earth, and is the interpreter of religion to all mankind").[51]

When Plotinus planned "Platonopolis" we may suppose that what he had in mind was, in effect, a university: an assembly—with supporting staff—of scholars dedicated to unraveling the truth, by various reasonable means. But we should take more seriously the thought that he had Plato's *Laws* in mind: a genuine city, all of whose citizens would share in the liturgical year.[52] "In the *Laws*," as Pickstock emphasizes, "it is the divine gift of the liturgical cycle with all the concomitant sustenance which the deities bring to these festivals, which distinguishes human beings from the wild animals which have no such gifts of order, rhythm or harmony."[53] The citizens of that great city are to *dance*.

What happens here is only, perhaps, an echo or reminder of the real world. The Delphic Oracle and Porphyry conclude their account of Plotinus's life with the expectation that he has joined those who "set the dance of immortal love."[54] "There the most blessed spirits have their birth and live a life filled full of festivity and joy; and this life lasts for ever, made blessed by the gods."[55] Did he expect his friends and followers to celebrate with songs and dances on the traditional birthdays of Plato and Socrates? Perhaps that would have been too much to ask of them! Did he wish them to consider human life a game?[56] Apparently so:

---

place was in the middle, while at the edges there might be two or three who could not sing at all, and who kept mum."

51. Plato, *Republic* 4.427c. See Frost, *Poetry*, 362: "We dance round in a ring and suppose, / But the Secret sits in the middle and knows" (1942).

52. Later Platonists conceived such a city as one to be built within us, or in the "far west" of the imagination. See Yates, *Giordano Bruno*, 372, 394, bringing together Campanella's "City of the Sun," Adocentyn (as described in *Picatrix*), Asclepius's city in the west—and Plotinus's Platonopolis. See Helm, "Platonopolis Revisited."

53. Pickstock, *After Writing*, 40. See Plato, *Laws* 2.653d ff.: "whereas the animals have no perception of order or disorder in their movements, that is, of rhythm or harmony, as they are called, to us, the Gods, who, as we say, have been appointed to be our companions in the dance, have given the pleasurable sense of harmony and rhythm; and so they stir us into life, and we follow them, joining hands together in dances and songs; and these they call choruses, which is a term naturally expressive of cheerfulness." Whether the Stranger in that dialogue always speaks for Plato himself is uncertain. The claim itself—that nonhumans have no sense of rhythm—is one still often endorsed by students of animal behavior. See Sacks, *Musicophilia*, 239–40.

54. "*Khoron sterixan erotos athanatou*" (Porphyry, *Life* 23.36–7, after 22.54–63).

55. Porphyry, *Life* 23.38–40. Did Porphyry suppose that this dance was the one enacted in the heavens, the dance of fixed and planetary stars? Or might Plotinus have passed even beyond the heavens?

56. See also Rahner, *Man at Play*, for a study of this trope in pagan, Jewish, and Christian tradition.

When men, mortal as they are, direct their weapons against each other, fighting in orderly ranks, doing what they do in sport in their war-dances [*purrichai*] their battles show that all human concerns are children's games, and tell us that deaths are nothing terrible, and that those who die in wars and battles anticipate only a little the death which comes in old age—they go away and come back quicker. (III.2 [47].15, 33–40)[57]

---

57. These are not the remarks of a mere "intellectual": Plotinus had served in an imperial army and was fully aware of the effects of military violence.

CHAPTER TEN

Remembering and Forgetting

But shall we remember these comings and goings?[1]
Memory, for Plotinus, was not a passive affair but an active use of imagination. The traditional notion that memories are, as it were, inscribed on mental tablets is an error (III.6 [26]. 2, 39–45). There is some evidence that Plotinus was familiar with "topical" techniques of memory, which involve the imaginative creation of a house or landscape within which appropriate mnemonic images can be placed. Porphyry notes Plotinus's remarkable capacity to pick up conversations and writings where he had left off to attend to something else.[2] And Plotinus refers often enough to temples, statues, and inner shrines to represent the workings of the soul to suggest that he may have established some such order. But the use he made of those images was not, after all, straightforwardly mnemonic. The point—as I have observed already—was to mold the statues (I.6 [1].9) and scrub them clean, clear away impedimenta, and at last go naked into the shrine, where there would be no statues.

We remember best what we are moved by: "the more strongly [the soul] is moved, the more lasting the presence" (IV.6 [41].3, 21). Plotinus's innovation was to distinguish two sorts of imagination, two organs of imagination (IV.3 [27].31): one is that by which, as bodily beings, we recall whatever is personal to us, and the other is that by which we recall the larger, eternal reality. Our "fall" into bodily, personal life, as Plato suggested, involves our forgetting that larger world. Conversely, our re-ascent to reality means that we must shed the merely personal, accidental memories of our lives here.

---

1. An earlier version of this chapter was presented at a conference on memory at Durham University and is due to be published as "Plotinus on Forgetting."
2. Porphyry, *Life* 8.8–19.

"Souls which migrate and change their state will also remember; for memory is of things which have happened and are past; but as for the souls to
which it belongs to remain in the same state, what could they remember?"
(IV.4 [28].6, 1–6). It is *forgetting* that is more significant for Plotinus than
this-worldly uses of the art of memory. Heracles's shadow might recall his
earthly life, but *Heracles himself* does not remember it (IV.3 [27].27).[3] The
souls of the stars need not remember where they've been (IV.4 [28].8, 41ff.).
Plato, in his Myth of Er, proposed that inferior souls drink their fill of the
river of Don't Care, while superior souls, aimed at enlightenment, restrain
their thirst—and remember. Plotinus, in effect, rewrites the story in a way
that Dante might approve.[4] Purification is a waking up from inappropriate
images (III.6 [26].5, 23ff.). Odysseus, in his final purification, must travel
so far from the sea (of matter) as to forget entirely what an oar might be.[5]
Oblivion allows us to awaken to the higher realm,[6] as stripping away all
images reveals the naked truth.[7]

These processes of descent and ascent are determined by whatever it is
that we most love: we are pulled away from reality by a wish to have things
all our own way (V.2 [11].2), and we return by attending first to images of
beauty. This is to forget ourselves, as an attentive reader or accomplished
dancer also has no attention to spare for herself (I.4 [46].10; IV.4 [28].33).
Even beauty may at last be forgotten: "like a man who enters into the sanctuary and leaves behind the statues in the outer shrine" (VI.9 [9].11, 18–9) or
like someone who wakes from dreaming.

The two movements, of remembering and forgetting, can also be linked
to Plotinus's use of astrological themes, especially that the soul acquires
various characters in its descent through the planetary spheres and must
relinquish them as it returns to its first material home, in the fixed stars.[8]
Although the astrological details cannot easily now be taken seriously, it

3. After Homer, *Odyssey* 11.601ff.; see also IV.3 [27].32, 24–5; I.1 [53].12, 32–40.
4. Plato, *Republic* 10.621; Dante Alighieri, *Divine Comedy: Purgatory* 33.91–9, 127–9
(Dante at the top of Purgatory peak drinks first of Lethe, banishing all memory of sin, and then
of Eunoë, restoring an objective, guiltless memory of what has been). The dual springs of Lethe
and Mnemosyne also appear in accounts of the Oracle of Trophonius at Lebadaea (Detienne,
Dionysos at Large, 84).
5. Porphyry, *De antro nympharum* 80.20 (Lamberton, *Homer the Theologian*, 131). Numenius also refers to matter as a troubled sea: T45, cited by Dodds, "Numenius," 18.
6. See Detienne, *Masters of Truth*, 181n107, citing IV.3.32, IV.4.1, after Schaerer, *Le héros*,
193–4. See also Warren, "Memory in Plotinus."
7. See Schroeder, "*Avocatio*," with particular reference to stripping "matter" out of the
imagined cosmos.
8. Macrobius, *Dream of Scipio*, 136 (I.13).

is worth noting that we may still put aside our this-worldly memories and concerns by attending to modern visions of astronomical immensity. The difference between Plotinus's vision and that modern, more nihilistic vision does not turn on the astrological details but on metaphysical and ethical commitments.

That there were "mental exercises" in common use in Plotinus's day is attested by his remarks on memory, designed to show that memory is not a passive matter. Remembering is a power of the soul that can be improved by exercise, "just like physical training of our arms and legs to make them do easily what does not lie in the arms or legs, but what they are made ready for by continuous exercise" (IV.6 [41].3, 29–30). The obvious reference is to the ordinary use of memory, though no Platonist can escape the association of "memory" with what Plato called *anamnesis*, recollection of real things. But even if these exercises do not empower us to do more than remember dates or data or persons' faces, it is worth considering what they were. Exercises for the arms and legs are not simply a matter of doing more of what one does in any case (as it might be, walking or lifting books). Rather those who exercise will train carefully with sticks or balls or dance or practice yoga. Just so, those who would improve their memory do not simply learn long lists, in the hope that this will somehow help them to remember dates or data or peoples' faces. Learning long lists may help, but only if we thereby learn *how* to remember, how to do something more than what comes naturally. "The Art of Memory" was well known in rhetorical and philosophical circles from the fifth century BC till well into the Renaissance and had more than "utilitarian" significance.[9]

The first step in remembering anything is to have it to remember, by attending to its first appearance. Children, Plotinus says, are better at remembering because they are more attentive, or less easily distracted by other things to think about (IV.6 [41].3, 22). We remember best what we are moved by: "the more strongly [the soul] is moved, the more lasting the presence" (IV.6 [41].3, 2). Remembering is primarily a function of the imagination, so that it will be easier to remember an image that excites us—which explains the violence and obscenity of myths intended to convey more abstract truths. But the images aren't simply fading impressions.

9. See Yates, *Art of Memory*. Mary Carruthers offers a more sympathetic account, criticizing Yates's assumption that the memorist aims to recall entire speeches verbatim: "the art of memory was not an art of recitation and reiteration, but an art of invention" (*Craft of Thought*, 8). See also Small, "Memory and the Roman Orator"; Small, *Wax Tablets of the Mind*.

There is no stamp impressed on it internally but it has what it sees and
in another way does not have it; it has it by knowing it, but does not
have it in that something is not put away in it from the seeing, like a
shape in wax. And we must remember that memories too do not exist
because things are put away in our minds but the soul awakes the power
in such a way as to have what it does not have. (III.6 [26]. 2, 39–45)

They are there even when they aren't recalled—and these "unconscious"
memories may have more effect than the conscious ones.[10] We might rely
simply on chance associations to revive them, but it is better to put them in
some accessible order so that we can remember where our forgotten images
are—and know what to do with them. Modern manuals often suggest that
they be ordered in a narrative or musical sequence, so that what needs to be
recalled is set to music or incorporated in a—precisely—*memorable* story.

Memory is not like a video record. It does not need images, and images
are never enough; moreover, our memories shade and patch and combine and delete. This thought leads to a second one: the best analogy to
remembering is storytelling. The metaphor for memory is narrative.[11]

The disadvantage is that things must then be remembered *in that order*,
and often the whole song or story must be recited to reach a later item.
Though memory does not *need* images, they help. The method preferred
in ancient manuals is the "topical," first devised—it is said—by the poet
Simonides of Ceos, who realized that he could recall where each member of his audience had been since he had a vivid visual memory of the
couches where they lay.[12] The technique he advocated (though he would
have had many predecessors, from the beginnings of human consciousness) was first to memorize a familiar building and then put mementos
around its imagined walls, windows, and niches. Everything could then
be relocated merely by going, in imagination, to that part of the building,
from any direction and starting point—very much as members of oral cultures identify stories with particular features of a landscape.[13] Medieval
cathedrals similarly contained sacred memories, embodied in pictures

10. Warren, "Memory in Plotinus," 255, after IV.4 [28].4, 7–14.
11. Hacking, *Rewriting the Soul*, 250.
12. It was good that he could, since the roof had fallen in while he was outside, and the
bodies were otherwise unidentifiable. See Cicero, *De oratore* 2.86.351–3. It may of course be
that this is itself an invented story, designed to advertise the principles of the art.
13. See Abram, *Spell of the Sensuous*, 173–5.

and carvings rather than mere words, very much as the Egyptian priests expressed *their* doctrines (IV.3 [27].11; V.8 [31].6). The further advantage of the system was that the architectural ordering itself might make new associations, and the images might change to reveal new aspects of the things remembered.[14] The metaphor is architectural and holistic rather than narrative and linear.

Commentators usually say that Plotinus has misunderstood the nature of Egyptian hieroglyphs—that they are not all ideograms but are rather a complex system combining ideograms and phonograms to expound what may be quite banal or commonplace remarks or stories.[15] But Plotinus may not be wrong.

> The mixed form of their [the Egyptians'] gods is nothing other than a hieroglyph, a way of "writing" not the name but the nature and function of the deity in question. The Egyptians do not hesitate to call hieroglyphs "gods," and even to equate individual signs in the script with particular gods; it is quite in keeping with their views to see images of the gods as signs in a metalanguage. As is true of every Egyptian hieroglyph, they are more than just ciphers or lifeless symbols; the god can inhabit them, his cult image will normally be in the same form, and his priests may assume his role by wearing animal masks.[16]

Hornung goes on to say that none of these images give any information about "the true form of a deity": "every image is an imperfect means of making a god visible," and "scarcely any important deity is restricted to a single form and manifestation."[17]

This may give a credible sense to the odd stories in which statues created by Egyptian priests moved.[18] It is possible that these were powered by technical tricks to deceive or amuse the faithful. Or else they were

14. It is better to recall the composite images, seeing what is the *same* in many different occasions, than simply to remember all the detail. See Draaisma, *Why Life Speeds Up*, 70, commenting on Borges's Funes (see Borges, "Funes the Memorious") and on the Russian mnemonist Shereshevsky: "their absolute memory destroyed any sense of continuity." Shereshevsky also had no sense of metaphor or poetry (68); see Luria, *Mind of a Mnemonist*.

15. See Hare, *Remembering Osiris*, 45–80, for an accessible account of the history of interpreting hieroglyphs, and a reminder that they do not, as some supposed, sidestep vocal utterances so as to represent "ideas" directly, without need of speech or other symbolic connections. See also Hornung, *Secret Lore*.

16. Hornung, *Conceptions of God*, 124.

17. Ibid., 125.

18. See *Asclepius* 24 (Copenhaver, *Hermetica*, 81).

perceived to be moving, as devout Hindus or Catholics may also see their statues giving signs of life. And insofar as the supposedly physical world is a composite or idealization of common perceptions, why should we be surprised that some can see what others don't, any more than we are surprised that some of us cannot distinguish red and green? Maybe the emperor Julian's favored teacher, Maximus, that "theatrical wonder-worker," really *did* make a statue of Hecate laugh and the torches in her hands light up— whether or not there were other material consequences.[19] Maybe Iamblichus was right to insist that "the divine images occur not only within the imagination of an inspired devotee, but may be apparent also to the observers of ritual."[20] But it is more helpful now to conceive of them as personally imagined statues, which could come to life in us. Such images could be drawn from public exhibition—Pheidias's Zeus, Praxiteles's Aphrodite, or allegorical depictions of *sophrosune* (roughly, "self-possession") or justice: the soul sees "them standing in itself like splendid statues all rusted with time which it has cleaned" (IV.7 [2].10, 47).[21]

The Romans, and their many imitators, chose to depict Virtues on their public monuments as clothed female figures: the four statues ornamenting the Library of Celsus in Ephesus, for example, are of *arete, ennoia, episteme,* and *sophia* (virtue, wit, knowledge, wisdom). Roman coins carry similar figures to represent equity, good faith, modesty, and the like. Whether those who admired the statues or glanced at the coins ever *invoked* these personified virtues, constructing moving images of them, is unknown, though it is likely that even what seem to us to be lifeless abstractions had some real emotional significance.[22] The virtues might be embodied in images of ancestors:

> How many images of the bravest men, carefully elaborated, have both the Greek and Latin writers bequeathed to us, not merely for us to look at and gaze upon, but also for our imitation! And I, always keeping them before my eyes as examples for my own public conduct, have endeav-

19. Eunapius, *Lives*, 435. See further Uzdavinys, *Philosophy and Theurgy*, 143–203.

20. Iamblichus, *De mysteriis* 3.8.117, 1–3, cited by E. Clarke, *Iamblichus' "De mysteriis,"* 100.

21. After Plato, *Phaedrus* 247d.

22. See Stafford, *Worshipping Virtues*, 26–7, on *Homonoia*. Stafford (27–35) discusses why these virtues are so often female: the very obvious answer she suggests (34) is that—at least for the heterosexual males who are the authors and artists of these images—it is the female form that is more attractive. The few *male* figures mostly fit the same pattern: if male, then also young and beautiful.

oured to model my mind and views by continually thinking of those
excellent men.[23]

Conversely, what seem to us to be anthropomorphic deities may have had
a more "impersonal" nature. Augustine, in a sermon in 404, gave voice to
a learned defender of pagan worship: "When I worship Mercury," we are to
suppose his saying, "I worship talent. Talent cannot be seen; it is something
invisible." Augustine allowed the gloss, contenting himself with inquiring
what it was that the "talent" in question did: "perhaps they err greatly who
think that talent is to be worshipped using an image of Mercury [the god
of thieves, tricksters, and traders]."[24] A similar question might be posed
of those who worshiped civic "virtues": what was it that these "virtuous
people" did? Are the conventionally "law-abiding" *virtuous* as "philosophers" count virtue?

   Invoking these exemplars is not merely to remind ourselves of how past
heroes have behaved, in the hope of imitating them. It is to *internalize* their
spirit by controlled and vivid imaginings, and so submit to their guidance, to
act as they would now act, not merely as once they did. We may still have
doubts about particular suggested spirits and their attendant virtues. Seneca
himself supposed that what actual Romans mostly honored were no more
than copies—and by implication misleading copies—of what is truly good.[25]
By Plotinus's own account even public, "civic" virtues can barely qualify as
human, and their exemplars can expect to be born again as ants or bees (VI.3
[44].16, 28ff.).[26] "Real" virtues—of which those civic virtues are themselves
no more than possibly misleading images—are not dependent on a fallen
world to give them sense (as the exercise of courage requires that there be
wars), and the truly virtuous themselves would wish *not* to have to exercise
their civic virtue in that way, "as if a physician were to wish that nobody
needed his skill" (VI.8 [39].5, 13–21).[27] *Sophrosune*, as seen by those who gaze
on the divine beauty, is "not the kind which men have here below, when
they do have it (for this is some sort of imitation of that other)" (V.8 [31].10,
14–6). But we have to start somewhere: to be virtuous even in ordinary civil

   23. Cicero, *Pro Archias* 6.14, cited by Bartsch, *Mirror of the Self*, 126. See also Seneca,
Epistles 11.8–10, after Epicurus: "take some man of high character, and keep him ever before
your eyes, living as if he were watching you, and ordering all your actions as if he beheld them"
(cited by Bartsch, *Mirror of the Self*, 201).
   24. Augustine, *Sermon* 26.24, cited by Ando, *Matter of the Gods*, 41.
   25. Seneca, *Epistles* 81.13.3, cited by Bartsch, *Mirror of the Self*, 202.
   26. See also VI.8 [39].5; Plato, *Phaedo* 82b.
   27. After Aristotle, *Nicomachean Ethics* 10.1178b7–22. See Rist, *Plotinus*, 132–3.

practice we must awaken a right spirit in us—one that is sleeping in us already. Imagining true virtue in ourselves we may, perhaps, become virtuous.

> God is near you, he is with you, he is inside you. I mean this, Lucilius: a holy spirit lives inside us, an observer and guardian of our good and bad deeds.[28]

Plotinus would not disagree. But the chief point of his art was to go naked into the shrine, beyond the statues, beyond our internal heroes. "Memory can play no part in well-being" (V.8 [31].10, 14). "We must certainly not attribute memory to God, or [to] real being or Intellect" (IV.3 [27].25, 13–4). Purification is a waking up from inappropriate images (III.6 [26].5, 23ff.), as dreams dissolve and are forgotten.[29] But in the heavens, he says, we may still remember enough to recognize our friends, "by their characters and the individuality of their behaviour" (IV.4 [28].5, 20), even if they have spherical bodies (i.e., even if they are stars),[30] and even if neither they nor we have any memory of our lives below. Nor do they need to *speak*. "For here below, too, we can know many things by the look in people's eyes when they are silent; but There all their body is clear and pure and each is like an eye, and nothing is hidden or feigned, but before one speaks to another that other has seen and understood" (IV.3 [27].18, 19–24).[31] But it is hard to see how this should matter: "the man of quality [*asteios*] would have his memories of [friends and children and wife] without emotion" (IV.3 [27].32, 3–4). And in going further "up," we forget even particular friends. The way down from the intelligible is when we acquire memory: that is, when we fell. "When the soul comes out of the intelligible world and cannot endure unity but embraces its own individuality and wants to be different and so to speak puts its head outside, it thereupon acquires memory" (IV.4 [28].3, 1–4). Does this speak

---

28. Seneca, *Epistles* 41.1–2 (addressing his friend Lucilius), cited by Bartsch, *Mirror of the Self*, 202.

29. See Detienne, *Masters of Truth*, 181n107, citing IV.3 [27].32, IV.4 [28].1, after Schaerer, *Le héros*, 193–4.

30. That the stars are *spherical* is not as obvious as we now might think: after all, to the astronomers of Plotinus's day they were visible only as *points* (see I.6 [1].1, 34–5). They are *spherical*, perhaps, because they travel in circles around the North Pole: their bodies are their transit across the sky, visible now by time-lapse photography and recognizable in memory before. Alternatively, a *point* is the smallest possible sphere or circle (on which, see chap. 13).

31. Plotinus may have recalled the stories of how pantomimes conveyed their meanings so lucidly that even a skeptical Cynic, after watching an unaccompanied performance of the scandalous story of Ares and Aphrodite, exclaimed, "This is not seeing, but hearing and seeing, both: 'tis as if your hands were tongues!" (Lucian, "On Pantomime," 256; Webb, *Demons and Dancers*, 73).

to the same ideal as the "objective glance" that I described before and reckoned that Plotinus would not approve?

The opposition—and occasional conjunction—of Truth (*aletheia*) and
Forgetfulness (*lethe*) is a rhetorical trope dating back at least to Hesiod. One
who sees and speaks the truth, *alethes*, is one who has not forgotten. Truth
lies, for the most part, in memory, *mnemosyne*, but "when the Muses [who
are the daughters of Memory] tell the truth, they simultaneously bring 'a
forgetting of ills and a rest from sorrows.'"[32] "The higher soul ought to be
happy to forget what it has received from the worse soul" (IV.3 [27].32, 10–1).
So also Maximus the Confessor (AD 580–662):

> We carry along with us the voluptuous images of the things we once ex-
> perienced. Now the one who overcomes these voluptuous images com-
> pletely disdains the realities of which they are images. In fact, the battle
> against memories is more difficult than the battle against deeds, as sin-
> ning in thought is easier than sinning in deed.[33]

There is more to be said about those images and the living statues that
"wise men of old" created. Here the point is only that there is another use
for "mental exercises" than their creators intended, a use that may explain
one of the oddest of Plotinus's similes:

> It is as if someone went into a house richly decorated and so beautiful, and
> within it contemplated each and every one of the decorations and admired
> them before seeing the master of the house [*tou oikou despotes*], but when
> he sees the master with delight, who is not of the nature of the images,
> but worthy of genuine contemplation, he dismisses those other things and
> thereafter looks at him alone. . . . And perhaps the likeness would keep
> in conformity with the reality if it was not a mortal who encountered the
> one who was seeing the sights of the house but one of the gods, and who
> did not appear visibly but filled the soul of the beholder. (VI.7 [38].35)

It is certainly not usual to find the master of a beautiful house more
beautiful than the house and ornaments, unless one is in love.[34] It is pos-

32. Detienne, *Masters of Truth*, 81–3, after Hesiod, *Theogony* 55–6.

33. Maximus the Confessor, "Four Hundred Chapters on Love" 1.63 (*Writings*, 41–2).

34. Though the claim is also made by Traherne, *Centuries*, 257 (2.93): "he that possesseth
the house is greater than the house." A similar respect is owed the figure of the Great King and
his court: V.5 [32].3.

sible to bring the notion more vividly to life by recalling how a respectable
Roman house was arranged: "the architecture of the Romans was, from first
to last, an art of shaping space around ritual."[35] The single entry point, *fau-
ces*, led directly to the *atrium* and, beyond that, past the pool where rain-
water was collected, to the *tablinum*. Rather than being casually welcomed
at the door, we are to imagine entering *ceremonially* as a guest or client
and advancing down the axis of the house to where the *paterfamilias* stood,
properly robed, to greet us.[36] That human figure, however fine the surrounding decorations, is more "beautiful" in the sense that it compels attention.
Correspondingly, if the house intended here is the imagined memory house,
we should attend to the *controller* of that house, the inspiring spirit, so
turning aside from images to let them wither.[37]

> Let every soul first consider this, that it made all living things itself,
> breathing life into them, those that the earth feeds and those that are
> nourished by the sea, and the divine stars in the sky; it made the sun
> itself, and this great heaven, and adorned itself, and drives it round itself,
> in orderly movement; it is a nature other than the things which it adorns
> and moves and makes live; and it must necessarily be more honourable
> than they. (V.1 [10].2, 1–7)

This can be read in at least two ways. It may be a cosmological thesis,
about the earth, sea, and stars and the creatures that inhabit them. It is
after all literally and clearly true that the whole world has been made and
constantly remade—soil and air as well as our fuel and food—by living
things, by the life in them. Maybe the ancients were wrong to extrapolate
that observation to the heavens (though it *may* also be true Out There).
But the story is also about the world that each of us severally creates, the
world as it is for us, our subjective worlds. We need to understand both
that the world of our immediate experience is personal to us, constructed

35. J. Clarke, *Houses*, 1.
36. Ibid., 4–6.
37. Compare Blake, *Marriage of Heaven and Hell*, pl. 12 (*Writings*, 153): "We of Israel
taught that the Poetic Genius . . . was the first principle and all the others merely derivative,
which was the cause of our despising the Priests and Philosophers of other countries, and proph-
ecying that all Gods would at last be proved to originate in ours and to be the tributaries of the
Poetic Genius." It may be relevant that Porphyry, according to Iamblichus, suggests that the
leading figure of a natal horoscope, its *oikodespotes*, master of the house, determines the subject's personal *daimon*. See Iamblichus, *De mysteriis* 9.2 (*Iamblichus, On the Mysteries*, 314);
Iamblichus, *Réponse à Porphyre*, 77–8. Iamblichus himself reckons this an error, as the *daimon*
is the one to help us *free ourselves* from fate, not fate's agent.

according to our own needs and fancies, and also that it is a *lesser* world than the one that guides and sustains us.[38] These revelations are not distinct: in realizing that I make my world I also realize that I *do not* make *myself*, that the power I display in attending to this or that, in populating my world with phantom memories and plans, lies deeper than I ordinarily conceive.

> Much as your body is built from the foods you eat, your mind is built from the experiences you have. The flow of experience gradually sculpts your brain, thus shaping your mind. Some of the results can be explicitly recalled: *This is what I did last summer; that is how I felt when I was in love.* But most of the shaping of your mind remains forever unconscious. This is called implicit memory, and it includes your expectations, models of relationships, emotional tendencies, and general outlook. Implicit memory establishes the interior landscape of your mind—what it feels like to be you—based on the slowly accumulating residues of lived experience.[39]

Hanson draws on modern neuroscience and Buddhist theory to suggest how this interior landscape can be reshaped once we recognize that memories are not fixed objects but part of an ongoing story or a house that can be rebuilt—though some of our mental structures have been fashioned long before our births and may be difficult to reform. Similarly, Plotinus's goal is not Remembrance but Forgetfulness, not because he was "ashamed to be in a body," as Porphyry supposed,[40] but because there were things better worth "remembering" than childhood fears or fancies, even than grown-up fears and fancies. It may sometimes be necessary to bring those unconscious memories to light, but only to deconstruct them.[41] By concentrating on what he wished to remember, on the very poetic genius that creates those images, "the master of the house," he could hope to cleanse the past—and also the future. Everyday life is conditioned by our hopes and memories: we must remember our mistakes in the hope of avoiding like mistakes, but

---

38. Wilson, *Philosopher's Stone*, 129: "Man is the first *objective* animal. All others live in a subjective world of instinct, from which they can never escape; only man looks at the stars or rocks and says 'How interesting . . .' instantly leaping over the wall of his mere identity." I am not so sure that we are the first or only such animals.

39. Hanson and Mendius, *Buddha's Brain*, 69.

40. Porphyry, *Life* 1.1–2.

41. See Volf, *End of Memory*, for an intelligent and moving discussion of the rights and wrongs, advantages and costs, of remembering evils done to us or by us.

the very memories remind us of the likeliest future, that we will mistake again.[42] If we are ever to change, we must change the way we see things. We must repopulate our inner landscape. And the first step in that process is forgetting.[43] Similarly Wilson: "to be possessed by a strong sense of purpose is to ignore ninety-nine per cent of your experience, and to forget all the un-important things that have happened to you."[44]

Medieval "mnemotechnicians" imagined the items written on papyrus and then burnt up.[45] Eco has suggested that this could only be a way of recalling that there is something that we wanted to forget—though it is not clear that he had attempted the technique.[46] Even writing something down—without the addition of any ceremonial burning—may at least *distance* ourselves from the memory, or even let us forget it—so that Thoth's invention was not, perhaps, as harmful as Ammon claimed![47] Eco's own suggestion for obscuring unwelcome memories, or forgetting whether this or that is true, is rather to overlay the memory. If we wished to forget the rhyme recalling the valid figures of the syllogism ("Barbara Celarent Darii Ferioque prioris" and the rest) we should recite some spurious version till we can't remember which is right, which wrong, so rendering them all ridiculous. Better perhaps follow Maimonides (AD 1135–1204), who proposed that the Law was also an overlay, a counter to "Sabian idolatry," the worship, as he supposed, of stars.[48] Is that also the point of learn-

---

42. See Ouspensky, *Strange Life of Ivan Osokin*: Osokin is magically permitted to go back to his schooldays and attempt to remake his life. He merely repeats the very same mistakes, even though he knows or half-knows what will happen. My thanks to Richard Lawrence for this reference.

43. Themistocles declared, "I would rather a technique of forgetting, for I remember what I would rather not remember and cannot forget what I would rather forget" (Cicero, *De finibus* 2.104).

44. Wilson, *Existential Criticism*, 56, commenting on Borges, "Funes the Memorious." See also Kerényi, "Mnemosyne-Lesmosyne: On the Springs of Memory and Forgetting," a text I have been unable to retrieve. Kerényi apparently proposed that forgetfulness allowed experiences to be let slip away, leaving behind the gap, the sheer presence, of awareness (see Hillman, *Dream*, 154–5).

45. See M. Carruthers, review of Bolzoni's *La stanza della memoria*. Luria, *Mind of a Mnemonist*, 66–71, reports that his mnemonist, Shereshevsky, found this technique unhelpful, but that he could simply will his images away.

46. Eco, "An Ars Oblivionalis?" Eco argues that there can be no real "art of oblivion" since all attempts to identify what is to be forgotten must inevitably bring it to mind. But this only really shows, at most, that the art requires a sort of indirection, not that we cannot learn or identify effective ways of forgetting.

47. Plato, *Phaedrus* 274c–275c.

48. See Maimonides, *Guide of the Perplexed*, bk. 3, chap. 29, 178: "the first purpose of the whole law is to remove idolatry and to wipe out its traces and all that belongs to it, even in memory." See also Assmann, *Moses the Egyptian*, 58.

ing entire "sacred" works by heart, whether Homer[49] or the Bible or the Koran?

A still easier technique for forgetting things like that is simply: not to remember them—as Plotinus declined to reminisce "about his race, his parents or his native country."[50] Students who once achieved distinctions for their memory of "Barbara," the formula for solving quadratic equations, or "the Causes of the Peloponnesian War" will forget them when their exams are over. Unfortunately, neither overlaying memories nor not recalling them is a foolproof way of forgetting more emotive matters: the memory of showing oneself an idiot at the age of seven (seventeen, twenty-seven, forty, or a week ago) is something likely to recur however we attempt to overlay the memory, and even after months or years of not recalling it. And most of us nowadays are plagued by memories of telephone numbers and pin codes that we haven't used for years. This indeed is one reason Plotinus had for rejecting the idea that memories are impressions: that wouldn't explain why we need to search for them, how we lose them for a while and then find them again (IV.6 [41].3, 27). "It is rather difficult to forget unwanted memories at will."[51] The only way of addressing this is somehow to live through the memories and "throw them away" or (in another spiritual tradition) "lay them on the Lord." We must redirect our attention to the beauties we have encountered, the living presences covered in rust or lichen or barnacles, and let them shake free. Or if this is too much to hope for, at least let us put aside the memories of past errors (and the fear of future ones) so as simply to return to the present moment: breathe in and breathe out; look at what is actually now happening; smile.[52] Then I shall at last be rid of Me.

> What an exceeding rest 'twill be
> When I can leave off being Me!
> To think of it!—at last be rid
> Of all the things I ever did![53]

---

49. Niceratus reports that his father, "being concerned to make him a good man, made him memorize all of Homer" (Xenophon, *Symposium* 3.5–6, in Xenophon, *Memorabilia*, 559; cited by Gerard Naddaf in Brisson, *Plato the Myth Maker*, xxviii).

50. Porphyry, *Life* 1.2–5.

51. Nørby, Lange, and Larsen, "Forgetting to Forget."

52. See Bernhard, *How to Be Sick*, 113–20.

53. Gilman, "Eternal Me" (1899) (*In This Our World*, 159). Cf. Tolle, *Power of Now*, 1: "'I cannot live with myself any longer.' This was the thought that kept repeating in my mind. Then suddenly I became aware of what a peculiar thought it was. 'Am I one or two? If I cannot live with myself, there must be two of me: the "I" and the "self" that "I" cannot live with.' 'Maybe,' I thought, 'only one of them is real.'"

Another mnemotechnical device is a further reminder of the significance of dance. Havelock proposed that in oral cultures memories might piggy-back on *body* memory: the flow of movement in a dance or other celebra-tion.[54] Naerebout's response, in his study of Greek dance, was that words were easier to remember by themselves than movements[55]—but this was uncharacteristically obtuse! Most of us are unable to describe how to tie our tie or our shoelaces—tasks that we perform daily from body memory—and many of us, incidentally, learnt the wrong way to tie those laces! We may need to unlearn the older way before we can ever easily manage the new, and must, for a time, be careful *not* to do what seems most natural. Dancers, and other people with a bias toward the bodily rather than (like Naerebout and myself) the verbal, learn their dances (and other bodily tasks), as Naere-bout himself acknowledges, by example and even corporeal manipulation. Their limbs are guided into the proper pose before they can feel what it's like to position them themselves.[56]

The world as we ordinarily experience it is private and delusional in a way that we can escape only by intellectual awakening: "the fool on the hill sees the sun going down, and the eyes in his head"—that is, the eye of reason—"see the world spinning round."[57] So far, so Stoical: is the advice just to abandon our *personal* perceptions, memories, and attitudes in favor of as *impersonal*, as *universal*, a stance as possible? Should we after all seek to see and feel things as "just anyone" would see and feel them, or at least as just anyone sane and sensible would, free of passion and unimportant detail? But Plotinus's notion of awakening, as I have suggested, is more pas-sionate, the drunkenness of intellect in love (VI.7 [38].35), nakedness to the world.

The beauty that such drunken lovers see has "penetrated through the whole of their soul," and they are not simply spectators—"as if someone possessed by a god, taken over by Phoebus or one of the Muses, could bring about the vision of the god in himself, if he had the power to look at the god in himself" (V.8 [31].10).[58] The lovers are so far involved in what is happen-ing that they "forget themselves," as dancers do when they dance well.[59]

54. Havelock, "Prehistory of the Greeks."

55. Naerebout, *Attractive Performances*, 201.

56. See Libanius, *Reply to Aristides* [*Orations* 64], 104–5; Webb, *Demons and Dancers*, 68, 91.

57. McCartney, "The Fool on the Hill" (1967) (*Poems and Lyrics*, 29–30).

58. After Plato, *Phaedrus* 246e ff.

59. Montero has cast some doubt on this familiar trope. See Montero, "Does Bodily Aware-ness Interfere with Movement?" But at least trained dancers are unlikely to be mouthing verbal mnemonics as they dance.

The dancer's intention looks elsewhere; his limbs are affected in accordance with the dance and serve the dance, and help to make it perfect and complete; and the connoisseur of ballet [i.e., the pantomime] can say that to fit a particular figure one limb is raised, another bent together, one is hidden, another degraded; the dancer does not choose to make these movements for no reason, but each part of him as he performs the dance has its necessary position in the dancing of the whole body. (IV.4 [28].33, 17–26)[60]

But we don't stay forgetful, unselfconscious, happily involved, for long. However gripping those moments, we forget *them* in their turn and imagine that the common world, the projection of our more parochial and personal fears, is real. Once again: "It is as if people who slept through their life thought the things in their dreams were reliable and obvious, but, if someone woke them up, disbelieved in what they saw with their eyes open and went to sleep again" (V.5 [32].11, 19–23).

Conversely, factors in our ever-changeful bodies cause us to forget what once we knew—and we can hope that "when they are removed and purged away the memory revives" (IV.3 [27].26, 52). Forgetting is of two sorts, just as there are two sets of memories, and two *phantastika*, the organs of imagination: one belongs to our real self, and one to the soul of the world as it moves and maintains us according to its own, quite proper, policies (IV.3 [27].27).[61] And the former is the more divine. So the straightforwardly *Stoical* version, despite appearances, is mistaken. Our real selves are to be found in admiration of beauty, and we must forget the very things that first seduced us from the *better* beauty. The lover, as Socrates said, "forgets mother, brothers, friends, all together, not caring about the loss of its wealth through neglect, and with contempt for all accepted standards of propriety and good taste."[62] How might this effort affect John and Mary? They will retain their intimate appreciation of each other if they stay "naked,"[63] needing no excuse for their own "unfitness" and remembering no occasions of offense.[64] "Getting naked" is the right sort of forgetting.

60. See also VI.9 [9].38. I examined this sort of unconsciousness in more detail in "How to Become Unconscious."

61. See Nikulin, *Matter, Imagination and Geometry*, 175–87.

62. Plato, *Phaedrus* 252a. Thanks to Andrea Carpa for the reminder of this passage, in her essay on "lyric oblivion" presented at the Durham conference on memory.

63. The metaphor is employed in this sense by Denise in *Naked Relationships*.

64. Cf. *Dante* Alighieri, *Divine Comedy: Purgatory* 33.91–9: Dante, having drunk of Lethe, no longer remembers that he was ever estranged from Beatrice—or his faithful memory of her.

So how shall we remember beauty and forget or put aside the bodily entanglements and confusions that the worldly count as reason? And what would it be like to live like that? It is—or at least it approximates—the life of stars, which need not remember where they've been (IV.4 [28].8, 41ff.). "[A]s for the souls to which it belongs to remain in the same state, what could they remember?" (IV.4 [28].6, 5–6). And this too is a way of guiding our minds and memories. Later mnemotechnicians sometimes used the constellations and the houses of the zodiac as their imagined building, to the scandal of the church. Plotinus may have done something similar—but what does the method amount to? The heavens, or the sphere of the fixed stars, move in a circle "because it imitates intellect" (II.2 [14].1), and the soul that animates the stars conveys a literally or spatially circular motion to them because she is herself "in orbit" around God (II.2 [14].2, 13ff.; II.2 [14].3, 20ff.), as also are our "real selves." We are to look toward the example of the heavens to get some sense of our real lives. Plato suggested that we "must correct the orbits in the head which were corrupted at our birth"[65] and so bring ourselves into line with the heavens. Plotinus supposed rather that our real selves were already thus "in orbit," and that only our lower selves needed the reminder—but what this means remains obscure. In what sense is the light from above divided "among the houses" (IV.3 [27].4, 21)? What does "circular motion" *mean*, in this spiritual sense? Why should we regret that our bodies do not "go round" or that "our spherical parts," our heads, don't "run easily, being earthy" (II.2 [14].2, 18–9)? *How* are we to "imitate the soul of the universe and of the stars" (II.9 [33].18, 32)? And should we draw any morals from *planetary* motions, whether from their visible shape or from the nested spheres that are postulated to predict how they will seem to us?

The intended motion, obviously, isn't spatial: "one must use 'centre' analogically" (II.2 [14].2, 10). "Circular motion" is—in principle—unending and is never nearer or farther from its goal. It is therefore more "perfect" than "linear motion," since its end and its beginning are the same: it has nowhere *else* to go. "Linear motion" is a process, culminating in arrival or completion (after which, it ceases). "Circular motion" is always already there and, because it needs nothing else to complete it, can be forever.[66] A

Beatrice teasingly observes that his not remembering so much indicates exactly how much he needed to forget!

65. Plato, *Timaeus* 90d.

66. In Plotinus's cosmology, it is rather that the visible heavens imitate the intellectual: they travel with a circular motion as models of the intellect (II.2 [14]).

similar distinction had been drawn by Aristotle, between "motions" (*kineseis*) and "activities" (*energeiai*)—a distinction which is not exactly mapped by the grammatical or semantic distinctions he offered but which had important ethical implications.[67] Nothing qualifies as the essential element of *eudaimonia*, the good life, if it must, of its nature, end and cannot, of its nature, be complete until that end.[68] *Eudaimonia* is an activity, not a motion, and its highest form is God's life. "On such a principle depend the heavens and the world of nature. And it is a life such as the best that we enjoy, and enjoy for but a short time. . . . So that life and *aion* continuous and eternal belong to the god, for this is what the god is."[69] So also Pseudo-Dionysius: "the soul moves in a circle [like the divine intelligences], that is, it turns within itself and away from what is outside and there is an inner concentration of its intellectual powers. . . . From there the revolution brings the soul the Beautiful and the Good, which is beyond all things, is one and the same, and has neither beginning nor end."[70] Even a more recent Neoplatonist tells us that "by contemplating the equivalence of the future and the past [in the circling heavens] we pierce through time right to eternity."[71]

> One must think that there is a universe in our soul, not only an intelligible one but an arrangement like in form to that of the soul of the world: so, as that, too, is distributed according to its diverse powers into the sphere of the fixed stars and those of the moving stars, the powers in our soul also are of like form to these powers, and there is an activity proceeding from each power, and when the souls are set free they come there to the star which is harmony with the character and power which lived and worked in them; and each will have a god of this kind as its guardian spirit, either the star itself or the god set above this power. (III.4 [15].6, 22–30)

The further associations of fixed and wandering stars will concern me later, as will the circles, spheres, and centers of Plotinus's spiritual geom-

67. See Aristotle, *Nicomachean Ethics* 10.1174a12–1174b33.
68. See I.5 [36].2: if we are always to be aiming to get more or better, "even the gods will be better off now than they were before, but they will not be perfectly well off; they will never be perfectly well off."
69. Aristotle, *Metaphysics* 12.1072b13–4.
70. Pseudo-Dionysius, "The Divine Names" 705a (*Works*, 78). See also Maximus the Confessor, *Writings*, 219n58 (*Scholia on the Divine Names* 257CD).
71. Weil, *Intimations of Christianity*, 96.

etry. One last gloss on forgetfulness is perhaps consoling—in its way: in Proclus's last illness "though he forgot almost all human things as the paralysis
advanced . . . he completed the hymns [he had asked to be chanted] and the
greater part of the Orphic verses . . . read out in his presence."[72] Those suffering from dementia and losing their "personal" memories may still be able
to sing.[73] Our predecessors would have inferred that this is what was worth
remembering.[74]

72. Marinus, *Life of Proclus*; M. Edwards, *Neoplatonic Saints*, 89.
73. See Sacks, *Anthropologist on Mars*; Sacks, *Musicophilia*, 371–86.
74. See my "Goals of Goodness" and *Biology and Christian Ethics*, 241–57.

CHAPTER ELEVEN

Standing Up to the Blows of Fortune

How shall we deal with assaults on our minds and bodies? "Stand up against the blows of fortune like a great trained fighter," Plotinus urges (I.4 [46].8, 25), and remember that "the law says those who fight bravely, not those who pray, are to come safe out of the wars" (III.2 [47].8, 37–42). We may reasonably suspect that Plotinus was here speaking from experience: his "religion" was not of the sort that expected the gods to assist us in our ordinary affairs or to spare us trouble. But fighting bravely and invoking the spirit of a great fighter (or rather—as I shall observe—an *athlete*) may still require an imaginative effort that differs hardly at all from prayer. Is it helpful to invoke that spirit, or may there be problems with such an image, in effect of the Heroic Self? Can we expect *Heracles*—or at least our image of Heracles—to help free us from our chains (IV.3 [27].14, 16–8)?

Consider the obvious congruence between that pagan hero and the Christian.[1] Both Heracles and Jesus were reputed sons of God, born of a mortal mother, required to labor in the service of humanity despite—or because of—being the rightful king. They were both tempted, and resisted the temptation, to take the easier, pleasanter path. They perished through the treachery or folly of a trusted friend but were raised up to Heaven and thereafter served as an ideal, an inspiration, even a supernatural aid. Both harrowed Hell. Their double nature led some to suppose that there were two of each—one in Heaven and the other (a mere shadow) in the land of the mortal dead. Christians preferred, in the main, to insist that there was only one such Jesus, with two natures united in one identity—a doctrine lying outside my present brief. The much easier option would have been to

---

1. See also my *Ancient Mediterranean Philosophy*, 161–4.

follow the Heraclean and Hellenic model, distinguishing one Heracles from another, or at least the archetype from the image: he was identified with a Mesopotamian god, Nergal, as well as with the Tyrian Melqart.[2] His name was also given to the First Born of creation.[3] Worshipers—for example, on Thasos—distinguished the Olympian, to whom they gave the sacrifices due an immortal, from the other, to whom "they delivered funerary honours as with a hero."[4] The Cynics especially took him as their patron, as one who had chosen the path of Virtue[5] and showed it was possible to live entirely by one's wits and courage, even in the face of celestial—that is, Hera's—malice.

> It is generally agreed that during the whole time which Heracles spent among men he submitted to great and continuous labours and perils willingly, in order that he might confer benefits upon the race of men and thereby gain immortality.[6]

Socrates had sworn by him, and Xenophon's band of mercenaries regularly prayed to "Zeus the Saviour and Heracles the guide."[7] He was honored in Carthage as well as Rome, and by emperors as well as wandering Cynics.

> The imperial theology of the greatest of the persecutors [e.g., Diocletian (AD 244–311)] had important features in common with the religion which they persecuted. Jupiter is the supreme god. His son, Hercules, acts as his executive representative, and is a benefactor of man. The resemblance to Christian theology is obvious.[8]

2. See Kingsley, *Ancient Philosophy*, 274–5.

3. According to Orphic testimony, the third principle after water and earth was "Unaging Time (Chronos), and also Heracles," conjoined with Ananke or Adrasteia (which is Necessity). Damascius, *Principles* 123 bis (i.317 R: Orpheus frag. 54), cited by West, *Orphic Poems*, 178, 180. West further suggests (192–4) that "Heracles' labours represent everything that happens in cosmic time," and that this allegory was probably originated by the Stoic Cleanthes.

4. Herodotus, *History* 2.44.

5. Xenophon, *Memorabilia*, 95–9 (2.1.21–34), quoting Prodicus.

6. Diodorus, *History*, vol. 1, 1.2.4.

7. Xenophon, *Anabasis* 4.8, 6.5.

8. Liebeschuetz, *Continuity and Change*, 242–3. There are also considerable differences, most obviously the absence in pagan thought and practice of any theology or practice of the Holy Spirit. Blois, *Policy of Gallienus*, 149–50, notes that it was Plotinus's patron Gallienus who revived Heracles as a focus for imperial loyalty and his own self-image (he also invoked Mercury, "Genius Populi Romani," Demeter, Zeus, and the Sun; 150–9). None of this is to suggest that Christians modeled their Christology on pagan templates: rather the reverse.

Are these associations—familiar enough in the third century AD—ones that Plotinus would have cared to recall? And should we understand the fabled horrors of Heracles's reputed life—for example, that in madness he killed his children—as literal reminders that even the greatest of heroic sages could be subject to external madness? "Suppose he is unconscious, his mind swamped by sickness or magic arts" (I.4 [46].9, 1–2)? Even then, Plotinus proposes, the sage's wisdom does not cease to exist merely because it is not reflected in the mirror of his soul, nor even if its reflection is very badly distorted (I.4 [46].10, 6–28).

More or less literal invocation will concern me in a later chapter. Here I seek instead to address the military *or athletic* image in its own right. Plotinus was not, of course, the first to offer such advice. Quintus Sextius, for example, suggests that we should form a mental image of an army marching in square formation to fend off enemies—that is, emotional assaults.[9] Cicero doubted that creating such images of virtues can cancel the bare truth that one is being tortured or the effects of torture.[10] They may nonetheless be helpful, both by recalling what such equanimity is like and, at the least, by diverting our attention: the mere sensation of injury or disease is only, we can sometimes feel (though not easily as the pain grows greater), a simple fact, to whose importunities we need not quite assent. That pain is an evil to be avoided, tempered, or averted is only an opinion, of rather doubtful value. Moderns may find this hard to accept: we have easy recourse, in ordinary life, to anesthetics and analgesics, whereas our ancestors had simply to endure. At best we can imagine *ignoring* the sensations or giving them a masochistic value—but neither practice is what dancers and athletes (or, rather, great trained dancers and athletes) use.[11] Perhaps unsurprisingly, not expecting the worst but believing that a situation can be faced, a problem dealt with, a project completed, makes it more likely that this will happen: in psychologist-speak this is labeled "self-efficacy,"[12] but this label may be misleading. The Self that copes may not always be simply our loquacious ego. Better to suppose, with Paul, that it is not I but—in his case—Christ that lives and acts in him.[13]

---

9. Quintus Sextius, *Epistles* 59.7, cited by Bartsch, *Mirror of the Self,* 128. See also Seneca, *Epistles* 74.7.

10. Cicero, *Tusculans* 5.5.13–4, cited by Bartsch, *Mirror of the Self,* 128.

11. Tesarz et al., "Pain Perception."

12. Bandura, "Self-Efficacy."

13. Paul, *Galatians* 2.20. In about AD 203 Felicity (a pregnant slave who could not—by Roman law—be executed till she had given birth) cried out during her labor pains in prison and was mocked by a servant of the jailers, asking her, "You who are in such suffering now, what

The fact that athletes, dancers, and fighters (and maybe martyrs) can cope better with pain partly because they believe they can, and at least do not *increase* their pains by imagining worse outcomes, may itself be damaging: pain, after all, is usually a signal of some bodily distress which it would be well, for our bodies' sake, to remedy. Dancing through the pain results in injuries rather greater than the usual—and of course many moderns also pity martyrs, thinking (like many Roman magistrates) that it would have been easier if they would have agreed to make some gesture of compliance. Whether humanity will long survive this general readiness to be bribed or bullied may be moot and is, at least, a question not to be settled here.

But I must return to the initial suggestion: of acting "like a great trained fighter," in Armstrong's version. What did Plotinus have in mind? The term *athletes* does not mean "fighter." Plotinus does make mention elsewhere of boxers, *puknikoi*, but only as an example, not a metaphor: how does the boxer "by nature" differ from one "by knowledge" (VI.1 [42]. 11, 12–3)? And what the athlete (the term has connotations rather of "prize-seeker" than "performer") does in "standing up to the blows of fortune" is to *resist* or to *defend* or simply to *continue* rather than "fight back." This is perhaps as well: an ancient boxing match had few rules, and the boxers wore weighted gloves to do as much damage as possible. The match ended in surrender, incapacity, or death—which can only be *our* death or incapacity if we must fight with fortune. Our goal must rather be to minimize the damage done, to dodge, and to survive. It may even be that what Plotinus has in mind are the lashes of the judges, used to rebuke athletes variously out of line. As in the earlier cases, of dancing, drunkenness, and love, Plotinus may be deliberately rebutting an educated perception of what "athleticism" is. Galen, for example, excoriates the "training" of professional athletes—a matter of sleeping, stuffing themselves with food, and following exactly prescribed muscle-building and programming exercises which will have a damaging effect in later life.[14] Athletes, it was a common claim since Plato, were useless as soldiers, who must—in contrast—be ready to perform in unison, on far too little food and sleep, in unexpected and irregular surroundings.[15]

---

will you do when you are thrown to the beasts, which you despised when you refused to sacrifice?" And she replied, "Now it is I that suffer what I suffer; but then there will be another in me, who will suffer for me, because I also am about to suffer for Him." Roberts and Donaldson, *Acts*, 704 (5.2).

14. See S. Miller, *Arete*, 174–7. See also Plato, *Republic* 3.410d; *Laches* 182e–184c.

15. Plutarch, *Lives*, vol. 10, 261–3 (3.2–4): "[Philopoemen, 253–183 BC] was thought to be a good wrestler, but when some of his friends and directors urged him to take up athletics,

Diodorus tells a story that slightly subverts the notion: Dioxippus, a Greek in Alexander's entourage, having quarreled with a Macedonian soldier, was required to duel with him. He faced the armored soldier naked, with a club, dodged a thrown spear, broke the soldier's sword, and quickly downed his opponent. The story ended unhappily for him, since Alexander was furious at the defeat: Dioxippus was constrained to kill himself.[16] So perhaps there was after all some merit in some sorts of athletic training, with a familiar moral: at least in single combat the victor may be the nimbler, both in wits and in movement, and this capacity is honed by constant practice—in effect, by dancing. And we can note in this context that the archetypal "strong man with a club"—namely, Heracles—accomplished almost all his tasks by guile and indirection, not brute strength.

"And when the pains concern others" (I.4 [46].8, 13–4)? Decent people nowadays care about others' pains, but Plotinus, like the Stoics, apparently thought it weakness to feel for others. "There is evidence for this in the fact that we think it something gained if we do not know about other people's sufferings, and even regard it as a good thing if we die first." That at least *is* weakness, to be avoided by facing up to what "ordinary nature normally finds terrible" (I.4 [46].8, 23–4). But modern moralists are likelier to feel that virtue lies in pity and fear, rather than in knowing that "though some natures may not like [such evils], one's own can bear them, not as terrors but as children's bogies." In the very next treatise that he wrote he added that "we should be *spectators* of murders, and all deaths, and takings and sacking of cities, as if they were on the stages of theatres" (III.2 [47].15, 44–5). Such things are no more than children's games: "one must not take weeping and lamenting as evidence of the presence of evils, for children, too, weep and wail over things that are not evils" (III.2 [47].15, 61). If children are being bullied the remedy must lie with them (III.2 [47].8, 16–21). If professed adults are fearful or distressed or greedy, they must discipline their "inner child."

---

he asked them if athletics would not be injurious to his military training. They told him (and it was the truth) that the habit of body and mode of life for athlete and soldier were totally different, and particularly that their diet and training were not the same, since the one required much sleep, continuous surfeit of food, and fixed periods of activity and repose, in order to preserve or improve their condition, which the slightest influence or the least departure from routine is apt to change for the worse; whereas the soldier ought to be conversant with all sorts of irregularity and all sorts of inequality, and above all should accustom himself to endure lack of food easily, and as easily lack of sleep." See S. Miller, *Ancient Greek Athletics*, 197–8.

16. Diodorus, *History* 17.100–2, cited by Miller, *Ancient Greek Athletics*, 197–8.

If sometimes when he is concerned with other things an involuntary fear comes upon him before he has time to reflect, the wise man [in him] will come and drive it away and quiet the child in him which is stirred to a sort of distress, by threatening or reasoning; the threatening will be unemotional, as if the child was shocked into quietness just by a severe look. A man of this sort will not be unfriendly or unsympathetic; he will be like this to himself and in dealing with his own affairs: but he will render to his friends all that he renders to himself, and so will be the best of friends as well as remaining intelligent [*meta ton noun ekhein*]. (I.4 [46].15, 17–25)

But perhaps our "inner child" also deserves some time to play. "Life must be lived as play," as Plato said,[17] and in telling us to think of our troubles merely as children's games, Plotinus is not disparaging our life here-now but offering a way of living it more lightly. This indeed is the message of all the metaphors and images I have so far considered, described, and deconstructed. Get naked: turn aside from everyday concerns and all received opinions. Welcome the greater gods—immortal presences of passion or delight—into your lives, and "shake yourself free" of lesser powers.[18] Let yourself be "turned": *metanoia*, it is worth noting, is not quite "repentance." When we "repent" we are wracked by guilt:

We do earnestly repent, and are heartily sorry for these our misdoings; the remembrance of them is grievous unto us; the burden of them is intolerable.[19]

Metanoia, on the other hand, is the moment when our heart is changed, and the burden lifted.[20] So allow yourselves to forget entanglements, resentments, follies, and live without concern for tomorrow. Allow yourselves to be "simplified into happiness." Dance with your eye on your leader, dodge when attacked, and learn from your repeated failures. Live, in essence, like a happy child, in a world perennially new.

'Tis the gift to be simple, 'tis the gift to be free
    'Tis the gift to come down where we ought to be,

17. Plato, *Laws* 7.796.
18. Remes, *Neoplatonism*, 168–9.
19. General Confession in *Book of Common Prayer* (1662).
20. See Verney, *Dance of Love*, 21–4.

And when we find ourselves in the place just right,
    'Twill be in the valley of love and delight.
When true simplicity is gained,
    To bow and to bend we shan't be ashamed,
To turn, turn will be our delight,
    Till by turning, turning we come round right.[21]

21. "Simple Gifts" (1848). The words and music were composed by Joseph Brackett (1797–1882), a Shaker elder. According to Roger Hall, "'Simple Gifts,'" "this song was really intended to accompany the vigorous dance movement that the Shakers called 'laboring,' or a religious 'exercise.' Even though Brackett's song may be quaintly worded, it wasn't meant to be sung as a lethargic lullaby as heard sometimes these days. His 'Simple Gifts' was made for some 'delight,' with Shakers dancing with great gusto, till they turned 'round right.'" My thanks to Jay Bregman and Roger Hall.

PART III

The Plotinian Imaginary

CHAPTER TWELVE

Platonic and Classical Myths

So far I have been addressing images and metaphorical procedures that do not entirely depend for their usefulness on any particular view of the universe at large, whatever mistakes Plotinus and his contemporaries may have made about the way things are. We can realize for ourselves what it is to be "drunk" with beauty or "strip naked." We can acknowledge the influence that familiar images and stories have on us, and even seek to rewrite or polish them. In the following chapters I shall speak instead of the "Plotinian Imaginary," as it can be distinguished from the world as *we* (as we "moderns") imagine it to be. Our Imaginary encompasses far more than can easily be perceived, or even proved: dinosaurs and dark matter, artificial minds and interstellar empires. But most of us are confident that demons and the Olympian gods are fictions, that magic and astrological predictions do not work, and that "the real world" is the one we ordinarily perceive (although we are also confident that the real world uncovered by scientific inquiry is unimaginably vaster and more odd than ever we suspected). The question in interpreting and developing the Plotinian story then becomes whether we can adapt his methods and conclusions to our own very different world, or whether instead we might profitably "imagine ourselves" back into his. We might even begin to wonder whether our world is very different from his.

First, what has he himself to say about the myths he uses? How far does he suppose them to be true reports? Or in what sense might they, in a way, be true? Do they have any authority of their own, or are they merely (even if significantly) opportunities to convey messages and doctrines that he has discovered or decided upon by other means?[1]

---

1. As Andrew Smith proposes in "Myth of Love."

Plotinus makes use of both traditional and Platonic myths, ranging from the gruesome tales of Kronos and his children to the humor of Plato's *Symposium* (though Plato does not himself call any of the *Symposium*'s fantasies "a myth"[2]). Plato, of course, had done so too, despite also insisting that those gruesome and overtly immoral tales about gods and heroes were corrupting.

> If we want our future guardians to believe that to quarrel with each other for trivial reasons is the greatest source of shame, we should not tell them stories or paint pictures of gigantomachies and the many and various enmities between gods and heroes and their relatives and close friends. . . . The divine combats which Homer wrote about should not be admitted into the city, whether they are presented in allegories [*huponoiai*] or without allegory.[3]

Philosophers of a rationalizing kind have usually sought to represent the myths as ornamental and potentially misleading: the real philosophy, they insist, is to be found in *arguments* of a strictly logical kind. The dialectician especially, interrogating different hypotheses to see which lead to contradiction or to falsehood and which may be flatly asserted as necessary truths, need not be influenced by fictions and folk stories. Poets, like accomplished rhetoricians, may produce memorable lines and images, but they must be challenged in at least two ways: what do those lines and images really mean, and what authority do their creators have to assert or emphasize them? Fictions stand or fall by their immediate impact and their ongoing influence on our nonrational souls. Genuine arguments are subject to more formal rules of inquiry: they may turn out to be fallacious and then lose their grip (or should). Modern analytical philosophers especially excerpt Plato's *arguments* (as they understand them) from the dialogues and rarely trouble even to read the *myths* in which he often sums up his thesis. Plotinus is often treated in the same way: even so sympathetic and knowledgeable a commentator as Armstrong was persuaded that Plotinus couldn't really be engaged by any of the myths he uses, and that they were there only, at best, to make his arguments seem more conventional than in fact they were. But

---

2. See Brisson, *Plato the Myth Maker*, 42–3, 141–4: he calls them "fabrications" (*poieseis*). See also Pépin, "Plotin et les mythes"; Brisson, *How Philosophers Saved Myths*.

3. *Republic* 2.378c1–d7. See Rousselle, "Images as Education." Porphyry disagreed with Plotinus by dismissing such brutal fables from even allegorical consideration. See Hadot, *Veil of Isis*, 51–3.

even the "realistic" narratives that contain and present the arguments matter more than moderns suppose. Perhaps, like Bible-reading Christians,[4]
those who attended Plotinus's salon *imagined* themselves into the narrative
of the dialogues and so discovered the "Thrasymachus" or "Callicles" or
"Cebes" in themselves, as well as Typhon and the cavalcade of souls. That
sort of "close reading" deserves more attention than I shall give it here.

Muthos and *logos* did not have very different connotations until the late
fourth century, when *muthoi* were gradually identified as stories passed on
by oral tradition, without any check on their truth or authority. In still later
usage "myths" are stories that have been made up to appeal to our feelings
and intuitions about what is right and proper, without regard to historical
verisimilitude. Plotinus himself identifies "myths" as separating in time
"the things of which they tell" and setting "apart from each other many
realities which are together, but distinct in rank or powers." Understanding them, we can "put together again that which they have separated" (III.5
[50].9, 24–9). So the story of creation in Plato's *Timaeus* (or in Genesis) is interpreted as showing how things *could* have been put together, but were not.
But are *logoi*, even if supported by plausible evidence and argument, necessarily more reliable (they must, after all, be plausible *to us*: that is, they
must appeal to our feelings and intuitions about what is right and proper)?
Even Plato, though he may distinguish them, does not automatically think
logoi are superior, either in truth or in authority.[5] My own proposal is that
arguments themselves, *logoi*, are rarely well defined by their merely formal
characteristics and have an ongoing influence by their appeal to images and
stereotypical responses that are better understood by poets than logicians.
The stronger the argument in logical terms—the more clearly one proposition implies another—the more it becomes a choice, whether to accept the
second proposition or deny the first! Which conclusion we pick will usually
depend on some unconscious bias, some appeal to our sense of beauty, fit-
ness, or propriety. *Logoi* do hang together, but perhaps not as firmly as rationalists suppose—and they gesture toward an *atemporal* connectivity

4. See Luhrmann, *When God Talks Back*, 175–84.

5. See Brisson, *Plato the Myth Maker*, for a detailed study of Plato's own usage of the
terms, and especially of the Atlantis myth of the *Timaeus*. *Mythoi*, typically, are stories passed
down by word of mouth and so subject to the constraints of *oral* tradition, by contrast with
those of literate culture. Havelock, for example, proposed that written texts were worded "so
as to replace agents by impersonal forces and the acts of agents performed upon other agents by
statements of relationships between impersonal entities" (see Havelock, "Linguistic Task of the
Presocratics," 21, cited by Naddaf in Brisson, *Plato the Myth Maker*, xvi). See further Ong, *Orality and Literacy*; Buxton, *From Myth to Reason?* (esp. Murray, "What Is a *Muthos* for Plato?").

which is itself more than abstract argument: it is something more like a living organism.[6] Stories, *muthoi*, in their turn must have a *narrative* logic to be convincing, or even memorable. The difference between "mythical" or "poetic" persuasion and the more "logical" or "rational" sort may be simply that the latter is aimed at a larger group which may not share as many unvoiced assumptions as those targeted by poets (and especially *oral* poets). The seemingly random events that occur around the heroes of some mythological tradition with which we aren't familiar (Polynesian or South American, for example) will either leave us completely cold or else encourage us to learn enough to guess what the stories are really about, how they function, how one thing leads to another. Sometimes there is good reason to want to check the stories "mathematically," to formalize and quantify the changes they describe. But "adding the numbers in" does not automatically make a story better worth believing. Sometimes there is good reason to notice apparent contradictions in a story—those same seeming contradictions may reveal a deeper unity. Evolutionary theorists in the late nineteenth century had to live with the knowledge that the best *physicists* of their day insisted that the sun could not possibly have been giving the earth light and warmth for long enough to allow the evolutionary processes they—and especially Darwinists—hypothesized. In the end, they were vindicated by the discovery that the sun and all the stars were working in quite another, unimagined, way. Before that discovery, their convictions were founded, not on a rationalistic grasp of "what must be" nor even a detailed grasp of what *biological* processes could be involved in merely Darwinian selection, but on the story's power to explain (or gesture at least toward a possible explanation) and inspire.

> There is grandeur in this view of life, with its several powers, having been originally breathed into a few forms or into one; and that, whilst this planet has gone cycling on according to the fixed law of gravity, from so simple a beginning endless forms most beautiful and most wonderful have been, and are being, evolved.[7]

That the story is entrancing, of course, does not make it certainly true—any more than Copernican heliocentrism must be thought true merely because the Sun is a more attractive center for planetary revolutions than dis-

---

6. Plato, *Phaedrus* 264c.

7. Darwin, *Origin of Species*, 490. The next edition, in 1860, added "by the Creator" after "originally breathed."

mal Earth. We need, so Plotinus thought, Reality because Reality is Beauty (I.6 [1].6, 21). And that too is a dogma which could be denied (though at some cost to sanity).

So Plato's stories, and Plotinus's, may not be merely ornamental.[8] Sometimes, for Plotinus, they contain some message that "the wise men of old"—Plato or some other named or unnamed sage—intended for us.[9] Sometimes he follows esoteric interpretations of stories that Plato himself despised: the stories, for example, of how Kronos castrated his father and consumed his children, until one luckier offspring, Zeus, defeated him in his turn.[10] Sometimes Plotinus himself appears to be twisting the story for his own ends, even reversing the usual valency (as he also does with Kronos):[11] in his version of Hesiod's Pandora myth, for example, it is Epimetheus ("Afterthought"), not his brother Prometheus ("Forethought"), who has grasped the truth that "a life lived more in the intelligible world is the better one" (IV.3 [27].14, 12–4).[12] Prometheus, thief of fire, is trapped—so now the allegory runs—in his own creation and has to be rescued by Heracles (or his own higher self). The story of the infant Dionysus's suffering at the hands of Titans becomes an allegory of the soul's descent.[13] As Origen declared (and asked for the same open-mindedness from pagan readers of the Gospels),

8. See Collobert, Destrée, and Gonzalez, *Plato and Myth*, for a recent and welcome discussion of the use Plato made of myth.

9. So Barfield, *Ancient Quarrel*, 53: "Plotinus takes on the myths of Plato as myths indeed—as places where truth breaks through uniquely in myth." There may sometimes be no other way of discovering truth than through imaginative fiction.

10. Plato, *Republic* 2.377e–378c, 10.599d–608b.

11. See, e.g., V.8 [31].12–3: Zeus is the one of Kronos's children who lives outside his father, for a good purpose (so that there might be "a beautiful image of beauty and reality"), but he is bound to be surpassed by those offspring that have stayed "within" the worlds that have not (yet) had temporal expression. See also *Hermetic Corpus* 5.9 (Copenhaver, *Hermetica*, 20): "He is himself the things that are and those that are not. Those that are he has made visible; those that are not he holds within him. . . . There is nothing that he is not, for he also is all that is, and this is why he has all names, because they are of one father, and this is why he has no name, because he is father of them all."

12. Armstrong, *Enneads*, vol. 4, 82, thinks that Plotinus's casual attitude to the stories shows how little he cares about them. Cf. Blumenberg, *Work on Myth*, 366–8, on Ficino's version of the allegory (which leaves out the rescue by Heracles).

13. See Linforth, *Arts of Orpheus*, 307–66 (who finds the story silly, bizarre, obscene, "repellent to the normal, healthy mind"; 364). He does not mention Plotinus's use of the story, though acknowledging that the Neoplatonists in general "read into [the Orphic poems], through their indomitable allegorizing, the meaning of their own elevated philosophy" (364). See further Plutarch, *Moralia* 389a; Diodorus, *History* 5.75.4; Plato, *Timaeus* 35bc; Proclus, *In Timaeum* 313c; Guthrie, *Orpheus and Greek Religion*, 107–8; A. Cook, *Zeus, God of the Dark Sky*, 1030–2. Origen mentions the story in *Contra Celsum*, 194 (4.17), noting the possibility of allegorizing it to be about the soul.

"anyone who reads the stories with a fair mind, who wants to keep himself from being deceived by them, will decide what he will accept and what he will interpret allegorically, searching out the meaning of the authors who wrote such fictitious stories, and what he will disbelieve as having been written to gratify certain people."[14] He could have found the suggestion in an earlier pagan writer, Cornutus:

> And so, my child, the rest of the material handed down in myth which appears to be about the gods you are now in a position to refer to the principles I have set out, convinced that the ancients were no ordinary men, but capable of understanding the nature of the cosmos and inclined to use symbols and riddles [sumbolon kai ainigmaton] in their philosophical discussions of it.[15]

Another way of considering the difference between "muthos" and "logos" is to reserve the latter title for the world of everyday, the "ordinary" world. "Myth," by contrast, deals with the world of dream, the unseen and unexpectable. "Myth is about a 'beyond' which must be located in a distant past or a space which is different from the one in which the narrator and his public reside."[16] Bellah makes use of one particular Aboriginal people, the Walbiri, to make the point that the myths (the stories those Aboriginals tell about the origins of people, life, and everything) do not refer to any *past* historical time but rather to an ever-present Dream. They are about the forms and personages that are continually to be met and re-met in the world the Aboriginals travel: rather, they *are* those forms and personages.

> According to Nancy Munn, the Walbiri "use the term *djugurba*, which also means 'dream' and 'story,' to denote . . . ancestral inhabitants of the country and the times in which they traveled around creating the world in which present-day Walbiri now live. The contrast term, *yidjaru*, de-

---

14. Origen, *Contra Celsum*, 39 (1.42). See Lamberton, *Homer the Theologian*, 81. See also Martens, *Origen and Scripture*, 82–3, citing Origen, *Contra Celsum*, 213 (4.38): "It is not treating the matter fairly to refuse to laugh at [the Hesiodic myth about Pandora] as being a legend, and to admire the philosophical truths contained in it, and yet to sneer at the biblical stories and think that they are worthless, your judgment being based upon the literal meaning alone."

15. Lucius Annaeus Cornutus (a first-century Stoic), *Greek Theology* 35, 75.18–76.5 Lang (cited by Boys-Stones, *Post-Hellenistic Philosophy*, 53). See Eusebius, *History* 6.19, quoting Porphyry (cited by Martens, *Origen and Scripture*, 37).

16. Brisson, *Plato the Myth Maker*, 7.

notes the ongoing present or events within living memory. It also refers
to 'waking experience in contrast to dreaming.' . . . Although *yidjaru* refers to the ordinary present, *djugurba* also becomes present during ritual
enactment or even when the myths are told."[17]

Those ancestral inhabitants are readily present as stories in the landscape
the Walbiri travel. Similarly, Plotinus distances himself from those who
supposed that, for example, the *Timaeus* myth was intended to describe a
temporal creation of the cosmos. *Nous* is eternally realized in worship of
the One, and Soul Herself is an eternal realization, in apparent discontinuity
and plurality, of the intelligible, unchanging world. There was never a time,
he thought, when there was no World, no Soul, no Time (III.2 [47].1, 20–1).[18]
The relations of One, *Nous*, Soul, Nature, and Matter are not chronological,
as if there were first one and then another of them: instead, they are all
always present, and always causally connected.

There are other Platonic myths that Plotinus ignores, it seems, entirely:
such as that the Mediterranean peoples are sitting like frogs around a pond
in the deeper and mistier crannies of a vaster world, the dodecahedron of the
Phaedo's concluding story.[19] Nor does he make much use of the *Phaedrus*
stories, either that Thoth (which is Hermes) invented writing,[20] or that our
souls were riding in a chariot drawn by two horses till they were tugged
away from the course of heaven by the unrulier of the two,[21] or that Athens

17. Bellah, *Religion in Human Evolution*, 147, citing Munn, *Walbiri Iconography*, 23–4.

18. See also V.8 [31].7, where he argues against any "literal" creation: "where could the
ideas of all these things come from to one who had never seen them? And if he received them
from someone else he could not carry them out as craftsmen do now, using their hands and
tools; for hands and feet come later."

19. Plato, *Phaedo* 110b1ff. See also II.9 [33].6, 13–4, on Gnostic borrowing of "the rivers
in Hades and the reincarnations," a notion that Celsus (and probably others) took to represent
the distinction between our phenomenal world and the real, eternal reality in the heavens. See
Origen, *Contra Celsum*, 417–9 (7.28–31). Origen in turn allegorized the promise of a "land flowing with milk and honey" (*Exodus* 3.8) to mean that same "holy and good earth and the city of
God in it" (419 [7.31]).

20. Plato, *Phaedrus* 274c–275b.

21. Ibid. 253c7ff. Plotinus does mentions "moulting" as a cause or occasion of our fall, at
IV.8 [6].1, 37. Proclus especially found fault with Plotinus on this point, contending that he was
wrong to suppose that any part of our soul remained "aloft" and unaffected by the fall; see Proclus, *Commentary on Timaeus* 3.333.29ff., cited by R. Van den Berg, "Myth of the Charioteer."
On the other hand, Iamblichus also interpreted the *Phaedrus* story as suggesting that "pure
and perfect souls [at any rate] enter into the bodies purely without passions and without being
deprived of intellection" (*De anima* 379.22–4)—so (as Van den Berg points out) Iamblichus at
least is closer to Plotinus than some have thought.

once fought a war with Atlantis, and Atlantis drowned.[22] He does not make
any innovative use of the analogy of soul and city, despite sometimes referring to our passions as if they were an unruly assembly (VI.4 [22].15). Nor
does he mention the "noble lie" that Socrates devised for his imaginary
city, that some people are innately golden, others silver, and the mass of
humanity mere iron or bronze,[23] nor the notion attributed to Protagoras
that Zeus endowed all human beings with a sense of shame and justice,[24]
nor yet the wilder fancy that there was ever an age when changes ran the
opposite way entirely (so that the elderly sprouted as whole organisms from
the ground and grew steadily younger).[25] He rarely mentions Plato's Cave,
merely equating it with "the den of Empedocles" as an image of the world
of sense to which we have been condemned and from which we may hope
to clamber.[26]

The Platonic myths that he chiefly uses are, first, the *Timaeus* story of
creation; second, the Myth of Er (from *The Republic*), with its implication
that we have each chosen our earthly lives[27] and can't reasonably now com-

---

22. Plato, *Timaeus* 26e4ff. Numenius seems to have interpreted this story as a battle
between the superior souls associated with Athena and those "concerned with generation" (and
Poseidon); see Lamberton, *Homer the Theologian*, 65. And Zoticus, one of Plotinus's companions, who died a little before him, wrote "a very good poem" on that subject (Porphyry, *Life*
7.12–7).

23. Plato, *Republic* 3.415c7ff., where it is described as a "Phoenician" sort of story, presumably after the story that Cadmus the Phoenician sowed the dragons' teeth from which the
Spartans sprang. See also *Laws* 2.663e.

24. Plato, *Protagoras* 320c3ff.

25. Plato, *Statesman* 269d9ff.; Plato, *Laws* 4.713a6. This trope turns up in modern speculative physics to describe what life would be like in an imagined reversal of cosmic expansion
(see Gold, "Arrow of Time"). The usual inference is that—from the inside—it would look
exactly like our present age! If everything is reversed, after all, so also would be the direction
of our memories. See Smart, "Temporal Asymmetry of the World." The aged persons who, in
Plato's story, are seen—by us—to be getting younger themselves remember being younger and
experience their plight as getting older. The implication is that "the direction of time" is an
illusion: all moments are equally real, and none (such as "the past" over "the future") have any
ontological priority. See Price, *Time's Arrow*, for a fuller discussion. We all simply are, at the
moments that we are. This in turn makes it difficult for moderns to denounce "teleological
explanation": future events are just as much an "explanation" of present reality as past events
(better still: all events are mutually and timelessly adjusted). But this is another story.

26. IV.8 [6].1, 24–37; II.9 [33].6, 9; Empedocles 31B120DK. As Meredith, "Plato's Cave,"
observes, Plato had not offered any story about the reasons for his prisoners' incarceration.
But he probably did intend to suggest that they were indeed "in prison" (as also *Phaedo* 95d;
Phaedrus 247d).

27. Plato, *Republic* 10.621b8ff.; see IV.3 [27].8, 9–11. As Lamberton, *Homer the Theologian*,
118–9, observes, Porphyry goes some way to humanizing this story, by emphasizing, in his allegory of Circe's island, the terror and confusion of discarnate souls before they are dragged away
to a fitting reincarnation.

plain; and, third, the conception and birth of Eros (from *The Symposium*).[28] What the omissions imply about seminar discussion in Plotinus's salon I cannot tell. Nor is it easy to see why he devotes so much attention to the "Birth of Love."[29] I have touched on that story several times and note now only one other possible association: the unwitting father, as Plato imagines, of Eros is Poros son of Metis, a deity otherwise unfamiliar but possibly reminiscent of Ploutos—which is to say, of Hades, whom Plato elsewhere identifies not simply with the Unseen but with the source of knowledge.[30]

Another grand omission is any clear reference to *Egyptian* myth, despite his admiration for "the wise men of old" and their hieroglyphic symbols, and despite the presence of Isis-worshipers in his circle.[31] Did he deliberately exclude the stories at least from his writings, not wishing to be stereotyped as another Egyptian guru? For allegorical or theological interpretation of the Isis stories we must go to Plutarch[32] or Apuleius's *Golden Ass* or—of course—the grand *Hermetic Corpus*. Does their presence in the background have any effects, either directly or indirectly? And what did Plotinus's successors make of them?

He did not limit himself to plainly classical myths: Cybele and her worship—a cult officially welcomed in Rome but conducted with scant regard for normal Roman decencies[33]—are invoked to make a point about the sterility of matter (III.6 [26].19, 26ff.)![34] It may be significant (but of what I cannot tell) that he does not mention the dismemberment of Osiris and the loss of *his* phallus. But most of the non-Platonic references are rather to

---

28. Plato, *Symposium* 203bc. There is an easy allegorical significance in making Poros a son of Metis (i.e., of clever strategy). What is odd is that any son of Metis is fated to surpass his father, and to avoid that outcome, Zeus swallows Metis, not knowing that she is pregnant with Athena.

29. Origen, *Contra Celsum*, 215 (4.39), observes that malicious literalists like Celsus ought to mock the myth, and that the "garden of Zeus" resembles the paradise of God in *Genesis* 2.8–9: maybe, Origen tentatively suggests, the story is borrowed from an Egyptian reading of the Jewish myth.

30. Plato, *Cratylus* 404b.

31. Porphyry, *Life* 10.15–31.

32. Plutarch, *De Iside et Osiride*, 149 (359a, chap. 20): "the present myth [the story of Isis, Osiris, Set, and Horus] is the image of a reality which turns the mind back to other thoughts." See also 159 (chap. 27): Isis "infused images, suggestions and representations of her experiences at that time [into the most sacred rites], and so consecrated at once a pattern of piety and an encouragement to men and women overtaken by similar misfortunes."

33. See Beard, "The Roman and the Foreign."

34. Proclus celebrated Cybele's rites every month (Marinus, *Life of Proclus* 19; M. Edwards, *Neoplatonic Saints*, 86) and made a point of honoring every nation's gods (M. Edwards, *Neoplatonic Saints*, 88), except presumably the Christian and Jewish (whose honor would have required him *not* to honor the others).

Homer and to Hesiod. "By my calculation there are in the works of Plotinus approximately twenty-eight passages, most of them very brief, in which some recognizable allusion is made to the content or language of the Homeric poems. Four other passages allude to Hesiod."[35] Most of the allusions seem not to import or imply any special interpretation, except (perhaps) to mark moments where Plotinus's mind is turning toward those sources. Lamberton notes that when Plotinus speaks of "the elders of the city seated in assembly" (as an analogue of conflict resolution in the individual soul) the Iliadic language must recall an "oasis of peace and reason in the absurd and violent context" of the Trojan War—but without any further development of the allusion.[36] We may be missing—we certainly must be missing—many further contextual allusions that would have made sense to his contemporaries. The two principal Hesiodic myths that he invokes are those of Pandora and the stories of Ouranos, Kronos, and Zeus that I have already mentioned: in both cases he chooses to distort or at least seriously disarrange the original stories.

Lamberton identifies other passages as having more Homeric force and influence. The first describes a hoped-for moment of enlightenment in terms of Athena's yanking Achilles around (VI.5 [23].7, 11–7);[37] the second is a reference to the rising of the sun "out of Ocean" as an analogue of sudden enlightenment ("what is the horizon which [he of whom the sun is an image] will mount above when he appears?"; V.5 [32].8, 7–9).[38] Plotinus further discusses what could be meant by the gods' "living at ease," "being drunk on the nectar," "feasting and banqueting," and so on (concluding that these are necessary ways to give us some sense of how much the noetic life is to be desired) (V.5 [32].4; VI.7 [38].30). Some of Homer's stories—for example, that the gods wander through many cities in disguise—are explained as references to lesser *daimones* (V.5 [32].12).[39] Others are taken still more seriously as evidence: such as that Minos was "a companion of Zeus" and so enabled to make laws for us lesser mortals (VI.9 [9].7, 23–6),[40] that there is something—on Plotinus's account, dead matter—that the gods hate (V.1

---

35. Lamberton, *Homer the Theologian*, 90.

36. Ibid., 91–5, after VI.5 [22].15 and Homer, *Iliad* 3.149.

37. After Homer, *Iliad* 1.199–200.

38. Lamberton, *Homer the Theologian*, 95–6. See also Philo, *Legum allegoriarum* 1.46 (*Collected Works*, vol. 1, 177): "right reason does not set, nor is quenched, but its nature is ever to rise."

39. *Pace* Plato, *Republic* 2.381d. Later Platonists developed a complex demonology to accommodate these stories—and also the observable presence of powers with their own priorities!

40. After Plato, *Minos* 319a; Plato, *Laws* 1.624.

[10].2, 24–7),⁴¹ and that Heracles exists both as an *eidolon* in Hades and as his real self among the gods.⁴²

The principal image that Plotinus borrows from the Homeric corpus is Odysseus, whom he interprets as "a type, symbolic of the highest class of humanity: those who have, in Plotinus's sense, reached home."⁴³ This was not Plotinus's own invention. In an earlier text, attributed to Plutarch, the witch Circe, whom Odysseus flees, is a "symbol of the cycle of *metensomatosis* [transmigration], to which 'the thinking man' (*ho emphron aner*) Odysseus is immune."⁴⁴ Nor was Plotinus the last to take the story so.

> Homer calls the cyclical progress and rotation of *metensomatosis* "Circe," making her a child of the sun, which is constantly linking destruction with birth and birth back again with destruction and stringing them together. The island of Aiaia is both the fate that awaits the dead and a place in the upper air. When they have first fallen into it, the souls wander about disoriented and wail and do not know where the west is "or where the sun that lights mortal men goes beneath the earth."⁴⁵

Such souls, as Plotinus also supposed, will find themselves reborn as asses or as wolves and the like, depending on their particular vicious disposition.

> Therefore where death is concerned, purity is just as important as in an initiation, and you must keep all base emotion from the soul, put all painful desire to sleep, and keep as far from the mind as possible all jealousy, ill will and anger, as you leave the body. Hermes with his golden

41. After Homer, *Iliad* 20.65.

42. IV.3 [27].27, 7–14; IV.3 [27].32, 24–8; IV.4 [28].1; I.1 [53].12, 32–40, after Homer, *Odyssey* 11.601–2. See Pépin, "Héracles et son reflet"; Sheppard, *Studies on the 5th and 6th Essays*, 135. Ananda Wood, in his reworking of the Upanishads, identifies a similar distinction: "within each heart, there seem to be two selves, experiencing the truth of moral action in the world. Of these two selves, one is described as a mere shadow or reflection of the other self: the real self, which shines by its own light, by its own pure intensity" (*Katha Upanishad* 3.1; Wood, *From the Upanishads*, 15). Wood's reworking makes the Upanishads more nearly intelligible to readers unfamiliar with ancient Hindu ritual and practice, but I am conscious that trying to uncover Plotinus's meaning by comparing his thought to the Upanishads is, for me, *obscurum per obscurius*. The more nearly *literal* version of the Upanishads in Olivelle's *Early Upanisads* may be less contentious as pure scholarship but is not helpful as philosophy.

43. Lamberton, *Homer the Theologian*, 107, after V.9 [5].1, 20–1. See also I.6 [1].8, 16–23.

44. Lamberton, *Homer the Theologian*, 41, after Pseudo-Plutarch, *De vita Homeri* 126. Further on Plato's use of Odysseus in *The Republic*, see Adluri, "Plato's Saving *Mūthos*."

45. Stobaeus, *Eclogae* 1.41.60, cited by Lamberton, *Homer the Theologian*, 116.

staff—in reality, reason (*logos*)—meets the soul and clearly points the way to the good. He either bars the soul's way and prevents its reaching the witch's brew or, if it drinks, watches over it and keeps it as long as possible in a human form.[46]

It is "reason" that allows our liberation from the cycle (but do we yet know what "reason" is?).

Porphyry's gloss on Circe and the role of Hermes is in keeping with Plotinus's own remarks. Whether one other and more famous allegorical interpretation, of the Cave of the Nymphs, could be considered Plotinian is less clear, though both Porphyry (his follower) and Numenius (his predecessor) used that episode. The cave is where, in the literal fiction, Odysseus returns to Ithaca from fairyland and where, in the allegorical, the soul is in transit between this material world and the eternal.[47]

Our own perception of Odysseus is likely to be a favorable one, even if we do not think of him as Everyman (or at least Every Philosopher) in search of an eternally satisfying truth. He resists both Circe, who would transform him into a beast, and Calypso, who would make him a god. He is wise enough to guard himself against the Sirens' offer to make him all-knowing.[48] In effect he follows what came to be the standard Greek advice: to think mortal thoughts, being mortal, rather than the philosophical.[49] There have also been more critical views: he might instead be reckoned treacherous, duplicitous, ambitious, and disastrously inquisitive. Probably Plotinus was merely relying on the more favorable perception and simply ignoring both the dominant Roman interpretation of their imagined ancestors' most successful foe[50] and the more subdued Greek reading. But it is also possible that this is another case where his analogy was meant at least to startle and perhaps to shock. For Plotinus and his followers at any rate, Odysseus is a friend of that same Athena who preserved Achilles's sense (and is represented by the olive tree in the Cave of the Nymphs); gentle toward his friends and fierce toward his foes, he had the philosophical temperament

---

46. Lamberton, *Homer the Theologian*, 116–7. The ass generally stands for lust; the wolf, for anger.

47. Homer, *Odyssey* 13.102–12; Lamberton, *Homer the Theologian*, 119–33. On the history of interpretation of this passage, see Lamberton, *Homer the Theologian*, 318–24.

48. Homer, *Odyssey* 12.190. Note that the Sirens do not seek to arouse Odysseus's mere desire, but his curiosity—the fault which Dante later chose to impute to him, alongside his giving of wicked advice (*Divine Comedy: Hell* 26).

49. Pindar, *Isthmian* 5.20; cf. Aristotle, *Nicomachean Ethics* 10.1177b31–4.

50. See W. R. Stanford, *Ulysses Theme*, 128–58.

that Plato required for the guardians of his Republic;[51] he struggled against monsters (though often at unnecessary cost), visited the Underworld, and resisted the temptation of an easy immortality—all in his progress back from exile. In the words of a later poet and theologian:

Nostrum est interim mentem erigere
et totis patriam votis appetere,
Et ad Jerusalem a Babylonia
Post longa regredi tandem exilia.[52]

I shall cite one final gloss to that return, matching an earlier exegesis:

Homer says that all outward possessions must be deposited in this cave and that one must be stripped naked and take on the persona of a beggar and, having withered the body away and cast aside all that is superficial and turned away from the senses, take counsel with Athena, sitting with her beneath the roots of the olive, how he might cut away all the destructive passions of the soul.[53]

Even the story of mass murder (of Penelope's suitors and the treacherous maidservants) is given a ready reading—very much as Christian and Jewish exegetes have dealt with the book of Joshua and other episodes in the recorded history or myth-history of Israel! Internalizing Odysseus and his adventures plays a similar role to Loyola's *Spiritual Exercises*.

51. So ibid., 32, citing Plato, *Republic* 2.375. Athena characterizes Odysseus, in *Odyssey* 13.332, as *"epetes, anchinoos, ekhephron"* (courteous, quick-witted, self-possessed).
52. Peter Abelard (1079–1142), "O quanta qualia sunt illa sabbata" (Davis and Calkins, *Hymns of the Church*, 47).
53. Porphyry, *De antro nympharum*, §16; Uzdavinys, *Heart of Plotinus*, 265; see Lamberton, *Homer the Theologian*, 130.

CHAPTER THIRTEEN

Spheres and Circles

Plotinus's use of dances as symbols—and examples—of the better life makes it evident that he can conceive and appreciate an *embodied* glory (even if he did not join in, at least in public). Some signs and symbols are merely arbitrary codes (as the word "gold" stands in for gold, by mere convention). Other signs and symbols are themselves what they convey (as a piece of gold may stand for gold in general: V.8 [31].3, 13–4). Dancing—literal dancing—is love's proper exercise: a clumsy version of eternal joy. What of his other principal image, the merely geometric? Does that lean in what we consider a more abstract, formal direction? I shall propose, on the contrary, that it is in imagining circles, and their centers, that he is at his most empirical!

That God is always doing geometry is, so Plutarch says, a genuinely Platonic thought, even if it is not stated in the Platonic texts.[1] Other Platonists and Pythagoreans made much of triangles, squares, pentagons, or hexagons in plane geometry and of the so-called "Platonic Solids" in solid geometry (tetraheda, cubes, octahedra, dodecahedra, icosahedra). Astronomy in turn could be viewed as the study of *motion* in three dimensions, and music itself as a final form of applied mathematics.[2] Little of this is visible in Plotinus's text (though he mentions that fire is made of pyramids[3]). His focus is rather upon spheres and circles—and their radii and centers. Intellect dances around the One, and Soul around intellect (I.8 [51].2, 23–32).[4]

One use of the imagery of circles that does not seem to appear in the Plo-

---

1. Plutarch, "Table Talk" 8.718c (*Moralia*, vol. 9, 127).
2. Plato, *Republic* 7.524d–535a, on the potential philosopher-kings' curriculum.
3. E.g., VI.6 [34].17, 32–3, after Plato, *Timaeus* 54d5ff.
4. See Plato, *Letter* 2.312e.

tinian text is that of Hierocles: each of us, it was proposed, is surrounded by concentric circles of attachment—our own bodies, our immediate family, uncles and aunts and cousins, and more-distant relatives. "Next upon this is the circle of the members of one's deme, then that of the members of one's tribe, next that of one's fellow citizens, and so, finally, that of those who border one's city and that of people of like ethnicity." The farthest out and largest one, which surrounds all the circles, is that of the entire race of human beings.[5] Our aim, Hierocles said, should be to draw the circles—concerning the behavior that is due to each group—together toward the center. The logical fulfillment of the process must presumably be to treat each and every human being as one would oneself, regardless of original connection, but—realistically—we may be surprised if foreigners are treated as well as fellow citizens, let alone loved as oneself (as the Hebrew scriptures required): "if a stranger sojourn with thee in your land, ye shall not vex him. But the stranger that dwelleth with you shall be unto you as one born among you, and thou shalt love him as thyself; for ye were strangers in the land of Egypt."[6]

This universal humanism is not endorsed in the Plotinian texts—partly, perhaps, because Platonists were readier than most philosophers to respect the nonhuman but also because there seems to be a still harder requirement, namely, to bring the god (*theos*) in each of us to meet the god (*theion*) in the all,[7] and so to "join ourselves at our own centres to something like the centre of all things" (VI.9 [9].8, 20). If we were, somehow, to achieve this, it would be as if we "had become someone else . . . having joined, as it were, centre to centre" (VI.9 [9].10, 15–7).[8] There would then be no question of "loving others as ourselves" (or even as our next-door neighbor), since there would be no distinguishable selves to love or to be loved. Nor, it seems, can we hope to say anything about the vision while it lasts—though Plotinus tries.

Is he here doing anything more than gesturing toward an experience

---

5. Stobaeus, *Anthology* 4.8.23 (Ramelli, *Hierocles*, 91). See also Long and Sedley, *Hellenistic Philosophers*, 349–50 (57G). While the story appeals to modern moralists influenced by Hamilton's rule on "kin selection" ("Genetical Evolution"), it is too schematic. As Augustine pointed out, many people care more for their dogs than for human foreigners (*City of God*, bk. 19, chap. 7) and for unrelated friends more than for their kin (*Confessions* IV.6.11).

6. *Leviticus* 19.33–4. See also *Exodus* 23.9: "thou shalt not oppress a stranger: for ye know the heart of a stranger, seeing ye were strangers in the land of Egypt."

7. Porphyry, *Life* 2.25–6: Plotinus's deathbed injunction to his friend Eustochius.

8. A modern version of the metaphor speaks of "our center of gravity" (a notion not available in a pre-Newtonian worldview) and the need to shift it inward "from [our] chattering ego-mind to a deeper self" (S. Taylor, *Waking from Sleep*, 105).

necessarily ineffable and unexpectable, something that only the gods can ever induce in us, and leave us bereft of speech? Possibly so, but there is more to the metaphors of spheres and circles than a gesture: there seems to be a program. Circles and spheres, in addition to their centers, have radii and circumferences—and it is these which Plotinus more frequently evokes.

Consider first the circumference, the route of circular motion, in the stars or in the soul. From his perspective in the Northern Hemisphere the stars orbit nightly round the pole. From a slightly wider perspective, stars orbit around Earth, with the planetary stars pursuing an epicyclic path, wheels rotating around points on their orbit. And of course from our modern, still wider perspective, the planets—including Earth—orbit instead around the sun (not in circular but in elliptical paths), while the sun itself traverses the outer reaches of our home galaxy. Circles and spheres are common features even of our world, though they no longer have the simple center or the perfect paths our ancestors imagined. But what matters to Plotinus about their circular orbit is that it can—in principle and, as he supposed, in fact—continue on forever. Linear movements from one place to another cannot be supposed to continue indefinitely: the implicit reasoning is probably Aristotelian. On the one hand, the available space in any direction is not *infinite*. On the other, all linear movement is a return to some "natural" place, where whatever it is that is moving will have no further reason, unless disturbed, to move. Substances mainly earthy find their home as close to the center of things as possible; fiery substances will naturally ascend—and finding nowhere further to go will circle endlessly around Earth (though this does not explain why they orbit in one direction rather than at whim around the sphere of heaven). Watery and airy substances will naturally lie in between—except that all are stirred up and removed from their favorite seats by the orbits of the sun and other planets. These astronomical speculations are, to us, no more than ancient jokes, nor are they among the more significant features of the Plotinian system, which fits more easily with Theophrastus's conception of the cosmos as a single, adaptive organism. Why do the stars go on forever? Because each stage of their motion leads around a circle, and they thereby imitate eternity. How are we to imitate the stars? Terrestrial life in general manages by repeatedly embodying the same forms, though not the same individuals—so that even terrestrial and human history will, in a way, go on forever, without ever breaking radically new ground. As individuals we may achieve a little more, by turning round upon ourselves, and taking our own selves as the objects of our thought. Only so shall we not be led astray by other, adventitious interests. Only so can we achieve a partial bond between the self as subject and the self as object—even though there is still an implicit duality.

> It is because of the circular revolutions of the heavens that generation returns in a circle upon itself and brings its unstable mutability into a definite cycle. If you divide bodiless things into soul and intellect, you will say that the circle has the character of Intellect, the straight line that of Soul. This is why the Soul, as it reverts to Intellect, is said to move in a circle.[9]

So the advice Plotinus gives us is to become aware of our own awareness, to stop drifting on from one *outward* object to another, and remember who and what we are. Other contemplative traditions have something like this aim: always to recall ourselves from passing thoughts and concentrate instead on our own concentration, bringing ourselves into a center. One technique often offered is to attend to our own breathing in and out—and Plotinus too employs exactly this example, though without making the suggestion explicit: "it seems that the breath which is around the soul moves in a circle. If God is in all things, the soul which desires to be with him must move around him, for he is not in any place" (II.2 [14]. 2, 21–3).[10] This may serve as a counter to that constituent of our bodily selves "which moves in straight lines" (II.2 [14].2, 18–20), following one thought and impulse after another without discernible end.

God is not in any place. This is already to begin to subvert the metaphor. How can we move around him if he has no place? Each point in a circle's circumference, or a sphere's surface, is as near or far from the center as any other. That indeed is what defines a circular or spherical form, that there are no privileged places at the edge, nowhere that is nearer or more like the center. But circles and spheres will ordinarily put some distance *between* the center and the edge, and thereby allow some points *within* the circle or sphere that are closer to the center. Lings recalls the image of the spider's web, in which "the concentric circles represent the hierarchy of the different worlds, that is, the different planes of existence . . . and the radii

---

9. Proclus, *Commentary on Euclid* 147.12, trans. G. R. Morrow (Wear and Dillon, *Dionysius*, 56).

10. After Plato, *Timaeus* 79a5–e9. Dodds, "Tradition and Personal Achievement," 7, insists, in line with his determination to present Plotinus as an *intellectual* mystic, that Plotinus "prescribes no breathing exercises, no navel-brooding, no hypnotic repetition of sacred syllables." He may not write explicitly of these, but that he made no use of them is unproven.

of the web on the other hand are images of the Divine Mercy."[11] This may be a thought that Plotinus could allow: at any rate he does occasionally insist that there is a natural hierarchy of souls which we should not ignore, though all have a connection to the center.

The metaphor of the king is put forward in the most explicit manner. The One is enthroned, veiled as the Great King (*ho megas basileus*) whose glorious, beautiful court advances in front simultaneously with His progress (*proodos*). Plotinus apparently reckons five ranks apart from the One itself, all arranged according to *timia* or *axia*, or, in Latin, *dignitas*, i.e. dignity, honour or worthiness (cf. V.4.1.39–41, VI.8.7.6–7). That the One or the Good has taken refuge in the realm of Beauty is mentioned in the *Philebus* (64e), and Plotinus has obviously (cf. I.6.9.14–15) been influenced more by the *Phaedrus* (254b) with its description of real Beauty (cf. I.8.2.7–9) enthroned on a pedestal next to Moderation. The ranking is very likely meant to accord with the four circles around the centre as described in the Platonic *Seventh Letter* (342a–343a), so there is more detail or probably yet another analogy in use in Plotinus' metaphorical account of the five ranks. Five ranks of men are, for instance, enumerated in the *Phaedo* (113d–114c), and in the *Republic* (544a–d) five different kinds of societies are correspondingly listed. The further details of the analogy are due to Plotinus' usual three-partitioned hierarchy of hypostases mixed with a description like the one in the *Phaedo* of persons with more or less mastery over themselves and correspondingly, therefore, of more or less worth (cf. II.3.13.20–24, VI.8.12.11–13). Intellect is made the pedestal of the One (cf. VI.7.17.34, VI.8.7.7, IV.8.1.5, Porphyry in *VP* [*Vita Plotini*] 23.12), and all the five ranks reckoned by Plotinus therefore must belong to the hypostasis of Soul, since in the metaphor they are all different kinds of men surrounding the king. First come the lesser ranks in the periphery; secondly, the greater; thirdly, the more majestic (*semnotera*, as appears from III.7.2.6–8: this as well as other predicates cannot be strictly used to designate the king himself, cf. *Parmenides* 142a); fourthly, the court with still more royal dignity (*basilikotera*); and fifthly, the ones who are honoured the most after the king. In the end, the great king of kings reveals himself to all those who have passed through the ranks to him and who did not give up by turning themselves into something less (cf. VI.8.8.8, VI.8.9.18–21, VI.7.42.8–12, *Sophist* 249a, *Second Letter* 312e–

---

11. Lings, *Symbol and Archetype*, 6, citing Schuon, *Treasures of Buddhism*, 34–5.

313a). And they all pray and prostrate themselves before him in an out-spoken Eastern fashion (V.5.3.13).[12]

But these ranks and hierarchies, however significant here and now, are still illusory. God—the One—is not far off from any one of us, nor to be reached only by successive steps up through an imperial bureaucracy. Nothing is really a "long way off" (IV.3 [27].11, 22–3). And God is—in a famous phrase—"a circle whose centre is everywhere and whose circumference nowhere."[13]

In a passage whose debt to Plotinus seems not to have been widely noticed, Buber comments as follows:

> Not the periphery, not the community comes first, but the radii, the common relation to the center. That alone assures the genuine existence of a community. The anchoring of time in a relation-oriented life of salvation and the anchoring of space in a community unified by a common center: only when both of these come to be and only as long as both continue to be, a human cosmos comes to be and continues to be around the invisible altar, grasped in the spirit out of the world stuff of the eon.[14]

The radii that connect the center to the circumference are everywhere the same, and none are longer or shorter than any other—or at least that must be the effect of bringing *our* centers into contact with the true center. *Nous* is King (alongside the One), "but we too are kings [*basileuomen*], when we are in accord with it; we can be in accord with it in two ways, either by having something like its writing written in us like laws, or by being as if filled

---

12. Ousager, *Plotinus on Selfhood*, 218–9. Ousager perhaps exaggerates the likely *political* connotations of this metaphor, though the association cannot be ignored. At any rate I find it implausible that there is any reference here to the ten-year anniversary for the reign of Emperor Gallienus in AD 263, as he reports from Wundt (1919). Did Plotinus even have the emperor in mind? The Greek-speaking East spoke of the emperor as king (*basileus*) though the Latin-speaking West refused to think of him as *rex*. What exactly was conveyed by the title we cannot tell: there were too many differing associations. See Millar, *Emperor in the Roman World*, 613. It is perhaps more likely that the subliminal association in the *Enneads* is the Persian king of kings, as imagined by Greek writers. Should we remember that Shapur defeated Gordian and enslaved Valerian or that Gallienus—Plotinus's patron—notoriously did not seek vengeance?

13. The first *known* use of the phrase is in the twelfth century: see Hudry, *Liber Viginti Quattuor Philosophorum*. The text may be a Latin translation of an Alexandrian handbook, and its assumed association with Hermetic sources may not be mistaken. See also Borges, "Pascal's Sphere." Borges concludes his essay with the comment "perhaps universal history is the history of the diverse intonation of a few metaphors."

14. Buber, *I and Thou*, 161.

with it and able to see it and be aware of it as present" (V.3 [49].4, 1–4). If we manage to be linked to the center, we shall be as gods, but one who stands far off from it is "a multiple human being and a beast" (*anthropos ho polus kai therion*; VI.9 [9].8, 9–10). The circle on which we live must turn back to the center (I.7 [54].1, 23–5), must contract into that center. And the closer we come, it follows, the *less* we shall be going round in circles: a change in the story's implications that I shall stress later, in considering the differences between pagan and Christian themes.

There is a similar Christian rhetoric—for example, in Maximus the Confessor:

> Just as at the center of a circle there is one single point where all the straight lines which come out from it are undivided, in the same way, whoever has been judged worthy of "seeing in God" knows, without concepts and with simple knowledge, all the ideas of created things.[15]

But whereas the Christian hope depends on an ethical commitment and explicit appeal to God through Christ, Plotinus offers instead an imaginative exercise (not unrelated to the ethical commitment). We are to invoke an unknown god by imagining the sphere containing all things stripped of matter, distance, bulk—and then the god will come (on which I shall have more to say below: V.8 [31].9).

But what does this mean in practice? What outcome is he envisaging? As to the latter question, the goal is "what has come into being may become equal, to the extent of its power, by its magnitude to the partlessness of its archetype: for greatness in the intelligible world is in power, here below in bulk" (II.9 [33].17, 8–11). On the one hand—and fitting the metaphor of the kingly court I mentioned—each soul has its own place in heaven; on the other, every one that acknowledges the center is as close to the One as any other—as Dante confirms for us in his *Divine Comedy*.[16]

But what *practice* is implied? We are first of all to orient ourselves in the circumference, breathing in and out, and recalling our attention constantly to the mere fact of attention. Then we are to conceive the cosmos as a sphere, stripped of its bulk and distance, and include ourselves within this image. "What the centre is like is revealed through the lines [i.e., the radii]"

---

15. Jean Hani, *Le symbolisme du temple chretien* (Paris, 1862), 126, quoted by Evdokimov, *Art of the Icon*, 4. See also *Art of the Icon*, 14, on Maximus's use of the image of concentric circles. See also Pseudo-Dionysius, "Divine Names" 821a (*Works*, 99).

16. Dante Alighieri, *Divine Comedy: Paradise* 3.61–96.

(VI.8 [39].18, 18).[17] We have no need to progress inward along the radii—no need, and possibly some harm in making the attempt. Rather, we are to lie open to the rays—and those rays are at once *different* from the One itself and just the same. "It is like a light dispersed far and wide from some one thing translucent in itself; what is dispersed is image, but that from which it comes is truth" (VI.8 [39].18, 35–6). This is a thought that seems to have a clear correspondence to some Upanishadic thought (which is not to claim that there was any historical influence either way, nor that the Upanishads can easily be mined for remarks that sound like Plotinus):

> As in a wheel, all spokes are joined together at the hub and rim; so too, all things, all gods, all worlds, all lives, all separate-seeming selves are joined together in the self.[18]

It is hard to put this vision (*theama*) into words—precisely because there is no duality there, where they have "come together" (VI.9 [9].10, 17–9). A closer historical connection than the Upanishadic is in the Hesychastic tradition of Orthodox Christianity: there is a difference between God's unknowable essence and his *energeiai*, his activity.[19] Those practiced in the Way may be illumined by the light that pours from him, may even *become* that light, but they are not therefore united with God's *essence*. Once again, what exactly this means in practice can only, at best, be discovered by those who practice.

Keiji Nishitani of the Kyoto school of Buddhism also employs the image of circle and circumference, with an added detail.

> One can draw a circle with a centre "A." Then on the circumference of this first circle, one can put a point "a." This point "a" can then become the center of a much smaller circle. Moving from point "A" to point "a," is like a person leaving his or her true Center or home-ground and estab-

---

17. See also V.1 [10].11, 8–15; VI.5 [23].4, 22–5.

18. *Brihadaranyaka Upanishad* 2.5.15 (Wood, *From the Upanishads*, 67). See also *Mundaka Upanishad* 2.2.6: "As in a wheel whose spokes revolve about the centre where they join, so too all feelings, thoughts and acts revolve about pure consciousness, still centre where all joins in one. It's here that differences begin, and here that differences must end. It's here that movement seems to start and come to rest in peace again. Think of this only as your self and cross all dark to light beyond" (Wood, *From the Upanishads*, 194).

19. See Palamas, *150 Chapters*, 243 (chap. 136): "If the substance does not possess an energy distinct from itself, it will be completely without actual subsistence and will be only a concept in the mind." On Palamas in general, see Meyendorff, *Palamas*, though Meyendorff underestimates Palamas's knowledge of the Platonic texts and his philosophical acumen.

lishing an alternative center. This second center, "a," is an ego-center on
the circumference of his or her true existence. . . . It is an identity that
distinguishes oneself from the other points on the circumference. One
appears, in this small circular field of experience, to be a distinct individual separate from others.[20]

And reversing this "fall" is to make the center of that "little circle" coincide
with the greater, acknowledging the *reality* behind our ego-consciousness.

One further problem: the usual point of "drawing a circle" around something is to divide the Inner from the Outer. But if everything is to lie *within*
the circle or the sphere, how can there be anything excluded, or any line of
demarcation? What is "outside" is Nothing—the darkness, perhaps, "that
the gods hate" (V.1 [10].2, 27–8). Or else what is excluded is our own, idiosyncratic, phantom world: "take away everything!" (*aphele panta*; V.3
[49].17, 39). By placing ourselves, in imagination, *within* the circle, we seek
to rid ourselves of private follies and so to reverse the fall in which each
soul, tired of being together, went only to its own (IV.8 [6].4, 10–2). As Heracleitos said, "the waking share one common world, whereas the sleeping
turn aside each man into a world of his own."[21] Time to wake up—but
how?

20. Mitchell, *Spirituality and Emptiness*, 34, after Nishitani, *Religion and Nothingness*, 145.
21. Heracleitos, 22B89DK, cited by Hillman, *Dream*, 133.

CHAPTER FOURTEEN

Charms and Counshcharms

"What art is there, what method or practice, which will take us up there where we must go? Where that is, that it is to the Good, the First Principle, we can take as agreed and established by many demonstrations; and the demonstrations themselves were a kind of leading up on our way [*anagoge tis en*]" (I.3 [20].1, 1–6).

The charms and countercharms that Plotinus urges on us, like those of Socrates in Plato's *Phaedo*, are sometimes rational arguments, which need to be repeated and reexamined and reaffirmed, even though we can see at once that they are valid and compelling. Our problem is that we don't stay convinced by any argument that runs counter to our fears or wishes and need to repeat them to ourselves as firmly as any child repeats his charm against the bogeys he does not believe in.[1]

> This is an illustration of the nature of true opinions: while they abide with us they are beautiful and fruitful, but [like Daedalus's images] they run away out of the human soul, and do not remain long, and therefore they are not of much value unless they are fastened by the tie of the cause; and this fastening [so Plato's Socrates tells Meno] is recollection.[2]

Seeing *why* something is true is needed to transform our opinion into "knowledge," but this seeing is also evanescent. We need constantly to recover it and bring its light into our ordinary doings. This isn't an entirely

---

1. Not children only: "there is a child within us to whom death is a sort of hobgoblin [*ta mormolukeia*]; him too we must persuade not to be afraid when he is alone in the dark" (Plato, *Phaedo* 77e).

2. Plato, *Meno* 98a; see Fine, "Knowledge and True Belief in the *Meno*."

"rational" endeavor. Even the most ardently atheistical or nihilistic thinkers—perhaps especially those ardent atheists—repeat their creeds, proclaim their faith, read and reread their holiest scriptures, denounce sin, gather in groups of the like-minded, and make a ritual of defying heaven, just in case they might be reinfected. Even intellectually, the problem with merely argumentative discourse is that we can never be persuaded by an argument which leads to a conclusion we are determined to resist: all such arguments amount, at best, to refutations of the proffered premises. But even if the balance of conviction momentarily left us believing, we easily lose our grip on premises and argument-form alike. Even if we continue to mouth the conclusion, we most probably reveal our unbelief by inappropriate action or inaction. Those who are fully identified with intellect may be free of all enchantments, "kings," but the rest of us are subject, for good or ill, to rhetoric, music, and the other "psychagogic" arts (IV.4 [28].31, 20–1).

Those arts include "a magical art of love," erotic sorcery,

> used by those who apply by contact to different people magical substances designed to draw them together and with a love-force implanted in them; they join one soul to another, as if they were training together plants set at intervals. They use as well figures with power in them, and by putting themselves in the right postures they quietly bring powers upon themselves, since they are within one universe and work upon one universe. . . . And there is a natural drawing power in spells wrought by the tune and the particular intonation and posture of the magician—for these things attract, as pitiable figures and voices attract; for it is the irrational soul—not the power of choice or the reason—which is charmed by music, and this kind of magic causes no surprise: people even like being enchanted, even if this is not exactly what they demand from the musicians. (IV.4 [28].40, 11–27)[3]

The power of rhetoric is the power of seduction—of exciting desire in its auditors. However firmly we insist to ourselves and others that we are and should be guided solely by rational argument, the lasting success of all such arguments still depends on our being moved to accept them, whether for good or for ill. Newman was right:

> Deductions have no power of persuasion. The heart is commonly reached, not through the reason, but through the imagination, by means

---

3. See also IV.4 [28].43, 16–26: "all practical action is under enchantment."

of direct impressions, by the testimony of facts and events, by history, by description. Persons influence us, voices melt us, looks subdue us, deeds inflame us. Many a man will live and die upon a dogma: no man will be a martyr for a conclusion. A conclusion is but an opinion; it is not a thing which is, but which we are "quite sure about"; and it has often been observed, that we never say we are sure and certain without implying that we doubt. To say that a thing must be, is to admit that it may not be. No one, I say, will die for his own calculations: he dies for realities.[4]

Even the strange art and principle of withholding judgment unless "compelled" to believe and act must be sustained by a yearning for serenity, for a stance immune to refutation, undisturbed by seeming contradiction.[5] Dogmatists have fallen in love with a dogma—but Skeptics are also in love, with a quiet mind. Deduction, even deduction from supposedly "first principles," can never persuade the unwilling. Even direct experience is unconvincing, since it is always up to us how we perceive and describe the experience! Persuasion is always advocacy and is always powered by desire, whether for good or for ill. How shall we understand the arts of rhetoric? How—sometimes—might we be immune to them if we wish to be? And is there any better sort of love?

By the fourth century CE, the Neo-Platonists, making parallels between love and magic, and sophistry, describe a rhetoric of universal sympathetic magic that enacts desire through the manipulation of imaginative images. These images are at one and the same time the physical perceptions of the realm of not-being, spiritual intimations of the realm of being, and the creative psychological capacity to shape responses to both perception and intimation. All relationships are lived through imaginative images that stimulate identity or difference by concretizing the erotic desires of people who define themselves as isolated or joined to others through their investments in and uses of the physical manifestations of those imaginative symbols. Investing themselves in images and their meanings, persons create themselves as rhetorical beings. Thus the authority of physical images rests not in their representation of reality. It consists instead of the lived experience of their meanings and values, their valence within a matrix of social, emotional, and intellectual spheres, which in turn charge the imaginative receptions of those

---

4. Newman, *Grammar of Assent*, 92–3.
5. On which, see my "Living the Pyrrhonian Way."

images, in essence investing them with the daemonic power of cognitive
and emotional force.[6]

Such charms are not used only by sexual predators: rhetoricians, poli-
ticians, advertisers, and con men all practice the art of seduction, and even
poets do. All such seducers tell us what we wish to hear. We need protec-
tion. The good man (the *spoudaios*) will dissolve those enchantments by
"counter-charms and counter-incantations" (though he may suffer death
or bodily illness; IV.4 [28].43, 8–9). Armstrong suggests that those counter-
charms are no more than the philosophical exhortations, the repetition of
sound arguments, so described by Plato in the *Charmides*.[7] Maybe so—but
we need to be clearer about what those exhortations are. Ovid's *Remedium
amoris* is, in a way, entirely rational, consisting of cynical reminders that
the beloved is not *really* beauty herself or a promise of eternity (and it is certainly no less obscene than his earlier *Ars amatoria* nor an apology to Augustus for the offense that, perhaps, he caused). But would Plotinus easily
agree that this "common sense" was accurate (despite his respect for common opinion and democracy)? Consider again Shestov's challenge:

> Many "truths," and the most important ones, cannot obtain recognition
> by all, and most often do not even pretend—this is the most significant
> point—to this recognition.[8]

It may well be that "contemplation" is immune to all enchantment
(IV.4 [28].44, 1), and that the "contemplative" is not seduced by any of
those arts that employ drugs, gestures, postures, or sympathetic forces for
a known end, nor yet by "the magic of nature" (IV.4 [28].44, 30). But this is
not because the contemplative has chosen to disassemble the known beauty
of the beloved, so as to see mere bodily parts or irritating mannerisms. Contemplatives, precisely, do not attend to the mere matter of the thing but
rather to its unity, its grace. They are freed from enchantment not because
they see all things as indifferent or ugly (as though they were "cynics" in a
more modern sense) but because every real thing is beautiful, and such as to
awaken joy in those who really see it. "They exist and appear to us and he
who sees them cannot possibly say anything else except that they are what

6. Marback, "Rethinking Plato's Legacy," 43. See also Marback, *Plato's Dream of Sophistry*.
    7. Armstrong, *Enneads*, vol. 4, 268, citing *Charmides* 156–7.
    8. Shestov, *Potestas Clavium*, pt.1, chap. 6.

really exists. What does 'really exist' mean? That they exist as beauties" (I.6 [1].5, 18–9). "Or rather, beautifulness is reality."[9]

Awakening oneself to the omnipresence of beauty and the grace shed on all real things by the One may be aided by discursive argument (perhaps by thinking through in honesty what our life must be like if we deny that beauty)—but it is more likely that Plotinus intends us to suppose, to realize, that contemplatives will simply *see* the real. John and Mary are mistaken, on Plotinus's account, only because they fail to understand that *every* soul, ambivalently, is Aphrodite (VI.9 [9].9, 28ff.), every creature a child of the One (II.9 [33].15, 33–II.9 [3].16, 10).

If we just have to *see* this, then there seems no advice to give, unless that given in Plato's *Seventh Letter*:

> One must point out to such men [those, that is, like the young tyrant Dionysius of Syracuse] that the whole plan is possible and explain what preliminary steps and how much hard work it will require, for the hearer, if he is genuinely devoted to philosophy and is a man of God with a natural affinity and fitness for the work, sees in the course marked out a path of enchantment, which he must at once strain every nerve to fol-low, or die in the attempt. Thereupon he braces himself and his guide to the task and does not relax his efforts until he either crowns them with final accomplishment or acquires the faculty of tracing his own way no longer accompanied by the pathfinder. When this conviction has taken possession of him, such a man passes his life in whatever occupations he may engage in, but through it all never ceases to practice philosophy and such habits of daily life as will be most effective in making him an intelligent and retentive student, able to reason soberly by himself. Other practices than these he shuns to the end. As for those, however, who are not genuine converts to philosophy, but have only a superficial tinge of doctrine—like the coat of tan that people get in the sun—as soon as they see how many subjects there are to study, how much hard work they involve, and how indispensable it is for the project to adopt a well-ordered scheme of living, they decide that the plan is difficult if not impossible for them, and so they really do not prove capable of practic-ing philosophy.[10]

9. "For this reason being is longed for because it is the same as beauty, and beauty is lov-able because it is being" (V.8 [31].9, 41).

10. Plato, *Letters* VII.340c, trans. Edith Hamilton and Huntington Cairns. That this letter (and the others) are by Plato is impossible to prove. At least they are part of the Platonic tradi-

Plato—if it was he—went on to say, in rebuke to anyone who thought
to offer a written summary of his philosophy, that "acquaintance with it
must come rather after a long period of attendance on instruction in the
subject itself and of close companionship, when, suddenly, like a blaze kin-
dled by a leaping spark, it is generated in the soul and at once becomes self-
sustaining."[11] Maybe all that we can do is hope, with Plotinus, that a god
will turn us round: "if someone is able to turn around, either by himself
or having the good luck to have his hair pulled by Athena herself, he will
see God and himself and the all. . . . He will stop marking himself off from
all being and will come to all the All without going out anywhere" (VI.5
[23].7, 9–10). Somehow the prisoner in Plato's Cave is to be released from
his chains, pulled round and led outside.[12]

Perhaps this was why Amelius wished to visit all the temples, in the
hope that human ritual or divine intervention would transform him. And
maybe Plotinus's reply was simply to be patient: it is up to the gods to
come to us or not.[13] But "it does no good at all to say 'Look to God,' unless one also teaches how one is to look" (II.9 [33].15, 33), nor yet to wait
upon the gods without any idea what those gods might be nor how to wait.
Even those who practice the Buddhism of "Sudden Enlightenment" have a
detailed discipline to prepare the way and at least some hints to help them
recognize enlightenment when they see it!

And perhaps there are other charms available, at least for the irrational
soul: particularly music (IV.4 [28].40, 23–5).

Pythagoras, when he once observed how lads who had been filled with
Bacchic frenzy by alcoholic drink differed not at all from madmen, ex-
horted the *aulete* who was joining them in the carousal to play his aulos
for them in the spondaic *melos*. When he thus did what was ordered,
they suddenly changed and were given discretion as if they had been
sober even at the beginning.[14]

---

tion accepted by Plotinus. That this letter in particular appears to contain a rebuttal of Plato's
own practice is no proof that it's not by Plato: so do *Phaedrus* and *The Republic*! If it is not
Plato's there was another Platonizing philosopher of considerable rhetorical skill and philosophical acumen sometime in the fourth or third centuries BC.

11. Plato, *Letters* VII.341d.
12. Plato, *Republic* 7.513c4–d7.
13. Porphyry, *Life* 10.37.
14. Sextus Empiricus, *Against the Mathematicians* 6.7, trans. Denise Davidson Greaves
(Mathiesen, *Source Readings*, 97). See also Sorabji, *Philosophy of the Commentators, vol. 1,*

In speaking of such charms and magical arts I am perhaps in danger of neglecting the original context of these terms: are they entirely metaphors? Porphyry tells us that "one of those claiming to be philosophers, Olympius of Alexandria, who had been for a short time a pupil of Ammonius, adopted a superior attitude to Plotinus out of rivalry. This man's attacks on him went to the point of trying to bring a star-stroke (*astrobolesai*) upon him out of magic."[15] The attempt, it was said, recoiled, and Plotinus made a joke of it. What happened, we can hardly say. It is at least notable that it seemed *plausible* that someone professing to be a philosopher should attempt such sorceries. Was Olympius possibly also "the teacher and guild-leader of the magicians from Egypt" who persuaded Emperor Valerian "to kill and persecute pure and saintly men as rivals who hindered his own foul, disgusting incantations"?[16] Eusebius, of course, had Christians in mind as those "pure and saintly men . . . [who] were able, by being present and seen, and simply by breathing on them and speaking boldly, to frustrate the schemes of the wicked demons." Gallienus reversed his father's policy once Valerian had been defeated, captured, and enslaved by Shapur (to Eusebius's satisfaction).

Plotinus, it is easy to suppose, had nothing to do with such games, but they were the context of remarks which we now read "metaphorically." Are we confident that there are no malevolent demons or inimical magicians? What grounds our conviction beyond the "common sense" of this particular age? Might we not remember that other ages had their own common sense?

> I remember reading, not without amusement, a severe and trenchant article in the *Hibbert Journal*, in which Christ's admission of demonology was alone thought enough to dispose of his divinity. The one sentence of the article, which I cherish in my memory through all the changing years, ran thus: "If he was God, he knew there was no such thing as diabolical possession." It did not seem to strike the *Hibbert* critic that this line of criticism raises the question, not of whether Christ is God, but of whether the critic in the *Hibbert Journal* is God.[17]

302–4 (13J), for further anecdotes about Pythagoras's use of music, in particular modes, to calm erotic and other frenzy.

15. Porphyry, *Life* 10.1–5 See Merlan, "Plotinus and Magic," and Armstrong's vehement response, "Was Plotinus a Magician?"

16. Eusebius, *History*, 226 (7.10.2).

17. Chesterton, *New Jerusalem*, 104.

At least there are demons in the human heart, and all manner of other beasts there too, as Socrates remarked.[18] The question is, how to tame, defeat, or evict them. And perhaps Plotinus was not entirely right in avoiding his friend's temple crawl. Maybe there was help available even in a short visit: according to Seneca, "Pythagoras declares that our souls experience a change when we enter a temple and behold the images of the gods face to face, and await the utterances of an oracle."[19]

18. Plato, *Phaedrus* 230a. See also *Macarian Homilies* 43.7 (Pseudo-Macarius, *Fifty Homilies*, 222): "The heart is but a small vessel; and yet dragons and lions are there, and there likewise are poisonous creatures and all the treasures of wickedness; rough, uneven paths are there, and gaping chasms. There also is God, there are the angels, there life and the Kingdom, there light and the apostles, the heavenly cities and the treasures of grace: all things are there" (cited by Ware, "How Do We Enter the Heart?," 14).

19. Seneca, *Letters* 94.42.

CHAPTER FIFTEEN

Invoking Demons

Oddly, even the modern philosopher Peter Carruthers, in the course of claiming—implausibly—that there can be no thought without language, acknowledges that "not for nothing have poets traditionally prayed to the Muses for inspiration; for we often have no idea where our genuinely novel ideas come from, nor is there much that we can do intentionally in order to get them. Sometimes a relaxing environment can help—a hot bath, a daydream, or a good night's sleep. But when ideas do come, they seem to us to come of their own accord, often with no discernible history."[1] It may be that Platonists can find better methods.

Plotinus had playful habits (III.8 [30].1). In considering time and its origins, he remarks that "one could hardly, perhaps, call on the Muses, who did not then exist, to tell us 'how time first came out': but one might perhaps (even if the Muses did exist then after all) ask time when it *has* come into being to tell us *how* it did come into being and appear" (III.7 [45].11, 7–10). The Muses are the daughters of Memory (a child of Earth and Heaven and so a sister of Kronos). The term for time, "*chronos*," is conventionally close to "Kronos," the name of the second-generation leader of Hesiod's divine dynasty. Mythographers early agreed that the Titan Kronos was the lord of the golden age before death, disease, and discipline set in, the archetypal melancholiac, and the lord of time. For Plotinus, Kronos is, symbolically, the Intellect, his name formed from "*koros*" (satiety) and "*nous*."[2] Asking Time

---

1. P. Carruthers, *Language, Thought and Consciousness*, 59, 138–9. The claim about thought and language is implausible since it makes the actual acquisition of language, by an individual or the human species, miraculous. This is probably not his intention.

2. III.8 [30].11, 37; V.1 [10].4, 8; V.1 [10].7, 33; V.9 [5].8, 8; after Plato, *Cratylus* 396b. Plutarch, *De Iside et Osiride*, 189 (368–9, chap. 44), suggests that the Egyptian Anubis seems

himself how time came to be amounts to asking Intellect and getting the answer, which Plotinus passes on, that *we* made time as an image of eternity.

> Since there was a restlessly active nature which wanted to control itself
> and be on its own, and chose to seek for more than its present state, this
> moved, and time moved with it; and so, always moving on to the "next"
> and the "after" and what is not the same, we made a long stretch of our
> journey and constructed time as an image of eternity [*aionos eikona ton
> chronon eirgasmetha*]. (III.7 [45].11, 14–9)

This was the first fall, when "we" wanted to be "on our own" (IV.8 [6].4,
11–2), when soul did not want the whole to be present to it all together and
so preferred linear, locomotive, merely local views. We abandoned Now in
favor of anticipated pleasures and remembered wrongs! The Way Back, accordingly, or at least the beginning of that way, is to invoke a vision of the
whole and the god who made it.

> Let us then apprehend in our thought this visible universe, with each of
> its parts remaining what it is without confusion, gathering all of them
> together into one as far as we can, so that when any one part appears
> first, for instance the outside heavenly sphere, the imagination of the
> sun and, with it, the other heavenly bodies follows immediately, and the
> earth and sea and all the living creatures are seen, as they could in fact
> all be seen inside a transparent sphere. Let there be, then, in the soul a
> shining imagination of a sphere, having everything within it, either mov-
> ing or standing still. Keep this, and apprehend in your mind another, tak-
> ing away the mass [*aphelon ton onkon*]: take away also the places, and
> the mental picture of matter in yourself, and do not try to apprehend an-
> other sphere smaller in mass than the original one, but calling on the god
> who made that of which you have the mental picture [*to phantasma*],
> pray him to come. And may he come, bringing his own universe with
> him, with all the gods within him, he who is one and all, and each god is
> all the gods coming together into one. (V.8 [31].9, 1–18)[3]

We have Dillon's testimony that this "works." But what is it, exactly, that
we are being asked to do, and how is the result related to another instruction?

---

to some to be Kronos: "hence he gives birth to everything from himself and conceives (*kyon*)
everything within himself, thus gaining the name of a dog (*kyon*)."

   3. See further Rappe, "Metaphor in Plotinus' Enneads V.8.9."

If one likens it to a living richly varied sphere, or imagines it as a thing all faces, shining with living faces, or as all the pure souls running together into the same place, with no deficiencies but having all that is their own, and universal Intellect seated on their summits so that the region is illuminated by intellectual light—if one imagined it like this one would be seeing it somehow as one sees another from outside; but one must become that, and make oneself the contemplation. But we should not remain always in that manifold beauty, but go on still darting upwards, leaving even this behind. (VI.7 [38].15, 25–VI.7 [38].16, 3)[4]

It would be premature (presumptuous, pretentious) to attempt any outline or description of what that transformation could be like. The question still is: what are we to imagine, and what does Plotinus think will follow? Someone else, as it were, will take up our lives and feeling, if we can persuade it to. Nelson cites one young man's "favorable experience with LSD":

At first the effects were merely interesting—paisley patterns wriggling across blank walls, birds leaving colorful trails as they flew overhead. But when I closed my eyes, something remarkable happened. I was able to see the whole of my worldly ego *from a distance*. I could examine objectively all the games I play to get what I want, the feelings I usually ignore, all the ways I sell out. It was easy to forgive myself, though, because I knew I'd be more authentic from now on. Then all that melted away and then I was confronted by an awesome presence that filled my being—no, it *is* my being, and it is also divine and infinitely loving. It was as if I had known of its presence inside me all along, but somehow had forgotten.[5]

Porphyry tells us that Plotinus once allowed a friend to invoke "a visible manifestation of his companion spirit," and that this turned out to be a

---

4. Armstrong, *Enneads*, vol. 7, 136, suggests that the image of many faces might have been inspired by the sight of "some small Indian image." It seems as likely that the inspiration was Ezekiel's vision of the four living creatures, each with four faces and four wings and each with a wheel full of eyes, before the throne of God (*Ezekiel* 1.4–28). *Merkabah* symbolism has a long Rabbinic history. Scholem remarks: "The throne-world is to the Jewish mystic what the *pleroma*, the 'fullness,' the bright sphere of divinity with its potencies, aeons, archons and dominions is to the Hellenistic and early Christian mystics of the period who appear in the history of religion under the names of Gnostics and Hermetics" (*Major Trends*, 44). Plotinus doesn't explicitly mention these various inmates of the *pleroma*—as it might be the Real Horse or Real Tree which he discusses in VI.7 [38].8–15, but they may be there in his imagination.

5. J. Nelson, *Healing the Split*, 148. Nelson emphasizes that these are not the only possible effects of LSD.

god.[6] This episode apparently led Plotinus to write "on our allotted guardian spirit" (i.e., our *daimon*), a treatise numbered by Porphyry as III.4 [15]. Armstrong prefers to think that his doctrine "has little to do with the superstitions of his time or even with the theology of spirits which is to be found in his Platonist predecessors and successors"[7]—another example of the wish to make Plotinus more "rational" than perhaps he was. As before, the issue is not necessarily to do with the "real world," the world as it was before and will be after us, the world accessible, perhaps, to physics. It has to do with the world of *our experience*. Maybe it will turn out to be relevant only to the world of third-century Mediterranean high society, but it would be rash to assume so. The point of reading ancient authors, after all, is to discover historical possibilities—and perhaps begin to see that our worlds aren't different after all. Phenomenologically, our world is still awash with gods and ghosts and demons. That "they aren't really there" (in the sense that they can't be trapped or weighed or photographed) is not the point. We don't *notice* them, or admit that we have noticed them, because we insist that only tangible creatures count and have forgotten exactly what gods, ghosts, and demons are. Our *actual* experience, rather than what we ordinarily report, flickers with remembered faces, fantasies, and reconstructed conversations.[8] Many of what we call "our thoughts" are not *ours*, as we can discover easily by attempting only the simple task of thinking through a problem or attending to an image: stray memories and random phrases almost always intervene. Learning to hear angels, or demons, is perhaps a matter of *interpreting* what we already hear as divine or daimonic communications,[9] sensing the *same character* in successive interruptions and intrusions into what we falsely imagined was *our* mind. Even our surroundings speak to us. This doesn't answer the question, what exactly did the celebrants in the temple of Isis see? They interpreted whatever it was in the light of literary and ritual convention. Maybe we would have seen things differently, or even suspected a scam.[10] What is it to see a god, a ghost, a *daimon*, or a demon? And if we don't know what it is, how do we know we are not seeing it?

6. Porphyry, *Life* 10. See Proclus, *Alcibiades*, 48 (73).

7. Armstrong, *Enneads*, vol. 3, 140. Cf. Lepajõe, "Demonology of Plotinus."

8. See Armstrong, "Elements," 15: "one of the most important things which [Plotinus] noticed was that there was a great deal in our selves and their experiences which we did not and sometimes could not notice, and that these unnoticed components were not at all insignificant."

9. As Luhrmann (*When God Talks Back*, 72–100) proposes in her investigation of American Baptist Christians, also emphasizing the deliberate *playfulness* of the process.

10. See Dodds, "Theurgy and Its Relationship to Neoplatonism," for a scholarly (and deeply unsympathetic) account of theurgy in general and the Isis story in particular (reprinted in

In the treatise that, perhaps, he wrote in response to the outcome of that séance, Plotinus suggests that for each of us our *daimon* operates at the level immediately above our own. "If the working principle is that by which we have sense-perception, the spirit is the rational principle [*ho daimon to logikon*]; but if we live by the rational principle, the spirit is what is above this, presiding inactive and giving its consent to the principle which works" (III.4 [15].3, 6–8). One in whom *Nous* itself is active is himself a *daimon*, or lives by the *daimon*, and his *daimon* is a god, above even Intellect. According to Iamblichus,

> We also perform such things as [our personal *daimon*] suggests to our intellect, and he continues to govern us till, through sacerdotal theurgy, we obtain a god for the inspective guardian and leader of the soul. For then the *daimon* either yields or delivers his government to a more excellent nature, or is subjected to him, as contributing to his guardianship, or in some other way is ministrant to him as to his lord.[11]

The implication is that Plotinus has so far followed his original *daimon*'s lead (even if he did not act out his "theurgical" discipline) and in so doing has encouraged some being of still higher order to take charge of him.

Armstrong translates *"theos"* as "God," rather than merely as "a god," suggesting that the One itself is all that is above *Nous* in Plotinus's ontology. But clearly the One itself cannot have appeared to order, and even if we neglect any literal reading of the story of the séance (hinting that the audience actually *saw* something), it seems very doubtful that Plotinus could reasonably think that just any good man (*spoudaios*) has only the One for his overseer—unless he means that such a saint lives only in the presence of that One, without any expectation of what to do or be (but that is perhaps quite rare). In our ascent to heaven, we may come to the star "which is in harmony with the character and power which lived and worked in [us] and each will have a god of this kind as its guardian spirit, either the star itself or the god set above this power" (III.4 [15].6, 27–30; see also VI.5 [23].12,

---

Dodds, *Greeks and the Irrational*, 289ff.). It is difficult not to suspect that the hero of Apuleius's *Golden Ass* was the victim of a priestly scam, even if he was also rescued from his ass-hood by divine grace. The gods he "saw," we suspect, were actors in disguise—but why is that incompatible with his really seeing gods? When Catholic Christians see the Eucharistic Christ, are they "in error" if others see only wafers? Are film buffs, even or especially those most inspired by their favorite films, being *deceived* by technological or dramatic artifice? See V. Nelson, *Secret Life of Puppets*, 35–44.

11. Iamblichus, *De mysteriis*, 321–2 (9.4)

32–4). So it is more likely that, at best, the good man's *daimon* is a star-god, not the One—or, rather, is the One only because the One is close to every one of us. Later Platonists, such as Iamblichus and Pseudo-Dionysius, developed complex hierarchies of angels, powers, and principalities to guard their spiritual ascent. Plotinus does not mention these in detail, but we cannot assume that he didn't have them in mind.

> If a man is able to follow the spirit [*daimon*] which is above him, he comes to be himself above, living that spirit's life, and giving the preeminence to that better part of himself to which he is being led; and after that spirit he rises to another, until he reaches the heights. For the soul is many things, and all things, both the things above and the things below down to the limits of all life, and we are each one of us an intelligible universe, making contact with this lower world by the powers of soul below, but with the intelligible world by its powers above. (III.4 [15].3, 18–24)[12]

Soul stretches from the One out to the least of things, and our ascent to heaven is a movement up that line: it would seem to follow that we should hope ourselves eventually to be spirits, or star-gods. We may *imagine* what a star-god or a guardian angel or a visitor from the Galactic Federation (endowed with whatever powers and virtues we admire) might say to us, and in *imagining* that advice we may gradually find it at work in us, may actually begin to see with those new eyes. The *daimon* that oversees us might then seem to be our own "higher self" rather than a distinct being whose life we might come to share.[13] This seems at least to have been what Marcus Aurelius thought: "the spirit which Zeus has given each man as his guardian and guide, a splinter of his own being, is each man's intellect and reason."[14] But it is more likely that Plotinus, like Proclus, thought of the *daimon* as someone or something other than our own self, assigned a more or less difficult role as overseer and, sometimes, guard.[15] We shall do well, perhaps, to test

12. See also VI.7 [38].6, 27–30: "he who is before the soul is more of a spirit (*daimonioteros*), or rather is a god, and a spirit is an imitation of a god, dependent on the god as man is on the spirit; for the being on whom man is dependent is not called a god" (but cf. Porphyry, *Life* 10.19–31). See Plaisance, "Cosmocrators and Cosmic Gods."

13. VI.7 [38].30, 36–9: "what is really worth aspiring to for us is our selves, bringing themselves back for themselves to the best of themselves; this is the well-proportioned and beautiful and the form which is not part of the composite and the clear, intelligent, beautiful life."

14. Aurelius, *Meditations* 5.27.

15. Proclus, *Alcibiades*, 50–1 (76–7): "Those who equate the individual intellect with the guardian spirit of man seem to me badly to confuse the specific character of intellect with the

ourselves against that presence, to act "in the light of eternity" rather than simply follow our own working principle, our usual preference, our own plan of life. The *daimon* probably won't speak to us directly—"to follow about in silence is characteristic of a guardian spirit"[16]—so it is up to us to imagine what it might say, what questions it might pose.

Whichever story we choose, how shall we invoke that *daimon* or that god? We are to gather the visible universe into "a shining imagination of a sphere" and then remove the mass (*aphelon ton onkon*) and the sense of place and matter. It may be that Plotinus's auditors would have heard in this some echo of the ritual for establishing a *templum*, originally a sacred space marked out in the heavens and on the land, from within which auguries may be taken (rather than from the building that might be erected within that sacred space).[17] Similar forms are found elsewhere, whether these are literally constructed or only imagined. How then are we to remove mass, place, and matter? A clue can be found elsewhere, in his description of the visible world's coming to be from the world of intellect: "just as in the formative principle in a seed all the parts are together and in the same place, and none of them fights with any other or is at odds with it or gets in its way; then something comes to be in bulk [*en onkoi*], and the different parts are in different places, and then one could really get in another's way, and even consume it" (III.2 [47].2, 19–23).[18] What is to be imagined away is whatever divides the unity against itself. "Bulk" is impenetrability: the factor that makes it impossible for things fully to occupy the same space. Spatiality is the difference of one place from another. Matter is the chance of being otherwise, so that every corporeal thing is subject to defect and decay. The corporeal world is that of our present experience but depends, so Plotinus thinks, on the intelligible, where nothing is at odds with anything but all together make the living world. *Imagining* this world is locating the real world in ourselves—or rather, it is elevating our own awareness to a level that can grasp the world, if only in imagination, in the hope that this will bring us close enough to God (i.e., the divine intellect).

---

substantial reality of spirit. . . . Souls enjoy intellect only when they turn towards it, receive the light therefrom, and unite their own activity with it; but we receive of the care of the guardian spirit as regards our whole life and existence and way of life, in all the decisions of fate and the provisions of universal providence."

16. Ibid., 110 (165).

17. See Varro, *De lingua Latina* 7.2: "in terris dictum templum locus augurii aut auspicii causa quibusdam conceptis verbis finitus." See Eliade, *Sacred and Profane*; J. Brown, "Templum and Saeculum."

18. See also III.7 [45].11, 22ff.

Consider another exercise:

> Let every soul first consider this, that it made all living things itself,
> breathing life into them. . . . Let it look at the great soul, being itself
> another soul which is no small one, which has become worthy to look
> by being freed from deceit and the things that have bewitched the other
> souls, and is established in quietude. Let not only its encompassing body
> and the body's raging sea be quiet, but all its environment: the earth
> quiet, and the sea and air quiet, and the heaven itself at peace. Into this
> heaven at rest let it imagine soul as if flowing in from outside, pouring
> in and entering it everywhere and illuminating it: as the rays of the sun
> light up a dark cloud, and make it shine and give it a golden look, so soul
> entering into the body of heaven gives it life and gives it immortality and
> wakes what lies inert. . . . Before soul it was a dead body, earth and water,
> or rather the darkness of matter and non-existence, and "what the gods
> hate," as a poet says. (V.1 [10].2, 1, 13–23, 26–8)[19]

The passage from which this is drawn is partly to be understood as argument. "One body lies in one place and one in another, and one is here and
another there; some are separated by being in opposite parts of the universe,
and others in other ways" (V.1 [10].2, 33–4). If they are to be unified, and
subject to a single law, it must be by some *nonmaterial* principle, called
"soul" (*psyche*), "and by its power the heaven is one, though it is multiple
with one part in one place and one in another, and the universe is a god
[i.e., an immortal beauty] by the agency of this soul" (V.1 [10].2, 39–41). In
the absence of such a principle, everything must fall apart, and leave not
even separate bodies—since even the smallest actual body must be unified
by just this nonmaterial, nonextended principle. Modern philosophers and
scientists too often forget how odd it is that things which are by definition
different should somehow embody the same law, that places so far apart
that there has been no contact between them since the very beginning can
nonetheless be sensibly assumed to be homogeneous. What is the glue that
binds all things together, either as individual items or as parts of the greater
whole? Plotinus's answer (and that of other Platonists) is that a nonmate-

19. Quoting the Homeric description of Hades, in *Iliad* 20.65. Elsewhere he suggests that
we might ourselves become "golden" like those who go up into the highlands (V.8 [31].10, 28),
in the desert light. It is more usual for him to suppose that we *are* golden, underneath. Gold is
valued as being incorruptible, however much mud may sometimes cover it: see I.6 [1].5, 43–58.
There was a story among Iamblichus's pupils that he levitated while praying and *turned golden*
(Eunapius, *Lives*, 365–6). Iamblichus thought this (the story) amusing.

rial principle ceaselessly informs all matter in accordance with a single, unified system, which he calls "Intellect and Being": intelligible reality. It is because there is such an order that we have any reasonable hope of understanding the world.[20] The reason there is such an intelligible reality, and one of exactly the form there is, must lie beyond that system. Each layer of Plotinus's universe is called into being in imitation of, or homage to, the higher: an *eikon* even if also quite unlike!

But this set of arguments, here sketchily presented, isn't the essence of the image. Plotinus asks us to *imagine* how "soul" animates what would otherwise be blank darkness, "corpses more throwable away than dung" (V.1 [10].2, 42).[21] The nonmaterial principle he invokes is, in effect, sentience, in all its forms. So also William James:

> We may, if we like, by our reasonings, unwind things back to that black and jointless continuity of space and moving clouds of swarming atoms which science calls the only real world. But all the while the world we feel and live in will be that which our ancestors and we, by slowly cumulating strokes of choice, have extricated out of this, like sculptors, by simply rejecting certain portions of the given stuff. Other sculptors, other statues from the same stone! Other minds, other worlds from the same monotonous and inexpressive chaos! My world is but one in a million alike embedded, alike real to those who may abstract them. How different must be the worlds in the consciousness of ant, cuttlefish or crab![22]

But Plotinus reckons that "the black and jointless continuity" is only what *would* be if there were no soul, no intellect (and even that much can be doubted: it is not "black and jointless" in any *sensible* way, but simply without observable detail or distinction). As it is, the worlds of our experience (and those of ant, cuttlefish, and crab) are ceaselessly being made by sentient involvement. All souls contribute to that work, within the context of the World Soul's action: there is, after all, a single world expanded and

20. The common response, that "universal law" is only a description of what happens universally (so that there must always be such a description, even if it turns out to be very complex), is inconsistent with any notion that such a law *explains* what happens. See Wittgenstein, *Tractatus*, 85 (6.371): "the whole modern conception of the world is founded on the illusion that the so-called laws of nature are the explanations of natural phenomena." See also Lewis, *Miracles*, 63, 90–1. This is not to say that there may not be a better understanding of "laws" as binding principles which *do* explain rather than just describe or—at best—indicate what needs explanation.

21. After Heracleitos 22B96DK.

22. James, *Principles of Psychology*, vol. 1, 288–9.

extended by the lesser souls. The phenomenal world is "an image, always in process of being made" (*ho kosmos eikon aei eikonizomenos*; II.3 [52].18, 17).[23] The soul which is always making and remaking it is "like a farmer who, when he has sown or planted, is always putting right what rainstorms or continuous frosts or gales of wind have spoiled" (II.3 [52].16, 34–5).

If only we can imagine this vast world, compounded of all possible points of view, and realize that there is, in soul and intellect, no *distance*[24] and no *competition* for space or for resources, then we may also achieve a sense of the world's beauty, the single intelligible reality that is ceaselessly mirrored in the awareness of all sentient beings. What would the material world have been like "before" there were individual souls less than the World Soul? What was it like "before" there were souls able to bind time and so recognize "the same thing" in different times and places? What was it like "before" there were even souls to experience the loss and anticipation that ground "past" and "future"? How short or long a time had passed "before" there were souls to count the minutes, hours, or centuries? The questions aren't of any moment for Plotinus, who supposed (in agreement with majority pagan opinion) that the world has been forever, whether it repeated itself or not.[25] The priority of the intelligible world over the many worlds of soul is not chronological. *We* may have a more serious problem, especially if we doubt that there is any single soul present in all the times and places of our universe: in that case, all that can unify experience is the network of souls, seeking common cause and arising out of nowhere. Our best guess, perhaps, is that any world "preceding" soul could only be intelligible reality itself, for which abstract, mathematical description seems the only option. But rather than advance that theory, Plotinus resorts again to prayer:

> Let us speak of it this way, first invoking God himself, not in spoken words, but stretching ourselves out with our soul in prayer to him, able in this way to pray [without distractions, to the One: *monous pros monon*]. The contemplator, then, since God exists by himself as if inside the temple, remaining quiet beyond all things, must contemplate what corresponds to the images already standing outside the temple, or rather that one image which appeared first. (V.1 [10].6, 9–15)

---

23. Armstrong omits a necessary comma between "an image" and "always in process of being made"—*eikonizomenos* qualifies *ho kosmos* (masculine), not *eikon* (feminine).

24. Nothing, as I remarked before, is really a "long way off": IV.3 [27].11, 22–3.

25. The universe "completes its course periodically according to everlastingly fixed rational principles, and everlastingly returns to the same state, period by period" (IV.3 [27].12, 14–5), though Plotinus has some doubts about this Stoic vision.

Why am I speaking of all this as "metaphor"? May it not be "literally" or "straightforwardly" the case that Plotinus expected God, gods, *daimones* to respond to his requests as easily as one man to another?[26] But even if there are "literal" spirits, as real as any other nonhuman creatures, our actual experience of their coming is less clear. Something happens that is *interpreted* as a coming, or an answer, which does not have exactly the same character as an ordinary answer. As I said before, it is not certain which is the more metaphorical: maybe ordinary answers strike us as such only because they have the same enlightening effect as what—to us—are stranger cases. The very first conviction that *there is Someone Else Out There* (whether this is a child's discovery or an adolescent's or just anyone's) is not entirely mediated by our senses. Stranger convictions (strange to us, that is), that the world is "full of signs," that the stars or other auguries can *speak*, may also be, in a way, veridical. So what is it like to "hear" them?

Maimonides, following in this the Arab interpreters of Neoplatonic discourse, supposed that prophets were illuminated by the single "Active Intelligence":

> It must be understood that the true character of prophecy is that of an emanation flowing from God by means of the Active Intelligence first upon the rational faculty and thence upon the imaginative faculty. This is the highest rank attainable by man and the utmost degree of perfection which can be found in his species.[27]

"Scholars of a speculative bent," he goes on to say, may find only their rational faculty affected; "prophetic dreamers," only their imaginations. True prophets are affected in both modes and preach or teach in ways that merely speculative scholars do not trouble themselves to do. Where Maimonides speaks of Moses, Plotinus invokes Minos (VI.9 [9].7), following in this a familiar trope:

> After the establishment of settled life in Egypt in early times, which took place, according to the mythical account, in the period of the gods and heroes, the first, they say, to persuade the multitudes to use written laws was Mneves, a man not only great of soul but also in his life the

26. See also III.8 [30].4, where he considers how "Nature" might respond if someone were to ask her why she makes: "You ought not to ask, but understand in silence." See also Wakoff, "Hushed by Beauty."

27. Maimonides, *Guide of the Perplexed*, 130 (2.36).

most public-spirited of all lawgivers whose names are recorded. According to the tradition he claimed that Hermes had given the laws to him, with the assurance that they would be the cause of great blessings, just as among the Greeks, they say, Minos did in Crete and Lycurgus among the Lacedaemonians, the former saying that he received his laws from Zeus and the latter his from Apollo. Also among several other peoples tradition says that this kind of a device was used and was the cause of much good to such as believed it. Thus it is recorded that among the Arians Zathraustes claimed that the Good Spirit gave him his laws, among the people known as the Getae who represent themselves to be immortal Zalmoxis asserted the same of their common goddess Hestia, and among the Jews Moyses referred his laws to the god who is invoked as Iao. They all did this either because they believed that a conception which would help humanity was marvellous and wholly divine, or because they held that the common crowd would be more likely to obey the laws if their gaze were directed towards the majesty and power of those to whom their laws were ascribed.[28]

Plotinus takes the story seriously, that lawgivers can indeed be inspired rather than merely resourceful. We cannot become such prophets by our own will, however conscientiously we might prepare the ground or polish up the statues. And where is Minos "now"? He is not merely a historical or mythicohistorical figure but our judge in "the underworld," the unseen, Hades, existing on the backside of the globe, or behind our backs.[29] He is himself a *story*, a myth to be woken up in being recounted.[30] And there are other gods to which we might appeal.

The guardian spirit of Socrates, possessing this sort of individual character, I mean one that is purificatory and productive of an undefiled life, and ranked under that power of Apollo which governs simply the whole of purification, restrains Socrates from relationship with the many and the life that extends towards multiplicity, leads him round to the inner portion of the soul and to activity undefiled by contact with the less perfect, and for this reason "never impels but ever deters him." For what else is "to deter" than to restrain him from the many activities that tend

---

28. Diodorus, *History* 1.94, 1–2. See Assmann, *Religio Duplex*, 56–9, on the trope's later history.

29. See also Hillman, *Dream*, 27–50.

30. Plato, *Statesman* 272d5. See Brisson, *Plato the Myth Maker*, 61.

towards externals? . . . The guardian spirit is analogous to Apollo, being
a follower of his, and Socrates' reason to Dionysos, since the intellect
within us is a product of the power of this god.[31]

According to Julian we need Dionysos's inspiration to avoid being shredded
and diverted into many channels.[32] We need, that is, to put an end to *time*,
and so appreciate the Eternal Now rather than—as we most of us mostly
do—waiting impatiently for something else to happen or reworking old
encounters.

But is there some reason to be worried about invoking demons (precisely
because some of them bring with them worries and complaints)? Boyd finds
fault with Augustine for, he says, adopting a Neoplatonic attitude to evil (as
mere negation) rather than acceding to the biblical story that this world is
full of rebel angels.[33] But this is both to misunderstand the role of matter,
and negation, in "evil" and to neglect the presence of "rebel angels" even in
pagan thought. Plotinus was well aware of the confusions that fragment and
surround us. "'Know Yourself' is said to those who because of their selves'
multiplicity have the business of counting themselves up and learning that
they do not know all the numbers and kinds of things they are, or do not
know any one of them, nor what their ruling principle is, or by what they
are themselves" (VI. 7 [38]. 41, 22–6).[34] Those who seek to follow the Delphic instruction—so Hesychios the Priest (c. eighth to ninth century) was to
say—find themselves, as it were, gazing into a mirror and sighting the dark
faces of the demons peering over their shoulders.[35] Porphyry agreed:

31. Proclus, *Alcibiades*, 54–5 (83). O'Neill, commenting on that passage, also cites Proclus,
In Cratylum 100.27–101.3: "Apollo unifies the multitude and gathers it into one: he uniformly
prepossesses every kind of purification, cleansing the whole heavens and birth and all intramun-
dane forms of life; he separates individual souls from the crass layers of matter."

32. Julian, *Oratio* 7.222ab (*Works*, vol. 2, 117).

33. Boyd, *God at War*, 47, 68.

34. Lucian, "On Pantomime," 256, records an anecdote about the pantomime: "seeing five
masks laid ready—that being the number of parts in the piece—and only one pantomime, [a
foreigner] asked who were going to play the other parts. He was informed that the whole piece
would be performed by a single actor. 'Your humble servant, sir,' cries our foreigner to the artist; 'I observe that you have but one body: it had escaped me, that you possessed several souls.'
Most necessary advice, this, for the pantomime, whose task it is to identify himself with his
subject, and make himself part and parcel of the scene that he enacts." There are risks attached
to the enterprise.

35. Palmer, Sherrard, and Ware, *Philokalia*, vol. 1, 123. See also Plato, *Phaedrus* 229b4–
230a6, where Socrates puts aside literal, physicalist interpretations of the creatures of Greek
myth, in favor of asking whether he is himself "a more complex creature and more puffed up
with pride than Typhon."

But wheresoever forgetfulness of God shall enter in, there must the evil spirit dwell. For the soul is a dwelling-place, as thou hast learnt, either of gods or of evil spirits. If the gods are present, it will do what is good both in word and in deed; but if it has welcomed in the evil guest, it does all things in wickedness. Whensoever then thou beholdest a man doing or rejoicing in that which is evil, know that he has denied God in his heart and is the dwelling-place of an evil spirit.[36]

Celsus suggested that whenever we "eat food and drink wine, and taste fruits, and drink even water itself, and breathe even the very air, [we are] receiving each of these from certain daemons, among whom the administration of each of these has been divided."[37] Origen denied the claim, taking "daemons" always to mean evil spirits with whom we feast only when we eat "sacred offerings" and drink wine poured out explicitly in libation to the daemons: it is, he supposed, the angels of God that supervise "the produce of the earth and also all flowing water and air."[38] Celsus and Porphyry alike acknowledged, though, that some features of our daily lives were likely to serve "demons" in the pejorative sense—and this is a notion which we can allegorize with ease. Our diet and more generally our way of life are made possible by our cooperation and compliance with customary institutions, whether or not these are in some way "literally" inspired by distinct spirits, and some of those institutions should be disowned. The problem is, how to do it. "Our wrestling is not against flesh and blood, but against the principalities, against the powers, against the world-rulers of this darkness, against the spiritual hosts of wickedness in the heavenly places."[39] Without a belief in God's providence, and the competing presence of good spirits, we will continue as a battleground of competing spirits, a broken image of the single soul.

> It is not one and the same Goodness that alwaies acts the Faculties of a Wicked man; but as many several images and pictures of Goodness as a quick and working Fancy can represent to him; which so divide his affections, that he is no One thing within himself, but tossed hither and thither by the most independent Principels and Imaginations that may be.[40]

36. Porphyry, *To Marcella*, §§21–2.
37. Origen, *Contra Celsum*, 472 (8.28).
38. Ibid., 474 (8.31).
39. Paul, *Ephesians* 6.12.
40. John Smith (1618–52), in Patrides, *Cambridge Platonists*, 172.

Hesychios's solution—and that of the Orthodox Christian tradition in general—was to invoke the name of Jesus constantly: "whenever we are filled with evil thoughts, we should throw the invocation of our Lord Jesus Christ into their midst. Then, as experience has taught us, we shall see them instantly dispersed like smoke in the air."[41] This solution was not available to pagan Platonists, but maybe they had some similar hopes of properly divine assistance.

41. Palmer, Sherrard, and Ware, *Philokalia*, vol. 1, 178–9. See also Bacovcin, *Way of the Pilgrim*, a nineteenth-century Russian exposition (composed around 1859) of the techniques and prayers advised in *Philokalia*. It is important to add that these techniques, notably the constant repetition of the Jesus Prayer, are to be placed within normal ecclesial discipline.

CHAPTER SIXTEEN

Images Within and Without

My question throughout has been, what is it like to *live* Plotinus's world? And how, and why, to do it? This is to put on one side the merely factual questions, such as whether the stars are living or whether we have many lives. But it is already also evident that mere *storytelling* is not quite the issue. Plotinus was, in his way, entirely naturalistic: "the law says those who fight bravely, not those who pray, are to come safe out of the wars" (III.2 [47].8, 37). Virtue "was not necessary when practising magic. The thought behind this is the firm conviction that magic is something entirely *natural*."[1] The causes and the cures of disease are physical and don't depend on charming demons in or out of us (II.9 [33].14). The very effort Plotinus puts into *imagining* the world depends on his belief that there is a world to imagine. So far from thinking that we can remake the world by reinterpreting it, he is adamant that we really want the truth.

> Certainly the good which one chooses must be something which is not the feeling one has when one attains it; that is why the one who takes this for good remains empty, because he only has the feeling which one might get from the good. This is the reason why one would not find acceptable the feeling produced by something one has not got; for instance, one would not delight in a boy because he was present when he was not present; nor do I think that those who find the good in bodily satisfaction would feel pleasure as if they were eating when they were not eating or as if they were enjoying sex when they were not with the one they wanted to be with, or in general when they were not active. (VI.7 [38].26, 17–25)

1. A. Smith, *Porphyry's Place*, 135.

Fantasy is not what we require, even though our knowledge of reality and our response to it depends on our *imagining* it. It is because he will not accept a merely conventional notion of the truth, that it is only what "we" commonly assert it is, that he rejects the arguments of Skeptics and insists that there is an epistemic condition, a state of soul, the Intellect, which fully contains whatever can be understood. Reality is not apart from Intellect, for if it were, even the Intellect could only appreciate an *image* of reality and never be able to compare what it imagined with the real thing (V.5 [32].1). We need to *believe* in intellect if we are even to reason rightly, since without it there is no right answer to any question we might ask.

> Since, then, there exists soul which reasons about what is right and good, and discursive reasoning which enquires about the rightness [*di-kaion*] and goodness [*kalon*] of this or that particular thing, there must be some further permanent rightness from which arises the discursive reasoning in the realm of soul. Or how else would it manage to reason? And if soul sometimes reasons about the right and good and sometimes does not, there must be in us Intellect which does not reason discursively but always possesses the right, and there must be also the principle and cause and God of Intellect. He is not divided, but abides, and as he does not abide in place he is contemplated in many beings, in each and every one of those capable of receiving him as another self, just as the centre of a circle exists by itself, but every one of the radii has its point in the centre and the lines bring their individuality to it. For it is with something of this sort in ourselves that we are in contact with god and are with him and depend upon him, and those of us who converge towards him are firmly established in him. (V.1 [10].11, 1–15)[2]

I considered the geometrical image in an earlier chapter. Here the question is: what can our imaginings have to do with intellect? Imagination, after all, is something we associate with "inner," "private" thoughts. It is through sense perception, so we now suppose, that we are linked to a common world. Just as we moderns easily succumb to hedonistic theories of value, so we also succumb to sensualist theories of experience and understanding.

But a moment's thought can show us that our *senses* are our own, and that the world revealed through them is *ours*. For each of us, the sense-

2. See my "Plotinian Account of Intellect."

world centers upon us. We see with our own eyes, hear with our own ears, feel with our own skin and organs. As far as sense goes, we are solitary or, at the least, alone: that is, we *might* be the only sentience there is, or else, for each of us, the most important. Of course, we *know* this is not true. From early in our infancy we are taught to say, and even partly to believe, that there are many other sentient beings around, that the world has many faces, that we are not, after all, its center (or not, at any rate, its *only* center). Only occasionally do we fully grasp this truth, realizing that we are also *objects*. This thought may be borne in on us by pain, which is at once a solitary affair and one that quickly convinces us that there are laws not of our choosing. But pain, for those very reasons, is ambivalent: we hardly believe, whatever we say, in *others'* pain, since—as I have remarked before—it plainly doesn't hurt as much (doesn't hurt *us* as much, that is). The route to a wider understanding is, in the end, through intellect—which is not to say, through abstract reasoning. It is our intellectual grasp of the real world that shows us the limits of our linear and parochial view—but to reach that intellectual moment (and it is likely only, in this life, to be a moment) we must reorder our imaginings. We *imagine* what we cannot ourselves sense and seek to bring our limited imaginings into line, as it were, with the universal, to join *our* center to *the* center. Because we can imagine "being someone else," or seeing from another angle, we can begin to form an image of the real things of which our senses give us only partial views.

The way things *look* to us is not the way things *are*. One response has been to think away all aspects of the way things *look* (or sound or feel) that can be shown to depend on us (their "secondary" qualities), till all that is left is "atoms and the void" (all else being merely convention).[3] A further function of this "denuding" or "disenchantment" is to remove all sense of beauty or justice or personal importance, till we "see" things only in the dry, "objective" light denounced by Chesterton, which "must at last wither up the moral mysteries as illusions":[4] the view from nowhere.

Plotinus's answer is different. Reality is "a thing all faces, shining with living faces" (VI.7 [38].15, 27). The right view is not from *nowhere* but from everywhere, or everywhere inhabited by soul. To get close to the real world we need not, on this occasion, pare our senses down but rather build them up. We make "models" of reality to lie behind and "explain" our sensa—and hope that these models "come to life." "The wise men of old . . . made

3. Democritus 68B9 (Sextus Empiricus, *Against the Mathematicians* 7.135); Waterfield, *First Philosophers*, 175–6.
4. Chesterton, *Poet and the Lunatics*, 70.

temples and statues in the wish that the gods should be present to them" (IV.3 [27].11): the temples and statues that they made were richly imagined ones, whether they were entirely "within their minds" or placed out in the world for all to see. The things they made "came alive" for them, and for other people: that is, their audience believed in them.

The soul, Plotinus went on to say, "acts as an interpreter of what comes from the sun to the intelligible sun and from the intelligible sun to this sun, in so far as this sun does reach the intelligible sun through soul" (IV.3 [27].11, 20–2). Maybe this is *merely* allegorical: the soul can use the visible sun to stand for abstract intellect (more easily if we believe the visible world was founded as an image of that "real" world). So also other planets might "stand for" certain values, and the whole array of stars provide a blueprint, properly interpreted, for spiritual growth. "[We] must correct the orbits in the head which were corrupted at our birth" and bring ourselves in line with the celestial pattern.[5] But there is, for the moment, a much simpler reading. The visible sun is and is not the *real* sun, and we become acquainted with that "real" sun by the exercise of controlled imagination. What we merely see, as we now understand it, is an image or echo of something vaster than the earth. *Pace* Heath it is easy to see what Plato meant "by the contrast which he draws between the visible broideries of heaven [the visible stars and their arrangement], which are indeed beautiful, and the true broideries which they only imitate and which are infinitely more beautiful and marvelous."[6] Whether or not it "stands for" something even greater need not be the first thing that we see: it is enough that it "stands for" a celestial being, burning away to itself for longer than terrestrial life. But even this "astronomical" sun is not well imagined without something more.

"What," it will be Question'd, "When the Sun rises, do you not see a round disk of fire somewhat like a Guinea?" O no, no, I see an Innumerable company of the Heavenly host crying "Holy, Holy, Holy is the Lord God Almighty." I question not my Corporeal or Vegetative Eye any more than I would Question a Window concerning a Sight. I look thro' it & not with it.[7]

5. Plato, *Timaeus* 90d.

6. Heath, *Greek Mathematics*, vol. 1, 285, cited by Livio, *Golden Ratio*, 64. Livio goes on to interpret Plato as making a distinction between "the beauty of the cosmos itself and the beauty of the theory that explains the universe." No doubt there is such a distinction, but the simplest distinction is between the stars we see (which are twinkling points of light) and the actual stars themselves, which are not.

7. Blake, "Vision of the Last Judgment" (1810) (*Writings*, 617).

Frye comments that "the Hallelujah-Chorus perception of the sun makes it a far more real sun than the guinea-sun, because more imagination has gone into perceiving it."[8] But the sun does not need our imagining to make it real. What Blake "saw" was the Sun as it is for its innumerable offspring, the totality of vision. The Sun is all around us, literally so, and its being rests not in what it would be if it were "unseen" but in its giving of itself to all within its sphere. The Sun Blake saw is the aggregate of all the suns in every living thing's sensorium, and more. So also with anything else we really try to "see." "There is no poverty or lack of resource there, but all things are filled full of life, and, we may say, boiling with life. They all flow, in a way, from a single spring" (VI.7 [38].12, 23–4).[9]

Were "the wise men of old" making their temples and statues so that the gods might "be present to them" (i.e., to themselves), building internal temples and statues of the sort that Plotinus regularly describes, or were they making, as we say, "actual" statues? The passage, as I remarked earlier, has often been interpreted with reference to the "ancient Egyptian practice of ritually animating statues,"[10] and we are then asked to imagine that later Neoplatonists, at least, expected their ritually animated statues "literally" to move or speak (though lacking all the tissues, organs, sinews that make such movements possible). "Life," we are to suppose, was thought to be a sort of magic fluid, transforming otherwise dull matter into motion. Perhaps all this is so (or perhaps Plotinus thought it was, or might be). But nothing in what he says requires this gloss. The wise men built these statues or these temples so that the gods should be present to them:[11] souls are more easily attracted to reflections of their own nature—that is to say, the souls of the observers or the makers are attracted, and so learn to refine their own image of what's real (and beautiful). John Chrysostom was alert to the dangers, specifically of "the image (*eidolon*) of the mime actress and its effect on the male soul":

8. Frye, *Fearful Symmetry*, 21.

9. See also III.3 [48].7, 10ff.

10. As by Armstrong, *Enneads*, vol. 4, 70–1, after *Asclepius* 37. Johnston, "Animating Statues," observes that the theurgic rituals described do not match known Egyptian practice. Actually, it is not altogether clear that even *Asclepius* refers to a "magical" operation upon objects made of stone, clay, or bronze: the "statues" that they animate may be the wise men themselves or their inner virtues.

11. See also Porphyry, *To Marcella*, §11: "Reason tells us that the divine is present everywhere and in all men, but that only the mind of the wise man is sanctified as its temple, and God is best honoured by him who knows Him best. And this must naturally be the wise man alone, who in wisdom must honour the Divine, and in wisdom adorn for it a temple in his thought, honouring it with a living statue, the mind moulded in His image."

Even when the show is over and she has gone away, the image of her is
stored up in your soul, her words, her gestures, her glances, the way she
walks, the rhythm, the enunciation, the lewd songs.

Webb adds that "Chrysostom is adapting a tradition in which the lover's
mental image of the beloved is depicted as moving and speaking."[12] So may
any of our images.

Even producing a *public* "art object" is a mystery. So Nilus the Scholastic puts words into the mouth of a sculpture: "I laugh because I marvel how,
put together out of all sorts of stones, I suddenly become a satyr."[13] When
what is intended is more than a fantasy, the matter becomes more serious
still. Nilus again: "How daring it is to picture the incorporeal! But yet the
image leads us up to spiritual recollection of celestial beings."[14]

Greatly daring was the wax that formed the image of the invisible Prince
of the Angels, incorporeal in the essence of his form. But yet it is not
without grace; for a man looking at the image directs his mind to a
higher contemplation. No longer has he a confused veneration, but im-
printing the image in himself he fears him as if he were present. The
eyes stir up the depths of the spirit, and Art can convey by colours the
prayers of the soul.[15]

Those who venerate, or at least attend to, icons know more or less what
they are doing. Others may internalize the animated images unconsciously,
and not always—as Chrysostom eloquently declares—to any good effect.
Among the images that we ourselves, in modern times, contain is that of
the hero, which we easily consider the ego[16] and make the subject of all our
endeavors. There is scope for this self-image in Plotinus: he urges us, as I
noted before, to "stand up against the blows of fortune like a great trained
athlete" (I.4 [46].8, 25). But this is not the only image, and not the real subject. So what *are* the images set up in the porch of the temple, or inside our-

12. Chrysostom, *De Davide et Saule* 3, *Patrologia Graeca* 54.697 (Webb, *Demons and
Dancers*, 179).
13. Nilus the Scholastic (fifth century), *Planudean Appendix* (Paton, *Greek Anthology*, bk.
16), epigram 247, quoted by Mathew, *Byzantine Aesthetics*, 76.
14. Nilus, "On an Image of the Archangel" (Paton, *Greek Anthology* 1.34, 1.33), quoted by
Mathew, *Byzantine Aesthetics*, 117.
15. Agathias (536–82) (Paton, *Greek Anthology* 1.34), quoted by Mathew, *Byzantine Aesthetics*, 78.
16. Hillman, *Re-visioning Psychology*, 178.

selves, for us to clean and venerate? Porphyry does not suggest that Plotinus himself had any *corporeal* images set up to venerate: rather the contrary, Plotinus refused Amelius's wish for a portrait of himself.[17] It was enough, apparently, to imagine them, and should have been enough for his disciples too. But such imagined images were probably drawn, as before, from public exhibition—Pheidias's Zeus, Praxiteles's Aphrodite, Heracles, or openly allegorical depictions of *sophrosune* or justice (IV.7 [2].10, 47).[18]

What in particular was Pheidias's Zeus? Molded in gold and ivory, cypress and citron-wood, in the late fifth century BC and stationed in Olympia, it represented Zeus in majesty:

> The god sits on a throne, and he is made of gold and ivory. On his head lies a garland which is a copy of olive shoots. In his right hand he carries a Victory, which, like the statue, is of ivory and gold; she wears a ribbon and—on her head—a garland. In the left hand of the god is a scepter, ornamented with every kind of metal, and the bird sitting on the scepter is the eagle. The sandals also of the god are of gold, as is likewise his robe. On the robe are embroidered figures of animals and the flowers of the lily.[19]

The throne was further surrounded by Victories, Graces, and Seasons, together with images of athletic contests, war, murder, and assault. Aemilius Paulus, according to Plutarch, "was moved to his soul, as if he had seen the god in person," and declared that Pheidias had molded the Zeus of Homer.[20] Did Homer intend what Pheidias intended? Did Aemilius, a Roman general who managed, by Plutarch's account, to combine military intelligence and generosity of spirit, intend the same as either? What did Plutarch himself, or Plotinus, see in the statue, or the verbal description? According to Dio Chrysostom (or at least according to an account he chose to offer—and subsequently deconstruct a little):

---

17. Porphyry, *Life* 1.5–20: Amelius apparently had a portrait drawn in secret by the painter Carterius, presumably to help his own imagination of the greater soul. Porphyry, it is implied, understood better than Amelius that it was Plotinus's *spirit*, not his bodily appearance, that deserved remembrance. See M. Edwards, "Portrait of Plotinus." A similar story is told of the Apostle John and his disciple Lycomedes in the apocryphal *Acts of John* 26–9 (second century). See Tsakiridou, *Icons in Time*, 210–1. John did not even recognize the portrait, never having seen his own reflection.

18. After Plato, *Phaedrus* 247d.

19. Pausanias, *Description of Greece*, vol. 2, 437 (5.11.1). The story went that Zeus himself registered his approval with a lightning strike (443 [5.11.9]).

20. Plutarch, *Aemilius Paulus*, chap. 28 (*Lives*, 431). See Homer, *Iliad* 1.528–30.

Even the irrational brute creation would be so struck with awe if they
could catch merely a glimpse of yonder statue, not only the bulls which
are being continually led to the altar, so that they would willingly submit themselves to the priests who perform the rites of sacrifice, if so
they would be giving some pleasure to the god, but eagles too, and horses
and lions, so that they would subdue their untamed and savage spirits
and preserve perfect quiet, delighted by the vision; and of men, whoever
is sore distressed in soul, having in the course of his life drained the cup
of many misfortunes and griefs, nor ever winning sweet sleep—even this
man, methinks, if he stood before this image, would forget all the terrors
and hardships that fall to our human lot. Such a wondrous vision did
you devise and fashion, one in very truth a "charmer of grief and anger,
that from men all the remembrance of their ills could loose!" So great
the radiance and so great the charm with which your art has clothed it.[21]

The "first conception of God" as Dio Chrysostom represented it
amounts to the elevation of human mind and judgment over the "brute
beasts" of passion and disorder—an elevation that has often been employed also to fight with foreigners and defend imperial control of recalci-
trant *human* populations. Dio perhaps recognized that unfortunate effect,
praising the owl of Athena for having, unavailingly, warned his fellow birds
against humankind's gradual advance in the arts of capture and control. But
the main import of his speech is to suggest that Pheidias displayed in art the
proper conception of God.

His sovereignty and kingship are intended to be shown by the strength
in the image and its grandeur; his fatherhood and his solicitude by its
gentleness and kindliness; the "Protector of Cities" and "Upholder of
the Law" by its majesty and severity; the kinship between gods and men,
I presume, by the mere similarity in shape, being already in use as a
symbol; the "God of Friends, Suppliants, Strangers, Refugees," and all
such qualities in short, by the benevolence and gentleness and goodness
appearing in his countenance. The "God of Wealth" and the "Giver of
Increase" are represented by the simplicity and grandeur shown by the
figure, for the god does in very truth seem like one who is giving and
bestowing blessings.[22]

21. Dio Chrysostom, "Man's First Conception of God" (at Olympia, in AD 97) (*Discourses*,
vol. 2, 57 [12.51]), citing Homer, *Odyssey* 4.221.
22. Ibid., 79–81 (12.77).

This account may subtly alter or diminish the meaning that Aemilius may have seen in the statue—the motif that Virgil epitomized as the duty of Rome, *"parcere subiectis et debellare superbos"* (to spare the defeated and beat down the proud).[23] Dio may also be offering a mild critique of those who thought that it was wrong to imagine the divine in animal, nonhuman, form, even while verbally endorsing that decree. "This unexpected knowledge [of the divine] is indeed more natural for the beasts and the trees than dullness and ignorance are for us"![24]

The chief moral of Dio's discourse, however, is his recognition that great artists like Pheidias fix an image for all those who follow after.

> In times past, because we had no clear knowledge, we formed each his different idea, and each person, according to his capacity and nature, conceived a likeness for every divine manifestation and fashioned such likenesses in his dreams; and if we do perchance collect any small and insignificant likenesses made by the earlier artists, we do not trust them very much nor pay them very much attention. But [Pheidias] by the power of [his] art first conquered and united Hellas and then all others by means of this wondrous presentment, showing forth so marvellous and dazzling a conception, that none of those who have beheld it could any longer easily form a different one.[25]

This may not be entirely a good thing, partly for Plato's reason (that the imagery gives us false expectations of authority) and partly because so successful an image, even if it contains a truth, diminishes too many other truths and spiritual ideals.

On the other hand, the image of Zeus that was internalized in Pheidias's followers might serve as opposition to another image described by Dio:

> [Some] men despise all things divine, and having set up the image of one female divinity, depraved and monstrous, representing a kind of wantonness or self-indulgent ease and unrestrained lewdness, to which they gave the name of Pleasure—an effeminate god in very truth—her they prefer in honour and worship with softly tinkling cymbal-like instru-

---

23. Virgil, *Aeneid* 6.853.

24. Dio Chrysostom, "Man's First Conception of God" (*Discourses*, vol. 2, 37 [12.36]).

25. Ibid., 59 (12.53). See also Purves, *Holy Smoke*, 19: "Sculpture, like music, has a peculiar power to start communicating at the place where logic and experience have to stop. Great statues, like music, speak to small children with a directness not to be underestimated."

ments, or with pipes played under cover of darkness—a form of entertainment which nobody would grudge such men if their cleverness went
only as far as singing, and they did not attempt to take our gods from us
and send them into banishment, driving them out of their own state and
kingdom, clean out of this ordered universe to alien regions, even as unfortunate human beings are banished to sundry uninhabited isles; and all
this universe above us they assert is without purpose or intelligence or
master, has no ruler, or even steward or overseer, but wanders at random
and is swept aimlessly along, no master being there to take thought for
it now, and no creator having made it in the first place, or even doing as
boys do with their hoops, which they set in motion of their own accord,
and then let them roll along of themselves.[26]

Dio's covert attack on an Epicurean and hedonistic materialism (very
unlike Epicurus's own proposals) would probably have been applauded by
Plotinus: neither the idea that the cosmos could be sensibly understood
as a mere confluence of random particles, nor that there is nothing left for
us to seek within this maelstrom than occasional sensual pleasures, could
earn his approval.[27] Neither would he approve the setting up of another deity, another standard. That Dio readily supposes that such an image would
be *female*—would, in effect, be Aphrodite—is not so easily to be endorsed.
"Aphrodite," for Plotinus as for Plato, is a double figure; she represents the
loveliness of every individual soul but may also become vulgar, "a kind of
whore" (VI.9 [9].9, 29–31)[28] if she is envisaged outside the influence of our
Father Zeus. As a much later Platonist remarked:

Visions of these eternal principles or characters of human life appear
to poets, in all ages; the Grecian gods were the ancient Cherubim of
Phoenicia; but the Greeks, and since them the Moderns, have neglected
to subdue the gods of Priam. These gods are visions of the eternal attributes, or divine names, which, when erected into gods, become destructive of humanity. They ought to be the servants, and not the masters of

26. Dio Chrysostom, "Man's First Conception of God" (*Discourses*, vol. 2, 41 [12.36–7]).
27. See, e.g., IV.7 [2].2; V.9 [5].1 (where Epicureans are mocked as heavy, flightless birds).
28. Plato (and Plotinus) seemingly reversed a more plausible evaluation of the double Aphrodite: strictly, the "heavenly" Aphrodite, as the late-born child of Ouranos, is a Titan (one of
the lawless powers whom Olympian Zeus displaced) and the "popular" one, as Zeus's daughter,
has a proper place within the Olympian order. Plato instead jokingly distinguished the "elite"
Aphrodite from the vulgar—possibly a nod toward Athenian aristocratic pederasty. This last
nuance seems not to be what Plotinus has in mind.

man, or of society. They ought to be made to sacrifice to Man, and not
man compelled to sacrifice to them; for when separated from man or
humanity, who is Jesus the Saviour, the vine of eternity, they are thieves
and rebels, they are destroyers.[29]

The Romans, and their many imitators, chose to depict Virtues as
clothed female figures: the four statues ornamenting the Library of Celsus
in Ephesus, remember, are of *arete, ennoia, episteme,* and *sophia.* But we
should remember that these "public" virtues, then and now, are not "real"
virtues. *Sophrosune,* as seen by those who gaze on the divine beauty, is
"not the kind which men have here below, when they do have it (for this is
some sort of imitation of that other)" (V.8 [31].10, 14–6). The detail of Plotinian ethical theory is another story, but we can get some way toward an
understanding of his pedagogic practice by enlisting the aid of more explicit
guides from other spiritual traditions. Consider, for example, Makransky's
summary of Tibetan Buddhist practice:

> Sitting in correct posture on a comfortable seat, one takes refuge (*skyabs
> 'gro*) in Guru, Buddha, Dharma and Saṅgha, receives their blessing envi-
> sioned as light and nectar, and generates the thought of enlightenment
> for the sake of all beings (*sems bskyed*). That thought is the highest pos-
> sible motivation for action (*karma*) of any kind. It directs all the ritual
> activity which follows toward the highest soteriological ends. One then
> recollects the field of karmic merit (*tshogs zhing gsal gdab pa*). A vast
> array of lineage gurus, tantric deities, buddhas, bodhisattvas, *pratyeka-
> buddhas, śravakas, ḍākas, ḍākinīs,* and protector deities is visualized
> and their presence invoked by ritual procedures. Each element of the vi-
> sualization has levels of signification based on Tibetan systematizations
> of Sūtra and Tantra, the whole array being viewed as a manifestation of
> enlightened mind, the gnosis of bliss and void, the inseparability of *bla
> ma (guru)* and *yi dam (iṣṭadevatā)*. Offering one's practices to that "field"
> is said to generate enormous karmic merit, to purify, and to bless, the
> three fundamentals of spiritual progress. In fact, from a Tibetan perspec-
> tive, no meditator is ever alone. A practitioner in "solitary" retreat not
> only visualizes the field of deities, but feels their presence, repeatedly
> entreating them for inspiration and blessing.[30]

29. Blake, "Descriptive Catalogue" (1809) (*Writings,* 571).
    30. Makransky, "Offering in Tibetan Ritual Literature," 318–9. See Beyer, *Cult of Tara.* I
make no apology for including the Tibetan terms: it is important to recognize that Tibetan Bud-

The historical question, whether Plotinus and his friends did something like this, is currently unanswerable and is less important than the psychological, whether such practices have the desired effect, or the philosophical, what they tell us about the way things are—or at least the way we are. The particular terms and images employed by Tibetan Buddhists, of course, are unlikely to be familiar to most inheritors of the European tradition, and there is no need to explore them here—except to note that "light" and "nectar" at least are metaphors we hold in common.

The first thing to note is that the "vast array" of apparently alien presences is nothing strange.

> "Know yourself" is said to those who because of their selves' multiplicity have the business of counting themselves up and learning that they do not know all of the number and kind of things they are, or do not know any one of them, not what their ruling principle is or by what they are themselves. (VI.7 [38].41, 22–7)

The point about visualizing this array is not to summon them from somewhere else but to identify the work they already do in us, and maybe to give them their appropriate ranks. "The Unity of Self" is something, in a way, to be achieved, or eventually uncovered, not merely, placidly, assumed. Finding a new way of seeing is also to find a new way of being.

> Not only must the practitioner visualize the deity as vividly as possible, but he must also, in any ritual of evocation (that is, whenever he generates himself as the deity), exchange for his own ordinary ego the ego of the deity, which is the subjective correlate of the exchange of ordinary appearances for the special appearance of the deity and his retinue of mandalas.[31]

Just as Tibetan Buddhists find a vocabulary for their multiplicity in "lineage gurus, tantric deities, buddhas, bodhisattvas, *pratyekabuddhas*, *śravakas*, *ḍākas*, *ḍākinīs*, and protector deities," so Plotinians found them in Hellenic myth, the myths of Plato, and contemporary culture. The very fact that Armstrong, for example, cited as evidence that Plotinus did not take myths seriously (namely, that he used them inconsistently or strained

dhism (and Buddhism in general) is, for us, an *alien* tradition—as alien indeed as late Hellenic culture—and also that it is still human.

31. Beyer, *Cult of Tara*, 76–7.

their sense) is rather evidence of the use he made of them. The images, the stories, are changed in action, to embody his particular meanings.

And the second thing to note is that for Plotinus as well as for Buddhists and for modern therapists all these images and opinions only float past our attention: they are not of our essence (III.6 [26].15) and must in the end be discarded (which they can't be if we don't know what they are). They are not *only* internal images but also *masks* such as those worn by dancers, and must at last be discarded.

> For while we have been created in the image and likeness of God, it is as a result of our own vice that we put on multiple masks. And just as on the theatrical stage, one and the same actor stands firm and shows Hercules and at another is soft and broken to become Venus, and now quivers as Cybele so do we . . . have as many counterfeit masks as we have sins.[32]

I offer one further gloss on the *sculptural* metaphor. On the one hand, statues are formed, Plotinus supposed, by carving away the unnecessary pieces, revealing the form that exists already within the marble (I.6 [1].9).[33] There is something deep within us that only needs to be revealed, "as the veins of the marble outline a shape which is in the marble before they are uncovered by the sculptor"[34]—a notion of sculpture that is now often forgotten or attributed to other, alien traditions.[35] On the other hand, Plotinus's mention of golden statues obscured by earth suggests a different notion, and a different technique of image-making. It is probable that his "muddy statues" are imagined as if they had been retrieved from a shipwreck or from being buried among ruins (I.6 [1].5, 43–58).[36] But some Neoplatonists might instead have the *cire perdue* technique in mind, in which a wax model is made, encased in clay, and baked.[37] Once the clay has hardened, the liquefied wax is allowed out through a convenient drain and molten gold poured in to set in the pattern fixed by the artist. Thus Herbert:

    32. Jerome, *To Marcella* 43.2.4 (Webb, *Demons and Dancers,* 164). See also Pallis, "Do Clothes Make the Man?," 146, on the actor's risk of "forgetting who he is": "it is only afterwards, when he is restored 'to his right mind' that he discovers the truth of the saying that, after all, 'clothes do not make the man.'"
    33. See also Sen, "Good Times and the Timeless Good"; Ganeri, "Return to the Self."
    34. Leibniz, *New Essays,* 86 (1.1.24).
    35. Harré, *Personal Being,* 88, describes a Kwakiutl theory to the same effect as unlike "our" idea.
    36. In IV.7 [2].10 he may be thinking chiefly of smelting the gold from ore.
    37. Plato, *Republic* 3.387c. See Brisson, *Plato the Myth Maker,* 109.

As Statuaries having fram'd in Clay
An hollow Image, afterwards convey
The molten mettle through each several way;
But when it once unto its place hath past,
And th'inward Statua perfectly is cast,
Do throw away the outward Clay at last,
So when that form the Heav'ns at first decreed
Is finished within, Souls do not need
Their Bodies more, but would from them be freed.
For who still cover'd with their earth would ly?
Who would not shake their fetters off, and fly,
And be, at least, next to, a Deity?
However then you be most lovely here,
Yet when you from all Elements are clear,
You far more pure and glorious shall appear.[38]

What would the moral be of this alternative vision? Whatever it is we make of ourselves is to be transformed into durable, incorruptible substance, revealed when our earthy tegument is broken. We shall all be changed. "Behold, I tell you a mystery; we shall not all sleep, but we shall all be changed, in a moment, in the twinkling of an eye, at the last trumpet; for the trumpet will sound, and the dead will be raised imperishable, and we shall be changed."[39] Or rather, the changes we have ourselves devised will be made permanent. "As the tree falls, so shall it lie."[40]

Or else, just possibly, there is one further possibility:

Flesh fade and mortal trash
Fall to the residuary worm; world's wildfire, leave but ash:
In a flash, at a trumpet crash,
I am all at once what Christ is, since He was what I am, and
This Jack, joke, poor potsherd, patch, matchwood, immortal diamond
Is immortal diamond.[41]

One figure that appears only once in Plotinus's virtual iconography is Hygieia (Health)—and we are likely to miss the reference:

38. Herbert, "The Idea" (1639) (*Poems*, 77–8).
39. Paul, *1 Corinthians* 15.50–52.
40. *Ecclesiastes* 11.3.
41. Hopkins, "That Nature Is a Heraclitean Fire" (*Poems*, 105).

Illness strikes our consciousness harder, but the quiet companionship of
health gives us a better understanding of it; for [she] comes and sits by
us as something which belongs to us and is united to us. Illness is alien
and not our own. (V.8 [31].11, 28–30)[42]

Armstrong's translation is misleading, making the remark frigidly allegorical: the original has a feminine *Hygieia*, and it is *she*, being quietly with us
(*erema sunousa*), who gives us understanding (*sunesis autes*). Is the reference of "*autes*" (of her) to Hygieia or to the soul? Does it make a difference?
Illness, disease, is distracting: the goddess, through her presence, allows us
an awareness that does not distinguish subject and object. It was perhaps
her snake that (it was said) slid under Plotinus's deathbed and disappeared
into a hole in the wall.[43]

42. See also VI.1 [42].10, 62–3.
43. Porphyry, *Life* 2.27–9: snakes were associated with dead heroes (see Bremmer, *Early
Greek Concept*, 80–1), but what Porphyry supposed the significance of this event, I have no idea.
On Hygieia, see Stafford, "Without You No-One Is Happy."

CHAPTER SEVENTEEN

Fixed Stars and Planets

Later Neoplatonists, practicing the art of memory, sometimes chose to use the zodiacal signs, or the thirty-six decans (ten-degree segments) of the zodiacal circle, as "places" to attach their memories.[1] In doing this, they were seen to be reviving an idolatrous devotion to the fixed and wandering stars, to the visible celestials. This "Chaldaean" or "Sabian"[2] religious doctrine seems to exist rather as a back-formation from monotheistic denunciation of idolatry than as any real religious practice. The Olympian gods may give their names to the wandering stars, the "planets" (a list that includes Sun and Moon but not—of course—Earth), and persons mentioned in Greek fables may be pictured in the constellations (irrespective of any merit), but even in Egypt, only the Sun is clearly identified with any god. But maybe there was more to the doctrine than we think.

> Because of those Sabian ideas they put up statues for the stars: golden statues for the sun and silver statues for the moon. . . . They built temples and placed images in them. They claimed that the powers of the planets were emanated onto these images, and those images spoke, understood what was spoken to them, reasoned, [and] gave revelations to people.[3]

1. Thirty-six is also the Pythagorean *tetraktys*, "the greatest oath among them, and was called by them the world, because it is made up of the first four even numbers and the first four odd numbers summed up together" (Plutarch, *De Iside et Osiride*, 239 [382a, §76]). See Origen, *Contra Celsum*, 496 (8.58), for an account of these "Egyptian" daemons, as described by Celsus, each with authority over some particular bodily part and invoked by names such as "Chnoumen, Chnachoumen, Knat," and so on.

2. This is the title that Maimonides accepts for pre-Islamic Arabic writings and for the religion in which Abram (before his name was changed) was at first brought up. See Maimonides, *Guide of the Perplexed*, 175–80 (3.29).

3. Ibid., 177.

Those images may have been those of the worshipers' imaginations (as above)—not magical automata. What is of interest is that the gods they supposedly summoned to themselves were also visible to them as stars. People in "premodern" times lived, literally, under the eyes of heaven. We hardly notice the stars—in part because our city lights obscure them but also because we live on the near side of a religious revolution and no longer easily think of stars as anything but corporeal (witness the problem we have with Blake). Not noticing them, we also do not notice that fixed stars and planets may not have the same significance.

Numenius (whom Plotinus was said by some to have copied) and Amelius (perhaps Plotinus's principal disciple) both seem to have suggested that the soul was corrupted in its descent through the planetary spheres.[4] It was a familiar notion of the time, to which Plotinus himself gestures in speaking of "stripping off" in our ascent to the higher world "what we put on in our descent" (I.6 [1].7, 5–6). The planets, so called because they did not keep the steady onward march of the "fixed stars," could easily be thought perverse, and so (perhaps) responsible for unwelcome features of our terrestrial souls. According to the Hermetic text *Poimandres*, in its ascent "the soul gives back the power of increase and decrease in the first sphere (i.e. the moon), evil plotting in the second (Mercury), lust in the third (Venus), the proud desire to rule in the fourth (the sun), impiety and audacity in the fifth (Mars), greed for wealth in the sixth (Jupiter) and malevolent falsehood in the seventh (Saturn), and escapes the rule of Fate."[5]

Plotinus himself gives a less detailed story—and one that he immediately qualifies:

> In the *Timaeus* the God who makes the world gives "the first principle of soul," but the gods who are borne through the heavens "the terrible and inevitable passions," "angers," and desires and "pleasures and pains," and the "other kind of soul," from which comes passions of this kind. These statements bind us to the stars, from which we get our souls, and subject us to necessity when we come down here; from them we get our moral characters, our characteristic actions, and our emotions, coming from a disposition which is liable to emotion. So what is left which is "we"? Surely, just that which we really are, we to whom nature gave power to master our passions. (II.3 [52].9, 7–16)[6]

---

4. Scott, *Origen and the Stars*, 85ff. See Couliano, *Out of This World*, 188–211.

5. *Poimandres* 1.25, cited by Scott, *Origen and the Stars*, 89. On Ficino's use of the story, see Moore, *Planets Within*.

6. After Plato, *Timaeus* 69c5ff.

Each of us is double, he goes on to say, and our liberty lies in rising to a "higher" world, beyond the planetary spheres or even the highest heavens. That progress upward can be conceived as a successive stripping away of the garments donned in the earlier descent from heaven through the planetary spheres or the four elements.[7] But Plotinus insists that "the sun and other heavenly bodies . . . communicate no evil to the other pure soul" (II.3 [52].9, 35–6), unless perhaps such evil comes from the mixed, double souls of those planets. According to Macrobius, we pick up "reason and understanding" in the sphere of Saturn; "in Jupiter's sphere, the power to act, called *praktikon*; in Mars' sphere, a bold spirit or *thymikon*; in the sun's sphere, sense-perception and imagination, *aisthetikon* and *phantastikon*; in Venus' sphere, the impulse of passion, *epithymetikon*; in Mercury's sphere, the ability to speak and interpret, *hermeneutikon*; and in the lunar sphere, the function of moulding and increasing bodies, *phytikon*."[8] These powers may not be needed while we are among the stars, but they aren't actively maleficent. Plotinus's schema may accommodate both opinions, the more positive one recorded by Macrobius and the negative account from the *Hermetic Corpus*: "what comes from the stars will not reach the recipients in the same state in which it left them" (II.3 [52].11, 1–3).

If it is a loving disposition it becomes weak in the recipient and produces a rather unpleasant kind of loving [*ou mala kalen ten philesin*]; and manly spirit, when the receiver does not take it in due measure, so as to become brave, produces violent temper or spiritlessness [*athumia*]; and that which belongs to honour in love and is concerned with beauty produces desire of what only seems to be beautiful, and the efflux of intellect produces knavery [*panourgia*]; for knavery wants to be intellect, only it is unable to attain what it aims at. So all these things become evil in us, though they are not so up in heaven. (II.3 [52].11, 4–10)

Recall Hildegard of Bingen's claim: before Adam fell, "what is now gall in him sparkled like crystal, and bore the taste of good works, and what is now melancholy in man shone in him like the dawn and contained in itself the wisdom and perfection of good works."[9] And Pseudo-Dionysius: "their fury of anger represents an intellectual power of resistance of which anger

7. Proclus, *Elements*, 307n2, on proposition 209. See also Rist, *Plotinus*, 190–1; IV.3 [27].15.

8. Macrobius, *Dream of Scipio*, 136 (I.13). Macrobius (fr. AD 400) frequently refers to Plotinus but may only have read Porphyry. The *Dream of Scipio* is a surviving story from Cicero's *De Republica* (bk. 6), known through the Middle Ages in Macrobius's commentary.

9. Klibansky, Panofsky, and Saxl, *Saturn and Melancholy*, 80, citing Hildegard of Bingen.

is the last and faintest echo; their desire symbolizes the Divine Love; and in short we might find in all the irrational tendencies and many parts of irrational creatures, figures of the immaterial conceptions and single powers of the Celestial Beings."[10] How are we to reform ourselves? Is it something we can do for ourselves, or must we wait—as Iamblichus, as well as mainstream Christian tradition, insists—for divine assistance? Can we invoke "an intellectual power of resistance" without being wickedly enraged?

Plotinus's objection to the astrology of his day was founded not merely on empirical observation but on his refusal to agree that even the planetary stars could intend any evil, or that we were ourselves bound by astral necessity to do or to be evil.[11] Maybe the stars could serve as *signs* of terrestrial events or characters, but they were not to be conceived as squabbling superpowers, intent on doing us harm, and our "ascent" should not be conceived as shaking off their influence, even if meant discarding or purifying our this-worldly parts.

But his account remains, by modern standards, weird. The stars, unlike all sublunary things, manage to live forever as the individual entities they are.[12] They are not composed, as Aristotle had suggested, of another element, the ether, but of pure fire, and they move in circles because there is nowhere else for them to go now that they are aloft (II.1 [40].3, 13–24).[13] A deeper cause of their motion is "because it imitates intellect" (II.2 [14].1), and the soul that animates them conveys a literally or spatially circular motion to them because she is herself "in orbit" around God (II.2 [14].2, 12–4; II.2 [14].3, 20–2), as also are our "real selves." We are to look toward the example of the heavens to get some sense of what our real lives should be like, or are like. Plato suggested that we "must correct the orbits in the head which were corrupted at our birth,"[14] and perhaps meant chiefly that we should not be distracted from our enjoyment of eternal truth. Plotinus supposed, rather, that our real selves were already thus "in orbit," and that only our lower selves needed the reminder—but what exactly all this means, especially to us, remains obscure.[15] I shall make some attempt to suggest

---

10. Pseudo-Dionysius, *Celestial Hierarchy*, 34. See Louth, *Denys the Areopagite*, 47.

11. See III.1 [3].6, 11: "how could a wicked character be given by the stars, who are gods?"

12. See II.1 [40]. Further on this treatise, see Wilberding, *Plotinus' Cosmology*.

13. Platonists in general opposed the Aristotelian introduction of a fifth element: Origen, *Contra Celsum*, 230 (4.56); Eusebius, *Praeparatio* 15.7.

14. Plato, *Timaeus* 90d.

15. One issue that I shall not address is the supposed contradiction between the truism that the Divine is present everywhere (but contained or restricted nowhere) and that, in some sense, "the heavens" are closer to the eternal. This is not, as Armstrong proposes, a sort of "creeping

what "circular motion" means, in this spiritual sense, and why we should regret that our bodies do not "go round," or that "our spherical parts," our heads, don't "run easily, being earthy" (II.2 [14].2, 18–9). But the problem of how we are to "imitate the soul of the universe and of the stars" (II.9 [33].18, 32) remains. And should we draw any morals from *planetary* motions, whether from the visible shape of their motions or from the nested spheres that are postulated to predict how they will seem to us?

> One must think that there is a universe in our soul, not only an intelligible one but an arrangement like in form to that of the soul of the world: so, as that, too, is distributed according to its diverse powers into the sphere of the fixed stars and those of the moving stars, the powers in our soul also are of like form to these powers, and there is an activity proceeding from each power, and when the souls are set free they come there to the star which is in harmony with the character and power which lived and worked in them. (III.4 [15].6, 22–8)

Other Neoplatonists might also suppose that we have a vehicle, our astral self, in which to "ascend."

> For Neo-Platonists, the vehicle [okhema] fulfills three functions: it houses the rational soul in its descent from the noetic realm to the realm of generation; it acts as the organ of sense-perception and imagination; and, through theurgic rites, it can be purified and lifted above, a vehicle for the rational soul's return through the cosmos to the gods.[16]

But Plotinus expressly and humorously denies the need for any such carriage (I.6 [1].8, 24).[17] We—or at least our true selves—are "There" already. One reason for supposing that we might after all need a "carriage" is also one that he implicitly rejects: our normal awareness does not contain all that we are or could be, and yet those other—currently unrealized—potentials must still have some continuous existence in what is, in effect, the "stuff" of our

---

spatiality" (*Enneads*, vol. 4, 88n1); for a somewhat different take, see Wilberding, "Creeping Spatiality."

16. Finamore, *Iamblichus and the Vehicle of the Soul*, 1.

17. See Corrias, "Imagination and Memory." Plotinus does allow the possibility that souls might be entering earthly bodies from fiery or airy ones (IV.3 [27].9, 5), and that *daimones* (which may be our own "higher" selves: III.4 [15].6) have such bodies (III.5 [50].6, 37). So maybe that is as much as to agree, after all, with a version of the need for a fiery or airy vehicle. See O'Daly, *Augustine's Philosophy of Mind*, 75–9; A. Smith, *Porphyry's Place*, 152–8.

souls. Whether that stuff is ordinarily material, of one substance with flesh
and blood, may be less certain: perhaps it is indeed the airy or fiery "body"
that other Platonists supposed.[18] But Plotinus would deny that—at their
purest—our souls need "remember" anything in that way: whatever is important to the discarnate soul is eternally present to it. Everything "There"
is lucid. Even if, at some lower level, our souls have access to currently
unrealized information, this need not require any distinguishable vehicles.
To use a modern analogy, not all our personal documents need be housed
on our very own PC! Most or all could reside, suitably tagged, within the
common Cloud.

One further descant on these notions would be to suppose that the planets or the planetary spheres represent lesser values, each with their place
and with their devotees. "[The planets] are there precisely for the sake of
the whole living thing, as, for instance, the gall is to serve the whole and in
relation to the part next to it; for it has to stir up the manly spirit and keep
the whole and the part next to it from excess" (II.3 [52].12, 27–9). Plotinus
does not clearly or explicitly give voice to this suggestion, but it may represent something familiar to his first audience. Both al-Farabi and Avicenna
(Ibn Sina), Islamic philosophers much influenced by Neoplatonic thought,
linked the different planetary spheres with descending (or ascending) intellectual forms, thus giving further evidence that astrological forms may embody psychological suggestions.[19] If we cannot quite manage that, we might
at least acknowledge that it is through contemplating the *fixed* stars and
their eternal recurrence that we begin to pass beyond the transient values
of our present life.

But there is a further problem. It is the sun that most often stands for
the proper intellectual value, and the sun that is the center of light for us all.
When Plotinus wishes to speak of the celestials, he names "the sun and the
gods in the sky" (II.9 [33].18, 19), seemingly classing the sun and the fixed
stars together. This now comes so naturally to us that we forget that the
sun, in Ptolemaic astronomy, is the fourth planet outward from the stable
Earth. It lies, in a way, "at the center" of the planetary spheres, but only
because there are three planets below and three above it.[20] And also—in

---

18. See Braude, *Immortal Remains*, 247–8, citing Broad, *Psychical Research*, on what Broad
calls "animism," the belief that souls require an underlying substance as the basis for their
potential.

19. See Netton, *Allāh Transcendent*, 115, 165.

20. Respectively, in the traditional order, Moon, Mercury (Hermes), and Venus (the Morn-
ing Star); Mars (the Fiery), Jupiter (Zeus), and Saturn (Kronos). The order of the planets also
explains the names assigned to the seven days of the week (by Plotinus's time this familiar

a way—the other planetary bodies seem to dance around it, sometimes in advance and sometimes behind, as Julian declared.[21] It would perhaps be symbolically better if the sun were also the center of the whole *material* system—as Copernicus reasoned. And it is the center of Plotinus's own symbology.

> One must not chase after it, but wait quietly till it appears, preparing oneself to contemplate it, as the eye awaits the rising of the sun; and the sun rising over the horizon ("from Ocean," the poets say) gives itself to the eyes to see. But from where will he of whom the sun is an image rise? What is the horizon which he will mount above when he appears? (V.5 [32].8, 3–8)

Plotinus is not unusual in thus honoring the sun as the primary sign and symbol of the first origin of all things. The sun was widely worshiped (or at least honored), by Essenes, by Apollonius of Tyana, and Emperor Vespasian.[22] The cult of Sol Invictus, absorbing Elagabal of Emesa as well as Sol Indigenes of Rome, was publicized under Emperor Aurelian (AD 270–5), after Plotinus's death, in an effort to find a focus for imperial dreams (the figure of the emperor himself having plainly failed to secure an abiding loyalty).[23] Julian, rejecting Constantine's appeal to the Christian churches for support, attempted to reinvent a solar paganism,[24] and some solar rhetoric and celebrations were absorbed into Christian ritual and rhetoric: "thine be the glory, risen, conquering Sun [or Son]."

So our "ascent" should not be conceived as shaking off the influence of the stars, even if we should eventually pass beyond them (III.4 [15].6, 31–3). We must bring the imagined sun within us—or realize that it is already there:

---

arrangement had displaced the earlier Roman eight-day pattern, probably as an astrological conceit rather than by Hebraic influence): each hour of the twenty-four-hour day had its own planetary ruler, following the traditional order around the clock, and the *first* hour of each day dictated which planet governed that particular day. Starting from Saturn, the rule then assigns Sun, Moon, Mars, Mercury, Jupiter, and Venus to each day following. See Zerubavel, *Seven Day Circle*, 16–7, after Dio Cassius, *Roman History* 37.17–9, who also offers, less convincingly, "the principle of the tetrachord" as a possible algorithm to settle the order of the days.

21. Julian, *Oratio 4: Hymn to Helios* 135bc (*Works*, vol. 1, 367).

22. See Stoneman, *Palmyra and Its Empire*, 145–6.

23. Halsberghe, *Sol Invictus*, 132, 135–75. Azize has argued in *Phoenician Solar Theology*, with citations from Mochus of Sidon and Philo of Byblos, that solar theology is a Phoenician invention.

24. Julian, *Oratio 4: Hymn to Helios* (*Works*, vol. 1, 353–442). See R. Smith, *Julian's Gods*, 139–62.

Were not the eye itself a sun,
No sun for it could ever shine:
By nothing godlike could the heart be won,
Were not the heart itself divine.[25]

But even that image must at last be stripped away in a forgetting not far removed from Maimonides's rejection of Sabian idolatry, a movement beyond
the images in the outer sanctuary.[26]

So also did Damascius, writing on *Phaedo* 66d, believe: "The last garment and the one most difficult to cast off is, on the appetitive level, ambition, and on the cognitive level, *phantasia*. Hence even the majority of
philosophers are hampered by these, and especially by *phantasia*. Therefore
Plato here bids the philosopher to strip himself even of this last garment."[27]

But how seriously can we take all this? We may take the *goal* seriously:
to recall and seek to live by the vision of beauty rather than by personal or
parochial concerns. The arts of memory and oblivion may help. We may
even, with some effort, wonder whether it might be right to think of the
stars as living and intelligent beings, with less reason than ourselves not to
be virtuous.

> Why should they not possess virtue? What hindrance prevents them
> from acquiring it? The causes are not present there which make people
> bad here below, and there is not badness of body, disturbed and disturb-
> ing. And why should they not have understanding, in their everlasting
> peace, and grasp in their intellect God and the intelligible gods? Shall our
> wisdom be greater than that of the gods in the sky? (II.9 [33].8, 33–8)[28]

But the specifically astrological aspects of the story are still likely to
be unconvincing. In Plotinus's day, and for many centuries thereafter, we
might meditate on the heavens and expect to get some measure of calm
from their example. The planetary spheres might offer a sort of checklist for

25. Goethe in Goethe and Schiller, *Minor Poems*, after I.6 [1].9, 30–2 (see also Plato, *Republic* 6.508b3–509a1). Douglas Hedley draws my attention to Beierwaltes's work (*Platonismus und
Idealismus*) on the German reception of Plotinus in Goethe and Novalis.

26. See VI.9 [9].11.

27. Cited by G. Watson, *Phantasia*, 125.

28. Origen, *Contra Celsum*, 272–4 (5.11–3), declines to worship the sun, moon, and stars,
but not because he supposes them mere "masses of hot metal." On the contrary, it is because
they too pray to God, through his only-begotten Son, and wait to be delivered from the bondage
of corruption (after Paul, *Romans* 8.19–21).

the things that we should take care to forget, abandon, or correct. But nowadays we know that it is the earth that is revolving (and orbiting a minor star). And we know that the superlunary realm does change: stars too have their predictable life-spans, even if they aren't—quite—living. This is not to repeat the familiar story that our predecessors thought that the earth was significantly central in the scheme of things. Their problem was that they thought that the earth was at the bottom, and *insignificant*.[29] Ours is that the visible heavens are no more than backdrop: we mind far more than our ancestors about *this* life and world, and hardly anyone seeks to remember what we say we believe even about the wider natural world. But it does seem that we can still—occasionally—be moved by thinking of what we still call the heavens. The larger world is the one from which we should take life and light, and learn to forget our troubles.

> Whenever life get you down, Mrs. Brown
> And things seem hard or tough
> And people are stupid, obnoxious or daft
> And you feel that you've had quite enu-hu-hu-huuuuff,
> Just remember that you're standing on a planet that's evolving
> And revolving at 900 miles an hour,
> That's orbiting at 19 miles a second, so it's reckoned,
> A sun that is the source of all our power.
> The sun and you and me, and all the stars that we can see
> Are moving at a million miles a day
> In an outer spiral arm, at 40,000 miles an hour,
> Of the galaxy we call the Milky Way.[30]

This is a more nihilistic and defeatist vision than the Plotinian instruction to "imitate the soul of the universe and the stars" (II.9 [33].18, 31), but it points toward one further way in which our imaginary differs from the ancient. We are in motion. The planetary spheres by which we used to think we were surrounded, and perhaps imprisoned, have vanished.

---

29. Scipio, on his ascent through the planetary spheres, saw "stars which we never see from here below, and all the stars were vast far beyond what we have ever imagined. The least of them was that which, farthest from heaven, nearest to the earth, shone with a borrowed light. But the starry globes very far surpassed the earth in magnitude. The earth itself indeed looked to me so small as to make me ashamed of our empire, which was a mere point on its surface." Cicero, *Republic*, bk. 6, chap. 3, trans. Andrew P. Peabody, accessed 23 December 2014, http://ancienthistory.about.com/library/bl/bl_text_cic_scipiodream.htm.

30. "The Galaxy Song," from Monty Python's *Meaning of Life* (Universal Pictures, 1983).

The novelist John Crowley evokes Bruno's inference from the Copernican Revolution:

> The sky had only begun to pale, and the dimmest stars—or those far-thest off—had disappeared, when the caravan began clambering up the path toward the summit. The great starless darknesses on either hand were not sky but mountains, coming suddenly clear as though they had just awakened and stood up. Between them in the azure there flamed the morning stars. Mercury. Venus. Wet to the knees with snow-melt, Giordano climbed toward them. Earth was a star as they were; and the bright beings who inhabited them, looking this way, saw not a cold stone but another like themselves, aflame in the sun's light. He hailed them: Brother. Sister. A strange and soundless hum seemed to be filling up his ears and his being, as though the dawn itself were to make a sound in breaking, continuous and irreversible. The star he rode was turning pell-mell toward the sun with all of them aboard it, dwarfish stolid carters, chairs, animals, and men; Bruno laughed at his impulse to fall and clutch the hurtling ball with hands and knees. Infinite. You made yourself equal to the stars by knowing your mother Earth was a star as well; you rose up through the spheres not by leaving the earth but by sailing it: by know-ing that it sailed.[31]

When the notion was first invented, "planets" were those points of light that moved in peculiar ways against the background of the supposedly "fixed stars." Our gradual discovery that both fixed and planetary (wan-dering) stars were the visible signs of vast material spheres, that "stars"—including now that planetary sphere, the Sun—shone with their own light, that the other planetary stars did not, and that none of them, except the Moon, revolved around Earth, obscured a still stranger change in intellec-tual perceptions.[32] We had supposed that the heavens were in orderly, cir-cular motion: even the planetary spheres danced backward and forward in a repeating pattern.

31. Crowley, *Aegypt*, 399. See also Eastham, *American Dreamer*, 35: "we are all astro-nauts." See also Galilei, "Starry Messenger" (1610), 45: Earth is "a wandering body surpassing the moon in splendour, and not the sink of all dull refuse of the universe" (cited by Pendergrast, *Mirror Mirror*, 87).

32. See Lewis, *Discarded Image*, for a scholarly and sympathetic account of the signifi-cance of medieval cosmology. M. Ward, *Planet Narnia*, has offered a persuasive argument that Lewis's seven Narnia books were composed to represent the seven planetary spirits, and that this is more than an antiquarian fancy.

Only the earth doth stand forever still:
Her rocks remove not, nor her mountains meet,
Although some wits enriched with learning's skill
Say heaven stands firm and that the earth doth fleet,
And swiftly turneth underneath their feet.[33]

Even now our sensory conviction is indeed that the earth stands still, "a foundation and firm support for those who stand upon it" (II.1 [40].7, 3–5) except when earthquakes happen. We are rarely even conscious that it is a *sphere*: instead, the land stretches out around us, under the dome of heaven.[34] The Other Side of the world, where the sun goes at night, is still Unseen, even though—intellectually—we are aware of the Antipodes, where live those men whose heads *do* grow beneath their shoulders.[35] The fable that "in the Middle Ages" people believed that the earth was flat[36] has this much unintended truth in it: that there were doubts about the Antipodes. Palamas, writing in the late fourteenth century, insisted that the inhabited world is an island, the protruding section of a globe of earth contained within an immensely larger globe of water (echoing here the Egyptian myth that the primeval mound, Atum, emerged from ocean). This was to avoid the possibility that there are other lands and peoples wholly disconnected from Adam's race, separated from us by the supposedly impassable heats of the tropics.[37] Augustine had had a similar

33. John Davies (Gardner, *New Oxford Book of English Verse*, 178).

34. Manilius, *Astronomica* 1.204–46 (writing before AD 14), proved Earth a sphere by noting that different constellations are visible in different latitudes, and that the rising of the moon (and sun) occurs at different times.

35. Shakespeare, *Othello* 1.3.167. Hillman, *Dream*, 39, mentions an Egyptian fable that digestion too is reversed there, so that excrement leaves through the mouths of the antipodean dead—a story making clear the parallel between Plato's reversed world (*Statesman* 269d9ff.) and the Antipodes, and the unvoiced implications of *his* fable.

36. A fable credulously believed by far too many semieducated writers even when it is pointed out that Dante founded his *Divine Comedy* precisely on the image of a spherical Earth! Some ancient writers—including Lucretius (see *On the Nature of Things*, 2)—did imagine that "down" was an absolute direction, and that we lived on the "top" of a cylindrical rock falling forever, along with everything else, but this was a minority opinion only (other writers who held to it were Lactantius and Cosmas Indicopleustes). See J. Russell, *Inventing the Flat Earth*; Numbers, *Galileo Goes to Jail*. See also Furley, "Greek Theory of the Infinite Universe."

37. Palmer, Sherrard, and Ware, *Philokalia*, vol. 4, 349–52 (Palamas, *150 Chapters*, 9–14). See also *Dream of Scipio*: "You perceive also that this same earth is girded and surrounded by belts, two of which—the farthest from each other, and each resting at one extremity on the very pole of the heavens—you see entirely frost-bound; while the middle and largest of them burns under the sun's intensest heat. Two of them are habitable, of which the southern, whose inhabi-

problem with the notion of Antipodeans.[38] Their problem lapsed when it was realized that neither tropic heats nor the wastes of water were really impassable barriers, but we may be similarly concerned, nowadays, by the notion of supposedly rational extraterrestrials: for Christians, the issue may be whether such creatures need redemption; for rationalists in general, whether creatures with an utterly distinct evolutionary history and biological context could reasonably be expected to be "rational" in any recognizably "human" way.

Plotinus and his contemporaries could recognize that they lived upon a sphere, even though they supposed that the heavens revolved around them, in an intelligible order, and that there were intelligences in the heavens with whom they could have some kinds of conversation. Human beings, *daimones* with airy or fiery bodies, planetary intelligences (including, especially, the Sun), and all the star-gods were alike in having contact with *Nous* (as other sublunary creatures maybe didn't). The world, the whole world, as I remarked earlier, was ours in a way that it wasn't for other creatures— since those other creatures had access only to their *own* worlds, their *Umwelten*. But what was the sphere we live on? The Earth that we now believe in rolls round the Sun alongside other planetary spheres: indeed, all those rocky or gaseous spheres we now identify as "planets" are only a subset of the circling rubble, now joined by dwarf planets (including Pluto), moons, asteroids, comets, meteors, and dust. On the empirical evidence yet available, biological organisms are immensely rare contaminants of an essentially unliving and unloving cosmos—and terrestrial life may even be unique. We may *hope* to find new life elsewhere, even new intelligence. We may even fantasize that our descendants could *bring* new life to otherwise unliving worlds. But the overriding myth of the modern West is still that we are alone, in an essentially unhuman world, and that the current condition even of this sublunary realm is molded entirely by chance and "natural selection."

How then shall we enter sympathetically into Plotinus's crowded, beautiful worldscape? How did he think and feel about the Earth we live on? Orthodox Christians rejected the idea that the stars were gods, or even living; likewise, that there was a World Soul. Plotinus apparently accepted both— and that Earth (Ge) is living and even sentient, despite not having the sort of organs that we do (IV.4 [28].26–7).

---

tants are your antipodes, bears no relation to your people" (Cicero, *De amicitia, and Dream of Scipio*, §6).

38. Augustine, *City of God*, 664 (16.9).

One should not consider an earthy body the same when it is cut off from the earth and when it remains connected with it, as stones show, which grow as long as they are attached to the earth but remain the size they were cut when they are taken away from it. One must therefore consider that each part has a trace of the generative soul, and the whole power of growth is diffused over this, and belongs no more to this part or that, but to the whole earth: then comes the nature of sense-perception which is no longer "mixed up with the body" but in contact with it from above; then the rest of the soul and its intelligence, which men, making use of divine revelation and a nature which divines such things, call Hestia and Demeter. (IV.4 [28].27, 8–18)[39]

That stones grow while still part of the earth is not as foolish an idea as Armstrong (for example) thinks it.[40] Stalactites and stalagmites grow in their limestone caverns. Sedimentary rocks have grown and are growing; so also crystals. The very earth is shifting: molten rock forces tectonic plates apart, and they in turn crash into and across each other, making new mountains. Mediterranean peoples, living in an active volcanic region, were more aware of growth and motion in the earth than peoples in the quieter North!

But how does earth live? And what is it to be earth? And what is the earth there [in the intelligible world] which has life? Or rather, first, what is this earth here? That is, what being does it have? It must certainly even here below be a pattern [*morphe*] and a forming principle [*logos*]. (VI.7 [38].11, 18–21)

That Earth is also sentient or intelligent is a more difficult fancy, but this too needs only a slight revisioning: Earth—the circuit of soil and water that we call the land, and also the bitter sea—is not merely *made* by living creatures but is itself, herself, a living system, existing in the interchange of parts, the adjustment of microbial and other action to the changing sunlight. The microbial population of Earth is less divided than are large eukaryotic creatures like ourselves: genetic and other information passes continually between bacteria (both eubacteria and archaebacteria). Any small sample of soil or sea contains unimagined multitudes of microbial and smaller eu-

39. See also VI.7 [38].11, 24–32. Is he distinguishing Hestia as the earth's Soul and Demeter as its Intellect? Probably not: though such allegories are not beyond him, there seems no obvious route to that distinction.

40. Armstrong, *Enneads*, vol. 4, 211.

karyotic life, all working together even when they are acting out the roles of prey or predator. Plants convey information to each other both by airborne chemicals and through the fungal network that connects their roots. "It is necessary that animals should eat each other; these eatings are transformations into each other of animals which could not stay as they are forever, even if no one killed them" (III.2 [47].15, 18–9).[41]

So Earth, considered as a complex of living systems rather than "a Globe rolling thro' Voidness,"[42] is living and responsive to solar, climatic, and internal change. We can reasonably also believe that patterns of response have been devised and selected over many millions of years, and that the memory of these patterns is still contained within the genetic codes we carry: that is, Earth responds to information, in accordance with selected *logoi*, principles. What else—especially for modern reductivists—is sentience or intelligence? The question for an older world system is whether this outward sentience and intelligence is symptomatic of an *interior* order: does Earth have dreams, intentions, reasonings, self-consciousness? Is there anything it is like to *be* Earth?[43] That, it seems, is something more than merely outer responsiveness—but that something more is rarely recognized by modern reductivists even in the case of their ordinarily human neighbors! Granted the difficulty of explaining how conscious experience could be expected to evolve from purely nonconscious beginnings, or life from the unliving (IV.7 [2].2, 16)[44] (and the corresponding absurdity of postulating a purely nonconscious cosmos as an *explanation* of our conscious experience), it may well seem that Plotinus—along with most ancient classical philosophers—has the better part.

But the issue here is not the metaphysical but the phenomenological: what is it like to realize oneself as living within and alongside a much vaster creature, like maggots (*eulai*) within a rotting tree (IV.3 [27].4, 26–30)?[45] And what does Plotinus intend specifically by *Hestia*? Demeter's nature is rela-

---

41. This is not, by the way, a reason for *us* to eat them: see Porphyry, *Abstinence*. Nor do I think Armstrong (*Enneads*, vol. 3, 91) is right to suppose that "for Plotinus man's game is the grim one of killing and being killed, which the wise man will not take seriously and cry over like a child, because it only affects his unimportant lower self." But this is another story.

42. Blake, *Milton* 29, 16 (*Writings*, 516).

43. A notion coined by Sprigge, "Final Causes," and used in the context of an interesting argument for panpsychism by Nagel in "What Is It Like to Be a Bat?"

44. See my *From Athens to Jerusalem*, 121–57; "Minds, Memes and Rhetoric"; "Nothing without Mind."

45. Strictly, it is only our "lower" parts, the body-soul composites we are here-now, that thus inhabit the world tree, while our "higher" or "real selves" might function instead as co-gardeners—but this is not something that most of us now feel.

tively straightforward, as goddess of growing things (and distraught mother
of the abducted Persephone), though this need not dictate the value Plotinus
placed on her (granted his carefree and deliberately shocking way with other
noted deities). But why should Hestia, goddess of the Hearth, the center
of both family and civic life, be identified as the soul of Earth? What does
that tell us about either Earth or Hestia? Popular myth-history about the
supposed dismemberment of a prehistoric Great Mother whose functions
were then distributed among a host of lesser female deities is unlikely to be
helpful here: the evidence for any such prehistorical, monotheistic matriar-
chy is limited, and Plotinus at least had no reason to have noticed it. When
he thinks of our "parent and original" it is as a *father* that he imagines it,
not as a *mother*. Nor is it clear that we can learn much from Jungian analysis, according to which "Hestian themes include sanctity, inwardness, and
deepening," and possibly conservative oppression too.[46] What did Hestia
mean to Plotinus? Hearths are where we sit to tell stories, where we keep
warm, and where we cook (especially, we cook what Demeter provides). According to Plato (if he was serious), Hestia is named either (or both) from *es-
sia* (existence) or from *ôsia* (pushing).[47] More helpfully, he names her as the
only deity to stay "at home in the house of heaven," not joining the grand
processional of the gods[48] (which is to say, she is right here). And Aristotle
identifies the *heart* as the hearth—and citadel—of the body.[49] But the most
obvious reference in Rome is to her Latin analogue, Vesta. Throughout the
classical world the principal hearth intended would be the civic, the center
of a state's devotion, served not by priests or priestesses but by the rulers
of the realm.[50] According to Cicero, "this is the goddess who presides over
our hearths and altars. We always make our last prayers and sacrifices to

46. Jennings, "Tending Hestia's Flame," 216. See also Paris, *Pagan Meditations*.

47. Plato, *Cratylus* 401cd. Vernant, "Hestia-Hermès," 48, makes more of this than can perhaps be justified. Vernant's main theme is to explain a common pairing of Hestia and Hermes,
who together guard the home (at the hearth and at the entrance respectively) and stand in Greek
thought for the contrasted necessities of stability and traffic.

48. Plato, *Phaedrus* 246.

49. Aristotle, *De partibus animalium* 3.670a23. Plotinus, I should acknowledge, sided with
Galen against Aristotle's followers in holding that it was the *brain* rather than the heart that
was the principal organ of perception: IV.3 [27].23. See Tieleman, "Plotinus on the Seat of the
Soul." It may still be true that, phenomenologically and psychologically, we had better think of
ourselves as arising in the heart than simply behind our eyes.

50. See Kajava, "Hestia Hearth, Goddess, and Cult," for the archaeological evidence, principally from second- and third-century AD Sparta. The title *"hestia poleos"* appears to belong not
to a priestess but to a chief lady of the city (perhaps a magistrate's wife or daughter?).

this goddess, who is the guardian of our most private lives."[51] Hestia, in brief, is the focus (which is again to say, "the hearth") of devotion, the sign of proper authority, within our most intimate occasions, and also—as Vernant points out—the place where the human household is joined with the divine.[52] And "Demeter," in this context, may have a similar flavor. Rather than assimilating Hestia to Demeter and reading both as merely forms of an Earth Mother (forgetting that neither Hestia nor Demeter nor the World Soul itself is conceptualized as our mother), it might be better to recall that Demeter too was associated with hearths, in virtue of her employment as a nurse for Demophon of Eleusis (founder of the Mysteries) during her long search for her daughter. She sought to make him immortal, burning away his mortality in the hearth until his suspicious mother interrupted her.[53] So in naming the soul and intellect of Earth as Hestia and Demeter, Plotinus was identifying the whole Earth as our common hearth: the source and sign of sovereignty, the most private place where we *might* be or become immortal, and where there is a link to heaven (as also Demeter promised, via the Mysteries at Eleusis). He is also suggesting implicitly that the whole cosmos is an *oikos*, a household. If that is part of the background meaning of these remarks, is it also significant that the ancient household was divided—or at least it was conventional to *say* that it was divided—between the men's and the women's apartments, the more public and the more private?[54] Or is it rather that the cosmos is a city, and all of us *cosmopolitai*, citizens of the one world?

How much of this can we recall or reconstruct? Is it better to live within

---

51. Cicero, *On the Nature of the Gods*, 150 (2.67). It is difficult to locate any hearths or central fires in Roman houses: in practice, Romans relied on movable braziers instead. So Hestia may be less present in the private house than Vesta in the city.

52. Vernant, "Hestia-Hermès," 48: "Pour le groupe domestique, le centre que patronne Hestia représente bien ce point du sol qui permet de stabiliser l'étendue terrestre, de la délimiter, de s'y fixer; mais il représente aussi, et solidairement, le lieu de passage par excellence, la voie à travers laquelle s'effectue la circulation entre niveaux cosmiques, séparés et isolés. Pour les membres de *l'oikos*, le foyer, centre de la maison, marque aussi la route des échanges avec les dieux d'en-bas et les dieux d'en-haut, l'axe qui fait d'un bout à l'autre communiquer toutes les parties de l'univers." P. Miller, *Biography*, 126–33, notes that Amelius identified Plotinus himself as "our familiar hearth" (Porphyry, *Life* 17.39–40).

53. *Homeric Hymn to Demeter*, 239ff. Plutarch tells a similar story of Isis: *De Iside et Osiride* 16.357c ff.

54. See Plato, *Timaeus* 70b–d, where the gods divide the human thorax "into two parts, as the women's and men's apartments are divided in houses, and placed the midriff to be a wall of partition between them." This division seems not to have been so firm in Roman houses, and even further east there is little evidence of a strong *architectural* barrier between the areas conventionally associated with men or with women. See Nevett, *Domestic Space*, 49; Hales, *Roman House*.

a Christian or post-Christian imaginary, or a revisioned pagan one of the sort that Julian—and Elagabalus[55]—attempted to create? On the former account, the world—the cosmos as a whole and this Earth especially—is only a field of endeavor, having neither authority nor goals of its own. On the latter, it is full of beauties, and its own—her own—program of achievement. On the former account, we may expect to discard Earth—whether by rising up to a real heaven (as Christians, maybe, hope) or by creating new worlds in the skies (as speculative transhumanists expect).[56] On the latter, even though there is an ideal and eternal world which is our real home, this world here is a splendid image of that reality, an inspiration and a real companion.

55. The young Elagabalus of Emesa was briefly emperor (AD 218–22) and sought to join Sol Invictus Elagabal (Emesa's tutelary deity) in marriage to Rome's Vesta (and himself sought to marry a Vestal Virgin). Perhaps rather more of symbolical, or even magical, importance was intended than later historians, insistent that Elagabal was a degenerate fool, could allow. See Halsberghe, *Sol Invictus*, 89–90.

56. See my *Philosophical Futures* and "Futures Singular and Plural."

CHAPTER EIGHTEEN

Waking Up

Socrates describes himself, in Plato's *Apology*, as a gadfly sent to Athens to wake Athenians from their sleep.[1] "Sleep," in this context, meant a failure to engage, even to wish to engage, with their real situation. Being asleep and dreaming, we are content with what *appears*, without asking whether it is true, and convinced accordingly that we *know* what's true. Socrates's task, whether by Apollo's order or his own determination, was to reveal the Athenians' ignorance (and by extension ours). Waking does not, in this case, imply a sudden recognition of any truth wider than our own ignorance: upon waking we know that we know very little, not even (it seems) exactly what we mean by "knowing," "truth," or "waking up." Rationalizing philosophers have sometimes spoken as if Socrates was advancing the claims of "reason" and the duty "to think for oneself": it might be more accurate to suggest that he revealed its limits, or the limits at least of what passes for *our* reason. Gadflies may startle us awake or into frantic action,[2] but the other effect, we are told, of Socrates's elenchus was to silence or to numb his victims, like an electric eel.[3] We wake to find ourselves frozen! Maybe he had larger hopes (or Plato did)—in Shestov's words:

> [Socrates] called himself a gadfly, declared that his role consisted, so to speak, in stinging men up, in transmitting the unrest of which he could not free himself. But even Socrates could not confine himself to this role;

---

1. Plato, *Apology* 30e.

2. According to Plato, *Republic* 9.577, a gadfly goads the soul afflicted by tyrannical desire, filling her with trouble and remorse, but this is not the voice of conscience: it is only that the "tyrannical soul" is never satisfied.

3. Plato, *Meno* 80a.

even he was burdened by the self-evident truths, which he did not dare attack. He awakened and stung men, but he also promised them truth, a new world, where none would sleep but all wake; in other words, he promised to free the old world from the magic of the evil powers.[4]

We may be stung "awake" (at least to the point of realizing that we had been asleep) by philosophical paradox.[5] "To him who is not a dialectician life is but a sleepy dream, and many a man is in his grave before he is well waked up."[6] But this matters only if there is some notion that we *might* at last be free. Maybe, after all, the soul *does* know the intelligibles "because it has them in some way and sees them and is them in a rather dim way, and becomes them more clearly out of the dimness [*ek tou amudrou*] by a kind of awakening [*hoion egeiresthai*], and passes from potentiality to actuality" (IV.6 [41].3, 13–6). But this may not be as easy as we hope.

That insects like the gadfly or the bedbug exist to wake us up was given a more literal meaning in Stoic sermons: what might seem at least a minor evil has its providential justification, in not letting us lie in bed.[7] Clement of Alexandria offered a similarly literal-minded interpretation of the Gospel warning to "watch, for you know not in what hour the Son of Man comes": it is a "warning about the enervating effects of lying too long in bed"![8] But there are other goads than gadflies: the bite of love being one,[9] which also leaves us baffled and speechless before reality, knowing only that till now we had never loved at all, or done anything much worth doing.

> I wonder, by my troth, what thou and I
> Did till we loved? Were we not weaned till then?
> But sucked on country pleasures childishly?
> Or snorted we in the Seven Sleepers' den?
> 'Twas so; but this, all pleasures fancies be.
> If ever any beauty I did see,
> Which I desired, and got, 'twas but a dream of thee.[10]

---

4. Shestov, *Job's Balances*, 3.6.

5. See VI.6 [34].12 on a question's "stabbing" and "striking."

6. Plato, *Republic* 7.534c.

7. Plutarch, *On Stoic Self-Contradictions* 1044d (Long and Sedley, *Hellenistic Philosophers*, vol. 1, 328 [540]); so also Plotinus, III.2 [47].9, 33–5.

8. Clement, *Paidagogos* 2.77–82 (about *Matthew* 25.13), cited by Chadwick, *Early Christian Thought*, 102.

9. VI.7 [38].22, 8–11, after Plato, *Phaedrus* 246a.

10. Donne, "The Good-Morrow" (1633) (*Poems*, 48).

We may hope that waking up will allow us to see things clearly, but perhaps that hope is only another dream: reality may silence us with the discovery that we cannot ourselves see straight.

> To know that one is dreaming is to be no longer perfectly asleep. But for news of the fully waking world you must go to my betters.[11]

Is any further comment possible, or plausible? We may at least make a distinction between, as it were, a humanistic reading of the story and a more strongly metaphysical one (the latter of which also has subjective implications). The simpler, former reading fits well with Aurelius's dictum that our ordinary life is "a dream and a delirium."[12] The world as we imagine it, as we daily interact with it, is full of false values and discriminations, and we are blind to almost everything that is going on, even to what—at some level—we *know* is going on. The normal signs of success, our normal priorities, the distinctions we make between more or less respectable people, more or less welcome organisms—none of these stand up to rational inquiry or Socratic challenge.

> We are unsubstantial dreams, impalpable visions, like the flight of a passing bird, like a ship leaving no track upon the sea, or a speck of dust, a vapour, an early dew, a flower that quickly blooms, and quickly fades.[13]

But "getting up with the body is only getting out of one sleep into another, like getting out of one bed into another" (III.6 [26].6, 73–4). What is needed is to wake up entirely from the body, as Plotinus said he had "often" done (IV.8 [6].1, 1–2),[14] and then found it strange to be once again attached to his particular place and time. This may be delusion: if it is to be reckoned real, we must suppose—as is in any case quite plausible—that the "real world" which is the ultimate occasion for our ordinary seemings is very

11. Lewis, *Four Loves*, 160. See also Rappe, *Reading Neoplatonism*: "Once [the dreamer] realizes the fact about his own creations [that he himself projects the *phantasmata* seen in the dream], he is no longer subject to them."

12. Aurelius, *Meditations* 2.17.1.

13. Gregory Nazianzen, *Orationes* 7.19 (Schaff, *Cyril of Jerusalem and Gregory Nazianzen*, 235).

14. Porphyry, *Life* 23.17–8, says that during Porphyry's stay in Rome, Plotinus attained his goal four times "in unspeakable actuality."

different from those seemings.[15] Strangely, that very notion may now seem more plausible even to would-be "hardheaded" materialists. We can reasonably infer from our progress in creating "virtual realities," shared dreams, that our descendants will be yet more adept at such creations and may be inclined themselves to enter them. From which it seems to follow that most experiences of this liminal century will be strictly fictional, and that we ourselves, here-now, are probably only actors in some highly colored version of our descendants' past![16] If that is imaginably true, maybe the older story is intelligible too.

The older story may even be more acceptable: the argument about the creation of virtual realities, after all, must also apply to any experience, even of the supposedly awakened intelligences of the End Time.[17] Subjective certainty will be something that they know how to engineer, to enable virtual tourists to enjoy a plausible experience of—say—twenty-first-century terrestrial life. The thought is bound to occur to them that their own subjective certainty, of living in the End Times, drawing their energy from any surviving black holes long after the last stars have guttered out, is also something that yet more powerful and alien beings could have engineered. Only when there is a direct and incorrigible connection between experience and reality is the skeptical doubt silenced: if intellect (*nous*) were not the same as what it intuited (*ta noeta*), there will be no truth, "for the one who is trying to possess realities will possess an impression different from the realities, and this is not truth" (V.3 [49].5, 23–5). Only then can we be sure that we are awake. Only when we are fully cognizant of all the *other* faces of the world can we claim to have woken up.

> The waking share one common world, whereas the sleeping turn aside each man into a world of his own.[18]

The people of Plotinus's day were—as we suppose—mistaken: they mistook their dreams for the real waking world and yet still struggled, hopefully, to escape into the unknown beyond. There seems little reason not to suspect that our descendants will reckon *us* mistaken too, in ways that—clearly—we can't now guess or readily predict. Maybe the world is really queerer than we can imagine, and our task here-now is simply not to for-

---

15. See my "Waking-Up."
16. See Bostrom, "Are You Living in a Computer Simulation?"
17. On whom, see Dyson, "Time without End."
18. Heracleitos DK22B89, cited by Hillman, *Dream*, 133.

get that fact. The value of Plotinus's psychotherapeutic strategies does not depend on the truth of his cosmology: rather the reverse—his cosmological speculations are therapeutic images. They may be a good way for us to think even if they are not, "literally," true. Alternatively, we can locate new images in contemporary cosmology, as expressing or transforming our distinctive ways of seeing. Classical stories are replaced by modern myths; recurrent patterns, by one-way transformations; magical manipulations, by mind-altering drugs; demons, by imaginary alien visitors; the planetary spheres, by galaxies bound together by unseen "dark matter"; even the thought that we are asleep and dreaming, by the insidious speculation that we are characters in a virtual drama, composed by the vast intelligences of the Very Far Future universe. What all those images mean for modern sensibility would take another volume to discover. It will be enough here simply to reiterate the strong Plotinian message: "bring back the god in you to the divine in the all."[19] Model your own soul and your view of the world together.

19. Porphyry, *Life* 2.26–7.

PART IV

Understanding the Hypostases

We are each a microcosmic echo of the Whole, containing or represent-ing images of all hypostases (III.4 [15].3, 22): which is to say, whatever realities are relevant to an understanding of the Whole. Although Plotinus names only three hypostases (One, *Nous*, Soul), there are, in effect, at least two others, two other significant players (Matter and Nature). Intellect is the Second Hypostasis of Plato's *Parmenides*, and Soul (our subjective, lin-ear, sensory experience) is the Third. The explanation and focus of both these is the First, the One. Proclus goes further than Plotinus in explain-ing—or radically reinterpreting—the *Parmenides*: form-at-work-in-matter and matter itself are the Fourth and Fifth Hypostases of that dialogue. The further hierarchical complications of later Platonism are beyond my com-petence to unravel: here I address only the Plotinian Five, and do so primar-ily in the *psychological*, rather than the metaphysical, context. This is not to say that metaphysics is unimportant, nor entirely to reject the Plotinian story about reality at large. The latter is at least *consistent* with everything we now think we know about reality and provides a framework and vocabu-lary that are better suited to rational exploration of reality than currently fashionable alternatives (especially naturalistic materialism), despite the as-pects of his world that are perhaps or even certainly mistaken. But whether or not this is true, it also provides a framework and vocabulary for the ra-tional exploration and revisioning of our own experience. "The hypostases are experiences; they are types of consciousness; while therefore they have abstract and objective properties, they have also what we call phenomeno-logical properties."[1] The further complication, which I shall address only tangentially, is that neither Matter nor the One can easily be conceived "hy-postases" at all, since neither have any strictly substantial being.

1. Lloyd, *Anatomy*, 126.

CHAPTER NINETEEN

Matter

A t the start of his treatise "on the three primary hypostases" Plotinus aims to remind us of our own soul's dignity and power, and especially how Soul—our own souls and soul in general—"made all living things itself, breathing life into them" (V.1 [10].2, 2). Accordingly, he asks us (as noted earlier), not only to let "the encompassing body [of the great soul] and the body's raging sea be quiet, but all its environment: the earth quiet, and the sea and air quiet, and the heaven itself at peace" (V.1 [10].2, 14–8). We can hardly avoid supposing this to be a desirable state, the silence needed if we are to attend on God, or so Augustine thought.[1] But Plotinus swiftly reverses the story.

> Let [us] imagine soul as if flowing in from outside, pouring in and illuminating it: as the rays of the sun light up a dark cloud, and make it shine and give it a golden look, so soul entering into the body of heaven gives it life and gives it immortality and wakes what lies inert. And heaven, moved with an everlasting motion by the wise guidance of soul, becomes a "fortunate living being" and gains its value by the indwelling of soul; before soul it was a dead body, earth and water, or rather the darkness of matter and non-existence, and "what the gods hate," as a poet says. (V.1 [10].2, 18–28)

The quiet he has asked us to imagine turns out to be the "darkness of matter and non-existence"—a reversal as shocking as his praise of nakedness, drunkenness, passionate love, dancing, athleticism, and Odysseus! Matter is the Unseen—but how, in that case, do we know enough about it

---

1. Augustine, *Confessions*, 171–2 (9.10 [25]).

to characterize it in the way he does, or to name it "the principle (or begin-ning) of evil" (I.8 [51].6, 33–4)?[2] An intellect that presumes to see "what is not its own" (namely Matter) is not, he says, really intellect (I.8 [51].9, 18–9). Only a sort of "bastard reasoning," in Plato's phrase,[3] can discover it. Seeing darkness amounts to not seeing anything (I.8 [51].4, 31)![4]

So how do we get to this strange notion? There are three aspects to "bare matter" that deserve examination: its passivity, its extension, and what our own interior materiality amounts to. The first two show that matter is a metaphor.

Things like animals or plants or statues are composed of some under-lying stuff organized into a particular shape and form: the animal is com-posed of flesh and blood, the statue of bronze or marble. That stuff can be reorganized—keeping some of its own nature but acquiring a different *substance* in the change. The stuff itself can be literally or theoretically decomposed into yet other stuffs and forms: flesh and blood turns out to be matter in solid or liquid form ("earth" and "water"); bronze is composed of copper and tin melded together into a new metal (VI.1 [42].20, 23–6). In many of these cases we can also distinguish the organized material and the surplus matter, cut or boiled or polished away or (in living organisms) excreted. That surplus may be put to other uses and, even if left alone to decompose still further, has its own shape and texture. Even excrement is not formless—though it may provide the hidden and misleading meta-phor for "matter-just-as-such."[5] Even the elemental states of matter (given their traditional names: earth, water, air, and fire) can be transformed one into another, as their underlying natures shift from dry to moist, or hot to cold, and back again. Aristotle extrapolated—though with many hesi-tations—to the notion of a "prime matter," a stuff underlying at least all sublunary transformations (for the superlunary ether is of another sort en-tirely[6]). Plato had already posited a Receptacle, an Empty Space, in which or on which all forms could be reflected or imposed—and this Emptiness

2. Corrigan, *Plotinus' Theory of Matter-Evil*, offers a detailed and helpful account of the metaphysical arguments about matter in Plotinus and his predecessors; see esp. II.4 [12]; II.5 [25]; III.6 [26]; I.8 [51].

3. Plato, *Timaeus* 52b2, referring to the reasoning that results in the notion of *chora* (space); see II.4 [12].10.

4. See Nikulin, *Matter, Imagination and Geometry*, 6–12.

5. See Wisdom, *Unconscious Origin of Berkeley's Philosophy*; N. Brown, *Life against Death*.

6. Later esotericists proposed that "ether" is the fifth essence, *pneuma*, central to the man-dala of the ordinary four elements. Mainstream Platonists usually ignored it. See Dillon, *Middle Platonists*, 170–1.

of pure receptivity came to be identified with Aristotelian Matter (ignoring the problem posed by ether).[7] In no case can we ever encounter such Mere Matter by itself: it is not a substance, counted alongside the things that it contains or composes, and can have no essential property of its own beyond its universal receptivity.[8] In essence, the initial state of things (not necessarily chronologically) is defined only by the notion that anything at all is possible since nothing is yet actual! But how can this be? All *actual* familiar possibilities rest, precisely, on some actual nature: it is *because* bronze has the nature that it does that it can be transformed into bronze spheres or statues or coins or whatever. If it were of the same nature, say, as sulfur or as wine, it would have quite other destinies. Because we are made of flesh and blood, this material may escape the control of the living being it composes, and we can grow old, sick, and disabled. An indefinitely malleable stuff has at least that much actual nature—that it is, for some reason, indefinitely malleable, a shapeshifter more versatile than Proteus himself, and immune to destruction. And if we emphasize instead that anything at all is always possible, we must ask why it does not seem that just anything at all will happen from one moment or one location to the next. "To attribute the being and structure of this All to accident and chance is unreasonable" (III.2 [47].1, 1–2).

Why does matter—even as this unfettered possibility—"exist" at all, and what is the cause of its adopting just the masks it wears, apparently consistently? And how can it be blamed for any *failure* of formation? If it is real enough to affect the forms of things, then it has its own actual nature—as Plutarch seems to have thought, attributing to "matter" a malevolent spirit at odds with the better creative agency.[9] What can Plotinus mean instead, since he rejects that moral and metaphysical dualism?[10] Is it

7. Plato, *Timaeus* 48e–53b; Aristotle, *Physics* 4.209b; Aristotle, *Generation and Corruption* 2.329a ff. On the late-antique developments of these doctrines, see Sorabji, *Philosophy of the Commentators*, vol. 2, 253–68. See also Algra, *Concepts of Space*; Gill, *Aristotle on Substance*.

8. Burnyeat's ("Idealism and Greek Philosophy") contention that no ancient philosopher could have been an "idealist" since they all admitted the independent existence of "matter" as the necessary partner of "form" founders on this one point: that matter, for Platonists, has no real substantial or mind-independent existence. See Moran, "Idealism in Medieval Philosophy," for the later development of Plotinian doctrine.

9. See Plutarch, *De Iside et Osiride*, 191–9 (chaps. 46–50), describing both Egyptian and Zoroastrian suggestions that there is an independent principle of evil in the world. Plato gave some support to the story, in *Laws* 10.896e ff. Philo more usually suggests that—if there is any "sublunar demiurge"—it must still be an aspect of the one and only God; see Dillon, *Middle Platonists*, 169–4.

10. II.4 [12].2, 9–10; VI.1 [42].10, 60–3; Armstrong, *Enneads*, vol. 6, 46–7. See also Corrigan, "Plotinus and St. Gregory."

not "just" a metaphor, an undue extrapolation from familiar cases? The materiality of any substance rests only in the possibility of its being something else: it does not follow that there is an independently existing stuff whose essence it is to have no actual essence.

> When, for instance, we see an ugly face in matter, because the formative principle in it has not got the better of the matter so as to hide its ugliness, we picture it to ourselves as ugly because it falls short of the form. But how do we know what has absolutely no part in form? By absolutely taking away all form, we call that in which there is no form matter; in the process of taking away all form we apprehend formlessness in ourselves, if we propose to look at matter. (I.8 [51].9, 12–8)

The nearest, at first sight, that we can come to imagining this is as the notion of bare extension, "Space," "three-dimensionality" (to trichei diastaton; VI.1 [42].26, 20–6[11]), the second aspect of "mere matter." Considered simply as a Void, this notion too is imponderable: Epicureans firmly insisted on its weird being, since (they said) motion would be impossible if there were no "empty space" into which more solid things (atoms) could move. A keener metaphysical sight might ask how it is that "atoms" exist at all, and whether in truth they "move": the unbreakable bits, with no internal gaps to make them fragile, may be of any size or shape or even speed (though in principle they all, it seems, fall in one direction, "downward"). The answer seems again to be the mere stipulation that whatever can "possibly" happen does (and so no explanation is ever needed for any particular happening). Stoics, insisting that what did not happen couldn't happen (a dogma logically equivalent to the Epicurean, but having—by conversational implicature—a less fertile crop of happenings), had other problems: there can be no such emptiness, no gaps, within the ordered Cosmos (for that would break the necessary connections between one part and another), but that Cosmos, they supposed, itself floated within emptiness, an infinite extension beyond the walls of the world. Why then, their critics asked, should the Cosmos exist in any one part of that Void and not another? Is it even possible to imagine such a Void, in which—by hypothesis—there are distinct places which yet are absolutely indistinguishable? Once loose in the Void, we cannot tell where we are, nor even how far away from us

---

11. Plotinus here rejects an equation between three-dimensionality and matter, but he may only be speaking of the Stoic conception (which includes "resistance," antitupia).

the Cosmos is! Or rather, the Cosmos is no distance at all from anywhere, since there is no way of "moving" detectably from one point to another, and nothing—precisely—in between any one point and another. Cartesian location too is a use of metaphor: an extrapolation from the simple task of locating one thing by its connections to another to an unimaginable pure location prior to all actual things.

Matter as a universal stuff and Matter as the universal Void itself, in brief, are both metaphors: extrapolations from intelligible relations within an ordered Cosmos, but themselves having no prior existence, either logically or chronologically. If there are things, there are places. If there are things, then there may be lesser things or scraps or scrapes. It does not follow that things are made up of scraps, nor that they occupy an earlier Void. More things are possible than are now actual, and for that very reason we require some explanation for what is *actual* beyond the blank statement that it, along with everything else, is *possible*.

> It may be absurd to strive for victory with so manifest an absurdity by showing that they [i.e., Stoics] give non-being the first rank as that which is most of all being and so rank the last first. The cause of this is that sense-perception became their guide and they trusted it for the placing of principles and the rest. For they considered that bodies were the real beings, and since they were afraid of their transformation into each other, they thought that what persisted under them was reality, as if someone thought that place rather than bodies was real being, considering that place does not perish. . . . The most extraordinary of all is that, though they are assured of the existence of each and every thing by sense-perception, they posit as real being what cannot be apprehended by sense. . . . But if they say they grasp it by intellect, it is an odd sort of intellect which ranks matter before itself and attributes real being to matter but not to itself. (VI.1 [42].28, 3–22)

That place, absence, nothingness are merely a shadow of real being is a radical thought—at odds with the very first beginnings of cosmological speculation in Egypt. The Egyptian story is that in the beginning there was (is) Nothing, within which (for no particular reason) Something, the primeval Atum, came into being and generated from itself four linked pairs of deities (or fundamental principles) that together with Atum make up the primordial Ennead. This in turn produced the many-million-fold extravaganza that we see (including the second Ennead, of Isis and Osiris and their kin). That first Being is the One who became a Million[12] and is bound in the end to be swallowed up again by Nothing (symbolized as the world snake but having no real substance of its own—obviously), since Nothing is the primordial condition and there is no *reason* for anything at all to be. The startling feature of this story, of course, is how closely it corresponds with modern cosmological theory, though respectable cosmologists nowadays would prefer to neutralize even the faint hints of "personality" and "agency" in the story that they tell. The metaphors that cosmologists use may vary: for whatever reason moderns typically refer to "the Big Bang" (while denying that this was an explosion into an existing, empty space), while the Egyptians spoke of Atum's ejaculation, and others might as easily have thought of the primordial bulb's blossoming. But the story—whatever its particular versions—has always been vulnerable to the obvious responses: if there was ever Nothing, how could it ever be Something? Even if we stipulate that the Nothingness somehow *allows* for Anything, there must by that very fact have been some tracery or pattern to promote those possibilities.[13] How indeed could we ever, without self-contradiction, speak as if there were once, or ever could be, Nothing, as if "Nothing" names another of the things there are? Parmenides's revelation was that there must, on the contrary, always be *Something*: there *being* Nothing is a contradiction.[14] Nor could there be gaps within that Something (as the Stoics also saw)—but also there could really be no *distance*. I may imagine that New Zealand is very far away, in the Antipodes, but—obviously—it is not *essentially* "far away": insofar as it exists at all, it exists in its own presence and locality. Nothing can ever "go away," because it is bound always to be "here."[15] Can we even place things in a Cartesian array, no longer judging them as being "near" or "far away"

12. See also Chittick, *Sufi Path*, 133: "though Being is One Entity, the entities of the possible things have made It many, so It is the One/Many (*al-wahid al-kathir*)." Cited by Samsel, "Unity with Distinctions," 210.

13. See Wood, *From the Upanishads*, 272 (*Rig Veda* 10.129.4): "what is this seeming nothingness? It is the absence of apparent things, not of reality."

14. "If any man thinks he Can think well Enough how there should be nothing I'll engage that what he means by nothing is as much something as any thing that ever he thought of in his Life"; Jonathan Edwards (1703–58) (*Basic Writings*, 45–6).

15. The *Blue Cliff Record* (*Hekiganroku*), a collection of Ch'an koans compiled in China by Yuanwu Kegin (1063–1135), contains the following story ("Case 53"): "When Great Master Ba (709–788) and Hyakujô were walking together, they saw a wild duck fly past. Master Ba said, 'What's that?' Hyakujô said, 'A wild duck.' Master Ba said, 'Where did it go?' Hyakujô said, 'It flew away.' Master Ba twisted Hyakujô's nose. Hyakujô cried out in pain. Master Ba said, 'Where has it ever flown away?'" See *Open Buddha*, accessed 23 December 2014, http://www.open buddha.com/resources/koans/blue-cliff-record.html. My gloss on this may not be the original intention nor the customary interpretation.

but only as occupying one mathematically defined locus or another? This too has its problems: if the loci are indeed distinct (and it is part of their very definition that they must be), how can it also be true that they must also obey the same laws as each other or allow the same properties to be instantiated? Why should one place be like any other if the very point and nature of a place are exactly *not* to be another?

The mistake is to imagine

> a space and place, a kind of vast emptiness, and then, when the space is already there, we bring this nature [being] into the place which has come to be or is in our imagination [*phantasia*], and bringing it into this kind of place we enquire in this way as if into whence and how it came here, and as if it were a stranger we have asked about its presences and in a way its substance, really just as if we thought that it had been thrown up from some depth or down from some height. Therefore one must remove the cause of the difficulty by excluding from our concentrated gaze upon it all place, and not put it in any place either as resting and settled in it or as having come to it, but [think of it] as being what it is (this is said by the necessity of speech), but that place, like everything else is afterwards, and last of all afterwards. (VI.8 [39].11, 15–28)

In imagining Being—in the exercise I have mentioned often before (V.8 [31].9, 1–15)—we must remove all sense of any prior *place* from it. We remove its mass or magnitude not by making it—in imagination—*smaller* but by removing any sense of size or scale or distance. Being itself is, in effect, the Place—which coincidentally is one of the Rabbinic terms for God: "Why is God called 'the Place' (*hamaqom*)? Because the universe is located in Him, not He in the universe."[16]

This may seem to be merely an abstract metaphysical, "theological" argument, with the sort of strange or "mystical" conclusion that we ignore in practice (even when it is couched in the "scientific" terms that we admire, and cosmologists remind us that the Big Bang didn't happen far away but *here*). As long as we regard the story "from outside" that is bound to be the result. Actually *attempting* the exercise has a different effect, and not one that can be easily summarized. But even without that attempt we can learn from asking one pressing question: why must Matter[17] and "form-

---

16. *Genesis Rabbah* 68 (Maccoby, *Philosophy of the Talmud*, 24).

17. As at VI.1 [42].27, 1–5: "shapeless, without share in life, and unintelligent and dark and indefinite."

lessness," as elements of our own lives and sensibility, be disparaged? Even if we agree that the phenomenal world is, as it were, a projection onto the blank screen familiar to us nowadays in cinema (or in Plato's Cave), that screen must have a particular form and function if it is to do its job, and why should we despise it, even if it might also distort the projection? When Plotinus describes the phenomenal world as a painted corpse (II.4 [12].5, 18), emphasizing that the paint does not affect the corpse itself, might that not indicate that, after all, the "bare matter" has an impenetrable nature of its own, wholly independent of the forms laid over it? And how could anyone reared in Egypt, as Plotinus was, not be echoing, in this phrase, the very obvious "painted corpses" of the Egyptian dead and the archetypal mummy which is Osiris, Lord of the Land of the Living? In the story recounted by Plutarch (and mostly congruent with Egyptian sources), the reunited body of Osiris was employed by Isis to beget his avenger Horus—that is, this painted corpse was fertile after all!

> We must not treat the myths as wholly factual accounts (as *logoi*), but take what is fitting in each episode according to the principle of likeness (to truth). Thus when we say "the material," we should not be carried away by the ideas of many philosophers and think of a kind of inanimate and characterless body which is idle and intrinsically without energy.[18]

In the Egyptian Underworld, the Duat, Ra and Osiris are united.[19] Whatever it is that underlies or contains the many million things it is Something more than Nothing, a real presence rather than an absence, even if it is Unseen. So why might we not welcome it as an immortal truth? If animals need not mind about being "transformed" when they are taken by predators, why might we not equally accept the transformations? In the words attributed to Chuang Tzu:

18. Plutarch, *De Iside et Osiride*, 211 (chap. 58).

19. See Uzdavinys, "Animation of Statues in Ancient Civilizations." Lachman, *Quest for Hermes Trismegistus*, 113, suggests that Suhrawardi's *Hūrqalyā* "is an objective inner world that, through prayer and meditation, one can 'travel' in and within which one can encounter equally objective spiritual beings, much as the Hermeticists could journey inwardly through the planetary spheres, or the Egyptian initiate could travel through the underworld. *Hūrqalyā* is in essence identical to the realm of the Duat, and also to the inner realm within which the author of the *Poimandres* encountered *Nous*.'" Shahab al-Din Yahya Ibn Habash Suhrawardi (AD 1154–91) was a Sufi philosopher, of Kurdish ancestry, who sought to revive "ancient Iranian wisdom," with notably Plotinian parallels. On Suhrawardi and Hūrqalyā (i.e., the "imaginal"—not the imaginary—world), see Corbin, Spiritual Body and Celestial Earth, 118–34.

When a skilled smith is casting metal, if the metal should leap up and say, "I insist upon being made into a Mo-yeh!" he would surely regard it as very inauspicious metal indeed. Now, having had the audacity to take on human form once, if I should say, "I don't want to be anything but a man! Nothing but a man!," the Creator would surely regard me as a most inauspicious sort of person. So now I think of heaven and earth as a great furnace, and the Creator as a skilled smith. Where could he send me that would not be all right? I will go off to sleep peacefully, and then with a start I will wake up.[20]

On these terms "Matter" is, after all, not a "principle of evil" but merely our name for the melting pot which allows so many and so various entities their time and place. "What is there dreadful about magnitude?" (VI.6 [34].1, 8). Evils may afflict individual entities, but from the point of view (so to speak) of the Mass, they are not evils. The "formlessness" underlying our own subjectivity may be of greater power than we suppose—and I shall return to that thought.

And yet, perhaps there is still something to be learnt from the Plotinian gloss. Our being is not exhausted by our materiality: we are not indefinitely transformable stuff, though that imagined stuff enables us to live and work here-now. Something really is lost, *pace* Chuang Tzu, in dying.

Chuang Tzu's wife died. When Hui Tzu went to convey his condolences, he found Chuang Tzu sitting with his legs sprawled out, pounding on a tub and singing. "You lived with her, she brought up your children and grew old," said Hui Tzu. "It should be enough simply not to weep at her death. But pounding on a tub and singing—this is going too far, isn't it?" Chuang Tzu said, "You're wrong. When she first died, do you think I didn't grieve like anyone else? But I looked back to her beginning and the time before she was born. Not only the time before she was born, but the time before she had a body. Not only the time before she had a body, but the time before she had a spirit. In the midst of the jumble of wonder and mystery a change took place and she had a spirit. Another change and she had a body. Another change and she was born. Now there's been another change and she's dead. It's just like the progression

---

20. Chuang, *Works*, 48 (§6). The words commonly attributed to "Chuang" seem to have been composed by one Kuo Hsiang in the third century AD and have only lately been associated with an active Taoist tradition: see Kirkland, *Taoism*, 33–9. They are still of interest in their own right.

of the four seasons, spring, summer, fall, winter. Now she's going to lie down peacefully in a vast room. If I were to follow after her bawling and sobbing, it would show that I don't understand anything about fate. So I stopped."[21]

This anecdote suggests that Chuang Tzu did himself acknowledge the reality, the real being that is never to be lost, of the woman who was his wife, but it can also be read as giving weight to the notion that there is nothing lost because Stuff is eternal and may take on "the same" shapes again, even without a strictly personal identity. The same form, at least, can be expected to reappear in the ever flowing cycle of events (as Plotinus suggests in his contrast between superlunary and sublunary existence: II.1 [40].1, 5–13). Stoics and Epicureans too, from distinct metaphysical beginnings, imagined the same outcome (though they had no clear notion of what such a repeating form might be, except "our" inclination to use the same words on—axiomatically—different occasions). The more modern, and far more depressing, mutation of this idea sees only "matter" in motion, whether we reckon it alive or dead.

But Plotinus reckons that there is not simply a metaphysical error in supposing that Matter is an independent principle, or that the material stuff of things is the one real existent, or conversely that there is no function for "matter" at all. Vice in the soul is caused by our association with Matter—a doctrine which Proclus rebuts. There must have been a flaw in the soul already for it, for her, to be tempted by material goods, and the more material entities cannot reasonably be judged morally worse than the less.[22] Minding about the material, about the amount of stuff we can accumulate and control—including viewing material entities as both morally and spatially distant opponents—is one chief way in which we display our errors. But "matter" as such does not *cause* these errors: rather the reverse, the errors cause things to appear as mere material. The more we can begin to envisage how it might be if all things are *present*, the more we can be detached from the illusion that we inhabit a world of competition and exclusion, the world of things that Buber called the It-world.[23] The less seriously we take the merely material, the more we can educate ourselves out of, as it were, seeing pigs merely as ambulatory pork, mice or monkeys as "animal

21. Chuang, *Works*, 140 (§18).
22. See Opsomer, "Proclus versus Plotinus."
23. Buber, *I and Thou*, 84.

preparations,"[24] trees as timber, and the living soil as excrement: mere stuff to be used or thrown away.

Wren-Lewis, writing as a lay-theologian in the 1960s to explain the error—as he saw it—that imagined "God" to name an entity somehow exterior to a universe stretched out in "space" and "time," observed that "the categories of distance and measured time are just the categories that you need when you are concerned with using things, with manipulating things, rather than with responding to the aesthetic quality of things or responding to their personal import. . . . The error comes in generalizing that view of things, in believing that is what reality is like; for what you are then doing is *to generalize your attitude,* saying in effect *that life is essentially a matter of manipulation, that essentially we are concerned (either as individuals or as collective groups) with the manipulation of the world, and this is what life is really about.*"[25] Turning this round, we need no longer think of the world as "merely a material system." Its reality lies with us—as I shall observe in considering the hypostasis of Soul.

Or is there a rather different moral intended, by at least some pagan philosophers? There was a strand of pagan thought considerably more ascetic than even Christian monasticism: even though pagans generally thought that this world here was to be admired, they might also wish to detach themselves from many natural goods, and thinking of them as *matter* was a way of doing so.

> How useful when roasted meats and other foods are before you to see them in your mind as here the dead body of a fish, there the dead body of a bird or pig. Or again to think of Falernian wine as the juice of a cluster of grapes, of a purple robe as sheep's wool dyed with the blood of a shellfish and of sexual intercourse as internal rubbing accompanied by a spasmodic ejection of mucus. . . . You must do this throughout life; when things appear too enticing, strip them naked, destroy the myth which makes them proud.[26]

Pause a moment longer on that notion of the excremental. Unsurprisingly, we dislike our excrement and gladly relegate the task of dealing with

24. An expression used by some vivisectors to defuse their anxiety about what they are doing. see Devereux, *From Anxiety to Method,* 234–5.

25. Wren-Lewis, *God in a Technological Age,* 78.

26. Aurelius, *Meditations* 6.13, as cited by Liebeschuetz, *Continuity and Change,* 213. See also Hypatia's tactic for discouraging a suitor, according to Damascius, *Philosophical History,* 128–9 (43A–D).

such stuff to others, whom we can then despise for their associations. Curing ourselves of that disgust is a significant step. According to Muslim tradition, "one day Jesus was walking with his followers, and they passed by the carcass of a dog. The followers said, 'How this dog stinks!' But Jesus said, 'How white are its teeth.'"[27] "To the pure all things are pure."[28] Aurelius's technique of disparagement may sometimes be effective—however, it is perhaps not one that *Plotinus* would endorse. What is on display in the world of our experience is not *only* (at least) an unknown, unknowable, disagreeable stuff, feebly disguised by shapes and colors that do not touch its essence. If we "turn around," we shall see instead the beauties whose reflections we had previously glimpsed and realize that it is the One that is more truly on display.

But there is more to be said about "matter" as it functions within our own soul and sensibility. What does our own materiality amount to? What phenomena are we speaking about in speaking of "mere material," and why is it that we so easily expect metaphysical materialists to be—ethically— hedonists of the simple-minded sort who find nothing odd or improper about scratching when they itch? Part of the answer, or at least a probable answer, I have given already: to intuit things merely as "material" is to treat them at once as valueless in themselves and as available for any use we can suppose—stuff to be used, ignored, or scrubbed away, fuel or food or excrement. Our own materiality lies in the accumulated detritus that stains our internal statues, the intrusive memories that pretend to be our very selves. Or else in the fearful possibility of our own moral collapse: we might turn out to be very different people than we think we are, easily corruptible by fear or by desire and hardly able to escape from our multiple, corporeal obsessions. Materiality, in us, is the possibility of being otherwise than we suppose we are, or should be. Its attraction is the delusive hope it offers that we are omnicompetent: that we can be *simultaneously* student, lover, householder, and sage and so need never suffer the pains of loss and choice. All those different possibilities, all those differing obsessions, are—so Proclus declares, in allegorizing Socrates's remark to Alcibiades about his many suitors—"an incoherent multitude," a mob.

Mobbing is evidence of a slovenly, confused way of life that drags the beloved to the materialized, fragmented and "manifold" kind of variety

27. Meyer, *Unknown Sayings of Jesus*, 140, after al-Ghazali, *Revival of the Religious Sciences* 3.108.
28. Paul (?), *Titus* 1.15.

of the emotions. Timaeus too called all forms of irrational behaviour a mob, as being indeterminate in themselves, discordant and disorderly, "the thronging mob that has later grown upon it, composed of fire and earth and air and water."[29]

Or else, equivalently, materiality lets us think that we need not trouble with the real world of real forms and beauties but instead prefer delusion. No one, said Plotinus, would want merely to *think* that he was with the one he loved (VI.7 [38].26, 20ff.)—but perhaps some people wish exactly that, since the actual beloved may be less accommodating than their fantasy, may indeed have his or her own wishes and fulfillments![30]

These multiple meanings—matter as food, as excrement, as unlimited possibility, as fantasized fulfillment—are themselves an indication of matter's multiplicity, and a reason not to look too far in that direction. Conversely—and choosing instead to wonder about the strange equivalence of Matter and the One (as I have indicated earlier, and will discuss again)—we may begin to notice our own Protean power, our pantomime. Turning around from gazing "down" at matter, we may recognize *ourselves* as "mere material" and open to revision.

---

29. Proclus, *Alcibiades*, 38 (57), also citing Plato, *Timaeus* 42c.

30. See Charles Williams, *Descent into Hell*: the character who thus damns himself acts out the familiar theme, being tired of being together (IV.8 [6].4, 11–2).

CHAPTER TWENTY

Nature

Consider yet again the passage I have already twice addressed: "before soul it was a dead body, earth and water, or rather the darkness of matter and non-existence, and 'what the gods hate'" (V.1 [10].2, 22–8). Conversely, if we eliminate all "form" from the phenomenal world we inhabit, we are confronted only by rubble—and less than rubble, since every individual piece of stone or dirt turns out, on examination, to possess a complex structure which we must eliminate in thought. "The name for order in movement is 'rhythm,' and order of voice, when high and low are mixed together, is given the name '*harmonia*': without these there is no more than noise."[1] Aristides Quintilianus recorded a further—possibly Peripatetic—moral:

> Some of the ancients described rhythm as male, melody as female, on the ground that melody is inactive and without form, playing the part of matter because of its capacity for opposite qualifications, while rhythm moulds it and moves it in a determinate order, playing the part of the maker in relation to the thing made.[2]

"Mere matter" stretches out indefinitely, without clear borders or any privileged position—indeed, without any privileged rhythm, scale, or moment. What is it that can mark out any particular region of this indefinite array as belonging closely together while being separate from adja-

---

1. Plato, *Laws* 2.665a, cited by Barker, *Musician and His Art*, 149, 164. *Harmonia*, remember, means, not "harmony," but some mode or key in music.
2. Aristides, *De musica* 1.19 (Barker, *Harmonic and Acoustic Theory*, 445). See also West, *Ancient Greek Music*, 129–30. "Melody" means, not a tune, but the array of available notes.

cent regions? What can mark any such region out as being significantly "the same" as any more distant region? Once we have eliminated—in imagination—any sense of significant borders in "mere matter," any sense that there is more to the cosmos than Extension, there seems no reason to expect that any one cluster in the array is marked out from another or that its innate and essential difference from all *other* clusters is moderated. There may or may not be a smallest-possible region, within which there can be no further spatial discrimination (though we have no clear imagination of this possibility). If there isn't, then there are not even smaller or larger regions: every region contains as many subregions as every other. What prevents an equally infinite range of possible states for those regions? If, on the other hand, there are smallest-possible regions, literally atomic, how can these atoms even be contiguous? If—*per impossibile*—one atom (and it does not matter whether this is a "filled" or an "empty" atomic region) touched another, they would both share a point distinguishable, in thought at least, from all other points essential to them. How then would they be parted? Or if there are no *other* points in any such literally atomic instant, then all of them touch each other at all their points: that is, they are coextensive and mutually indistinguishable. Conversely, it seems, adjacent regions cannot *not* touch, since there would then be a distinct region shared by neither of the adjacent regions. Mere matter, again, appears incomprehensible.

So also with Time: nothing in the mere succession of instantaneous states requires their division into seconds, minutes, hours, days, months, or years. I may—correctly—say that as I write these words it is Wednesday, 13 March 2013, at about the eleventh hour since midnight. But nothing "in nature" dictates that "days" begin at midnight, that there are so-and-so many duodecimal divisions in each identified period. We cannot nowadays even be sure that our notion of what constitutes "the *same* time" is universally applicable, or that "everywhere" so-and-so many chronons (being the smallest identifiable unit of succession) have "now passed" since the Very Beginning (if there was one). Even the great polarities of light and darkness exist *because* we have adopted different lives and senses for the light and dark, not simply because there is an abrupt distinction in the level of light as the earth turns round and orbits the sun. Other forms of life might not distinguish night and day at all, nor need to change their habits as the nights grew cold.[3] All our familiar divisions, whether in time or space (succession or extension), are—as Democritus would say—merely "by convention." In reality, he added, there are only "atoms and the void"—but even

---

3. See my "End of the Ages"; and its revised version in *Philosophical Futures*, 91–114.

that much demands formal addition to the merely undifferentiated stuff of worlds, and especially an absolute and unexamined distinction between "filled" and "empty" space. Nor is there much chance of finding a truly "objective" difference between "the earlier" and "the later" (any more than between "the lower" and "the higher")—not even that "later" states within any identifiable sequence are more "disordered" or more homogeneous than "the earlier."

It has occasionally been suggested that we are at liberty to describe things as we please—that everything is as amenable to redescription as marital status, the age of consent, the value of an economic unit, our nationality, or the date. Nilus the Scholastic, remember, gave a sculpture words: "I laugh because I marvel how, put together out of all sorts of stones, I suddenly become a satyr."[4] Of course, we can respond, the pile of stones has "become a satyr" only because "we" are disposed to impose that fancy on the pile. Can the same apply outside the world of art? Do successive rabbit parts or rabbit phases only count as "a rabbit" because we choose to say so? And who or what are "we"? It has even been suggested that this thought—that "we" can change the world by redescribing it—is a welcome "charter of liberty."[5] There is no "fact of the matter" whether modern France is "the same" as ancient Gaul, whether a sixty-five-year-old Stephen is "the same" as a five-year-old, or whether an embryo is "part" of its mother or of its father. Do caterpillars *become* or *give birth to* butterflies? There are no boundaries in nature (though there may be immune systems) and so no entities in a familiar sense at all. A merely impersonal and material account would be entirely other than any familiar words, and probably incomprehensible (so that there is in practice a weird congruence between consistent materialists and atheistical idealists). This matches Rorty's conclusion. "Truth," he said, or the only truth that we could mind about, is "what it is better for us to believe, rather than the accurate representation of reality."[6] After all, how could we ever tell that our representations accurately described reality when the latter can be known to us only in those very representative ideas? As well check one copy of a newspaper against another. Why should we even think that accurate representations must be consistent—or seem to be consistent—with each other? Substance itself is utterly unknown: all that we can manage is to know the world we find. Our scientific conviction that

4. Nilus the Scholastic (fifth century), *Planudean Appendix* (Paton, *Greek Anthology*, bk. 16), epigram 247, quoted by Mathew, *Byzantine Aesthetics*, 76.
5. Findlay, *Language, Mind and Value*, 30.
6. Rorty, *Philosophy and the Mirror of Nature*, 10.

the real world is best described in "objective" terms, without recourse to values or substantial forms, is itself a metaphysical or methodological one that cannot be established "scientifically." The accolade "Reality" is given to what "we" affirm—and we affirm it because of our own evolutionary, sociohistorical, or personal needs. Such "postmodernism" is often deeply oppressive in its implications: if only what "we" say counts, and "we" are those with access to the public forum, it is inevitable that what anyone else says must be "false" (i.e., be different from what "we" say). A consistent Darwinian materialism may also be oppressive. "The sub-conscious popular instinct against Darwinism was," as Chesterton remarked,

> that when once one begins to think of man as a shifting and alterable thing, it is always easy for the strong and crafty to twist him into new shapes for all kinds of unnatural purposes. The popular instinct sees in such developments the possibility of backs bowed and hunch-backed for their burden, or limbs twisted for their task. It has a very well-grounded guess that whatever is done swiftly and systematically will mostly be done by a successful class and almost solely in their interests.[7]

But it seems deeply implausible that *everything* is open to our manipulations or reinterpretations. Such a conclusion is as vulnerable as Protagorean relativism to the arguments of Plato: the very claim that *this* (the postmodern vision) is how things "really are" is in conflict with almost everything that almost everyone would say. The world we seem to inhabit cannot simply be a painted corpse, without real boundaries or repeating patterns. Even a corpse has a structure and needs to be carved, as Plato said, at the joints![8] There are real joints and real divisions, even if (especially if) we do not always get them right, and even if the borders between one entity and another, one age and another, are often disputed. I shall have more to say about intelligible form, reality, in a later chapter, on *Nous*: here it is enough to draw attention to the forces, or single Force, we see at work around us.

All of us live in one and the same world, whatever our personal views of that one world may be. Europeans and Asians, humans and caterpillars, terrestrials and whatever weird beings inhabit distant nebulae—all of us are subject to the very same physical laws, and all of us could be considered simply fragments of that single world. In Winchell's words (in 1883):

7. Chesterton, *What's Wrong with the World*, 259.
8. Plato, *Phaedrus* 265e; Plato, *Statesman* 287c. See also Chuang, *Works*, 19 (§3).

We have neighbours; they live beyond impassable barriers, but they gaze on the same galaxy, and we know they are endowed with certain faculties which establish a community between them and us. However conformed bodily, whatever their modes and means of organic activity, we know that they reason as we reason, and interpret the universe on the same principles of logic and mathematics as ourselves. The orbits which their planetary homes describe are ellipses; they have studied the same celestial geometry as ourselves; they have written their treatises on celestial mechanics; they have felt the impact of the luminous weave of ether; they have speculated on the nature of matter and energy; they have interpreted the order of the cosmical mechanism as the expression of thought and purpose; they have placed themselves in communion with the Supreme Thinker who is so near to all of us that his voice is audible alike to the ear of reason in all the worlds.[9]

Winchell may have been too confident, but he did at least, as a theist, have some reason for his belief: atheistical naturalists cannot easily suppose that we chance-evolved primates have hold of a universal theory, or that every technologically competent alien will think and feel as we do. But philosophical tradition has generally emphasized this fact or dangerous fancy: the Truth is One, and no one's truth, no one's *real* truth, is truly at odds with another's. The thought also applies—and perhaps more plausibly—in morals. Nothing is really *true* or *just* on one side of a border but *untrue* or *unjust* on the other.[10] To entertain this thought, of course, it is necessary to distance ourselves from our own immediate feelings and perceptions. The very fact of experience—that "being empty, or again full, of food and drink gives the imaginations shape, and one who is full of semen has different imaginations" (VI.8 [39].3, 12–5)—is evidence of a world *outside* and not dependent on our imagining. Philosophers, who aspire to genuine understanding, may hope to achieve some knowledge of that one real world and reckon the little local worlds of custom or species-prejudice are only fantasies. Truth is what is true for everyone and everything,

9. Winchell, *World Life*, 507–8, cited by Guthke, *Last Frontier*, 344.

10. "Reason and justice grip the remotest and the loneliest star. Look at those stars. Don't they look as if they were single diamonds and sapphires? Well, you can imagine any mad botany or geology you please. Think of forests of adamant with leaves of brilliants. Think the moon is a blue moon, a single elephantine sapphire. But don't fancy that all that frantic astronomy would make the smallest difference to the reason and justice of conduct. On plains of opal, under cliffs cut out of pearl, you would still find a notice-board, 'Thou shalt not steal'"; Chesterton, "The Blue Cross" (1911), in *Father Brown*, 27.

whether they know it or not. We cannot *make* things to be true merely by saying that they are or by choosing our words carefully. Wisdom comes by accepting what is *real*. It cannot be true, for example, that "pigs feel pain" means only that "pigs should be included in our moral universe,"[11] since one important reason why they should be is that they do. The discovery that they do, and should be, is a revelation of an Otherness beyond the lies we spin. The demand that we be objective is, exactly, a moral demand.

> We must see things objectively, as we do a tree; and understand that they exist whether we like them or not. We must not try and turn them into something different by the mere exercise of our minds, as if we were witches.[12]

Mainstream philosophical (and scientific) tradition also claims that there are no privileged observers, times, scales, or places. The fact that we, here-now, can perceive only this one particular moment does not mean that there are no other moments. On the contrary, we know perfectly well— even if we can't always remember it—that there are people far away and long ago for whom *their* moments feel just as real as ours. There are certainly creatures living at a microbial scale, and there may be entities far vaster than ourselves. Finding the truth demands that we put aside our local and personal prejudices and step out from illusion. Here and Now is not more real than any other place and time (equivalently, *Here and Now* is the *only* reality, which innumerable distinct episodes and regions share). *Our* point of view is only one perspective.

But the world stripped of illusion and separate perspectives is obviously not the world we readily experience, nor is it safe—in science or morality—so to strip away all usual associations. That may indeed be the "dry light shed on things" which will "wither up the moral mysteries as illusions."[13] At least it leaves us without any secure basis for our judgments. Insisting that the world we *don't* experience, or that can be imagined only as an unperceived continuum, is the only *real* world may itself be an ideological prejudice. As Berkeley wryly remarked: "the Wall is not white, the Fire is not hot etc—we Irishmen cannot attain to these truths."[14] Experience teaches us better, and so does biological science. It was this that

---

11. Rorty, *Philosophy and the Mirror of Nature*, 190.
12. G. K. Chesterton (1913), in *Complete Works*, vol. 29, 589.
13. Chesterton, *Poet and the Lunatics*, 70.
14. Berkeley, *Commentaries* B392 (*Works*, vol. 1, 47).

Uexkuell was speaking about when he suggested that "biological theory seeks to draw to the attention of the naive person the fact that he sees much too little, and that the real world is much *richer* than he supposes [whereas the physicist seems to suggest that it's much poorer] because there is spread out around every living thing its own world of appearance, which is like his world in its basic traits but which nonetheless manifests so many variations that he could devote his whole life to the study of these worlds without there ever being an end in sight."[15]

So even if we cannot remake the worlds simply by redescribing them, may it be that something is always making and remaking them, and that each little world—the sort of world we actually experience—is constructed on an earlier framework, at once a composite of all the little worlds of those who came before and some underlying pattern? The Soul of the All, Plotinus says, draws a "preliminary outline" for individual souls to follow and fill out, "as the dancer does to the dramatic part given him" (VI.7 [38].7, 12–7). The tracery of that outline is an echo of Soul's activity, even in places where we detect no actual *living* creature.

> Few phenomena gave me more delight than to observe the forms which thawing sand and clay assume flowing down the sides of a deep cut on the railroad through which I passed on my way to the village. . . . When the frost comes out in the spring, and even in a thawing day in the winter, the sand begins to flow down the slopes like lava, sometimes bursting out through the snow and overwhelming it where no sand was to be seen before. Innumerable little streams overlap and interlace with one another, exhibiting a sort of hybrid product, which exhibits halfway the law of currents, and halfway that of vegetation. As it flows it takes the form of sappy leaves or vines, making heaps of pulpy sprays a foot or more in depth, and resembling, as you look down on them, the laciniated, lobed and imbricated thalluses of some lichens; or you are reminded of coral, of leopard's paws or birds' feet, of brains or lungs or bowels and excrements of all kinds. . . . You find thus in the very sands an anticipation of the vegetable leaf. No wonder that the earth expresses itself outwardly in leaves, it so labors with the idea inwardly. The atoms have already learned this law, and are pregnant by it.[16]

---

15. Uexkuell, *Theoretical Biology*, 62. See also his "Stroll through the Worlds of Animals and Men."

16. Thoreau, *Walden*, 544–6. Mud, though Socrates was too embarrassed to admit it (at least, according to Plato, *Parmenides* 130d), does have a form!

Nowadays we interpret rock patterns resembling skeletons or other seemingly biological structures precisely as fossil evidence of past life-forms. Our predecessors sometimes thought of them as indications of what might be *future* life-forms, struggling to be born! We can at least agree that patterns of the sort that we associate with living forms are also to be found elsewhere—evidence of a different sort of living, or evidence that the cosmos is prepared for life.[17]

So "Nature," on this account, is both the underlying and unconscious tracery that supports all living things and the result of the activity of all those living things, especially the vast microbial population of the little Earth. Whether the rest of the cosmos is also the work of living artists we don't know—though even those cosmologists who would overtly deny the claim fall easily into speaking of the expectable *life stories* of galaxies and stars. At least such individuals have histories, whether or not they are so far "animated" as also to have interior imaginations or subtle senses that are denied to us. In a way, modern cosmologists see *more* of an analogy between such astronomical entities and sublunary life-forms than Plotinus did, since he denied that the lives of stars had either ends or beginnings. Our modern thought is that all things will change, dissipate, decay, and die in time, leaving only a bland homogeneity behind—something as close to the mere matter "that the gods hate" as we can imagine.

> Then star nor sun shall waken,
>   Nor any change of light:
> Nor sound of waters shaken,
>   Nor any sound or sight:
> Nor wintry leaves nor vernal,
> Nor days nor things diurnal;
> Only the sleep eternal
>   In an eternal night.[18]

Cosmologists eager to dispel this horror have hoped either that the cosmos would eventually recycle itself and be renewed through the Conflagration or Big Crunch (an idea that seems not to be consistent with evidence of a cosmos whose expansion is now accelerating) or else that the cosmos is only one of many, maybe born out of the black holes into which some stars, and

---

17. See Kauffman, *At Home in the Universe*.
18. Swinburne, "The Garden of Proserpine" (1866) (*Poems*, 139).

galaxies, collapse.[19] These—literally—metaphysical speculations are further evidence of the power of Myth to direct and rule our hearts![20]

So how are we to address Nature in the outer world and in ourselves, this *eikon aei eikonizomene*, this image always imaging itself?[21] Are we to live as if it goes on forever or as if it is a finite image of the real Eternal? Is it wholly composite of individual creatures, each with its own integrity and purpose, or is there something underlying and preceding all those separate becomings? Is there anything in ourselves and in our world that we can conceive as "natural," as something born with each of us, as a given nature independent of our purposes and fictions? Plotinus sometimes seems to insist that Nature has no moral purpose of its own, and that we all take water from the same river, whether for good or ill (IV.4 [28].42, 15–6).[22] On other occasions it seems that Soul has no need to interfere in natural events:

> The forming principle [*ho logos*] compels the better things to exist and shapes them; the things which are not so, are present potentially in the principles, but actually in what comes to be; there is no need then any more for soul to make or to stir up the forming principles as matter is already, by the disturbance which comes from the preceding principles, making the things which come from it, the worse ones; though it is none the less overruled towards the production of the better. (II.3 [52].16, 47–8)

Can we get guidance from Nature, whether this is the effect of one great soul, our elder sister, or the unintended result of the many-million-fold of "lesser" creatures? Must we *accept* Nature, whatever and however it/she is, or may we hope for a remaking? On the one hand, that hope can seem like arrogance, one of the faults that Plotinus finds in Gnostics (II.9 [33].4, 25–32). On the other, we are not *simply* slaves, incapable of any different role.

According to Hillman,

---

19. Smolin, *Life of the Universe*.

20. According to Plutarch, *De Ei* 9.388e, the indestructible divinity that undergoes transformations is known as Apollo (i.e., *a-polla*, "not many") in the Conflagration and as Dionysus (or cognate identities) when he is rent apart and distributed "into winds, water, earth, stars, plants and animals" (Linforth, *Arts of Orpheus*, 317–8).

21. After II.3 [52].18, 17.

22. Staal, *Advaita and Neoplatonism*, 166–7, interprets this and similar passages as suggesting that prayer is an impersonal, ritualistic technique, as it is for the Brahmanas: "in the idea of the ritual act (*sat*) . . . it is the exactness (*satyam*) which counts and not the intention of the sacrificing priests."

"Nature" is only a psychological perspective, one of the fantasies of the soul and itself an imaginal topography, whose description changes through the centuries in accordance with shifting archetypal dominants. Western history shows many such fantasies: nature as a clockwork machine; as an enemy; as wild and beautiful asking to be tamed or to be left unspoilt, virginal; as a harmonious rhythm; as red in tooth and claw, everything competing for survival; as the very face of God.[23]

If we remove these fantasies, must we be left alone with Matter as an empty sheet for our imaginings? Or shall we accept, at least as a guiding fantasy, what seems Plotinus's main theme? "All things aspire to contemplation" (III.8 [30].1, 2–3).[24] All things play at being. They do not operate merely "mechanically" (in the metaphor of a later day), nor simply by pushing and pulling, "for what kind of thrusting or levering can produce this rich variety of colours and shapes of every kind?" (III.8 [30].2, 5–7). The cosmos is, as it were, a tree, comprising not only roots, fruits, and leaves but also the bacterial, fungal, and animal life that feeds and lives within it (we are, remember, "maggots"! [IV.3 [27].4, 26–30]): all things flower out from a single root, and "those that are closer to the root [which is to say, the stars] remain for ever [emenen aei], and the others are always coming into being [egineto aei], the fruits and the leaves" (III.3 [48].7, 16–7).[25] The tree that Plotinus imagines has its roots up in the heavens, and all the things "down here" blossom, decay, and blossom once again. Modern cosmologists have accepted that even the stars have finite lives and are also subject to time and chance, like us, but it is still true that our natural origins are "up there." We are, in the most literal sense, stardust, composed of elements forged only in the stars.

This claim can be carried too far: if we are *only* "dust," and our every act is reducible to the result of whatever movement our separate atoms make, then we are living in an illusion. As Galen caustically remarked a century earlier than Plotinus,

> Some [atomists] have even expressly declared that the soul possesses no reasoning faculty, but that we are led like cattle by the impression of our senses, and are unable to refuse or dissent from anything. In their view,

23. Hillman, *Dream*, 72.

24. For more on the notion that nature herself "contemplates," see Wildberg, "World of Thoughts."

25. Armstrong's translation of *"egineto aei"* as "come into being for ever" (*Enneads*, vol. 3, 137) is misleading. See also III.8 [30].10 for the same metaphor, "the life of a huge plant."

obviously, courage, wisdom [*phronesis*], temperance [*sophrosune*], and self-control [*enkrateia*] are all mere nonsense, we do not love either each other or our offspring, nor do the gods care anything for us.[26]

Indeed, it is not clear that "we" exist at all, still less that we can have "reasoned" our way to this conclusion. Common sense—and even the possibility of this very theory—suggest otherwise. As Augustine observed, if you deny that you have a will, there can be no reasoning with you, "because I do not have to answer your questions unless you want to know that you are asking. Furthermore, if you have no desire to attain wisdom, there should be no discussion with you about such matters. Finally, you can be no friend of mine if you do not wish me well."[27]

"Nature," on the contrary, "acts throughout in an artistic and equitable manner,"[28] whether or not there is a *conscious* maker behind its activity. But Dio Chrysostom spoke for many pagans in seeing the world as a shrine, and our life in it as an initiation:

It is very much the same as if anyone were to place a man, a Greek or a barbarian, in some mystic shrine of extraordinary beauty and size to be initiated, where he would see many mystic sights and hear many mystic voices, where light and darkness would appear to him alternately, and a thousand other things would occur; and further, if it should be just as in the rite called enthronement, where the inducting priests are wont to seat the novices and then dance round and round them—pray, is it likely that the man in this situation would be no whit moved in his mind and would not suspect that all which was taking place was the result of a more than wise intention and preparation, even if he belonged to the most remote and nameless barbarians and had no guide and interpreter at his side—provided, of course, that he had the mind of a human being? Or rather, is this not impossible? impossible too that the whole human race, which is receiving the complete and truly perfect initiation, not in a little building erected by the Athenians for the reception of a small company, but in this universe, a varied and cunningly wrought creation, in which countless marvels appear at every moment, and where, furthermore, the rites are being performed, not by human beings who are

---

26. Galen, *On the Natural Faculties*, 47–9 (1.12).
27. Augustine, *De libero arbitrio* 1.24 (*Teacher*, 95).
28. Galen, *On the Natural Faculties*, 49 (1.12).

of no higher order than the initiates themselves, but by immortal gods who are initiating mortal men, and night and day both in sunlight and under the stars are—if we may dare to use the term—literally dancing around them forever—is it possible to suppose, I repeat, that of all these things his senses told him nothing, or that he gained no faintest inkling of them, and especially when the leader of the choir was in charge of the whole spectacle and directing the entire heaven and universe, even as a skilful pilot commands a ship that has been perfectly furnished and lacks nothing?[29]

The leader, probably, is the Sun—around whom, as Julian said,[30] the visible gods perform their dances.

And what of the nature we encounter most immediately, the nature at work in our own physical (precisely) being? Falling in love, remember, is understood as our "consent" to that "other soul" that wraps us round (IV.4 [28].43). Going along "with nature" is allowing "what happens of itself" its head. Mainstream opinion about our *human* nature is that we alone, among all other animals, can and even must "step back" from what we "naturally" do. What we "want" and what we come to see as good are not always just the same. Indeed, it often seems that they are contrary. At least we can realize that the world, the whole world that surrounds and sustains us, is more than the simple "life-world," the array of threatening or tempting things that natural creatures variously see. And yet it may also be appropriate at times to "live along with nature," to allow the world and its abiding nature to manifest in us. Our very realization that the world, the real world, is larger than our hopes and fears, more complicated than our simple stratagems, may give us reason not to get in the way of its workings. We could not, of our own wit and reason, manage even the simplest of bodily processes: how well can we manage even our wit and reason?

Conversely, for those unpersuaded of the need for a single immaterial principle, "a shadow of soul" (IV.4 [28].18, 8),[31] to manage the one world, may we interpret that notion as itself a metaphor, drawn from our own experience of our own living bodies? We *feel* ourselves in possession of our

29. Dio Chrysostom, "Man's First Conception of God" (*Discourses*, vol. 2, 35–7 [12.31–4]).

30. Julian, *Oratio 4: Hymn to Helios* 135bc (*Works*, vol. 1, 367) (not because they, as planetary bodies, *orbit* the sun, but because the planetary points of light are sometimes ahead and sometimes behind the sun in its passage across our sky).

31. On the argument for such a shadow or "trace," see Noble, "How Plotinus' Soul Animates His Body."

bodies, despite doubts that we control that whole, and despite a tendency to disown the parts we do not like. That *feeling*, perhaps, provides a metaphor or model for the life of the whole, even if we had no intellectual reason to believe that there is indeed "a universe,"[32] a whole of which we are, in part, subsidiary parts. Even if there isn't, perhaps we had better believe or feel there is.

32. See Jaki, *Is There a Universe?*

CHAPTER TWENTY-ONE

Soul

If it is hard to discern what "Matter" or "Nature" may mean in our experience, surely it should be easier to understand what "Soul" is in our experience: is not Soul, exactly, our experience—subjective, linear, piecemeal? And yet perhaps it is not after all so easy to experience: we are all much likelier to be distracted from our own being, entangled in the web of time and place. That is why Plotinus finds it necessary to remind us that "soul made all living things itself" and is present everywhere (V.1 [10].2, 1–7, 35–8). In attending only to the things around us we may imagine that they are the primary reality, that they exist in their own right, and constrain us to obey their rules. Realizing instead that we have brought them into being ourselves, we may feel free also to remake them. Witness Yeats's somewhat inaccurate summary of Berkeley's philosophy:

> God-appointed Berkeley that proved all things a dream,
> That this pragmatical, preposterous pig of a world, its farrow that so
>   solid seem,
> Must vanish on the instant if the mind but change its theme.[1]

In another context it may be important to unravel this as an *ontological* argument, a thesis to the effect that the "merely material" cannot be a sufficient cause of the "mental": at any rate if we first define the *material* as what exists apart from "mind," it is no surprise that such material properties cannot explain the mental. At best it could only be a brute fact that such-and-such material bodies "give rise" to mental properties—and such brute

---

1. Yeats, "Blood and the Moon" (1928) (*Poems*, 201). See also Coleridge, "Dejection: An Ode" (1802) 4.47–8 (*Poems*, 308).

facts are knowable only from experience and are not "rationalizable."[2] But the issue here is not ontological but—exactly—psychological: what does it mean *for our experience of ourselves* to attend to our own experiencing rather than the multiple objects of our experience, whether those in their turn can be typed as "material," existing at particular places, or as "mental," existing over time but without independent locations? What happens when we cease to identify with our bodies, or even with the thoughts, feelings, and images that cross our minds, and become aware instead of our own awareness? Separating ourselves from sense perceptions and desires and passions and all such flummery, we find ourselves an image of *Nous*, as the light of the sun images the sun itself (V.3 [49].9, 3–10).

Plotinus does occasionally offer a familiar image for the relation of soul and body: that soul lives "in" body as the captain in a ship and must take care not to be pulled down in any shipwreck (IV.3 [27].17, 23–8). We might similarly be concerned not to be entangled in the net of material nature—an image familiar to Socrates, who described the body of a dangerously attractive courtesan as "a closely woven net."[3] Orphic poetry also speaks of the formation of a living creature as the knitting of a net.[4] But when Plotinus uses this image, it is to say that the body floats within the sea of soul—and soul is *not* entangled, any more than the sea is hampered by a net (IV.3 [27].9, 40–2). Remember Watts, on the networks we impose on "the real wiggly world."[5]

The world Watts has in mind is the *experienced* world, prior to our rationalizations and schematic orderings—and *separate bodies* are part of the familiar, misleading schema. These images make our situation clear. On the one hand, our attention can be "fettered by the bonds of magic" (*goeteia*), dragged down or sinking willingly into the material realm, into the delusion that we and others exist as separate bodies. On the other, we may recall our own existence as the ocean within which all such illusions float. There is a part of the soul, or a mode of soul, that does not "descend"—a notion that Iamblichus and other later Platonists abandoned. It is not so much that we should seek to disentangle ourselves as that we should realize that we have never been entangled!

But what is the ocean of Soul? An easy and familiar inference would be

2. See my "Plotinus: Body and Mind" and *From Athens to Jerusalem*, 121–57.

3. Xenophon, *Memorabilia* 3.11. See Scheid and Svenbro, *Craft of Zeus*, for more on the weaving image.

4. West, *Orphic Poems*, 10, cites the Orphic poem "Net" (frag. 26 Kern); see also Plato, *Timaeus* 78b.

5. A. Watts, *Taboo against Knowing*, 59.

that each of us is no more than a wave or current or arbitrary region of a homogeneous ocean—but Plotinus expressly denies that we are "parts" of any larger soul. Soul is not a stuff to be divided, nor can we think of ourselves merely as subordinate cells or segments within the world organism (though that may be what our bodily natures are). Each soul, including the World Soul, is a version of Soul-as-Such, equal in dignity and capacity, even if also currently confined or focused on some particular reality. Soul's experience is piecemeal, linear, localized, whether in its "higher" or its "lower" reaches.

> If a man is able to follow the spirit [daimon] which is above him, he comes to be himself above, living that spirit's life, and giving the preeminence to that better part of himself to which he is being led; and after that spirit he rises to another, until he reaches the heights. For the soul is many things, and all things, both the things above and the things below down to the limits of all life, and we are each one of us an intelligible universe, making contact with this lower world by the powers of soul below, but with the intelligible world by its powers above. (III.4 [15].3, 18–24)

Soul is also, and by its nature, confronted by genuinely *other* souls: we can see those others in the glance of another's eyes or the motion of their bodies. "For here below, too, we can know many things by the look in people's eyes when they are silent; but there [i.e., when we see things in the light of the spirit] all their body is clear and pure and each is like an eye, and nothing is hidden or feigned, but before one speaks to another that other has seen and understood" (IV.3 [27].18, 19–24). We see ourselves, remember, in the eyes of our beloveds—but this is as much as to say that we realize our—as it were—own soulishness alongside theirs. In glimpsing, momentarily, how things seem to another soul, we are reminded both that we are souls ourselves and that there is a world vaster and more beautiful than any we see when confined to our own fantasy. Yeats, in praising his quartet of properly "Irish" sages, speaks of "Whiggery" as

> A levelling, rancorous, rational sort of mind
> That never looked out of the eye of a saint
> Or out of a drunkard's eye.[6]

---

6. Yeats, "The Seven Sages" (*Poems*, 204). Yeats identifies Goldsmith, Burke, Swift, and Berkeley as men who understood that "wisdom comes of beggary."

We existed, as it were, before the play of life, and bring our own selves to it (III.2 [47].17, 27–8). Our fall into the world defined only by its use to us, or its obstructiveness, is occasioned, not by our creation as separate individuals, but by our being tired of "being together" (IV.8 [6].4, 11–2). The penalty is that we find ourselves carried along by the currents set in motion by the stars above, rediscovering our own singular identities only as we begin to stir from sleep (II.1 [40].5). One version of that awakening, that "return," is when we acknowledge, accept, enjoy the reality that there is already someone "looking out" of the eyes of others. Nor is that soulishness restricted to the simply *human*.[7] The cat, the lizard, or the octopus is suddenly *looking back at us*. The jolt of awakened consciousness, our recognition of the Uncanny, comes with the realization "It's Alive!"[8] Buber proposed that this may even apply to trees:

> The tree is no impression, no play of my imagination, no aspect of a mood; it confronts me bodily and has to deal with me as I must deal with it—only differently. One should not try to dilute the meaning of the relation: relation is reciprocity. Does the tree then have consciousness, similar to our own? I have no experience of that. But thinking that you have brought this off in your own case, must you again divide the indivisible? What I encounter is neither the soul of a tree nor a dryad, but the tree itself.[9]

Each living thing, each soul, including the World Soul, is an emanation or reflection of *Nous*, in one of its many faces (V.1 [10].3,8):[10] not that each individual bodily being has an eternal form (for the soul of Socrates may also be the soul of many other living beings), but that each such transmigrating soul is the image or echo in time of an eternal aspect of reality. "Our life is divided and we have many lives, but *Nous* has no need of another life or other lives" (V.3 [49].9, 23–5). I may live, successively or contemporaneously, as a boy and a girl, a bush and a bird, and a dumb fish in the sea.[11] And so may others.

---

7. See III.4 [15].2; IV.3 [27].12; VI.7 [38].6–7; Plato, *Phaedo* 80b; *Republic* 10.612a.

8. See my "Moments of Truth."

9. Buber, *I and Thou*, 58–9.

10. For Soul as *eikon* of *Nous*, see V.2 [11].1, 15. For *Nous* as *eikon* of the One, see V.1 [10].7, 1–2—though this latter claim is odder than the former. Whereas soul and *Nous* are, in a way, alike, *Nous* and the One cannot be thus *alike*, as the One isn't "like" anything. The better term for the relation, perhaps, would be *agalma* (V.8 [31].6, 7)—the "image" rather than the "likeness" of God.

11. Empedocles DK31B117 (Hippolytus, *Refutation of All Heresies* 1.3.2, 3–4).

CHAPTER TWENTY-TWO

Nous

A nd what exactly is *Nous*? One common misinterpretation of the Platonic tradition is that Platonists must prefer "abstractions" to "real experience," the formula to the fact, the blueprint to the building, the musical score to the performance. There is some ground for the interpretation, but it is still—fairly clearly—wrong.[1] What is known in *Nous* are the realities of which we only, when relying on our senses, receive the barest and—literally—most abstracted sign. Even—or especially—materialist philosophers need to admit as much: the real world of their imaginings is an array of atoms bouncing back and forth, bound together by unfamiliar forces, in a ceaseless exchange of energies. Organisms like ourselves sense only what we need, on whatever relevant scale. As James said, "my world is but one in a million alike embedded, alike real to those who may abstract them. How different must be the worlds in the consciousness of ant, cuttlefish or crab!"[2]

The Real World, not dependent on our various sensings, must at least *allow* for the existence of those sensings and cannot in reason be wholly alien to them (so leaving us with no explanation at all of *why* things look the way they do, to us or to cuttlefish, nor any good reason even to believe in the way things look). The first step in our revisioning is to recognize that reality, whatever else it is, must include those different visions, as in the grand metaphor of Indra's Net of jewels (first attested in the *Atharva Veda* and amplified in the *Avatamsaka Sutra*), each reflecting all the others.

---

1. "Forms are not universals because universals are ontologically posterior to that of which they are predicated. A universal is just what many things have in common, whereas a Form is that in virtue of which many things can correctly be called by the same name": Gerson, "Metaphor as an Ontological Concept," 259.

2. James, *Principles of Psychology*, vol. 1, 288–9.

> Each There has everything in itself and sees all things in every other,
> so that all are everywhere and each and every one is all and the glory is
> unbounded; for each of them is great, because even the small is great;
> the sun There is all the stars, and each star is the sun and all the others.
> (V.8 [31].4, 5–12)[3]

But reality is not simply that collection of differing visions: somehow they
all rest upon or else depend upon one central order. If it were not so, we
would have no ground to expect to find "the same principles" at work in all
regions of reality (even those regions that, on current theory, have not been
in touch with each other since the very beginning). And if we are to have
any confidence in our own ability somehow to transcend the seemings, we
must somehow believe, in line with ancient tradition, that something in
us—that we call "reason"—really mirrors or echoes or embodies the very
order of the real world. There is a *noumenal* reality, as well as the *phenomenal* realities.

> The Stoic philosopher Poseidonius attributed the intelligibility of the
> world's structure to the fact that the designing intelligence, God, and
> human intelligence shared the same thought processes, since human
> souls were *apospasmata* of God.[4]

The very same notion is explicit in modern Catholic theology and implicit in all our scientific practice. In Pope Benedict's words, "the objective structure of the universe and the intellectual structure of the human
being coincide; the subjective reason and the objectified reason in nature are
identical. In the end it is 'one' reason that links both and invites us to look
to a unique creative Intelligence."[5] But how shall we attain this insight?
Scientific reasoning, the ordering of propositions *about* reality, so as to display their interconnectedness, perhaps their mathematical unity, is of great
importance, but Plotinus is clear that *Nous* is not the same as *dianoia*, and
the objects of "noetic insight" are not merely propositions, not even *mathe-*

---

3. So also Numenius T33 (Dodds, "Numenius," 23). See F. Cook, *Hua-Yen Buddhism*;
Odin, *Process Metaphysics and Hua-Yen Buddhism*; Malhotra, *Indra's Net*; McEvilley, "Plotinus and Vijñānavāda Buddhism."

4. Rappe, *Reading Neoplatonism*, 40, some way after Diogenes, *Lives* 7.143.

5. Benedict XVI to Archbishop Rino Fisichella, on the occasion of the international congress "From Galileo's Telescope to Evolutionary Cosmology," 30 November–2 December 2009,
http://www.vatican.va/holy_father/benedict_xvi/messages/pont-messages/2009/documents
/hf_ben-xvi_mes_20091126_fisichella-telescopio_en.html.

matical propositions. Trusting ourselves to merely formal mechanisms, deducing one truth from another according to clearly stated principles of reasoning, may help us to avoid mere wishful thinking or other emotional prejudices, but this sort of "theorizing" is not the same as *theoria*.

Naydler, commenting on ancient Egyptian thought, mistakes the Platonic:

> The concept of the First Time is comparable to that of the realm of being in which the Platonic Ideas exist. In Egyptian thought, though, it is not abstract ideas that are to be found here, but living gods and archetypal relationships that obtain among them. The First Time is the realm of metaphysical realities conceived in terms of symbolic images and myths. These are the patterns that are reflected in the mundane world and that need to be participated in if mundane events are to be filled with archetypal power.[6]

But since Plotinus asserts the *union* of each Form with the Intellect's grasp of it, his Forms are also active knowers, not merely passive objects of knowledge.[7] And each of us is hanging on to one particular face or facet of the divine *Nous*: each of us, that is, in our "soulish" state is an emanation or echo or follower of one particular god or angel—as Plato too had suggested in his story of the cavalcade of Heaven.[8]

The cosmological story, by which *Nous* and Being are together "the true and first universe" (III.2 [47].1, 27–8), is a recurrent theme in the development of science: reality is not confined to the "merely sensible" world, nor yet to the "merely material" spatiotemporally divided world. There is Something from which all sensible and material entity is derived, which all sensible and material entity "reflects" or "echoes." That Something itself contains all distinguishable archetypes, all Forms—which is why Plotinus reckons that the Creator does not *make* such eternal realities:

> It is already clear that the thought of a horse existed if [God] wanted to make a horse; so that it is not possible for him to think it in order to make it, but the horse which did not come into being must exist before that which was to be afterwards. (VI.7 [38].8, 6–9)

---

6. Naydler, *Temple of the Cosmos*, 93, cited by Uzdavinys, "Animation of Statues in Ancient Civilizations," 126–7.

7. See also Barfield, *Ancient Quarrel*, 97: "Proclus took the divine ideas of Plotinus and made them into gods that can not only be known (as in Plotinus) but can also know. Dionysius makes them into angels. Thus it is that the Forms of Plato become the Angels of Christendom."

8. Plato, *Phaedrus* 246e–249d.

The patterns according to which sensible and material reality are modeled, in other words, are themselves "begotten and not made." The point is also at the root of orthodox Christian insistence that the Word of God is not a *created* thing: "He is external to the things which have come to be by will, but rather is Himself the Living Counsel of the Father, by which all these things have come to be."[9] The Divine Intellect, the *Logos*, contains all Forms as eternal realities: "it lived not as one soul but as all, and as possessing more power to make all the individual souls, and it was the 'complete living being,' not having only man in it: for otherwise there would only be man down here" (VI.7 [38].8, 29–32).

> Plotinus's divine mind is not just a mind knowing a lot of eternal objects. It is an organic living community of interpenetrating beings which are at once Forms and intelligences, all "awake and alive," in which every part thinks and therefore is the whole; so that all are one mind and yet each retains its distinct individuality without which the whole would be impoverished. And this mind-world is the region where our own mind, illumined by the divine intellect, finds its true self and lives its own life, its proper home and the penultimate stage on its journey, from which it is taken up to union with the Good.[10]

But though the *Logos* contains all eternal Forms, we must suppose (or at least Plotinus supposes) that our humanity has this privilege: that we too can thus contain them all. The divine *Nous* is king.

> But we too are kings [*basileuomen*], when we are in accord with it; we can be in accord with it in two ways, either by having something like its writing written in us like laws, or by being as if filled with it and able to see it and be aware of it as present. (V.3 [49].4, 1–4)[11]

9. Athanasius, *Orations against the Arians* 3.64; discourse 3 is available at http://www .newadvent.org/fathers/28163.htm, revised and edited for New Advent by Kevin Knight. See also my *God's World and the Great Awakening*, 29–81.

10. Armstrong and Markus, *Christian Faith and Greek Philosophy*, 27. See also Kant, "Perpetual Peace," 107, who reports—attempting to suggest some intercourse between Tibetan Buddhism and the Hellenic Mysteries—that Tibetan lamas told Francesco Orazio della Penna (1680–1745) that "God is the community of all the holy ones."

11. But note that, strictly, it is the One—and not "just" *Nous*—that is the Great King. See Ousager, *Plotinus on Selfhood*, 218–9. If either the One or *Nous* is to be considered a "king," it is because it is the source of all power and honor and the focus of our proper admiration. That "we too are kings" is as paradoxical a claim as Traherne's (*Centuries*, 177 [1.29]), that each of us

This has more than an epistemological significance. It indicates that humanity can be taken up into the godhead, not only to *see* the Truth but to embody it. So also Macarius of Egypt (c. AD 300–91):

> Those upon whom the divine law is written, not with ink and letters, but implanted in hearts of flesh, these, having the eyes of their mind enlightened, and reaching after a hope, not tangible and seen, but invisible and immaterial, have power to get the better of the stumbling-blocks of the evil one, not by themselves, but from the power that never can be defeated.[12]

What can this experience be like? Clearly and confessedly I cannot offer any testimony of my own in answer, but it may be possible still to identify some answers, and even judge them. Weil, for example, speaks of realizing

> the beauty of a landscape just at the moment when no-one is looking at it, absolutely nobody. . . . To see a landscape such as it is when I am not there. When I am anywhere, I pollute the silence of earth and sky with my breathing and the beating of my heart.[13]

This thought is not to be taken lightly. It is difficult not to see in it one aspect of Weil's fatal anorexia, but her insights should not be ignored merely because, as it so often does, "the disease" (i.e., the demon) took advantage of them. When she wrote that "I cannot conceive of the necessity for God to love me, when I feel so clearly that even with human beings affection for me can only be a mistake. But I can easily imagine that he loves that perspective of creation which can only be seen from the point where I am. . . . I must withdraw so that he can see it. I must withdraw so that God may make contact with the beings whom chance places in my path and whom he loves,"[14] the disease was speaking. How could it be that God

---

is "sole heir of all the world." So also Philo, *Quod omnis probus liber sit* 3.20 (*Collected Works*, vol. 9, 21): "he who has God alone for his leader, he alone is free, though to my thinking he is also the leader of all others, having received the charge of earthly things from the great, the immortal King, whom he, the mortal, serves as viceroy." See also Diogenes, *Lives* 7.122.

12. Macarius, *Fifty Spiritual Homilies*, 178 (25.1). I owe the reference to Mark Armitage of the Orthodox Christian blog *Enlarging the Heart*, accessed 23 December 2014, http://enlarging theheart.wordpress.com/.

13. Weil, *Notebooks*, vol. 2, 423.

14. Weil, *Gravity and Grace*, 88. See Lippitt, "True Self-Love and True Self-Sacrifice." On the history of anorexia, see Bell, *Holy Anorexia*; Brumberg, *Fasting Girls*. For a victim's viewpoint, see Green, *Lighter than My Shadow*.

loved everything but Weil? But there is still some value in considering this vision of the whole world. The world is not to be measured by my qualms, my simple-minded discriminations, even my appreciation of its beauty or its terror.

Dante, considering Fortune as the presiding principle of terrestrial life (as distinct from those that—so he imagined—propel the planetary spheres), declared that

> This is she that hast so curst a name
> Even from those who should give praise to her—
> Luck, whom men senselessly revile and blame.
> But she is blissful and she does not hear;
> She, with the other primal creatures gay,
> Tastes her own blessedness, and turns her sphere.[15]

I must put aside my own interests if I am to have any hope of seeing things straight, and such glimpses as I have of that reality may in turn assist me in putting aside my interests. It feels, at any rate, as if we might occasionally and obscurely be inhabited by a "higher" self or *daimon*—which is how so many of the ancients regarded *nous* itself, as the very *daimon* that can make us *eudaimones*.[16] Our task, as Aristotle concluded, is *ton theon theorein kai therapeuein*—that is, to love and serve the Lord.[17]

So what is it like to feel that *nous*—even if it is only one facet of the whole divine *Nous*—within one's heart and mind? How are we to awaken to its presence? *Theoria* is not the same as theorizing, any more than *Nous* is the same as *dianoia*, the power to "think things through," to eliminate contradiction and parochial assumptions. Nor are Forms merely "universals," shared properties or shared descriptions. But "thinking things through" may still be the best route to an awakening—unless our thoughts are always and already so contaminated that the results of our thinking lead

---

15. Dante Alighieri, *Divine Comedy: Hell*, 112–3 (7.91–6). See also Philo, *Quod Deus sit immutabilis*, 176–7 (*Collected Works*, vol. 3, 97): "circlewise moves the revolution of that divine plan [*logos ho theios*] which most call fortune. Presently in its ceaseless flux it makes distribution city by city, nation by nation, country by country. What these had once, those have now. What all had, all have. Only from time to time is the ownership changed by its agency, to the end that the whole of our world should be as a single [*polis*], enjoying that best of constitutions, democracy. So then, in all wherewith men concern themselves there is no solid work, no [*pragma*], only a shadow or breath which flits past, before it has real existence." (Colson and Whitaker translate *polis* as "state" and *pragma* as "matter": both terms are at least misleading.)

16. Plato, *Timaeus* 90.

17. Aristotle, *Eudemian Ethics* 8.1249b20.

us further away from truth. May we hope for assistance "from above"? "To trust God is a true teaching, but to trust our vain reasonings is a lie."[18] But how shall we recognize and welcome that true teaching for what it is? Is there some special sign that all of us may individually recognize? Or must we trust instead merely in "the wisdom of crowds," the result of many separate intelligences united only in their *desire* for truth? Maybe there is merit simply in *measuring* what happens by some commonly agreed standard?

> What would be the saving principle of human life? Would not the art of measuring be the saving principle; or would the power of appearance? Is not the latter that deceiving art which makes us wander up and down and take the things at one time of which we repent at another, both in our actions and in our choice of things great and small? But the art of measurement would do away with the effect of appearances, and, showing the truth, would fain teach the soul at last to find rest in the truth, and would thus save our life. Would not mankind generally acknowledge that the art which accomplishes this result is the art of measurement?[19]

It seems possible, at any rate, to dismiss whatever seeming vision of reality is overtly self-contradictory: we cannot sanely agree that we are incapable of ever recognizing truth, nor that we cannot will to welcome it. Nor can we suppose that *only* our own experience of the world is real. More controversially, we cannot sensibly suppose that our own present spatial or temporal location is the only real location. All times and places are equivalently Here and Now and cannot ever be separated from themselves so as to be Distant or Not-Present.[20] As living souls we may be bound to experience things piecemeal and to make distinctions between what is Near and Far, Present and Past, and Yet-to-Come. But it seems that these distinctions are unreal: not merely relative and transient but positively incorrect. All times, all places, are available to us:

> The contemplation of Eternity maketh the Soul immortal. Whose glory it is, that it can see before and after its existence into endless spaces. Its Sight is its presence. And therefore in the presence of the understanding

---

18. Philo, *Legum allegoriarum* 3.229 (*Collected Works*, vol. 1, 457).
19. Plato, *Protagoras* 357a; see also *Republic* 10.602d–603a.
20. See IV.3 [27].11, 22–3: "nothing is a long way off or far from anything else."

endless, because the Sight is so. . . . No creature but one like unto the
Holy Angels can see into all ages.[21]

This, to be sure, is "only" in imagination, and only makes successive moments available to us. But the imagination is still of something real and
indicates to us that all those moments, all those places, are Present to themselves and to the Divine. We may not ourselves, as living souls, be capable
of intuiting or holding in our hearts that eternal, unlocalized vision. Even
the attempt may be an error, in that it serves to set the world apart from us:
on the one hand, the seemingly abstract map or chart of places and events;
on the other, our observation of that map. Only when we—by occasional
grace—realize our own presence in the eternal, nonlocal world do we bridge
that seeming gap between observer and observed. Only then "will [we] stop
marking [ourselves] off from all being and will come to all the All without
going out anywhere" (VI.5 [23].7, 9–10).

It seems that this notion—of the equal reality of all times and places—is
a very ancient one.[22] According to Australian Aboriginals, past, present,
and future are not differentiated in the Dreaming: there is only, in Stanner's
apt term, "everywhen."[23] Cosmologically, the "universal living being" that
is Reality contains all living beings, including the sky and stars, and "earth
is there also, not barren, but much more full of life, and all animals are in
it, all that walk on and belong to the land here below, and, obviously, plants
rooted in life; and sea is there, and all water in abiding flow and life, and all
the living beings in water, and the nature of air is part of the universe there,
and aerial living things are just as the air itself is" (VI.7 [38].12, 4–13). Our
ordinary perception of all these living things may be—variously—delusory,
but that is only to say that we do not see things whole, and straight, and
in full appreciation of their beauty. So also psychologically: to see things
whole and straight we must refer our ordinary perceptions back to that
seemingly abstract vision. It may not be one that we can long maintain as
we struggle to escape "from the bitter wave of this blood-drinking life, from
its sickening whirlpools, in the midst of its billows and sudden surges."[24]

---

21. Traherne, *Centuries*, 189 (1.55).

22. "Let us say that 'being' neither at any time 'was,' nor ever can 'become,' but always 'is'
in a definite time, the present only"; Numenius, cited by Eusebius, *Praeparatio*, 525 (11.10).

23. Bellah, *Religion in Human Evolution*, 148, citing Stanner, "Dreaming." Stanner quotes
a native Australian as saying, "White man got no dreaming, Him go 'nother way. White man,
him go diffirent, Him got road belong himself." No doubt this is not entirely fair to Europeans.

24. This is the oracle offered to Amelius after Plotinus's death, as recorded by Porphyry,
Life 22.31–3 (Armstrong, *Enneads*, vol. 1, 67). See Lamberton, *Homer the Theologian*, 133.

But at least the *memory* of that living world may help us to continue. For us, *Nous* exists in the vision.

> To think well is to serve God in the interior court: To have a mind composed of Divine Thoughts, and set in frame, to be like Him within. To conceive aright and to enjoy the world, is to conceive the Holy Ghost, and to see His Love: which is the Mind of the Father.[25]

---

25. Traherne, *Centuries*, 169 (1.10).

CHAPTER TWENTY-THREE

The One

Soul is the linear and piecemeal experience with which we are all acquainted, and *Nous* is our recognition of a world far larger and more intricate than we can separately experience. Soul may be more or less engaged by sensual and material illusions but can be recalled to its unfallen state in realizing that much larger world as one experienced or intuited by very many Others. How shall we interpret or experience or realize the presence of the last and highest of the hypostases, the One, "a wakefulness [*egregoresis*] and a thought transcending thought [*hypernoesis*] which exists always" [VI.8 [39].16, 32]?

Abstract argument—which may itself be a spiritual practice—posits "the One" as the ultimate explanation and goal of all things. Neither Matter nor Nature offers any such explanation, though both have sometimes been invoked as such. We cannot sensibly say that things happen simply because they can (because Matter allows anything at all to happen), nor because they are what always or for the most part happens (because Nature does whatever it does more or less consistently). Even Soul is inadequate: granted that Soul as a singular but divided principle both makes and experiences all things, the question remains why it exists itself, and how it can thus engineer its own experience. *Nous*, considered as both Intellect and Reality, can be described as a self-consistent formal system, but there are two remaining objections to taking it as the ultimate explanation: even if Intellect and Being are combined, as Subject and Object, still they are *dual* and cannot themselves explain their own conformity; and even if this *Nous* dictates what *can* be, it does not, of itself, explain why anything of what *can* be actually is. What is it that "breathes fire into the equations"? What grounds the eternal being of the realities described in those equations? The

Platonic answer is that all things strive to realize the Good, the focus of all endeavor, and exist only inasmuch as they achieve—both as individuals and as members of the whole—a partial unity.[1] Not that they can "come into being" because they want to—that notion makes no sense—but that their being eternally is a yearning toward the Good.

What is it in us that constitutes an "experience" of the One, when any such experience, setting oneself over against another object, is untrue to the very nature of that One? How can we talk about something that, by hypothesis, cannot be meaningfully described or discriminated from anything else? "It is truly ineffable: for whatever you say about it, you will always be speaking of a 'something'" (V.3 [49].13, 1–2). What is this wordless glimpse into a reality higher even than the infinite web of forms, and how—if we can't speak about it—do mystics (and Plotinus) fill so many pages? What do they carry away from the experience, and how might they advise we seek it? "How can the self that knows be known?"[2]

One answer—inadequate as it is—might be that we recognize that "knowing self" in others. Realizing that the world we inhabit is molded to our own preconceptions and interests may be occasioned by a prior recognition that other people, other creatures, are experiencing things very differently, that *their* worlds are likewise molded to their own interests and preconceptions, and that The World Itself is larger and more intricate than they—or we—imagined. That shock of recognition may lead us no further than a glimpse of the encompassing reality and of our own involvement in it. But there may be more to say. Buber echoes Plotinus in his discussion of what he called the I-Thou relationship.

> In every sphere, in every relational act, through everything that becomes present to us, we gaze toward the train of the eternal You; in each we perceive a breath of it, in every you we address the eternal You, in every sphere according to its manner. All spheres are included in it, while it is included in none. Through all of them shines the one presence.[3]

The Other that we occasionally acknowledge is not another object in the world, conditioned and contained by our own viewpoint—or even by the real nature of the actual, natural objects.

---

1. See my "Cosmic Priority of Value"; Leslie, *Value and Existence.*
2. *Brihadaranyaka Upanishad* 4.5.15 (Wood, *From the Upanishads,* 99).
3. Buber, *I and Thou,* 150 (see also Bellah, *Religion in Human Evolution,* 105).

Whoever says You does not have something for his object. For wherever
there is something there is also another something; every It borders on
other Its; It is only by virtue of bordering on others. But where You is said
there is no something. You has no borders. Whoever says You does not
have something; he has nothing. But he stands in relation.[4]

A real encounter with any Other is the discovery of what is meant, in the
Jewish tradition at least, by "God":

> The sacred is here and now. The only God worth keeping is a God that
> cannot be kept. The only God worth talking about is a God that can-
> not be talked about. God is no object of discourse, knowledge or even
> experience. He cannot be spoken of, but he can be spoken to; he cannot
> be seen, but he can be listened to. The only possible relationship with
> God is to address him and to be addressed by him, here and now—or,
> as Buber puts it, in the present. For him the Hebrew name of God, the
> Tetragrammaton (YHVH), means HE IS PRESENT. *Er ist da* might be
> translated He is there; but in this context it would be more nearly right
> to say: He is here.[5]

What is always and everywhere Here cannot be pointed to, cannot be discovered by its *absence* (since it is never absent). But though this Here cannot ever be really absent, it may be overlaid and forgotten. We forget that
we too are Here, and need to be reminded to withdraw our attention from
the panorama of seeming events "outside over there." We are still all Here
together—though our souls' fall into seeming, into the illusion of separate identities, material distances, was because we were "tired of being together." The discovery—call it the revelation—that we have *not* escaped
from Here, nor from "the Presence of God," is also the discovery of its supreme generosity, its openness to whatever happens, its being—precisely—
the "power of all things" (III.8 [30].10).

One further gloss is suggested by the distinction drawn especially in Orthodox Christian theology between Nature and Person.

> A person is a mystery, never totally circumscribed by a definition, that
> is, as an essence or a "what." A person is not a "what" but a "who," and
> "who" you are, just as Who God is, is ultimately indefinable, undeter-

---

4. Buber, *I and Thou*, 55.
5. Kaufmann in ibid., 25.

mined, and of infinite depth. To say "what" something is, is to circum-
scribe that something in terms of essence or essential definition; to say
"who" is to speak, not of some "thing" which can be defined in terms
of its essence, but of some "one," an ultimately uncircumscribable and
indefinable "who."[6]

The precise theological dimensions of this distinction need not trouble
us.[7] It is enough to note that we need not consider ourselves, or any other
creature (not merely any other person), simply as creatures of a particular
sort or suppose that all we do and think is a product or by-product of our
natures. There is something in us and all things that is not confined by any
account of our nature, a pure will better conceived as "personal" than as
"impersonal," simply because the "impersonal" is associated with notions
of predetermination, of mechanical expression. Each creature, insofar as it
is a real identity, is the current expression of something that transcends
all such descriptions and predictions. How shall we represent that to ourselves? How did our predecessors?

> God appears and God is light to those poor souls who dwell in night,
> But does a human form display to those who dwell in realms of day.[8]

Rather than viewing this as a metaphysical claim, consider it an ethical
or psychological one: what is most to be respected is not simply order in
ourselves or others, not even beautiful order, but an openness to being, the
grace that makes even an apparently ugly living creature more beautiful
than the best-crafted statue (VI.7 [38].22). It is that unnameable, uncondi-
tioned element that we need to respect and cultivate. It must come by revelation rather than by "reason."

But of course the metaphysical claim is never far away, if only because
we model our picture of the World on our own experience of the world as
it is for us. If Soul makes all the many worlds, and *Nous* encapsulates the
whole Reality that Soul refracts and constitutes, what is it that lies beyond
them both? Ancient Egyptian thought seems to have imagined that the primeval Darkness surrounds and will in the end consume the One that be-

6. Rossi, "Presence, Participation, Performance," 79.

7. See Zizioulas, *Being as Communion*. It is the almost universal opinion of Christendom
that "animals" are all *somewhats* rather than *someones*. My view is otherwise—but that is another and lengthier story.

8. Blake, *Auguries of Innocence* (1803), lines 129–32 (*Writings*, 434).

came a Million.[9] This may seem as nihilistic in effect as any modern myth about the End of Days, when proton decay and cosmic expansion reduce everything to an undifferentiated, uncreative emptiness. But perhaps there is a different reading of the Dark. On the one hand, Hades stands for the world of phenomenal dream into which the soul may plunge and lose herself (I.6 [1].8, 15). On the other, Hades is the Invisible, but also what "knows all beauties" (at least according to Plato's *Cratylus*),[10] which stands behind us, out of sight. Zeus Chthonios (another name of Hades, the Unseen) is the other half of heaven, where the sun goes at night, beyond the circular horizon. And it is that Darkness which stands behind us.

The Divine Intellect can be conceived as a Trinity in Unity: it is "lovable and love and love of himself" (*erasmion kai eros ho autos kai autou eros*; VI.8 [39].15, 1). Or else it is knower, object known, and knowledge (V.3 [49].5, 44). In both cases the seeming division is the condition of there being anything else at all. When we are "simplified into happiness," the divisions vanish, together with any way of speaking about the experience until it is over.

> There is no deceit There; or where could it find any thing truer than the truth? What it speaks, then, is that, and it speaks it afterwards, and speaks it in silence. (VI.7 [38].34, 27–30)

Is this so unfamiliar? Consider the experience recounted by Wren-Lewis, the lay-theologian I mentioned earlier, who lost his faith—in his career, his marriage, and his professed beliefs. He was saved from penury, as he says, "by the fact that [his] writings apparently contained sufficient insights of inspirational or scholarly value to cause people in various parts of the world to want [his] occasional services as a teacher."[11] He began to travel in the company of his second wife, Ann Faraday, herself the author of a work on dream therapy (*Dream Game*), and by 1983 he was unhappily convinced that there was no chance of finding any transcendental or even *apparently* transcendental element in human experience. Then, on a bus in Thailand during a joint investigation of shamanic practices among the Senoi, he was poisoned almost to death and had a near-death experience which transformed his life.

---

9. Cf. Hornung, *Conceptions of God*, 172–85.

10. Plato, *Cratylus* 404b. Heracleitos 22B15DK identifies Hades and Dionysos, with what moral is unclear. See Wildberg, "Dionysos in the Mirror of Philosophy."

11. Wren-Lewis, "Mystical Awakening," 119. I have written at greater length about Wren-Lewis in "Atheists and Idolaters."

I came round with a radically "altered state of consciousness" wherein the mundane shell of so-called ordinary human life was completely gone. Subjectively the state was utterly different from anything I'd experienced with psychedelics (or for that matter in experiments with trance or meditation), but more significantly, it has remained with me ever since, an effect not found with any drug yet known. In fact this consciousness feels so utterly natural that terms like "drugged" or "tranced" seem more appropriate for my earlier life, and I now know firsthand, from more than ten years' continuing daily (and nightly) experience, why at the mystical core of most religious traditions there is found the notion of "awakening" from an age-long collective human nightmare. I also know from firsthand experience why those who've actually experienced mystical wakening so often resort to paradox or negation when trying to say anything about it, and frequently resort to terms like "ineffable." Almost all human speech derives from that old collective nightmare of separate individuals struggling in an alien space-time world for survival, satisfaction and meaning, whereas I now experience myself and everyone else—indeed every thing else—as more like the continuous dance-like activity of a universal, truly infinite Consciousness/Aliveness whose very nature is satisfaction and "meaning" in an eternal Presentness, from which Separation (space) and activity (time) are continuously created.[12]

In other and still more detailed attempts to talk around the unsayable—reminiscent indeed of Plotinus's humorous efforts to do the same—Wren-Lewis described his experience as of a "dazzling darkness."

It was as if I'd emerged freshly made (complete with all the memories that constitute my personal identity) from a vast blackness that was somehow radiant, a kind of infinitely concentrated aliveness or pure consciousness that had no separation within it, and therefore no space or time.[13]

---

12. Wren-Lewis, "Mystical Awakening," 121–3. Jill Taylor (*Stroke of Insight*), with a somewhat similar experience, acknowledges both its neurological aspect and its deep significance.

13. See also Wren-Lewis, "Near-Death Experience," http://www.capacitie.org/wren/archive.htm (maintained by Simon Mann); also Wren-Lewis, "Darkness of God." The phrase "dazzling darkness" seems to be derived from Henry Vaughan, "The Night" (1650): "there is in God (some say) / a deep but dazzling darkness." See Vaughan, *Poems*, 290, after Pseudo-Dionysius, *Mystical Theology* 997ab (1.1) (*Works*, 135).

Most of us must take these accounts on trust: certainly I make no claim to any such revelation. But the Plotinian structure of hypostases, confessedly metaphorical, accommodates so much of my own and others' experience as to seem, at least, a worthy project: not merely a subject for learned examination or comparison with Upanishadic or Orthodox or Sufi theories and stories but a guide to further exploration, further revisioning of our experience. And this will still be true even if we must wait for God or the gods to come in their own time and energy. Matter, Nature, Soul, *Nous*, and the singular presence that unites them all are all ways of organizing both our lives and our theory about those lives—and loves.

What then is the One (if that is a possible question)? One answer seems to be "the productive power of all things" (III.8 [30].10).[14] Matter is in one way "potentially everything," since it can be formed into anything. The One is power in another sense: the power of everything to live, to act, to generate ("this is common to all that exists, to bring things into likeness with themselves"; IV.3 [27].10, 35–6). Plotinus shows how intellect is carried out of itself—how we depend on myths and theurgic meditations and the passion of love—to fall in love at last with Love Himself. The One is unique, indeed—but not solitary. The One is everywhere—but not because it fills a preexistent space. Rather, every place and every entity exist in love. The One *is* Love, at once beloved, lover, and the love between them (*erasmion kai eros ho autos kai autou eros*; VI.8 [39].15).

---

14. See Perl, "Power of All Things." See also *Hermetic Corpus* 5.9 (Copenhaver, *Hermetica*, 20): "He is himself the things that are and those that are not. Those that are he has made visible; those that are not he holds within him. . . . There is nothing that he is not, for he also is all that is, and this is why he has all names, because they are of one father, and this is why he has no name, because he is father of them all."

PART V

The Plotinian Way

The first step on the way as Plotinus defines it is for each of us to realize the power and dignity of our own souls, and of Soul in general.[1] It is Soul, metaphysically, that continually constructs the spatiotemporal cosmos as a piecemeal representation of the total intelligible realm that is housed in *Nous*. It is our own soul, individually, that has responsibility for the phenomenal realm we individually inhabit. As Coleridge declared—misleadingly:

> We receive but what we give
> And in our life alone does Nature live.[2]

This is misleading as a response to depression, as it tends to confirm the—very depressing—notion that there is no world, no Nature, worth our worship. Subjectivity, as Benson said, *is* depression![3] Better believe, whatever else we may believe, that there is high beauty far beyond the shadows, a beauty that will survive our own collapse, even if it may do nothing more to help us than remind us of its own existence.

> Beyond all towers strong and high,
> Beyond all mountains steep,
> Above all shadows rides the Sun

1. See V.1 [10].2.
2. Coleridge, "Dejection: An Ode" (1802) 4.47–8 (*Poems*, 308).
3. Benson, *Spiritual Letters*, 3: "the cause of depression is subjectivity, always. The Eternal Facts of Religion remain exactly the same, always. Therefore in depression the escape lies in dwelling upon the external truths that are true anyhow; and not in self-examination, and attempts at acts of the soul that one is incapable of making at such a time."

And Stars for ever dwell.
I will not say the day is done
Nor bid the stars farewell.[4]

But though Coleridge's verse may mislead, it contains a truth: what the world is like *for us* depends a lot on us. It may even be that Plato and Plotinus were correct, and each of us has *chosen* our whole lives,[5] whether prenatally or at each passing moment of our earthly existence. It is up to us, to each of us, how the world of our experience will develop, how far "through" it we shall see and to what end. Bernhard, in her Buddhist-inspired guide for the chronically ill (including, of course, herself), cites the *Dhammapada*: "with our thoughts we make the world."[6] Learn to question those thoughts, demand to know their authority, ask what our world would be like if we could banish or ignore them. The idea is not only Buddhist: Stoics too remind us that it is our assent to, our cultivation of, the thoughts and feelings that constantly arise in us that can make our worlds happy or unhappy. But this advice—choose to be different, choose to look the "other way," choose *not* to assent to these overwhelming thoughts and feelings—is inadequate on its own. Our problem is that we are turned away from truth and cannot easily—or at all—reform ourselves, any more than an alcoholic can be content with one glass of whisky, an anorexic simply eat a cake, or a depressive just "cheer up." We are dependent on God's intervention: Athena gripping us by the hair (VI.5 [23].7, 9–10) or the gods' sending down a solid shaft of light.[7] This is also not much help. How might we prepare ourselves for the intervention, or at least not ward ourselves against it?

Most of us had better begin with bodies, their care and maintenance. Plotinus himself refused some of the treatments and medications on offer in his day: "he refused to take medicines containing the flesh of wild beasts, giving as his reason that he did not approve of eating the flesh even of domestic animals."[8] Nor would he submit to enemas for his bowel complaints, saying that the treatment was not for the elderly. This suggests, in both cases, that he minded about keeping his body clear of improper influences (as he supposed), but he placed no general bar on enemas and the like. On the contrary, he mocked those who preferred magical exorcisms of the

---

4. Tolkien, *Return of the King*, 185. See also Tolkien, *Silmarillion*, 103. On both occasions a song, barely heard, awakens and encourages a captive.
5. Plato, *Republic* 10.614–21. See also IV.3 [27].8.
6. Bernhard, *How to Be Sick*, 104.
7. Porphyry, *Life* 23.18–20.
8. Ibid., 2.6.

demons of sickness to the use of laxatives (II.9 [33].14)![9] We are not only souls, he insisted, but also ensouled bodies and should take note of bodily influences on our mood and character: some people are more prone to anger when they are ill than when they are healthy, and when they have not tasted food than when they have eaten, and so on (IV.4 [28].28, 37–52). These bodily conditions may, of course, in their turn be occasioned by the soul's own choices—but here and now it is those "traces of soul" that we have to deal with, to live through, and perhaps eventually amend. The influence of "blood and bile" may be diminished by careful attention to our diet, our physical surroundings, and bodily exercises. He himself seems to have relied on daily massage, an element of Galen's therapeutic regimen.[10] By Porphyry's account his failure to maintain that treatment when his masseurs died allowed his condition to get worse—and this may perhaps embody the advice Plotinus himself conceived as wise in his later years, to "reduce and gradually extinguish his bodily advantages by neglect" (I.4 [46].14, 20). Maybe sickness was, as Plato advised, something he thought it necessary to experience: "now the most skilful physicians are those who, from their youth upward, have combined with the knowledge of their art the greatest experience of disease; they had better not be robust in health, and should have had all manner of diseases in their own persons."[11]

On the other hand, there may simply have been no masseurs available in the time of plague (and no clear evidence, *pace* Porphyry, that massage did anything but at best alleviate some symptoms). Plotinus generally sounds more realistic, less melancholiac, than Porphyry: his point is merely that the wise—or even the ordinarily sane—have other priorities than merely corporeal health, even when their corporeal health is poor.[12] Musicians who

---

9. M. Williams, *Rethinking Gnosticism*, 132–4, remarks that Plotinus's own recommendations against disease (to avoid overwork, overeating, malnutrition, and so on) could be followed only by an elite. The masses might well prefer to think that diseases were caused by an invasion of living organisms that might perhaps be evicted, at not too great an expense. We would all much rather there was a magic pill.

10. Porphyry, *Life* 2.6–8. See Galen, *Hygiene*.

11. Plato, *Republic* 3.408de.

12. One of the most irritating of Internet memes is a notice requiring everyone "who cares" to pass on the declaration that people with cancer have only one goal (i.e., to defeat the cancer). This is plainly both false and offensive, carrying with it the implications that those who die have been insufficiently strong-minded, and that they wasted their last months and years. The battle metaphor is unhelpful in any case. What is certain is that cancer victims have many other goals (e.g., world peace, the health and safety of their families and friends, the completion of whatever project they have in hand, a really good cup of coffee and a bagel). To have no other aim than corporeal survival is to have died in spirit long before one's death.

can no longer play a lyre will find another instrument or sing without accompaniment (I.4 [46].16, 23–30).[13]

Plotinus was also realistic—or so it may seem—in his advice to Porphyry. Noticing that Porphyry was thinking of suicide, "he came to me unexpectedly . . . and told me that this lust for death did not come from a settled rational decision but from a bilious indisposition, and urged me to go abroad [my translation]."[14] Travel—or at least a change of scene—has indeed often been offered as a remedy for melancholia[15] and may appeal precisely as a way to "get away from one's self." It is not certainly a successful remedy, though Porphyry seems to have found it helpful. Evagrius of Pontus (AD 345–99) identified the urge to travel as simply another gambit of the "demon of *acedia*, also called the noonday demon, . . . [who] uses every device in order to have the monk leave his cell and flee the stadium."[16] Unfortunately, the route back home—"back to our own well-ordered country" (V.9 [5].1, 22)—is not a journey for the feet but a change of outlook (I.6 [1].8, 16–28).

We may reasonably suppose, with Plotinus, that we need to care for our immediate bodily selves, as being the present locus of our endeavors. We are stationed here to look after our particular segment of the corporeal world and to do our best to keep it fit for purpose in the ongoing life of nature.

> If some boys, who have kept their bodies in good training, but are inferior in soul to their bodily condition because of lack of education, win a wrestle with others who are trained neither in body or soul and grab

13. See G. Clark, "Health of the Spiritual Athlete."

14. Porphyry, *Life* 11.13–6: Armstrong has "go away for a holiday." This suggests a modern social practice rather than an ancient one. *Apodemesai* is simply "to go abroad," not necessarily "on vacation" or even—despite the connotations of the cognate Latin term "peregrination"—"on pilgrimage." Armstrong (*Enneads*, vol. 1, 320) also very oddly remarks that since I.9 [16] was written before Porphyry joined Plotinus, "it cannot represent the arguments Plotinus used to discourage Porphyry from suicide (*Life* 11)." It is true that Plotinus does change tack a little between I.9 [16] and I.4 [46], the latter of which concedes that there will be occasions when suicide is at least permissible (when it is impossible to live well in slavery or when one's pains are entirely too much to bear), though not obligatory.

15. Klibansky, Panofsky, and Saxl, *Saturn and Melancholy*, 45; though cf. I.4 [46].16, 14–6.

16. "The Monk: A Treatise on the Practical Life," chap. 12 (Sinkewicz, *Evagrius of Pontus*, 99). See also John Cassian (AD 360–435), *Institutes* 10.2: the monk afflicted by acidie (i.e., the slothful conviction that there is nothing worth doing) "cries up distant monasteries . . . as more profitable and better suited for salvation; and besides this he paints the intercourse with the brethren there as sweet and full of spiritual life" (accessed 24 December 2014, http://www .documentacatholicaomnia.eu/03d/0360–0435,_Cassianus,_Institutes_Of_The_Coenobia_And _The_Remedies_Vol_3,_EN.pdf). In brief, he imagines that life would be much better in another monastery, with nicer monks. My thanks to Gillian Clark for this reference and associated gloss.

their food and their dainty clothes, would the affair be anything but a
joke? Or would it not be right for even the lawgiver to allow them to
suffer this as a penalty for their laziness and luxury? (III.2 [47].8, 16–21)

The bullies themselves, of course, will suffer for what they let themselves become, but Plotinus has no sympathy for wimps—including, perhaps, his own past self! We are here to help build "the moving image of
eternity," not to indulge ourselves, either by excess or by defect. There is a
danger in being too attached to bodily sensations, and to the worlds we variously invent within that larger whole, but we are not simply to abandon the
attempt and flee, in "disgust, or fear, or anger" (I.9 [16].1, 10–1). Even if our
personal worlds and even the world of nature are only *images* of eternity,
still we are bound to feel affection, precisely, for those images. "For anyone
who feels affection for anything at all shows kindness to all that is akin to
the object of his affection, and to the children of the father that he loves. But
every soul is a child [specifically, a *daughter*] of That Father" (II.9 [33].15,
33–II.9 [33].16, 10).

Purgation, peregrination, purification may not always be appealing or
persuasive remedies for mortal ills. They may tip over very easily into a
form of slow suicide, as they have in anorexics and also in some ascetics.[17]
They are worth remembering, if only as a counter to the methods that we
may ourselves prefer. Some spiritually informed therapists and healers resort too readily to the notion that "healing" is to be regarded as a way of
"becoming whole," or reintegrating a fractured self, and so acknowledging
the good in all creation. This in turn may have a form of contentment as its
goal, to be "at one" with Nature and so forth. Those who undertake what
they regard as a "spiritual" path sometimes seem to be aiming mainly to be
"comfortable with themselves," to be reconciled to their own past misdeeds
and follies—but not to pay for them.

> Your self-satisfaction ill becomes you. Have you never heard the saying,
> "A little leaven leavens all the dough"? The old leaven of corruption is
> working among you. Purge it out, and then you will be bread of a new bak-
> ing. As Christians you are unleavened Passover bread; for indeed our Pass-
> over has begun; the sacrifice is offered—Christ himself. So we who ob-

17. See Porphyry, *Abstinence*, 114 (4.18), describing "Samanaeans" (probably referring to
Hindu "renouncers," to be contrasted with the inherited status and culture of Brahmins). The
practice of deliberate, world-renouncing starvation, the "ritual fast to death," is still found
among Jains. See Dalrymple, *Nine Lives*, 5–6.

serve the festival must not use the old leaven, the leaven of corruption and wickedness, but only the unleavened bread which is sincerity and truth.[18]

Plotinus's imagery, and Paul's, is purgative: it is necessary to purify ourselves as gold is purified (I.6 [1].5, 5off.). On the one hand, it is absurd to pretend that "the bull of Phalaris" (a notorious instrument of torture) could be considered "pleasant" (I.4 [46].13, 7–8) or that everything which happens in this world here and now is right. On the other, it may be necessary simply to give some things up rather than pretend to sublimate or integrate them. Food is necessary for life—but too much food damages the soul as well as the body. Sex is a compelling force for most of us—but celibacy will probably do no harm (unless it merely conceals a nagging interest in all things sexual), and it is better to be chaste: "if [lovers] remain chaste there is no error in their intimacy with the beauty here below, but it is error to fall away into sexual intercourse" (III.5 [50].1, 36–7).

So the initial stages of the Plotinian way are marked by a moderate asceticism: we are not to scorn our bodies, or the world at large, but we are also not to let ourselves be distracted. A moderate asceticism may help keep us healthy, but no one is immune to sickness and poor fortune. Maybe some ill fortunes are a just response to past wickedness or a spur to future virtue—but maybe, on the other hand, they are only opportunities to deal with troubled times (or not). There are usually two ways for people to make sense of sickness: either disease is promoted by an enemy from without (a witch or a demon), or else it is an effect of the victim's own misdoings. There were elements of both ideas afloat in Plotinus's day. It was rumored that he had himself been cursed by a rival, Olympius of Alexandria, and shrugged off the attack.[19] Conversely, he considered sympathetically the notion that we were "once the doer of that which [we] now suffer" (III.2 [47].13, 11ff.). Neither explanation seems entirely happy, even in more sophisticated forms. Better—perhaps—simply to see what happens as opportunity. Blindness is not an effect of sin but an occasion for the Lord to show His power (not only in the cure but in endurance).[20] The Lord makes his rain to fall on the just and the unjust;[21] the wicked as well as the virtuous draw water from the river (IV.4 [28].42, 15–6; see also IV.3 [27].16).

18. Paul, *1 Corinthians* 5.6–8. See also *Matthew* 18.8: "If it is your hand or foot that is your undoing, cut it off and fling it away; it is better for you to enter into life maimed or lame, than to keep two hands or two feet and be thrown into the eternal fire."

19. Porphyry, *Life* 10.1–14.

20. *John* 9.1–3. See my "Progress and the Argument from Evil."

21. *Matthew* 5.45.

The law says that those who fight bravely, not those who pray, are to come safe out of wars; for, in just the same way, it is not those who pray but those who look after their land who are to get in a harvest, and those who do not look after their health are not to be healthy; and we are not to be vexed if the bad get larger harvests, or if their farming generally goes better. (III.2 [47].8, 37–42)

We are not to be vexed partly because these things don't matter very much and partly because this is only what we should expect of a natural universe that is not guided in every detail by a moral purpose, to make whatever happens something that is "deserved." Nor is the "principle of evil" a malevolent or even an essentially active force: materiality merely provides the opportunity for things to happen otherwise than might at first seem decent.

These medical, or more generally dietetic, suggestions need not be, in detail, what we now approve. We may need to inquire more carefully what each of us should do to make and keep our bodies fit for purpose. We do not know, in any detail, what pattern Plotinus himself followed, save that he was vegetarian, avoided the public baths (and hence contagion), kept his body fit by massage rather than vigorous exercise (though he had served in Gordian's army, not necessarily just as a court philosopher). It may be (as I have proposed above) that he followed other simple exercises: breathing calmly in and out, engaging in the dances he describes, and enjoying (even if not playing) music:

> Pythagoras advised people that when they arose at dawn, before setting off on any activity, they should apply themselves to music ["the Muse"] and to soothing melody, so that the confusion of their souls resulting from arousal out of sleep should first be transformed into a pure and settled condition and an orderly gentleness, and so make their souls well-attuned and concordant for the actions of the day. It also seems to me that the fact that the gods are invoked with music and melody of some sort— with hymns and *auloi*, for instance, or with Egyptian *trigonoi*—shows that we desire them to listen to our prayers with kindly gentleness.[22]

Perhaps Plotinus even employed the customs Plutarch attributed to Egyptian priests, of burning resin at dawn, myrrh at noon, and a fragrant

---

22. Ptolemy, *Harmonics* 3.100 (Barker, *Harmonic and Acoustic Theory*, 379). *Auloi* are double pipes; *trigonoi* are triangular harps.

mixture of perfumes at dusk[23]—which would add significance to his occasional mention of perfume to illustrate the presence and influence of the
One (V.1 [10].6, 36–8). There is no direct evidence here (why should we expect it?), but the techniques are common in most spiritual paths, and later
Platonists did explicitly follow them. Consider, for example, Walker's image
of how Ficino sought to manage his Saturnine temperament:

> He is playing a *lira da braccio* or a lute, decorated with a picture of
> Orpheus charming animals, trees and rocks; he is singing . . . the Or-
> phic Hymn of the Sun; he's burning frankincense, and at times he drinks
> wine; perhaps he contemplates a talisman; in day-time he is in sunlight,
> and at night he "represents the sun by fire."[24]

This may sound merely restful, but it had a more serious aim than re-
laxation. Other classical ascetics—Pythagorean, Cynic, or Christian—often
followed more rigorous rules, not so much to maintain their bodily health
(they sometimes, obviously, didn't), but to practice a moral virtue which
most of us have long forgotten.

> The man who belongs to this world may be handsome and tall and rich
> and the ruler of all mankind (since he is essentially of this region), and
> we ought not to envy him for things like these, by which he is beguiled.
> The wise man will perhaps not have them at all, and if he has them will
> himself reduce them, if he cares for his true self. He will reduce and
> gradually extinguish his bodily advantages by neglect, and will put away
> authority and office. He will take care of his bodily health, but will not
> wish to be altogether without experience of illness, nor indeed also of
> pain. (I.4 [46].14, 14–23)

"Moral purpose," nowadays, will often have a hedonistic ring: the supposedly *moral* agent acts "for the good of others" rather than her own, and
that good will usually amount to sparing them serious pain and helping
them achieve (sensible) pleasures. We are, however, not all strict "utilitarians," concerned only to maximize the satisfaction of as many desires as
possible for as many sentient beings as possible (or—less consistently—only
for as many members of our species, nation-state, or tribe as possible). Indeed, hardly anyone—even among professed utilitarians—adopts this prin-

---

23. Plutarch, *De Iside et Osiride*, 245–7 (383a–384a, chaps. 79–80).
24. Walker, *Spiritual and Demonic Magic*, 30.

ciple: we distinguish between desires and pleasures that we can endorse and those we choose to ignore or damn, and we rely on inherited prejudice to tell us what the likely effects of different sorts of action are. But despite these caveats, rather few of us fully endorse the notions that pain (our own as well as others') does not matter much to really virtuous people, and that pleasure itself is mostly a temptation, to be refused or disciplined. Even when we do advise ourselves and others against indulgence or in favor of friendly feeling, it is almost always from fear of painful consequences, natural or social—a fear that our predecessors would have considered childish! As Chesterton remarked, warnings about the perils of this or that activity "only affect that small minority which will accept any virtue as long as we do not ask them for the virtue of courage. Most healthy people dismiss these moral dangers as they dismiss the possibility of bombs or microbes."[25]

The Plotinian account of civil virtue emphasizes instead a ban on self-indulgence, in favor of ordered life within a world governed by an impartial natural law and within a civil society governed by the precepts devised by the wise men of old (or brought to us by Minos: VI.9 [9].7), so that we may all display some trace at least of the beauty those wise men acknowledged and have at least some feeling for the realities among which we live. But there is a still higher sort of virtue, not dependent on social approval, nor much concerned about embellishing this world here:

> For what can true self-possession [*sophrosune*] be except not keeping company with bodily pleasures, but avoiding them as impure and belonging to something impure? Courage, too, is not being afraid of death. And death is the separation of body and soul; and a man does not fear this if he welcomes the prospect of being rid of superfluity [*monos genesthai*]. Again, greatness of soul is despising the things here: and wisdom [*phronesis*] is an intellectual activity which turns away from the things below and leads the soul to those above. (I.6 [1].6, 7–13)[26]

25. Chesterton, *Heretics*, 30.

26. See also I.2 [19].5, 6ff. I have amended Armstrong's translation of *sophrosune* as "self-control" and of *monos* as "alone." The soul that is *monos* is stripped of everything unnecessary for its flight—the point is not that the virtuous live in solitary. The phrase itself is attested earlier, *perhaps* with the implication of privacy (Numenius frag. 11, cited by Dodds, "Numenius," 16–7)—but especially in Numenius another resonance may be with the Hebrew notion that Moses spoke "face-to-face" with God (*Exodus* 33.11: *enopios enopio*, in the Septuagint). Here again the point is the intimacy of the communication ("as a man speaks with a friend") and nothing about being lonely. Elsewhere the emphasis is on *purity*, not solitude. See I.6 [1].5, 52–8: "This is the soul's ugliness, not being pure [*kithara*] and unmixed [*eilikrines*], like gold, but full of earthiness; if anyone takes the earthy stuff away the gold is left, and is beautiful, when it is

And if you are wronged, what is there dreadful in that to an immortal? (II.9 [33].9, 15–6)

But virtuous activity, even virtuous forbearance in the face of danger and temptation and virtuous resistance to the demon of depression, is not itself the goal: a truly courageous person (say) would not want to display courage—since that depends on there being wrongs to resist or even wars to fight—"as if a physician were to wish that nobody needed his skill" (VI.8 [39].5, 19–21). "Pity would be no more, if we did not make somebody poor"[27]—unless pity (or better, *liberality*) is the name of something better than its practical performance in this world. And Saturnine depression may be a gateway to a higher world.

Saturn is also the planetary influence associated with "academic" life itself, and it is proper to conclude my study of the Plotinian Way by remembering how Plotinus chose to spend his own time in Rome: in reading and discussing well-established texts and in encouraging backward-and-forward *argument*. It is important to remember the medical, ceremonial, and ethical context within which he, his friends, and his disciples lived and worked, especially as modern philosophers often forget that context. But it would also be a mistake to forget the *arguments* and the spirit of dialectical discussion. Precisely because we all so easily confuse our own dreams, fears, and wishes with reality, it is helpful to follow arguments where they lead, even if they lead to surprising or unwelcome places. Precisely because our imaginations and our intuitions are often parochial or confused, it is helpful to put our trust instead in abstract reasoning. Angelic intellects presumably have no difficulty in just *seeing* the answer to every arithmetical question, even those involving numbers larger than any empirical set: most of us can barely intuit even simple addition of numbers beyond a hundred. Arithmetical savants can recognize prime numbers on sight: even the ordinarily gifted must rely on Eratosthenes's Sieve to pick them out.[28] Our failing intuitions are even less reliable when we deal with questions about

---

singled out [*monoumenos*] from other things and is alone [*mone*] by itself. In the same way the soul too, when it is separated from the lusts which it has through the body with which it consorted too much, and freed [*monotheisa*] from its other affections, purged of what it gets from being embodied, when it abides alone [*mone*] has put away all the ugliness which came from the other nature." Plotinus also encourages us to pray *monoi pros monon* (V.1 [1].2, 35).

27. Blake, "Human Abstract," in *Songs of Experience* (*Writings*, 217). See Aristotle, *Nicomachean Ethics* 10.1178b7ff.

28. So named by Nicomachus of Gerasa (c. AD 100) in his *Introduction to Arithmetic*, 204–6 (1.13).

our or others' "welfare" or questions about unseen realities far off—as we suppose—in space or time. So both painstaking work on paper and argumentative exchanges in the seminar are likely to be essential aids—if not always in achieving truth, at least in avoiding error. We do not need to believe that crowds are always right, in either what they assert or what they deny, to suspect that at least we do—as individuals—have something to gain from an external view of our most cherished conclusions and presumptions.

Holding back from self-indulgence, offering our thoughts for comment and rebuttal, continually recalling who and what we are—all these provide an almost-effective discipline. Whether many of us can maintain it in the face of danger and temptation seems uncertain. "The first beginning [of error], the sudden impulse, if it is overlooked, even produces a settled choice of that into which one has fallen" (III.2 [47].4, 42–3).[29] Perhaps we must hope instead—as Plotinus did—that the gods will come to help us, "sending down a solid shaft of light"[30] or seizing us by the hair to turn us round (VI.5 [23].7, 9–10). We can perhaps get comfort from imagining and cleaning up our internal statues, waiting for them to move within us. We can internalize the stories of heroes, saints, and sages and so discover—mostly to our alarm—that more is possible for us than we had thought. We can force ourselves to *listen* to our rivals, partners, and—most of all—our foes. But all these images and stories must in the end be swallowed up: we must learn to turn in circles, unified and purified in the awareness of our own awareness. "Shut your eyes, and change to and wake another way of seeing, which everyone has but few use" (I.6 [1].8, 28). Imitate the stars: let both past and future go.

And though I have, in this volume, been emphasizing the significance of imagination, we must also remember that "if the shapes that men imagine in their minds could achieve Release for them, then surely men could become kings by means of the kingdom that they get in their dreams."[31] Our images can only prepare the way.

It is at least in line with Plotinus's style to offer one last reversal: "circular" reasoning may represent an ideal way, but it may also be a trap. Strictly circular reasoning, after all, can reach no answer that is not already assumed in the argument's own premises: "if *p*, then *p*" is a logically sound argument

29. Once we have decided either to do or to believe one out of the many options, we routinely *defend* that choice against all comers, even if we must use arguments that would not have worked to persuade us in the past!

30. Porphyry, *Life* 23.18–21.

31. *Mahanirvana Tantra* (c. eighteenth century), cited by Doniger, *Hindus*, 406.

(and "begging the question" is not a *logical* fallacy but only a rhetorical failing), but it gets us nowhere. If our initial premise is mistaken, we are merely repeating error. Even if it is not, we are not achieving any novel insight. We need, precisely, to break out of the circle.

> A man cannot think himself out of mental evil; for it is the organ of thought that has become diseased, ungovernable, and, as it were, independent. He can only be saved by will or faith. The moment his mere reason moves, it moves in the old circular rut; he will go round and round his logical circle, just as a man in a third-class carriage on the Inner Circle will go round and round the Inner Circle unless he performs the voluntary, vigorous, and mystical act of getting out at Gower Street.[32]

In still more mythological terms, we shall continue to go round the circle of incarnations till we wake up, and so return from our long exile. Once we have brought the center of our circle into accord with the One center, we need no longer (we can no longer) circle around the circumference: there is a moment when we can establish some quite other new direction.

Another route to the same result arises from the Mirror metaphor. Our error is to identify with, to fall in with, *images*, and the way to correct the error is to disengage ourselves. When we are afflicted by anger, greed, or depression, we may instead merely *take note* of these emotions, as we might also *note* the passage of a cloud across the sun or a butterfly among the flowers. As long as we do not *notice* that we are, for example, in a fearful temper, the temper absorbs us entirely. *Noticing* the rage (the greed, the despairing voice) is the first step to discarding it. Noticing it, we may also remember that it will pass, and that it has of itself no power to help or hurt us.[33] Remembering also that these feelings are *reflections*, we can—perhaps—identify the real things they represent: "the fury of anger represents an intellectual power of resistance of which anger is the last and faintest echo; desire symbolizes the Divine Love; and in short we might find in all the irrational tendencies and many parts of irrational creatures, figures of the immaterial conceptions and single powers of the Celestial Beings."[34] Every reflective image that we see, from which we must disengage ourselves, will prove also to be a reminder of the heavenly presences among which, perhaps, we shall live. But perhaps not yet.

---

32. Chesterton, *Orthodoxy*, 11.
33. This technique of detachment is explored in several of Tolle's works: see esp. *New Earth*.
34. Pseudo-Dionysius, *Celestial Hierarchy*, 34.

What and where is the Other Country, our Homeland, to which Plotinus beckons in this volume's epigraph? Later poets reckoned it a country "afar beyond the stars,"[35] which was—by the very fact of thus being
wholly *outside* our world—very close to each of us. In most of this volume
I have sought to represent it rather as a discovery of the one real world, and
our "migration" to it as merely (though significantly) a change of outlook.
"Flight, [Plato] says, is not going away from earth but being on earth 'just
and holy with the help of wisdom'; what he means is that we must fly from
wickedness" (I.8 [51].6, 10–3).[36] But perhaps it is time to acknowledge that
Platonists did often intend a more definite departure—even though it was
not a "journey for the feet," or even for a carriage or "*ti thalattion*" ("sea-
going somewhat"). Even so, my final comments are rather to do with the
significance of a belief in a real Other Country. The injunction is—as it
were—to live as like a Narnian as we can, even if there is no Narnia![37] The
problem with this, as a practical matter, is that the enterprise must then
seem more like a temporary fad or hobby than a dedicated form of life: to
sustain the latter over a lifetime it may be necessary to confirm it through
shared ceremonial, shared readings, a shared project—and a shared *belief.*

Plotinus himself seems not to have troubled with shared ceremonial,
though he would presumably have endorsed whatever festivals Pythian
Apollo decreed for Platonopolis.[38] He commented favorably on the methods
of "the wise men of old" but emphasized that acting out the internal
imagery was a sign of weakness. His successors were less refined, choosing
instead to practice theurgical rituals to ask the gods to help us. They also
rejected Plotinus's conviction that some part of our own soul did not "descend," and so was available to us even in this sublunary life: Iamblichus—
and in this he agreed with mainstream Christians—was persuaded that we
were fallen entirely away from the divine and needed far more help than we
could muster for ourselves. Our return needed more than simply to turn
round (not that Plotinus thought this easy): it really did need God's help.

Public ceremonials of a theurgical or sacramental kind, bringing—at
least—a *perception* of the gods into our working lives, have always been
at the center of the religious life. Plotinus's standing aside from Roman

35. Vaughan, "Peace," in *Silex Scintillans* (1650) (*Poems,* 184–5). See Holmes, *Vaughan and
the Hermetic Philosophy.*

36. After Plato, *Theaetetus* 176–7.

37. Lewis, *Silver Chair,* 191. Plotinus might not have agreed: he insists, remember, that no
one "would . . . delight in a boy because he was present when he was not present" (VI.7 [38].26,
21–2). Reality matters (and so, of course, insisted Lewis on many other occasions).

38. See Plato, *Laws* 8.828a: the magistrates are to offer sacrifice on each day of the year.

ritual does not mark him as irreligious: he may have preferred other ceremonials or supposed that the Roman sort were—for him—contaminated
by unwanted associations. He may have had a hankering for the rites of
Platonopolis. But whatever Plotinus himself managed, we may ourselves
find public ceremonial important. By Durkheim's account of religion, most
actual believers "feel that the real function of religion is not to make us
think, to enrich our knowledge, nor to add to the conceptions which we owe
to science others of another origin and another character, but rather, it is to
make us act, to aid us to live." He does also acknowledge that religion "is
not merely a system of practices—but also a system of ideas whose object is
to explain the world."[39] But—Durkheim continues—the primary purpose
of "religion," in its broadest sense, is protreptic rather than epistemic.

> The believer who has communicated with his god is not merely a man
> who sees new truths of which the unbeliever is ignorant; he is a man
> who is stronger. He feels within him more force, either to endure the tri-
> als of existence, or to conquer them. It is as though he were raised above
> the miseries of the world, because he is raised above his condition as a
> mere man; he believes that he is saved from evil, under whatever form
> he may conceive this evil. The first article in every creed is the belief in
> salvation by faith.

To cultivate and maintain that faith we need the cult, and the common life:

> Whoever has really practised a religion knows very well that it is the cult
> which gives rise to these impressions of joy, of interior peace, of seren-
> ity, of enthusiasm which are, for the believer, an experimental proof of
> his beliefs. The cult is not simply a system of signs by which the faith
> is outwardly translated; it is a collection of the means by which this is
> created and recreated periodically. Whether it consists in material acts or
> mental operations, it is always this which is efficacious.[40]

Porphyry leaves the impression that Plotinus was not concerned with
this—but this may be an error, too easily believed by philosophers and
scholars with a distaste for public ceremonial! The most widespread form
of divine service is now poorly understood by post-Copernican urbanites
like ourselves. "In this city [of the world] virtue is honoured and vice has its

---

39. Durkheim, *Elementary Forms*, 416.
40. Ibid., 416–7.

appropriate dishonour, and not merely the images of gods but *gods them-selves* look down on us from above" (II.9 [33].9, 19–22; my italics). Serving the visible gods, the stars of heaven, is sharing in the complex dance that they perform above and around us, and so sharing in a simulacrum of eternity (IV.4 [28].8).

The same movements are endlessly repeated, but neither the stars nor the people embedded in the ritual year need remember the merely linear, endless process. Seedtime and harvest, Christmas and Easter, and "the passionless Sundays after Trinity, neither feast-day nor fast,"[41] are permanent realities. Nothing serious is ever really lost, since circular motion is unending without being infinite. Obviously, post-Copernicans look out on an entirely different sidereal universe, and even if we manage to believe the speculative cosmologists who imagine an infinity of worlds or aeons, we know that our own personal and terrestrial history passes irrevocably from a far beginning to a distant end. Urbanites expect strawberries at any time of the year, and only play at the repeating seasons.

Plato, Plotinus, and other Platonists were both closer to the ceremonial year and readier to acknowledge the presence of the visible gods, the stars, and the periods they ruled.

> General opinion makes the Hours goddesses and the Month a god, and their worship has been handed on to us: we say also that the Day and the Night are deities, and the gods themselves have taught us how to call upon them.[42]

But they were also ready, as it were, to allegorize that ancient sidereal religion, and we too can glimpse what they saw in it. "By contemplating the equivalence of the future and the past we pierce through time right to eternity."[43] As *souls*, or as fallen souls, we see things only from particular angles, at particular moments, and are easily persuaded that the world as we see it is all the world there is. But even materialists know better: there are no privileged places, moments, or timescales, and the *real* world is the one discovered, if at all, through reason, as the complete, well-ordered content of the Intellect. Learning to detach ourselves from sensory illusions, to live in the understanding that each of us is only one *version* of reality, an entity

---

41. Falkner, "After Trinity" (1910); Betjeman, *Altar and Pew*, 42.

42. Proclus, *In Timaeum* 248d, quoted by Cumont, *Astrology and Religion*, 61, accessed 23 December 2014, http://www.sacred-texts.com/astro/argr/argr09.htm.

43. Weil, *Intimations of Christianity*, 96.

wholly dependent on its membership in that real world and without any special status, is both an epistemological and a moral exercise. We serve the gods by pleasing them. We please them by sharing, sometimes, in their life and dismissing the charms that bind us to our sensual, solitary delusions.

There are at least three roads onward from Plotinus's own stance: the first, to keep apart from the public, as Porphyry suggests he did, relying wholly on our own resources of imagination, reason, and devotion; the second, to follow the available public cult (until recently, in Western and Eastern Christendom, this would be, mostly, Christian in its various sorts); the third, to see what can be done with pagan Hellenism of the sort that Julian preferred. This last option, for most of us, must seem bizarre: only a few devoted cultists suppose they can recover this (and even they will usually not wish to reinstate the sacrifice of oxen, sheep, and pigs). It is not a practical option—but it may still be worth considering what would be lost or gained in it, and how far distant such practices may be from what Plotinus (and just possibly Gallienus)[44] really wanted.

The obvious difference—already intimated—is that Plotinus did not suppose that "animals" were ours to sacrifice. Maybe he even supposed, as Porphyry did, that killings of that sort were pleasing only to the more malevolent demons, that they summoned the *wrong* spirits to our imagined aid (and actual destruction). "An intelligent, temperate man will be wary of making sacrifices through which he will draw such beings to himself."[45] This might be true even if—as, of course, it is now eccentric to dispute—there really are no demons outside the human heart. The attitudes and axioms, the programmed behavior patterns that we encourage in ourselves, may end by having more influence on us than we at first expected. Bloodless sacrifices, of herbs or flowers or crystals, might be a better focus, or hymns to the stellar or the domestic divinities. These were the spiritual recourse of many later Platonists, like Yeats. By creating a particular mood Yeats hoped to gain access to powers that were more than moods—and at least help to dispel incipient psychoses (as we now consider them): clinical depression, paranoia, manic outbursts, whether of rage or drunken excitement. Maybe we can even *imagine* a helper, a higher self, into existence: "the yogic subtle body is an object our imagination has to create."[46]

44. As proposed by A. Alföldi, *Studien zur Geschichte der Weltkrise des dritten Jahrhunderts* (1967), cited by Blois, *Policy of Gallienus,* 185–93, who argues against the suggestion.

45. Porphyry, *Abstinence,* 73 (2.43).

46. Bharati, *Light at the Centre,* 164, cited by Singleton, *Yoga Body,* 51. See also Corbin, *Creative Imagination in Ibn Arabi.*

But even bloodless sacrifices have a meaning beyond such magics: to sacrifice something is to make it "sacred," to put it out of our reach, for good or ill. What should we sacrifice, and to whom? And how shall that sacrifice be secured against any later change of mind or office? Dead cattle, though some part of them may be consumed by fire, are made meat, whether for the priestly classes or for all devotees—which is why there was an issue for the early Christian Church about the consumption of animals sacrificed to idols.[47] Eating them was to share a feast prepared—it was supposed—for demons. In Jewish law, strictly interpreted, only animals killed in the Temple at Jerusalem were edible, as it was only by dedicating their deaths to God that their flesh was made available (but not their blood). A complete sacrifice could only be a whole offering, with nothing left for our advantage—and perhaps it would be better thus to "sacrifice" by simply letting the victims free.

On these terms, the proper "sacrifice" is simply to abandon any claim to possess or control the thing—as Weil remarked:

> It may be that vice, depravity and crime are nearly always, or even perhaps always, in their essence, attempts to eat beauty, to eat what we should only look at. . . . If [Eve] caused humanity to be lost by eating the fruit, the opposite attitude, looking at the fruit without eating it, should be what is required to save it.[48]

To sacrifice is to give up or give away, to let some other control the thing—but it is very easy then to allow a priestly or imperial class that power, exercised (perhaps) "on behalf" of an unseen deity. It does not seem that a Plotinian pagan would be happy with that outcome, unless perhaps the Platonic philosopher-kings were present. In their absence, there can be no single worthy authority, no viceroy or intermediary. Whether such a viceregal or priestly role can even be ascribed simply to any *human being* with respect to the nonhuman world must be uncertain. That human beings are created "in the image of God" may once have meant exactly this: that every individual human was created as a living representative—as many eastern kings erected statues of themselves throughout their dominions, requiring the same respect for them as for themselves. On these terms every earthly thing is to be subject to a human will (though that will should be exercised with more genuine humanity than most of us

47. See Paul, *1 Corinthians* 8.4–13; *Revelation* 2.14, 2.20.
48. Weil, *Notebooks*, vol. 1, 121.

have ever managed). But though there are traces even in Plotinus of such a high account of what it is to be human—for only human beings are ever *consciously* in touch with their own divinity[49]—it may be just as reasonable a development to remember instead that all creatures are our brothers and our sisters, and all are partial images of an eternal Beauty, brought to life and light by Soul. Setting all such creatures free of our control may be the sacrifice that we are required to make if we are ever to return back home.

Precisely because we are human—that is, the author and readers of this book are human even if, imaginably, some future readers are of different descent and habits[50]—we must reason and imagine our way to a proper understanding and appreciation of reality. Through philosophical conversation we may slowly come to recognize the images and received opinions that have governed our lives together, and learn how to pass beyond them. In particular we must surrender our attachment to the "beasts within." Someday, perhaps, "the wolf shall live with the sheep, and the leopard lie down with the kid; the calf and the young lion shall grow up together, and a little child shall lead them"[51]—and all our interior selves shall be integrated. But in this age of the world we had better put such dreams aside and not allow either the wild beasts or the tame too loud a voice in us.

> Man is a lump, where all beasts kneaded be,
> Wisdom makes him an ark where all agree;
> The fool, in whom these beasts do live at jar,
> Is sport to others and a theatre,
> Nor 'scapes he so, but is himself their prey;
> All which was man in him is eat away,
> And now his beasts on one another feed,
> Yet couple in anger, and new monsters breed;

49. So Gerson, "Metaphor as an Ontological Concept," 269: "Whereas nature contemplates by operating according to an image of *Nous*, only a person can recognize that he himself is an image and that he is thinking with the images of *Nous*. The recognition by the perceptible Socrates that he is not the real Socrates, a recognition that must of course occur in a language that is ineluctably metaphorical, is more than mere assent to a proposition about Socrates." That the perceptible Socrates is not the *real* Socrates is less paradoxical than Gerson implies—of course, the real Socrates is more and other than the impressions others have of him, or even than the impression he has of himself.

50. As I remarked, after Aristotle, in *Aristotle's Man*, 25: "hydrocarbon arachnoids are men [*sic*] as well as we, if they can converse with us and we with them."

51. *Isaiah* 12.6.

How happy is he, which hath due place assigned
To his beasts, and disafforested his mind!⁵²

Taming them may be beyond us: expelling them entirely may be, paradoxically, the easier option. "We must act like a human being, not like a sheep,
however gentle, nor violently like a wild beast."⁵³ Even "nobler" beasts
are not what we should embody: astronomers may be reborn as high-flying
birds, and kings as eagles, lofty predators, but this is a sign of their stupidity,
or at least their lack of sound philosophy (III.4 [15].1, 25)! The really self-
willed bury their heads in the earth, as plants (V.2 [11].2)!⁵⁴ It is the star-
gods that we should hope, at first, to imitate or incarnate, and we may hope
to do this by taking a less parochial view of things.

> But those which have come to be outside have transcended the nature of
> spirits and the whole destiny of birth, and altogether what is in the vis-
> ible world. (III.4 [15].6, 31–3)

I have sought throughout this work to show how Plotinus would have us
live here-now, and what the world of our experience might seem if we re-
formed our wills and imagination, whether or not the universe is as he
argued that it was. Even his most metaphysical utterances can be given a
therapeutic and this-worldly reading. Even when there is a more "literal"
and cosmological significance in what he says or quietly assumes, the "metaphorical" meanings offer effective recipes for remodeling our lives. But it
would be misleading not to acknowledge Plotinus's own last written words:

> We must say that life in a body is an evil in itself, but the soul comes
> into good by its virtue, by not living the life of the compound but sepa-
> rating itself even now. (I.7 [54].3, 20–4)

We shall live better in this world, and this body, on the understanding that
this world, this body, are neither entirely good nor even entirely real. Ploti-

---

52. Donne, "To Sir Edward Herbert" (1610) (Poems, 271).

53. Epictetus, Discourses, 168 (III.23.4). One popular self-help book, much admired by
athletes, chooses to describe our "lower, emotional self" as "the Chimp" and urges readers to
identify themselves entirely with "the Human" (Peters, Chimp Paradox). This is a rather less
subtle image than Epictetus's.

54. This echoes the line of descent in Plato's Timaeus 91c (see also Aristotle, De partibus
animalium 4.686a25ff.).

nus's last spoken words were "try to bring back the god in you to the divine in the All!"[55] That is not only a psychotherapeutic maxim but a considered judgment about the metaphysical. This world here-now when properly conceived is also the World Eternal—but this world here-now, as we perceive and live it, is still something to be abandoned. The one real world, Plotinus taught, is There. If we are also real (though not as we perceive ourselves here-now), we shall join, we have "already" joined, the Dance. Those who consider Plotinus's account to be *merely* metaphorical, or even *merely* therapeutic, are perhaps still missing his intended moral.

---

55. Porphyry, *Life* 2.26–7. See also VI.9 [9].11, 48–51.

Abram, David. *The Spell of the Sensuous*. New York: Pantheon, 1996.

Adamson, Peter. *The Arabic Plotinus: A Philosophical Study of the "Theology of Aristotle."* London: Duckworth, 2003.

Addey, Crystal. *Divination and Theurgy in Late Antiquity: Oracles of the Gods*. Farnham: Ashgate, 2014.

———. "Mirrors and Divination: Catopromancy, Oracles and Earth Goddesses in Antiquity." In *The Book of the Mirror*, edited by Miranda Anderson, 33–46. Cambridge: Cambridge Scholars, 2007.

Adluri, Vishwa. "Plato's Saving *Mūthos*: The Language of Salvation in the *Republic*." *International Journal of the Platonic Tradition* 8 (2014): 3–32.

Aesop. *The Complete Fables*. Translated by Olivia Temple and Robert Temple. New York: Penguin, 1998.

Alexander, Loveday A. "The Living Voice: Scepticism towards the Written Word in Early Christian and in Graeco-Roman Texts." In *The Bible in Three Dimensions*, edited by D. J. A. Clines, S. E. Fowl, and S. E. Porter, 221–47. Sheffield: Sheffield Academic Press, 1990.

Alexander, Samuel. *Space, Time and Deity*. London: Macmillan, 1920.

Alexander of Aphrodisias. *On Fate*. Translated by R. W. Sharples. London: Duckworth, 1983.

Algra, K. A. *Concepts of Space in Greek Thought*. Leiden: Brill, 1995.

Ando, Clifford. *The Matter of the Gods: Religion and the Roman Empire*. Berkeley: University of California Press, 2008.

Armstrong, A. H. "The Background of the Doctrine 'That the Intelligibles Are Not outside the Intellect.'" In *Sources de Plotin*, 391–413. Entretiens Hardt 5. Geneva: Fondation Hardt, 1960.

———. "Elements in the Thought of Plotinus at Variance with Classical Intellectualism." *Journal of Hellenic Studies* 93 (1973): 13–22.

———. *Enneads*. See Plotinus.

———. "Plotinus." In *Cambridge History of Later Greek and Early Mediaeval Philosophy*, edited by A. H. Armstrong, 195–271. Cambridge: Cambridge University Press, 1967.

————. "Was Plotinus a Magician?" *Phronesis* 1 (1955–6): 73–9.

Armstrong, A. H., and R. A. Markus. *Christian Faith and Greek Philosophy*. London: Darton, Longman, and Todd, 1960.

Assmann, Jan. *Moses the Egyptian*. Cambridge, MA: Harvard University Press, 1997.

————. *Religio Duplex: How the Enlightenment Reinvented Egyptian Religion*. Translated by Robert Savage. Cambridge: Polity, 2014.

Athanasius. *De incarnatione*. Translated by Penelope Lawson. New York: St. Vladimir's Seminary Press, 1989.

————. *Orations against the Arians*. Translated by John Henry Newman and Archibald Robertson. Nicene and Post-Nicene Fathers, 2nd ser., edited by Philip Schaff and Henry Wace, vol. 4. Buffalo, NY: Christian Literature, 1892.

Augustine. *City of God*. Translated by Henry Bettenson. Harmondsworth, UK: Penguin, 2003.

————. *Confessions*. Translated by Henry Chadwick. Oxford: Oxford University Press, 1992.

————. *On Christian Teaching*. Edited by R. P. H. Green. New York: Oxford University Press, 2008.

————. *The Teacher, the Free Choice of the Will, and Grace and Free Will*. Translated by R. P. Russell. Washington, DC: Catholic University of America Press, 1968.

Aurelius, Marcus. *Meditations*. Translated by C. R. Haines. Loeb Classical Library. London: Heinemann, 1930.

Azize, Joseph. *The Phoenician Solar Theology: An Investigation into the Phoenician Opinion of the Sun Found in Julian's Hymn to King Helios*. Piscataway, NJ: Gorgias Press, 2005.

Bacovcin, Helen, trans. *The Way of the Pilgrim*. New York: Doubleday, 1985.

Balthasar, Hans Urs von. *The Glory of the Lord: A Theological Aesthetics*. Vol. 4 of *The Realm of Metaphysics in Antiquity*. Translated by Brian McNeil, Andrew Louth, Johan Saward, Rowan Williams, and Oliver Davies. Edited by John Riches. Edinburgh: T. and T. Clark, 1989.

————. *Theo-Logic I: The Truth of the World*. Translated by Adrian J. Walker. San Francisco: Ignatius Press, 2000.

Bandura, Albert. "Self-Efficacy: Toward a Unifying Theory of Behavioral Change." *Psychological Review* 84, no. 2 (1977): 191–215.

Barber, Elizabeth Wayland, and Paul T. Barber. *When They Severed Earth from Sky: How the Human Mind Shapes Myth*. Princeton, NJ: Princeton University Press, 2004.

Barcan, Ruth. *Nudity*. Oxford: Berg, 2004.

Barfield, Raymond. *The Ancient Quarrel between Philosophy and Poetry*. Cambridge: Cambridge University Press, 2011.

Barker, Andrew, ed. *The Musician and His Art*. Vol. 1 of *Greek Musical Writings*. Cambridge: Cambridge University Press, 1984.

————. *Harmonic and Acoustic Theory*. Vol. 2 of *Greek Musical Writings*. Cambridge: Cambridge University Press, 1989.

Bartsch, Shadi. *The Mirror of the Self: Sexuality, Self-Knowledge, and the Gaze in the Early Roman Empire*. Chicago: University of Chicago Press, 2006.

Bates, Brian. *The Way of the Actor: A Path to Knowledge and Power*. Boston: Shambhala, 1988.

Bauckham, Richard. *Jesus and the Eyewitnesses: The Gospels as Eyewitness Testimony*. Grand Rapids, MI: William B. Eerdmans, 2006.

Beard, Mary. "The Roman and the Foreign: The Cult of the 'Great Mother' in Imperial Rome." In *Shamanism, History and the State*, edited by Nicholas Thomas and Caroline Humphrey, 164–90. Ann Arbor: University of Michigan Press, 1996.

Beierwaltes, Walter. *Platonismus und Idealismus*. Frankfurt: Klostermann, 1972.

Bell, Rudolph M. *Holy Anorexia*. Chicago: University of Chicago Press, 1987.

Bellah, Robert N. *Religion in Human Evolution: From the Paleolithic to the Axial Age*. Cambridge, MA: Harvard University Press, 2011.

Benjamin, J. D. "A Method of Distinguishing and Evaluating Formal and Thinking Disorders in Schizophrenia." In *Language and Thought in Schizophrenia*, edited by J. S. Kasanin, 65–90. New York: Norton, 1944.

Benson, R. H. *Spiritual Letters*. New York: Longmans Green, 1915.

Berger, John. *Ways of Seeing*. Harmondsworth, UK: Penguin, 1972.

Berkeley, George. *Works*. Edited by A. A. Luce and T. E. Jessop. 8 vols. London: T. Nelson, 1948–56.

Bernhard, Toni. *How to Be Sick: A Buddhist-Inspired Guide for the Chronically Ill and Their Caregivers*. Boston: Wisdom Publications, 2010.

Betjeman, John, ed. *Altar and Pew: Church of England Verses*. London: Edward Hulton, 1959.

Beyer, Stephan. *The Cult of Tara: Magic and Ritual in Tibet*. Berkeley: University of California Press, 1973.

Bharati, Agehananda. *The Light at the Centre: Context and Practice of Modern Mysticism*. Santa Barbara, CA: Ross-Erikson, 1976.

Blake, William. *Complete Writings*. Edited by Geoffrey Keynes. Oxford: Oxford University Press, 1966.

Blois, Lukas de. *The Policy of the Emperor Gallienus*. Leiden: E. J. Brill, 1976.

Blumenberg, Hans. *Work on Myth*. Translated by Robert M. Wallace. Cambridge, MA: MIT Press, 1985.

Bonfante, Larissa. "Nudity as a Costume in Classical Art." *American Journal of Archaeology* 93 (1989): 543–70.

Borges, J. L. "Funes the Memorious." In *Labyrinths*, edited by Donald A. Yates and James E. Irby, 87–95. Harmondsworth, UK: Penguin, 1970.

———. "Pascal's Sphere." 1951. In *Other Inquisitions, 1937–1952*, translated by Ruth L. C. Simms, 6–9. Austin: University of Texas Press, 1993.

Bostrom, Nick. "Are You Living in a Computer Simulation?" *Philosophical Quarterly* 53 (2003): 243–55.

Boswell, James. *The Life of Samuel Johnson*. 1791. Edited by David Womersley. London: Penguin, 2008.

Bowersock, Glenn. "The Hellenism of Zenobia." In *Greek Connections: Essays on Culture and Diplomacy*, edited by John T. A. Koumoulides, 19–27. Notre Dame, IN: University of Notre Dame Press, 1988.

Boyd, Gregory A. *God at War: The Bible and Spiritual Conflict*. Downers Grove, IL: Intervarsity Press, 1997.

Boyle, Marjorie O'Rourke. "Pure of Heart: From Ancient Rites to Renaissance Plato." *Journal of the History of Ideas* 63 (2002): 41–62.

Boys-Stones, George. *Post-Hellenistic Philosophy: A Study of Its Development from the Stoics to Origen*. Oxford: Oxford University Press, 2001.

Braude, Stephen E. *Immortal Remains: The Evidence for Life after Death*. New York: Rowman and Littlefield, 2003.

Bremmer, Jan. *The Early Greek Concept of the Soul*. Princeton, NJ: Princeton University Press, 1983.

Brisson, Luc. *How Philosophers Saved Myths: Allegorical Interpretation and Classical Mythology*. Translated by Catherine Tihanyi. Chicago: University of Chicago Press, 2004.

———. *Plato the Myth Maker*. Translated by Gerard Naddaf. Chicago: University of Chicago Press, 1998.

Broad, C. D. *Lectures on Psychical Research*. London: Routledge and Kegan Paul, 1962.

Brown, John Pairman. "The Templum and the Saeculum: Sacred Space and Time in Israel and Etruria." *Zeitschrift für die Alttestamentliche Wissenschaft* 98 (1986): 415–33. Revised version in John Pairman Brown, *Israel and Hellas*, vol. 2 (Berlin: W. de Gruyter, 2000), 199–234.

Brown, Norman. *Life against Death: Psychoanalytical Meaning of History*. Middletown, CT: Wesleyan University Press, 1959.

Brumberg, Joan Jacobs. *Fasting Girls: A History of Anorexia Nervosa*. 2nd ed. Boston: Vintage Books, 2001.

Buber, Martin. *I and Thou*. Translated by Walter Kaufmann. New York: Simon and Schuster, 1996.

Burkert, Walter. *Ancient Mystery Cults*. Cambridge, MA: Harvard University Press, 1987.

———. *Lore and Science in Ancient Pythagoreanism*. Translated by Edwin L. Minar. Cambridge, MA: Harvard University Press, 1972.

Burnyeat, M. F. "Idealism and Greek Philosophy: What Descartes Saw and Berkeley Missed." *Philosophical Review* 91 (1982): 3–40.

Bussanich, John. "Socrates the Mystic." In *Traditions of Platonism: Essays Presented to John Dillon*, edited by John Cleary, 29–51. London: Ashgate, 1999.

Buxton, Richard, ed. *From Myth to Reason? Studies in the Development of Greek Thought*. Oxford: Oxford University Press, 1999.

Caldecott, Stratford. "Liturgy and Trinity: Towards an Anthropology of the Liturgy." In *Looking Again at the Question of the Liturgy with Cardinal Ratzinger*, Proceedings of the July 2001 Fontgombault Liturgical Conference, edited by Alcuin Reid. Farnborough: St. Michael's Abbey Press, 2003. http://www.secondspring.co.uk/articles/scaldecott34.htm.

Cardenal, Ernesto. *Love*. Translated by Dinah Livingstone. London: Search Press, 1974.

Carruthers, Mary. *The Craft of Thought: Meditation, Rhetoric, and the Making of Images, 400–1200*. Cambridge: Cambridge University Press, 2000.

———. Review of *La stanza della memoria: Modelli letterari e iconografici nell'età della stampa*, by Lina Bolzoni. *Speculum* 71 (1996): 689–92.

Carruthers, Peter. *Language, Thought and Consciousness: An Essay in Philosophical Psychology.* Cambridge: Cambridge University Press, 1996.

Chadwick, Henry. *Early Christian Thought and the Classical Tradition.* Oxford: Clarendon Press, 1966.

Chase, Michael, Stephen R. L. Clark, and Michael McGhee, eds. *Philosophy as a Way of Life.* New York: Wiley-Blackwell, 2013.

Chesterton, G. K. *Complete Works.* Vol. 29. San Francisco: Ignatius Press, 1988.

———. *Fancies versus Fads.* London: Methuen, 1923.

———. *The Father Brown Stories.* London: Cassell, 1929.

———. *Heretics.* New York: John Lane, 1905.

———. *The New Jerusalem.* Sioux Falls, SD: NuVision Publications, 2007.

———. *Orthodoxy.* Thirsk, UK: House of Stratus, 2001.

———. *The Poet and the Lunatics.* London: Darwen Finlayson, 1962.

———. *St. Francis of Assisi.* London: Hodder and Stoughton, 1996.

———. *Tremendous Trifles.* London: Methuen, 1904.

———. *What's Wrong with the World.* London: Cassell, 1910.

Chittick, William C. "Jami on Divine Love and the Image of Wine." *Studies in Mystical Literature* 1, no. 3 (1981): 193–209.

———. *Science of the Cosmos, Science of the Soul: The Pertinence of Islamic Cosmology in the Modern World.* Oxford: Oneworld, 2007.

———. *The Sufi Path of Knowledge: Ibn al-'Arabi's Metaphysics of Imagination.* New York: SUNY Press, 1989.

Chuang Tzu. *Complete Works of Chuang Tzu.* Translated by Burton Watson. New York: Columbia University Press, 2013.

Cicero. *The Academic Questions, De finibus and Tusculan Disputations.* Translated by C. D. Yonge. London: Bell, 1880.

———. *De amicitia, and Dream of Scipio.* Translated by Andrew P. Peabody. Boston: Little, Brown, 1884. (Reissued, London: Forgotten Books, 2013.)

———. *On Fate.* Translated by J. E. King. Loeb Classical Library. Cambridge, MA: Harvard University Press, 1927.

———. *On the Nature of the Gods.* Translated by Horace C. P. McGregor. Harmondsworth, UK: Penguin, 1972.

Clark, Gillian. "The Health of the Spiritual Athlete." In *Health in Antiquity*, edited by Helen King, 216–29. London: Routledge, 2005.

———. "'In the Foreskin of Their Flesh': The Pure Male Body in Late Antiquity." In *Roman Bodies*, edited by A. Hopkins and M. Wyke, 43–54. London: British School at Rome, 2005.

Clark, Kenneth. *The Nude: A Study of Ideal Art.* Harmondsworth, UK: Penguin, 1956.

Clark, Stephen R. L. *Ancient Mediterranean Philosophy.* London: Bloomsbury, 2013.

———. *Aristotle's Man: Speculations upon Aristotelian Anthropology.* Oxford: Clarendon Press, 1983.

———. "Atheists and Idolaters: The Case of John Wren-Lewis." In *Atheisms*, edited by Victoria Harrison and Harriet Harris. London: Ashgate, forthcoming.

———. *Biology and Christian Ethics.* Cambridge: Cambridge University Press, 2000.

———. "Charms and Counter-Charms." In *Conceptions of Philosophy*, edited by Anthony O'Hear, 215–31. Royal Institute of Philosophy Supplementary Volume 65. Cambridge: Cambridge University Press, 2010.

———. Conclusion to Vassilopoulou and Clark, *Late Antique Epistemology*, 289–301.

———. "The Cosmic Priority of Value (Aquinas Lecture, Leuven)." *Tijdschrift voor filosofie* 62 (2000): 681–700.

———. "Deconstructing the Laws of Logic." *Philosophy* 82 (2008): 25–53.

———. "Discerning the Spirits: Healing and the Moral Problems of Efficacy." In *Spiritual Healing: Science, Meaning, and Discernment*, edited by Sarah Coakley. Grand Rapids, MI: Eerdmans, forthcoming.

———. "Does 'Made in the Image of God' Mean Humans Are More Special than Animals?" In *A Faith Embracing All Creatures*, edited by Tripp York and Andy Alexis-Baker, 138–49. Eugene, OR: Cascade Books, 2012.

———. "The End of the Ages." In *Imagining Apocalypse: Studies in Cultural Crisis*, edited by David Seed, 27–44. New York: St. Martin's Press, 2000.

———. "Folly to the Greeks: Good Reasons to Give Up Reason." *European Journal for Philosophy of Religion* 4 (2012): 93–113.

———. *From Athens to Jerusalem*. Oxford: Clarendon Press, 1984.

———. "Futures Singular and Plural." In *Towards the Noosphere*, edited by Tim Addey, 29–67. Westbury, Wiltshire: Prometheus Books, 2013.

———. *G. K. Chesterton: Thinking Backward, Looking Forward*. Philadelphia: Templeton Foundation Press, 2006.

———. "The Goals of Goodness." *Studies in World Christianity* 4 (1998): 228–44.

———. "God, Good and Evil." *Proceedings of the Aristotelian Society* 77 (1977): 247–64.

———. *God, Religion and Reality*. London: SPCK, 1998.

———. *God's World and the Great Awakening*. Oxford: Clarendon Press, 1991.

———. "Going Naked into the Shrine: Herbert, Plotinus and the Constructive Metaphor." In *Platonism at the Origins of Modernity*, edited by Douglas Hedley and Sarah Hutton, 45–61. Dordrecht, Neth.: Springer, 2008.

———. "How to Become Unconscious." In *The Metaphysics of Consciousness*, edited by Pierfrancesco Basile, Julian Kiverstein, and Pauline Phemister, 21–44. Royal Institute of Philosophy Supplementary Volume 67. Cambridge: Cambridge University Press, 2010.

———. "Living the Pyrrhonian Way." In *The Science, Politics, and Ontology of Life-Philosophy*, edited by Scott Campbell and Paul Bruno, 197–210. London: Bloomsbury, 2013.

———. "*The Mind Parasites*: Wilson, Husserl, Plotinus." In *Around the Outsider: Essays Presented to Colin Wilson*, edited by Colin Stanley, 42–62. Alresford, UK: O-Books, 2011.

———. "Minds, Memes and Rhetoric." *Inquiry* 36 (1993): 3–16.

———. "Moments of Truth: The Marginal and the Real." *European Legacy* 17, no. 6 (2012): 769–78.

———. "Nothing without Mind." In *Consciousness Evolving*, edited by James H. Fetzer, 139–60. Advances in Consciousness Research, vol. 34. Amsterdam: John Benjamins, 2002.

———. "Personal Identity and Identity Disorders." In *Oxford Handbook of Philosophy and Psychiatry*, edited by K. W. M. Fulford, Martin Davies, George Graham, John Z. Sadler, Giovanni Sanghellini, and Tim Thornton, 911–28. Oxford: Oxford University Press, 2013.

———. *Philosophical Futures*. Frankfurt: Peter Lang, 2011.

———. "A Plotinian Account of Intellect." *American Catholic Philosophical Quarterly* 71 (1997): 421–32.

———. "Plotinian Dualisms and the 'Greek' Ideas of Self." *Journal of Chinese Philosophy* 36 (2009): 554–67.

———. "Plotinus: Body and Mind." In *Cambridge Companion to Plotinus*, edited by Lloyd Gerson, 275–91. Cambridge: Cambridge University Press, 1996.

———. "Plotinus on Remembering and Forgetting." In *Greek Memories*, edited by Luca Castagnoli and Paola Ceccarelli. Cambridge: Cambridge University Press, forthcoming.

———. "The Possible Truth of Metaphor." *International Philosophical Studies* 2 (1994): 19–30.

———. "Progress and the Argument from Evil." *Religious Studies* 40 (2004): 181–92.

———. "Therapy and Theory Reconstructed." In *Philosophy as Therapy*, edited by Clare Carlisle and Jonardon Ganeri, 83–102. Royal Institute of Philosophy Supplementary Volume 66. Cambridge: Cambridge University Press, 2010.

———. "Waking-Up: A Neglected Model for the After-life." *Inquiry* 26 (1983): 209–30.

Clarke, Emma C. *Iamblichus' "De mysteriis."* London: Ashgate, 2001.

Clarke, John R. *The Houses of Roman Italy, 100 BC–AD 250*. Berkeley: University of California Press, 1991.

Clement of Alexandria. *Stromata (Miscellanies)*. Translated by Alexander Roberts and James Donaldson. http://www.earlychristianwritings.com/clement.html.

Cohen, Barry M., and Carol Thayer Cox. *Telling without Talking: Art as a Window into the World of Multiple Personality*. New York: Norton, 1995.

Coleridge, Samuel Taylor. *The Complete Poems*. Edited by William Keach. Harmondsworth, UK: Penguin, 1997.

Colet, John. *An Exposition of St. Paul's Epistle to the Romans: Delivered as Lectures in the University of Oxford about the Year 1497*. Edited and translated by J. H. Lupton. London: Bell and Daldy, 1873.

Collobert, Catherine, Pierre Destrée, and Francisco J. Gonzalez, eds. *Plato and Myth: Studies on the Use and Status of Platonic Myths*. Leiden: Brill, 2012.

Congdon, Lenore O. Keene. *Caryatid Mirrors of Ancient Greece: Technical, Stylistic and Historical Considerations of an Archaic and Early Classical Bronze Series*. Mainz: Philip von Zabern, 1981.

Conick, April D. de, and Jarl Fossum. "Stripped before God: A New Interpretation of Logion 37 in the Gospel of Thomas." *Vigiliae Christianae* 45 (1991): 123–50.

Connor, W. R. "Seized by the Nymphs: Nympholepsy and Symbolic Expression in Classical Greece." *Classical Antiquity* 7 (1988): 155–89.

Cook, A. B. *Zeus, God of the Dark Sky*. Vol. 2 of *Zeus, a Study in Ancient Religion*. Cambridge: Cambridge University Press, 1925.

Cook, Francis H. *Hua-Yen Buddhism: The Jewel Net of Indra*. University Park: Pennsylvania State University Press, 1977.

Copenhaver, Brian P. *Hermetica*. Cambridge: Cambridge University Press, 1992.

Corbin, Henry. *Avicenna and Visionary Recital*. Translated by Willard R. Trask. Irving, TX: Spring Publications, 1980.

———. *Creative Imagination in the Thought of Ibn Arabi*. Princeton, NJ: Princeton University Press, 1969.

———. *Spiritual Body and Celestial Earth: From Mazdean Iran to Shi'ite Iran*. Translated by Nancy Pearson. Princeton, NJ: Princeton University Press, 1977.

Corrias, Anna. "Imagination and Memory in Marsilio Ficino's Theory of the Vehicles of the Soul." *International Journal of the Platonic Tradition* 6 (2012): 81–114.

Corrigan, Kevin. "Plotinus and St. Gregory of Nyssa: Can Matter Really Have a Positive Function?" In *Cappadocian Fathers, Greek Authors after Nicaea, Augustine, Donatism, and Pelagianism*, edited by Elizabeth A. Livingstone, 14–20. Studia Patristica 27. Leuven: Peeters, 1993.

———. *Plotinus' Theory of Matter-Evil and the Question of Substance: Plato, Aristotle and Alexander of Aphrodisias*. Leuven: Peeters, 1996.

———. *Reading Plotinus*. West Lafayette, IN: Purdue University Press, 2005.

Corthright, Brant. *Psychotherapy and Spirit*. New York: SUNY Press, 1997.

Couliano, I. P. *Out of This World: Otherworldly Journeys from Gilgamesh to Albert Einstein*. Boston: Shambhala, 1991.

Coulter, James A. *The Literary Microcosm: Theories of Interpretation of the Later Platonists*. Leiden: Brill, 1976.

Croall, J. *Peter Hall's "Bacchae": The National Theatre at Work*. London: Oberon, 2002.

Crowley, John. *Aegypt*. London: Gollancz, 1987.

———. *Love and Sleep*. New York: Bantam Books, 1994.

Cumont, Franz. *Astrology and Religion among the Greeks and Romans*. New York: Dover, 1960.

Cutsinger, James S., ed. *Paths to the Heart: Sufism and the Christian East*. Bloomington, IN: World Wisdom, 2004.

Dalrymple, William. *Nine Lives: In Search of the Sacred in Modern India*. London: Bloomsbury, 2009.

Dalton, Joseph. "The Development of Perfection: The Interiorization of Buddhist Ritual in the Eighth and Ninth Centuries." *Journal of Indian Philosophy* 32 (2004): 1–30.

Damascius. *The Philosophical History*. Edited by Polymnia Athanassiadi. Athens: Apamea Cultural Association, 1999.

Dante Alighieri. *The Divine Comedy: Hell*. Translated by Dorothy L. Sayers. London: Penguin, 1949.

———. *The Divine Comedy: Paradise*. Translated by Dorothy L. Sayers and Barbara Reynolds. London: Penguin, 1962.

———. *The Divine Comedy: Purgatory*. Translated by Dorothy L. Sayers. London: Penguin, 1955.

D'Arcy, Martin C. *The Mind and Heart of Love: Lion and Unicorn, a Study in Eros and Agape*. London: Faber, 1945.

Darwin, Charles. *The Life and Letters of Charles Darwin*. Edited by F. Darwin. London: Murray, 1887.

———. *On the Origin of Species by Means of Natural Selection; or, The Preservation of Favoured Races in the Struggle for Life*. London: John Murray, 1859.

Davidson, Donald. "What Metaphors Mean." *Critical Inquiry* 5 (1978): 31–47.

Davidson, James. *Courtesans and Fishcakes: The Consuming Passions of Classical Athens.* London: HarperCollins, 1997.

Davies, John. *The Poems of Sir John Davies.* 1596. Oxford: Clarendon Press, 1975.

Davis, William Vail Wilson, and Raymond Calkins, eds. *Hymns of the Church: New and Old.* New York: A. S. Barnes, 1912.

Deck, John N. *Nature, Contemplation, and the One: A Study in the Philosophy of Plotinus.* Toronto: University of Toronto Press, 1967.

Denise, Jan. *Naked Relationships.* Charlottesville, NC: Hampton Roads, 2002.

Descartes, René. *Philosophical Letters.* Edited by Anthony Kenny. Oxford: Oxford University Press, 1970.

Detienne, Marcel. *Dionysos at Large.* Translated by A. Goldheimer. Cambridge, MA: Harvard University Press, 1989.

———. *The Masters of Truth.* Translated by Janet Lloyd. New York: Urzone, 1996.

Devereux, George. *From Anxiety to Method in the Behavioral Sciences.* The Hague: Mouton, 1967.

Dillon, John M. "An Ethic for the Late-Antique Sage." In *Cambridge Companion to Plotinus,* edited by Lloyd Gerson, 315–35. Cambridge: Cambridge University Press, 1996.

———. *The Golden Chain.* Aldershot, UK: Variorum Press, 1990.

———. *The Middle Platonists: A Study of Platonism, 80 BC to AD 220.* London: Duckworth, 1977.

———. "The NeoPlatonic Exegesis of the Politicus Myth." In *Reading the Statesman: Proceedings of the III Symposium Platonicum,* edited by C. Rowe, 364–74. Sankt Augustin, Ger.: Academia Verlag, 1995.

———. "Plotinus and the Chaldaean Oracles." In *Platonism and Late Antiquity,* edited by Stephen Gersh and Charles Kannengiesser, 131–40. Notre Dame, IN: University of Notre Dame Press, 1992.

———. "Plotinus and the Transcendental Imagination." In *Religious Imagination,* edited by J. P. Mackey, 55–64. Edinburgh: Edinburgh University Press, 1986.

Dio Chrysostom. *Discourses.* Translated by J. H. Cohoon. Loeb Classical Library. London: Heinemann, 1939.

Diodorus Siculus. *Library of History.* Translated by C. H. Oldfather. Loeb Classical Library. Boston: Harvard University Press, 1933.

Diogenes Laertius. *Lives of Eminent Philosophers.* Translated by R. D. Hicks. Loeb Classical Library. London: Heinemann, 1989.

Dodds, E. R. *The Greeks and the Irrational.* Berkeley: University of California Press, 1951.

———. "Numenius and Ammonius." In *Sources de Plotin,* 1–61. Entretiens Hardt 5. Geneva: Fondation Hardt, 1960.

———. "Theurgy and Its Relationship to Neoplatonism." *Journal of Roman Studies* 37 (1947): 55–69.

———. "Tradition and Personal Achievement in the Philosophy of Plotinus." *Journal of Roman Studies* 50 (1960): 1–7.

Doniger, Wendy. *The Hindus: An Alternative History.* Oxford: Oxford University Press, 2009.

Donne, John. *Complete English Poems*. Edited by C. A. Patrides. London: J. M. Dent, 1985.

Douglas, Mary. "A Distinctive Anthropological Perspective." In *Constructive Drinking: Perspectives on Drink from Anthropology*, edited by Mary Douglas, 3–15. Cambridge: Cambridge University Press, 1987.

Draaisma, Douwe. *Metaphors of Memory: A History of Ideas about the Mind*. Translated by Paul Vincent. Cambridge: Cambridge University Press, 2000.

———. *Why Life Speeds Up as You Get Older: How Memory Shapes Our Past*. Translated by Arnold Pomerans and Erica Pomerans. Cambridge: Cambridge University Press, 2004.

Durkheim, Emile. *Elementary Forms of the Religious Life*. London: Allen and Unwin, 1915.

Dyson, Freeman. "Time without End: Physics and Biology in an Open Universe." *Review of Modern Physics* 51 (1979): 447–60.

Eastham, Scott. *American Dreamer: Bucky Fuller and the Sacred Geometry of Nature*. Cambridge: Lutterworth Press, 2007.

Eco, Umberto. "An Ars Oblivionalis? Forget It!" *Publications of the Modern Language Association of America (PMLA)* 103 (1988): 254–61.

Edwards, Jonathan. *Basic Writings*. Edited by O. E. Winslow. New York: New American Library, 1966.

Edwards, Mark J. *Culture and Philosophy in the Age of Plotinus*. London: Duckworth, 2006.

———. "Gnostic Eros and Orphic Themes." *Zeitschrift für Papyrologie und Epigraphik* 88 (1991): 25–40.

———, trans. *Neoplatonic Saints: The Lives of Plotinus and Proclus by Their Students*. Liverpool: Liverpool University Press, 2000.

———. "A Portrait of Plotinus." *Classical Quarterly* 43 (1993): 480–90.

Eliade, Mircea. *The Sacred and the Profane*. Translated by Willard R. Trask. New York: Harcourt Brace Jovanovich, 1959.

———. *Shamanism: Archaic Techniques of Ecstasy*. Translated by Willard R. Trask. Princeton, NJ: Princeton University Press, 1951.

Epictetus. *Discourses and Selected Writings*. Translated by Robert Dobbin. London: Penguin, 2008.

Eunapius of Sardis. *Lives of the Sophists and Philosophers*. Translated by Wilmer C. Wright. Loeb Classical Library. London: Heinemann, 1921.

Eusebius. *History of the Church*. Translated by G. A. Williamson. Edited by Andrew Louth. London: Penguin, 1989.

———. *Praeparatio evangelica*. Translated by E. H. Gifford. Oxford: Clarendon Press, 1903.

Evdokimov, Paul. *Ages of the Spiritual Life*. Translated by Michael Plekon. New York: St. Vladimir's Seminary Press, 1998.

———. *The Art of the Icon: A Theology of Beauty*. Translated by Steven Bigham. Pasadena, CA: Oakwood Publications, 2011.

Falkner, John Meade. *Collected Poems*. Kings Newton, UK: John Meade Falkner Society, 2008.

Faraday, Ann. *The Dream Game.* New York: Harper and Row, 1974.

Ferwerda, R. "Pity in Plotinus." In *Plotinus amid Gnostics and Christians*, edited by David T. Runia, 53–72. Amsterdam: Free University Press, 1984.

———. *La signification des images et des métaphores dans la pensée de Plotin.* Groningen, Neth.: J. B. Wolters, 1965.

Feyerabend, Paul. *Against Method.* 3rd ed. London: Verso, 2000.

Feynman, Richard. *The Feynman Lectures on Physics.* New York: Basic Books, 2011.

Finamore, John F. *Iamblichus and the Theory of the Vehicle of the Soul.* Chico, CA: American Philological Association and Scholars Press, 1985.

Findlay, J. N. *Language, Mind and Value.* London: Allen and Unwin, 1963.

Fine, Gail. "Knowledge and True Belief in the *Meno.*" *Oxford Studies in Ancient Philosophy* 27 (2004): 41–81.

Florovsky, Georges V. *The Byzantine Fathers of the Fifth to Eighth Centuries.* London: Gregg, 1972. http://www.holytrinitymission.org/books/english/fathers_florovsky_2 .htm.

Fowden, Garth. *The Egyptian Hermes.* Cambridge: Cambridge University Press, 1986.

Frank, Susan. *Glass and Archaeology.* London: Academic Press, 1982.

Frankfort, H. *The Art and Architecture of the Ancient Orient.* Harmondsworth, UK: Penguin, 1956.

Freud, Sigmund. *Civilization and Its Discontents.* Translated by David McClintock. Harmondsworth, UK: Penguin, 2002.

Frost, Robert. *The Poetry of Robert Frost.* Edited by Edward Connery Lathem. New York: Henry Holt, 1969.

Frye, Northrop. *The Educated Imagination.* Bloomington: Indiana University Press, 1964.

———. *Fearful Symmetry.* Princeton, NJ: Princeton University Press, 1947.

Furley, David. "The Greek Theory of the Infinite Universe." *Journal of the History of Ideas* 42 (1981): 571–86.

Galen. *Hygiene.* Translated by Robert Montraville Green. Springfield, IL: Thomas, 1951.

———. *On the Natural Faculties.* Translated by A. J. Brock. Loeb Classical Library. London: Heinemann, 1916.

Galilei, Galileo. *Dialogues concerning Two New Sciences.* 1638. Translated by H. Crewe and A. De Salvo. New York: Dover Publications, 1952.

———. "The Starry Messenger." 1610. In *Discoveries and Opinions*, translated by Stillman Drake, 21–58. New York: Doubleday, 1957.

Galinsky, G. Karl. *The Heracles Theme.* Oxford: Blackwell, 1972.

Ganeri, Jonardon. "A Return to the Self: Indians and Greeks on Life as Art and Philosophical Therapy." In *Philosophy as Therapy*, edited by Clare Carlisle and Jonardon Ganeri, 119–36. Royal Institute of Philosophy Supplementary Volume 66. Cambridge: Cambridge University Press, 2010.

Gardner, Helen, ed. *New Oxford Book of English Verse.* Oxford: Clarendon Press, 1972.

Gennep, A. van. *The Rites of Passage.* Translated by Monika B. Vizedom and Gabrielle L. Caffe. Chicago: University of Chicago Press, 1960.

Gerson, Lloyd. "Metaphor as an Ontological Concept: Plotinus on the Philosophical Use of Language." In *Logos et langage chez Plotin et avant Plotin*, edited by Michel Fattal, 255–70. Paris: L'Harmattan, 2003.

Gill, Mary Louise. *Aristotle on Substance: The Paradox of Unity*. Princeton, NJ: Princeton University Press, 1991.

Gilman, Charlotte Perkins. *In This Our World, and Uncollected Poems*. Edited by Denise Knight and Gary Scharnhorst. New York: Syracuse University Press, 2012.

Gödel, Kurt. "Some Basic Theorems on the Foundations of Mathematics and Their Philosophical Implications." 1951. In *Collected Works*, edited by S. Feferman, J. Dawson, W. Goldfarb, C. Parsons, R. Solovay, and J. van Heijenoort, vol. 3, 304–23. Oxford: Oxford University Press, 1995.

Goethe, Johann Wolfgang von, and Friedrich Schiller. *Select Minor Poems: Translated from the German of Goethe and Schiller*. Translated by John S. Dwight. Boston: Hilliard, Gray, 1839.

Gold, Thomas. "The Arrow of Time." *American Journal of Physics* 30 (1962): 403–10. http://dx.doi.org/10.1119/1.1942052.

Graf, Fritz. *Magic in the Ancient World*. Cambridge, MA: Harvard University Press, 1999.

Graves, Robert. *Collected Poems*. London: Cassell, 1975.

Green, Katie. *Lighter than My Shadow*. London: Cape, 2013.

Gregory, R. L. *Mirrors in Mind*. Basingstoke, UK: W. H. Freeman, 1997.

Grmek, M. D. *Diseases in the Ancient World*. Baltimore, MD: Johns Hopkins University Press, 1983.

———. "Les maladies et la mort de Plotin." In *Porphyre: La vie de Plotin*, edited by Luc Brisson, vol. 2, 335–53. Paris: J. Vrin, 1989.

Gruen, Erich S. *Heritage and Hellenism: The Reinvention of Jewish Tradition*. Berkeley: University of California Press, 1998.

Guthke, Karl S. *The Last Frontier: Imagining Other Worlds from the Copernican Revolution to Modern Science Fiction*. Translated by Helen Atkins. Ithaca, NY: Cornell University Press, 1990.

Guthrie, W. K. C. *The Greeks and Their Gods*. London: Methuen, 1950.

———. *Orpheus and Greek Religion: A Study of the Orphic Movement*. Princeton, NJ: Princeton University Press, 1952.

Hacking, Ian. *Rewriting the Soul: Multiple Personality and the Sciences of Memory*. Princeton, NJ: Princeton University Press, 1995.

Hadot, Pierre. "Ouranos, Kronos and Zeus in Plotinus's Treatise against the Gnostics." In *Neoplatonism and Early Christian Thought: Essays in Honour of A. H. Armstrong*, edited by H. J. Blumenthal and R. A. Markus, 124–52. London: Variorum, 1981.

———. *Plotinus; or, The Simplicity of Vision*. Translated by Michael Chase. Chicago: University of Chicago Press, 1993.

———. *The Veil of Isis: An Essay on the History of the Idea of Nature*. Translated by Michael Chase. Cambridge, MA: Harvard University Press, 2006.

———. *What Is Ancient Philosophy?* Translated by Michael Chase. Cambridge, MA: Harvard University Press, 2002.

Haldane, J. B. S. *Possible Worlds and Other Essays*. London: Chatto and Windus, 1927.

Hales, Shelley. *The Roman House and Social Identity*. Cambridge: Cambridge University Press, 2003.

Hall, Peter. *Exposed by the Mask: Form and Language in Drama*. London: Oberon Books, 2000.

Hall, Roger L. "Joseph Brackett's 'Simple Gifts.'" *Sonneck Society for American Music Bulletin* 23, no. 3 (1997). http://www.american-music.org/publications/bullarchive /ha11233.htm.

Halsberghe, Gaston H. *The Cult of Sol Invictus.* Leiden: Brill, 1972.

Hamilton, W. D. "The Genetical Evolution of Social Behaviour." *Journal of Theoretical Biology* 7, no. 1 (1964): 1–16.

Hanson, Rick, and Richard Mendius. *Buddha's Brain: The Practical Neuroscience of Happiness, Love and Wisdom.* Oakland, CA: New Harbinger Publications, 2009.

Hare, Tom. *Remembering Osiris: Number, Gender and the Word in Ancient Egyptian Representational Systems.* Stanford, CA: Stanford University Press, 1999.

Harré, Rom. *Personal Being.* Cambridge, MA: Harvard University Press, 1984.

Harrington, Michael. "The Drunken *Epibole* of Plotinus and Its Reappearance in the Work of Dionysius the Areopagite." *Dionysius* 23 (2005): 117–38.

Harris, J. Rendel, ed. *The Odes and Psalms of Solomon.* Cambridge: Cambridge University Press, 1909.

Harris, Marvin. *Cows, Pigs, Wars, and Witches.* New York: Vintage Books, 1989.

Harrison, Andrew. "Metaphor." In *Philosophy and the Arts: Seeing and Believing*, 203–47. Bristol: Thoemmes Press, 1997.

Havel, Vaclav. *Letters to Olga.* Translated by Paul Wilson. London: Faber, 1988.

Havelock, Eric A. "The Linguistic Task of the Presocratics." In *Language and Thought in Early Greek Philosophy*, edited by Kevin Robb, 7–82. La Salle, IL: Hegeler Institute, 1983.

———. "The Prehistory of the Greeks." *New Literary History* 8 (1976–7): 369–71.

Hawking, Stephen. *A Brief History of Time.* London: Bantam, 1988.

Heath, Thomas. *A History of Greek Mathematics.* Oxford: Clarendon Press, 1921.

Heerink, Mark A. J. "Echoing Hylas: Metapoetics in Hellenistic and Roman Poetry." Doctoral thesis, Leiden University, 2010. http://hdl.handle.net/1887/16194.

———. "Going a Step Further: Valerius Flaccus' Metapoetical Reading of Propertius' Hylas." *Classical Quarterly* 57 (2007): 606–20.

Hekster, Olivier. *Rome and Its Empire, AD 193–284.* Edinburgh: Edinburgh University Press, 2008.

Helm, R. M. "Platonopolis Revisited." In *Neoplatonism and Contemporary Thought*, edited by R. Baine Harris, pt. 2, 81–92. New York: International Society for Neoplatonic Studies and SUNY Press, 2002.

Henry, P. "The Place of Plotinus in the History of Thought." 1962. In *Plotinus—"The Enneads,"* translated by S. MacKenna, 4th ed., revised by B. S. Page, xlii–lxxxiii. London: Faber, 1969.

Herbert, Edward (Earl of Cherbury). *De veritate.* 1624. Translated by M. H. Carré. Bristol: Arrowsmith, 1937.

———. *The Poems English and Latin of Edward, Lord Herbert of Cherbury.* Edited by G. C. Moore Smith. Oxford: Clarendon Press, 1923.

Hillman, James. *The Dream and the Underworld.* New York: Harper and Row, 1979.

———. *Re-visioning Psychology.* New York: HarperCollins, 1975.

Historia Augusta. Translated by David Magie. 3 vols. Loeb Classical Library. Cambridge, MA: Harvard University Press, 1921–32.

Holmes, Elizabeth. *Henry Vaughan and the Hermetic Philosophy.* Oxford: Blackwell, 1932.

Homeric Hymn to Demeter. Edited by N. J. Richardson. Oxford: Oxford University Press, 1963.

Hopkins, Gerard Manley. *Complete Poems.* Edited by W. H. Gardner and N. H. Mackenzie. 4th ed. London: Oxford University Press, 1967.

Hornung, Erik. *Conceptions of God in Ancient Egypt: The One and the Many.* Translated by John Baines. Ithaca, NY: Cornell University Press, 1982.

———. *The Secret Lore of Egypt: Its Impact on the West.* Translated by David Lorton. Ithaca, NY: Cornell University Press, 2001.

Hudry, Françoise, ed. *Liber Viginti Quattuor Philosophorum.* Paris: J. Vrin, 2009.

Hui Neng. *Platform Sutra of the Sixth Patriarch.* Translated by Philip B. Yampolsky. New York: Columbia University Press, 1967.

Huizinga, Johan. *Homo Ludens: A Study of the Play Element in Culture.* Boston: Beacon Press, 1950.

Hutton, Ronald. *The Pagan Religions of the Ancient British Isles.* Oxford: Blackwell, 1991.

Iamblichus of Chalcis. *The Letters.* Translated by John M. Dillon and Wolfgang Polleichtner. Writings from the Greco-Roman World. Atlanta, GA: Society of Biblical Literature, 2009.

———. *On the Mysteries.* Translated by Thomas Taylor. London: Bertram Dobell, 1821.

———. *On the Pythagorean Life.* Translated by Gillian Clark. Liverpool: Liverpool University Press, 1989.

———. *Réponse à Porphyre: De mysteriis.* Edited by H. D. Saffrey and A.-P. Segonds. Paris: Les Belles Lettres, 2013.

Ibn al-Fārid, 'Umar. "The Wine Song." Translated by Martin Lings. In *Sufi Poems: A Medieval Anthology,* edited by Martin Lings, 68–74. Cambridge: Islamic Texts Society, 2004.

Jaki, Stanley L. *Is There a Universe?* Liverpool: University of Liverpool Press, 1994.

James, William. *The Principles of Psychology.* New York: Macmillan, 1890.

———. *The Varieties of Religious Experience.* London: Longmans, Green, 1902.

Jennings, Janis. "Tending Hestia's Flame: Circumambulating the Sacred Feminine." *Psychological Perspectives* 51 (2008): 208–22.

Johnson, Aaron P. *Religion and Identity in Porphyry of Tyre: The Limits of Hellenism in Late Antiquity.* Cambridge: Cambridge University Press, 2013.

Johnston, Sarah Iles. "Animating Statues: A Case Study in Ritual." *Arethusa* 41, no. 3 (2008): 445–77.

Jonas, Hans. *The Gnostic Religion.* 2nd ed. Boston: Beacon Press, 1963.

———. *The Phenomenon of Life: Towards a Philosophical Biology.* Chicago: University of Chicago Press, 1982.

Jones, Rufus. *The Flowering of Mysticism and the Friends of God in the 14th Century.* New York: Macmillan, 1939.

Julian. *Works.* Translated by W. C. Wright. Loeb Classical Library. London: Heinemann, 1913.

Jung, Carl. *Psychology and Alchemy.* London: Routledge, 1980.

Kajava, Mika. "Hestia: Hearth, Goddess, and Cult." *Harvard Studies in Classical Philology* 102 (2004): 1–20.

Kant, Immanuel. "Perpetual Peace." In *Kant's Political Writings*, translated by H. B. Nisbet, edited by Hans Reiss, 93–130. Cambridge: Cambridge University Press, 1970.

Kauffman, Stuart. *At Home in the Universe: The Search for Laws of Self-Organization and Complexity*. New York: Oxford University Press, 1996.

Kauntze, Mark. "Seeing through a Glass Darkly: The Interpretation of a Biblical Verse in Augustine of Hippo." In *The Book of the Mirror*, edited by Miranda Anderson, 60–9. Cambridge: Cambridge Scholars, 2007.

Kaza, Stephanie, and Kenneth Kraft, eds. *Dharma Rain: Sources of Buddhist Environmentalism*. London: Shambhala, 2000.

Keats, John. *Poetical Works*. Edited by H. W. Garrod. London: Oxford University Press, 1956.

Kerényi, Karl. "Mnemosyne-Lesmosyne: On the Springs of Memory and Forgetting." Translated by Jay Stoner. In *Spring: An Annual of Archetypal Psychology and Jungian Thought*, 120–30. New York: Spring Publications, 1977.

Kidd, I. G. *Poseidonius*. Vol. 3, *The Translation of the Fragments*. Cambridge: Cambridge University Press, 1999.

King, Cynthia. *Musonius Rufus*. Createspace (Amazon Publishing), 2011.

Kingsley, Peter. *Ancient Philosophy, Mystery, and Magic: Empedocles and Pythagorean Tradition*. Oxford: Clarendon Press, 1995.

———. *Story Waiting to Pierce You: Mongolia, Tibet and the Destiny of the Western World*. Point Reyes Station, CA: Golden Sufi Center, 2010.

Kirkland, Russell. *Taoism: The Enduring Tradition*. London: Routledge, 2004.

Klibansky, R., E. Panofsky, and F. Saxl. *Saturn and Melancholy*. Edinburgh: Nelson, 1964.

Kofman, Sarah. *Nietzsche and Metaphor*. Translated by D. Large. London: Athlone Press, 1993.

Krishnamacharya, Tirumalai. *Yoga Makaranda*. Madurai, India: CMV Press, 1935.

Kuhn, Annette. *The Power of the Image*. London: Routledge and Kegan Paul, 1985.

Kupperman, Jeffrey S. *Living Theurgy: A Course in Iamblichus' Philosophy, Theology and Theurgy*. London: Avallonia, 2014.

Lachman, Gary. *The Quest for Hermes Trismegistus*. Edinburgh: Floris Books, 2011.

Lada-Richards, Ismene. *Silent Eloquence: Lucian and Pantomime Dancing*. London: Duckworth, 2007.

Laing, R. D. *The Divided Self*. Harmondsworth, UK: Penguin, 1965.

Lakoff, George, and Mark Johnson. *Metaphors We Live By*. Chicago: University of Chicago Press, 1980.

Lamberton, Robert. *Homer the Theologian: Neoplatonist Allegorical Reading and the Growth of the Epic Tradition*. Berkeley: University of California Press, 1986.

Lankila, Tuomo. "Proclus, Erototokos and 'the Great Confusion': Neoplatonist Defense of Polytheistic Piety in Early Byzantine Athens." Doctoral thesis, University of Jyväskylä, 2012. http://urn.fi/URN:ISBN:978–951–39–5145–0.

Lawler, Lilian B. *The Dance in Ancient Greece*. London: Adam and Charles Black, 1964.

———. "Proteus Is a Dancer." *Classical Weekly* 36 (1943): 116–7.

Lawley, James, and Penny Tompkins. *Metaphors in Mind: Transformation through Symbolic Modelling*. London: Developing Co. Press, 2000.

Leibniz, G. *New Essays on Human Understanding*. Edited by P. Remnant and J. Bennett. Cambridge: Cambridge University Press, 1981.

Lepajõe, M. "On the Demonology of Plotinus." *Folklore* 9 (1998): 7–16.

Leslie, John. *Value and Existence*. Oxford: Blackwell, 1979.

Levenson, Carl. *Socrates among the Corybantes: Dionysian Spirituality and the Philosophy of Plato*. Putnam, CT: Spring Publications, 1997.

Lewis, C. S. *The Discarded Image: An Introduction to Medieval and Renaissance Literature*. Cambridge: Cambridge University Press, 1964.

———. *The Four Loves*. London: Bles, 1960.

———. Introduction to Athanasius, *De incarnatione*, trans. Lawson.

———. "Meditations in a Toolshed." In *Essay Collection*, edited by Lesley Walmsley, 199–202. London: HarperCollins, 2000.

———. *Miracles*. 2nd ed. London: Fontana, 1974.

———. *The Silver Chair*. New York: HarperCollins, 2001.

Lewy, Hans. *Chaldaean Oracles and Theurgy*. Cairo: L'Institut français d'archéologic orientale, 1956.

———. *Sobria Ebrietas*. Giessen, Ger.: Töpelmann, 1929.

Ley, Hermann de. *Macrobius and Numenius*. Brussels: Revue d'études latines, 1972.

Liebeschuetz, J. W. W. G. *Continuity and Change in Roman Religion*. Oxford: Clarendon Press, 1979.

Linforth, Ivan M. *The Arts of Orpheus*. Berkeley: University of California Press, 1941.

Lings, Martin. *Symbol and Archetype: A Study of the Meaning of Existence*. Louisville, KY: Fons Vitae, 2006.

Lings, Martin, and Clinton Minnaar, eds. *The Underlying Religion: An Introduction to the Perennial Philosophy*. Bloomington, IN: World Wisdom, 2007.

Lippitt, John. "True Self-Love and True Self-Sacrifice." *International Journal of Philosophy of Religion* 66 (2009): 125–38.

Livio, Mario. *The Golden Ratio*. New York: Broadway Books, 2002.

Lloyd, A. C. *The Anatomy of Neoplatonism*. Oxford: Clarendon Press, 1990.

Long, A. A., and D. N. Sedley, eds. *The Hellenistic Philosophers*. Cambridge: Cambridge University Press, 1987.

Long, A. G. *Conversation and Self-Sufficiency in Plato*. Oxford: Oxford University Press, 2013.

Louth, Andrew. "Augustine." In *The Study of Spirituality*, edited by Cheslyn Jones, Geoffrey Wainwright, and Edward Yarnold, 134–45. London: SPCK, 1992.

———. *Denys the Areopagite*. London: Continuum, 1989.

Loyola, Ignatius. *The Spiritual Exercises*. Translated by Joseph Tetlow. New York: Crossroads, 1992.

Lucian of Samosata. "On Pantomime." In *Works*, translated by H. W. Fowler and F. G. Fowler, vol. 2. Oxford: Clarendon Press, 1905. http://www.sacred-texts.com/cla/luc/wl2/wl219.htm.

———. *Selected Dialogues*. Translated by C. D. N. Costa. New York: Oxford University Press, 2006.

Lucretius. *On the Nature of Things*. Translated by W. E. Leonard. New York: Dutton, 1921.

Luhrmann, Tanya M. *Persuasions of the Witch's Craft: Ritual Magic and Witchcraft in Present-Day England.* Oxford: Blackwell, 1988.

———. *When God Talks Back: Understanding the American Evangelical Relationship with God.* New York: Vintage Books, 2012.

Luria, A. R. *The Mind of a Mnemonist: Little Book about a Vast Memory.* Translated by L. Solotaroff. 2nd ed., introduced by Jerome Bruner. Cambridge, MA: Harvard University Press, 1986.

Lutz, Cora E., ed. *Musonius Rufus: The Roman Socrates.* Yale Classical Studies 10. New Haven, CT: Yale University Press, 1947.

Macarius. *Fifty Spiritual Homilies.* Translated by A. J. Mason. London: SPCK, 1921. See also Pseudo-Macarius.

Maccoby, Hyam. *The Philosophy of the Talmud.* London: Routledge, 2002.

MacCoull, L. S. B. "Plotinus the Egyptian?" *Mnemosyne*, 4th ser., 52 (1999): 330–3.

Macrobius. *Commentary on the "Dream of Scipio."* Translated by William Harris Stahl. New York: Columbia University Press, 1952.

———. *Saturnalia.* Translated by Percival Vaughan Davies. New York: Columbia University Press, 1969.

Madell, Geoffrey. *The Idea of the Self.* Edinburgh: Edinburgh University Press, 1985.

Maimonides, Moses. *A Guide of the Perplexed.* Translated by Chaim Rabin. Indianapolis: Hackett, 1995.

Makransky, John. "Offering (mChod pa) in Tibetan Ritual Literature." In *Tibetan Literature—Studies in Genre: Essays in Honor of Geshe Lhundup Sopa*, edited by José Ignacio Cabezón and Roger R. Jackson, 312–30. Ithaca, NY: Snow Lion, 1995. http://www.thlib.org/encyclopedias/literary/genres/genres-book.php#!book=/studies-in-genres/b18/.

Malhotra, Rajiv. *Indra's Net: Defending Hinduism's Philosophical Unity.* Noida, Uttar Pradesh: HarperCollins, 2014.

Manilius. *Astronomica.* Translated by G. P. Goold. Loeb Classical Library. London: Heinemann, 1972.

Marback, Richard C. *Plato's Dream of Sophistry.* Columbia: University of South Carolina Press, 1999.

———. "Rethinking Plato's Legacy: Neoplatonic Readings of Plato's *Sophist*." *Rhetoric Review* 13 (1994): 30–49.

Martens, Peter W. *Origen and Scripture: The Contours of the Exegetical Life.* Oxford: Oxford University Press, 2012.

Mathew, Gervase. *Byzantine Aesthetics.* London: John Murray, 1963.

Mathiesen, Thomas J. *Apollo's Lyre.* Lincoln: University of Nebraska Press, 1999.

———, ed. *Source Readings in Music History.* Vol. 1, *Greek Views of Music.* New York: W. W. Norton, 1998.

Maximus the Confessor. *Selected Writings.* Translated by George C. Berthold. London: SPCK, 1985.

Mazur, Zeke. "Having Sex with the One: Erotic Mysticism in Plotinus and the Problem of Metaphor." In Vassilopoulou and Clark, *Late Antique Epistemology*, 67–83.

McCartney, Paul. *Poems and Lyrics, 1965–99.* Edited by Adrian Mitchell. London: Faber, 2001.

McEvilley, Thomas. "Plotinus and Vijñānavāda Buddhism." *Philosophy East and West* 30, no. 2 (1980): 181–93.

McGilchrist, Iain. *The Master and His Emissary: The Divided Brain and the Making of the Western World*. New Haven, CT: Yale University Press, 2009.

McNeice, Louis. *Collected Poems, 1925–48*. London: Faber, 1949.

McNeil, W. G. *Plagues and People*. New York: Anchor Books, 1998.

Meredith, Anthony. "Plato's Cave (*Republic* vii.514a–517e) in Origen, Plotinus and Gregory of Nyssa." In *Cappadocian Fathers, Greek Authors after Nicaea, Augustine, Donatism, and Pelagianism*, edited by Elizabeth A. Livingstone, 49–61. Studia Patristica 27. Leuven: Peeters, 1993.

Merlan, Philip. *From Platonism to NeoPlatonism*. The Hague: Martinus Nijhoff, 1960.

———. *Monopsychism, Mysticism, Metaconsciousness*. The Hague: Martinus Nijhoff, 1963.

———. "Plotinus and Magic." *Isis* 44 (1953): 341–8.

———. "Religion and Philosophy from Plato's *Phaedo* to the Chaldaean Oracles; Appendix: Plotinus and the Jews." *Journal of the History of Philosophy* 2 (1964): 15–21.

Merton, Thomas. *Conjectures of a Guilty Bystander*. New York: Doubleday, 1966.

Meyendorff, John. *A Study of Gregory Palamas*. Translated by George Lawrence. Leighton Buzzard, UK: Faith Press, 1964.

Meyer, Marvin. *The Unknown Sayings of Jesus*. Boston: Shambhala, 1998.

Michelson, Andreas, et al. "Effects of Phlebotomy-Induced Reduction of Body Iron Stores on Metabolic Syndrome: Results from a Randomized Clinical Trial." *BMC Medicine* 10 (2012): 54. doi:10.1186/1741-7015-10-54.

Midgley, Mary. *Science and Poetry*. London: Routledge, 2001.

Miles, Leland. *John Colet and the Platonic Tradition*. London: Allen and Unwin, 1961.

Miles, Margaret R. *Carnal Knowing: Female Nakedness and Religious Meaning in the Christian West*. Tunbridge Wells, UK: Burns and Oates, 1989.

———. *Plotinus on Body and Beauty: Society, Philosophy and Religion in Third-Century Rome*. Oxford: Blackwell, 1999.

Millar, Fergus. *The Emperor in the Roman World: 31 BC–AD 337*. London: Duckworth, 1977.

Miller, James. *Measures of Wisdom: The Cosmic Dance in Classical and Christian Antiquity*. Toronto: University of Toronto Press, 1986.

Miller, Patricia Cox. *Biography in Late Antiquity: A Quest for the Holy Man*. Berkeley: University of California Press, 1983.

———. "In Praise of Nonsense." In *Classical Mediterranean Spirituality: Egyptian, Greek, Roman*, edited by A. H. Armstrong, 481–505. New York: Crossroad, 1986.

Miller, Stephen G. *Ancient Greek Athletics*. New Haven, CT: Yale University Press, 2004.

———. *Arete: Greek Sport from Ancient Sources*. 2nd ed. Berkeley: University of California Press, 1991.

Milne, A. A. *Now We Are Six*. London: Methuen, 1927.

Mitchell, Donald W. *Spirituality and Emptiness*. New York: Paulist Press, 1991.

Mohan, A. G., and Ganesh Mohan. *Krishnamacharya: His Life and Teachings*. Boston: Shambhala, 2011.

Molloy, Margaret E. *Libanius and the Dancers*. Hildesheim: Olms-Weidmann, 1996.

Montero, Barbara. "Does Bodily Awareness Interfere with Highly Skilled Movement?" *Inquiry* 53 (2010): 105–22.

Montiglio, Silvia. *Silence in the Land of Logos*. Princeton, NJ: Princeton University Press, 2000.

Moore, Thomas. *The Planets Within: The Astrological Psychology of Marsilio Ficino*. Great Barrington, MA: Lindisfarne Books, 1989.

Moran, Dermot. "Idealism in Medieval Philosophy: The Case of Johannes Scottus Eriugena." *Medieval Philosophy and Theology* 8 (1999): 53–82.

Morgan, Christopher. *R. S. Thomas: Identity, Environment, Deity*. Manchester: Manchester University Press, 2003.

Munn, Nancy D. *Walbiri Iconography: Graphic Representations and Cultural Symbolism in a Central Australian Society*. Ithaca, NY: Cornell University Press, 1973.

Murray, Penelope. "What Is a *Muthos* for Plato?" In Buxton, *From Myth to Reason?*, 251–62.

Naerebout, F. G. *Attractive Performances: Ancient Greek Dance—Three Preliminary Studies*. Amsterdam: J. C. Gieben, 1997.

Nagel, Thomas. *Mind and Cosmos: Why the Materialist Neo-Darwinian Conception of Nature Is Almost Certainly False*. New York: Oxford University Press, 2012.

———. "What Is It Like to Be a Bat?" *Philosophical Review* 83 (1974): 435–50. Reprinted in Thomas Nagel, *Mortal Questions* (Cambridge: Cambridge University Press, 1979).

Naydler, Jeremy. *Temple of the Cosmos: The Ancient Egyptian Experience of the Sacred*. Rochester, VT: Inner Traditions International, 1996.

Nelson, John E. *Healing the Split*. New York: SUNY Press, 1994.

Nelson, Victoria. *The Secret Life of Puppets*. Cambridge, MA: Harvard University Press, 2001.

Netton, Ian Richard. *Allāh Transcendent: Studies in the Structure and Semiotics of Islamic Philosophy, Theology and Cosmology*. Richmond, UK: Curzon Press, 1994.

Nevett, Lisa C. *Domestic Space in Classical Antiquity*. Cambridge: Cambridge University Press, 2012.

Newman, John Henry. *An Essay in Aid of a Grammar of Assent*. London: Longmans Green, 1903.

Nicomachus of Gerasa. *Introduction to Arithmetic*. Translated by Martin Luther D'Ooge. New York: Macmillan, 1926.

Nietzsche, Friedrich. *Beyond Good and Evil*. Translated by R. J. Hollingdale. Harmondsworth, UK: Penguin, 1973.

Nikulin, Dimitri. *Matter, Imagination and Geometry: Ontology, Natural Philosophy and Mathematics in Plotinus, Proclus and Descartes*. Aldershot, UK: Ashgate, 2002.

Nishitani, Keiji. *Religion and Nothingness*. Berkeley: University of California Press, 1982.

Noble, Christopher. "How Plotinus' Soul Animates His Body: The Soul-Trace at Ennead. IV.4.18." *Phronesis* 58, no. 3 (2013): 249–79.

Nørby, Simon, Martin Lange, and Axel Larsen. "Forgetting to Forget: On the Duration of Voluntary Suppression of Neutral and Emotional Memories." *Acta Psychologica* 133 (2010): 73–80. doi:10.1016/j.actpsy.2009.10.002.

Norman, N. "Hurt: The Actor with the Atom Brain." *Face* 69 (1986): 20–4.

Numbers, Ronald L., ed. *Galileo Goes to Jail and Other Myths about Science and Religion*. Cambridge, MA: Harvard University Press, 2009.

Numenius of Apamea. *Fragmenta*. Edited by Edouard des Places. Paris: Les Belles Lettres, 1973.

Nye, Edward. *Mime, Music and Drama on the Eighteenth-Century Stage: The Ballet d'Action*. Cambridge: Cambridge University Press, 2011.

Nygren, Anders. *Agape and Eros*. Translated by Philip S. Watson. London: SPCK, 1953.

O'Brien, Elmer, ed. *The Essential Plotinus*. New York: New American Library, 1964.

O'Daly, Gerard. *Augustine's Philosophy of Mind*. London: Duckworth, 1987.

Odin, Steve. *Process Metaphysics and Hua-Yen Buddhism: A Critical Study of Cumulative Penetration vs. Interpenetration*. New York: SUNY Press, 1982.

Olivelle, Patrick, ed. *The Early Upanisads: Annotated Text and Translation*. New York: Oxford University Press, 1998.

O'Meara, Dominic. *Platonopolis*. Oxford: Clarendon Press, 2003.

O'Neill, William. *Proclus, "Alcibiades I": A Translation and Commentary*. The Hague: Nijhoff, 1965.

Ong, Walter J. *Orality and Literacy: The Technologizing of the Word*. London: Methuen, 1982.

Opsomer, Jan. "Proclus versus Plotinus on Matter (*De malorum substantia* 30–7)." *Phronesis* 46 (2001): 154–88.

Origen. *Contra Celsum*. Translated by Henry Chadwick. Cambridge: Cambridge University Press, 1953.

Ousager, Asger. *Plotinus on Selfhood, Freedom and Politics*. Aarhus, Den.: Aarhus University Press, 2005.

Ouspensky, P. D. *Strange Life of Ivan Osokin*. London: Stourton Press, 1947.

Owen, G. E. L. "Tithenai ta phainomena." 1961. In *Logic, Science, and Dialectic*, by G. E. L. Owen, edited by Martha Nussbaum, 239–51. Ithaca, NY: Cornell University Press, 1986.

Palamas, Gregory. *The 150 Chapters*. Translated by Robert E. Sinkewicz. Toronto: Pontifical Institute of Mediaeval Studies, 1988.

Pallis, Marco. "Do Clothes Make the Man? The Significance of Human Attire." In *The Way and the Mountain*, 141–59. London: Peter Owen, 1960.

Palmer, G. E. H., P. Sherrard, and Kallistos Ware, eds. *The Philokalia*. Vol. 1. London: Faber, 1979.

———, eds. *The Philokalia*. Vol. 4. London: Faber, 1995.

Paris, Ginette. *Pagan Meditations: The Worlds of Aphrodite, Hestia, and Artemis*. Translated by G. Moore. Dallas, TX: Spring Publications, 1986.

Parsons, William B. *The Enigma of the Oceanic Feeling: Revisioning the Psychoanalytic Theory of Mysticism*. New York: Oxford University Press, 1999.

Paton, W. R., trans. *Greek Anthology*. Loeb Classical Library. London: Heinemann, 1916. http://www.ancientlibrary.com/greek-anthology/.

Patrides, C. A., ed. *The Cambridge Platonists*. Cambridge: Cambridge University Press, 1980.

Pausanias. *Description of Greece*. Translated by W. H. S. Jones and H. A. Ormerod. Loeb Classical Library. London: Heinemann, 1926.

Peirce, Charles Sanders. "A Neglected Argument for the Existence of God." *Hibbert Journal* 7 (1908): 90–112. Reprinted in *Collected Papers of Charles Sanders Peirce*, edited by Charles Hartshorne and Paul Weiss (Cambridge, MA: Harvard University Press, 1935), vol. 6, paras. 452–85.

Pendergrast, Mark. *Mirror Mirror: A History of the Human Love Affair with Reflection.* New York: Basic Books, 2003.

Pépin, Jean. "Héracles et son reflet dans le Néoplatonisme." In *Le Néoplatonisme*, 167–99. Paris: CNRS, 1971.

———. "Plotin et le miroir de Dionyse." *Revue internationale de philosophie* 92 (1970): 304–20.

———. "Plotin et les mythes." *Revue philosophique de Louvain* 53 (1955): 5–27.

Perl, Eric D. "The Power of All Things." *American Catholic Philosophical Quarterly* 71 (1997): 301–13.

Peters, Steve. *The Chimp Paradox: The Mind Management Programme to Help You Achieve Success, Confidence and Happiness.* London: Ebury, 2012.

Philo of Alexandria. *Collected Works.* Translated by F. H. Colson, G. H. Whitaker, et al. 10 vols. Loeb Classical Library. London: Heinemann, 1929.

———. *Supplementary Works.* Translated by Ralph Marcus. 2 vols. Loeb Classical Library. London: Heinemann, 1953.

Pickstock, Catherine. *After Writing: On the Liturgical Consummation of Philosophy.* Oxford: Blackwell, 1998.

Plaisance, Christopher A. "Of Cosmocrators and Cosmic Gods." In *Daimonic Imagination and Uncanny Intelligence*, edited by Angela Voss and William Rowlandson, 64–85. Newcastle: Cambridge Scholars, 2013.

Plantinga, Alvin. *Warrant and Proper Function.* New York: Oxford University Press, 1993.

Plato. *The Collected Dialogues of Plato, Including the Letters.* Translated by Edith Hamilton and Huntington Cairns. Princeton, NJ: Princeton University Press, 1982.

———. *The Dialogues of Plato Translated into English with Analyses and Introductions by B. Jowett, M.A. in Five Volumes.* 3rd ed. rev. and corrected. Oxford: Oxford University Press, 1892. http://oll.libertyfund.org/titles/166.

Pliny. *Natural History.* Translated by H. Rackham. Loeb Classical Library. London: Heinemann, 1952.

Plotinus. *The Enneads.* Translated by A. H. Armstrong. 7 vols. Loeb Classical Library. Cambridge, MA: Harvard University Press, 1966–88.

———. *The Enneads.* Translated by Stephen MacKenna. Edited by John Dillon. Harmondsworth, UK: Penguin, 1991. (Abridged ed. of the original Faber 1956 ed.)

———. *Plotin traités 1–6.* Edited by Luc Brisson and Jean-François Pradeau. Paris: Flammarion, 2002.

Plutarch. *De Iside et Osiride.* Edited by J. Gwyn Griffiths. Cardiff: University of Wales Press, 1970.

———. *Moralia.* Translated by E. L. Minor, F. H. Sandbach, and W. C. Helmbold. Loeb Classical Library. London: Heinemann, 1961.

———. *Plutarch's Lives.* Edited by Bernadotte Perrin. Loeb Classical Library. London: Heinemann, 1918.

Polanyi, Michael. *Personal Knowledge: Towards a Post-critical Philosophy*. Chicago: University of Chicago Press, 1958.

Porphyry of Tyre. *Letter to Marcella*. Translated by Alice Zimmern. Introduction by David Fideler. Grand Rapids, MI: Phanes Press, 1986.

———. *On Abstinence from Killing Animals*. Translated by Gillian Clark. London: Duckworth, 2000.

Price, Huw. *Time's Arrow and Archimedes' Point: New Directions for the Physics of Time*. New York: Oxford University Press, 1996.

Proclus. *Commentary on Alcibiades I*. Translated by William O'Neill. The Hague: Martinus Nijhoff, 1965.

———. *The Elements of Theology*. 2nd ed. Edited by E. R. Dodds. Oxford: Clarendon Press, 1963.

Pseudo-Dionysius. *The Celestial Hierarchy*. Whitefish, MT: Kessinger, 2004.

———. *The Complete Works*. Translated by Colm Luibheid and Paul Rorem. London: SPCK, 1987.

Pseudo-Macarius. *The Fifty Spiritual Homilies and the Great Letter*. Edited by George A. Maloney. New York: Paulist Press, 1992. See also Macarius.

Ptolemy. *Almagest*. 2nd ed. Translated by G. J. Toomer. Princeton, NJ: Princeton University Press, 1998.

Purves, Libby. *Holy Smoke: Religion and Roots*. London: Hodder and Stoughton, 1998.

Quasten, Johannes. *Music and Worship in Pagan and Christian Antiquity*. Translated by Boniface Ramsey. Washington, DC: National Association of Pastoral Musicians, 1983.

Rahner, Hugo. *Man at Play; or, Did You Ever Practice Eutrapelia?* Translated by Brian Battershaw and Edward Quinn. London: Burns and Oates, 1965.

Ramelli, Ilaria. *Hierocles the Stoic: Elements of Ethics, Fragments and Excerpts*. Translated by David Konstan. Atlanta: Society of Biblical Literature, 2009.

Rappe, Sara. "Metaphor in Plotinus' Enneads V.8.9." *Ancient Philosophy* 15 (1995): 155–72.

———. *Reading Neoplatonism*. Cambridge: Cambridge University Press, 2000.

Remes, Pauliina. *Neoplatonism: From Neglected Relic to Ancient Treasure*. Berkeley: University of California Press, 2008.

Rich, A. N. M. "Reincarnation in Plotinus." *Mnemosyne* 10 (1957): 232–8.

Ricks, Stephen D. "The Garment of Adam in Jewish, Christian and Islamic Tradition." In *Judaism and Islam: Boundaries, Communication, and Interaction—Essays in Honour of William M. Brinner*, edited by Benjamin H. Hary, John L. Hayes, and Fred Astren, 203–26. Leiden: Brill, 2000.

Rist, J. M. *Plotinus: The Road to Reality*. Cambridge: Cambridge University Press, 1967.

Roberts, Alexander, and James Donaldson, trans. *Acts of Perpetua and Felicitas*. 1885. Ante-Nicene Fathers, vol. 3. New York: Cosimo, 2007.

Rohr, Richard. *Immortal Diamond: The Search for Our True Self*. London: SPCK, 2013.

Rorty, R. M. *Philosophy and the Mirror of Nature*. Oxford: Blackwell, 1980.

Rosan, L. J. *The Philosophy of Proclus*. New York: Cosmos, 1949.

Rosenstock-Huessy, Eugen. *Out of Revolution: Autobiography of Western Man*. Windsor, Vic.: Argo, 1969.

Ross, Stephen David. *Metaphysical Aporia and Philosophical Heresy*. New York: SUNY Press, 1989.

Ross, W. D., ed. *Select Fragments*. Vol. 12 of *Works of Aristotle*. London: Oxford University Press, 1952.

Rossi, Vincent. "Presence, Participation, Performance: The Remembrance of God in the Early Hesychast Fathers." In Cutsinger, *Paths to the Heart*, 64–111.

Rousselle, Aline. "Images as Education in the Roman Empire." In *Education in Greek and Roman Antiquity*, edited by Yun Lee Too, 373–404. Leiden: Brill, 2001.

Russell, Bertrand. *Mysticism and Logic*. New York: Norton, 1929.

Russell, Jeffrey Burton. *Inventing the Flat Earth: Columbus and Modern Historians*. Westport, CT: Greenwood Press, 1991.

Ruysbroeck, Jan van. *The Adornment of the Spiritual Marriage; The Book of the Supreme Truth; The Sparkling Stone*. Translated by C. A. Winschenk. London: J. M. Dent and Sons, 1916.

Sacks, Oliver. *An Anthropologist on Mars: Seven Paradoxical Tales*. New York: Alfred A. Knopf, 1995.

———. *Musicophilia: Tales of Music and the Brain*. 2nd ed. New York: Vintage Books, 2008.

Samsel, Peter. "A Unity with Distinctions: Parallels in the Thought of St. Gregory Palamas and Ibn 'Arabi." In Cutsinger, *Paths to the Heart*, 190–224.

Sansonese, J. Nigro. *The Body of Myth*. Rochester, VT: Inner Traditions International, 1994.

Santillana, Giorgio de, and Hertha von Dechend. *Hamlet's Mill: An Essay on Myth and the Frame of Time*. Cambridge, MA: Harvard University Press, 1969.

Satlow, Michael L. "Jewish Constructions of Nakedness in Late Antiquity." *Journal of Biblical Literature* 116 (1997): 429–94.

Schaerer, René. *Le héros, sage et l'événement*. Paris: Aubier, 1965.

Schaff, Philip, ed. *Cyril of Jerusalem and Gregory Nazianzen*. Nicene and Post-Nicene Fathers, 2nd ser., vol. 7. Grand Rapids, MI: Christian Classics Ethereal Library, 1893.

Scheid, John, and Jesper Svenbro. *The Craft of Zeus: Myths of Weaving and Fabric*. Boston: Harvard University Press, 1996.

Scheinberg, S. "The Bee Maidens of the Homeric Hymn to Hermes." *Harvard Studies in Classical Philology* 83 (1979): 1–28.

Scholem, G. G. *Major Trends in Jewish Mysticism*. New York: Schocken Books, 1954.

Schroeder, Frederic M. "*Avocatio*, Rhetoric and the Technique of Contemplation in Plotinus." *Dionysius* 30 (2012): 147–60.

Schuon, Frithjof. *Treasures of Buddhism*. Bloomington, IN: World Wisdom, 1993.

Scott, Alan. *Origen and the Life of the Stars*. Oxford: Clarendon Press, 1991.

Séjourné, Laurette. *Burning Water: Thought and Religion in Ancient Mexico*. London: Thames and Hudson, 1957.

Sellars, John. "Marcus Aurelius and the Tradition of Spiritual Exercises." In *The Oxford Handbook of Roman Philosophy*, edited by R. Fletcher and W. H. Shearin. New York: Oxford University Press, forthcoming.

Sells, Michael A. *Mystical Languages of Unsaying.* Chicago: University of Chicago Press, 1994.

Sen, Joseph. "Good Times and the Timeless Good." *International Journal of Neoplatonic Studies* 3 (1995): 3–25.

Seneca, Lucius Annaeus. *Moral Epistles.* Translated by Richard M. Gummere. Loeb Classical Library. Cambridge, MA: Harvard University Press, 1917–25.

Shaw, Gregory. "Eros and Arithmos: Pythagorean Theurgy in Iamblichus and Plotinus." *Ancient Philosophy* 19 (1999): 121–43.

———. *Theurgy and the Soul.* University Park: Pennsylvania State University Press, 1995.

Sheppard, Anne. *Studies on the 5th and 6th Essays of Proclus' Commentary on the "Republic."* Gottingen: Vandenhoeck und Ruprecht, 1980.

Shestov, Lev. *In Job's Balances.* Translated by Camilla Coventry and C. A. Macartney. Edited by Bernard Martin. Athens: Ohio University Press, 1975. http://www.angelfire.com/nb/shestov/ijb/jb_o.html.

———. *Potestas Clavium.* Edited and translated by Bernard Martin. Athens: Ohio University Press, 1968. http://www.angelfire.com/nb/shestov/pc/pc_o.html.

Siegelmann, Ellen. *Metaphor and Meaning in Psychotherapy.* London: Guilford, 1990.

Singleton, Mark. *Yoga Body: The Origins of Modern Posture Practice.* New York: Oxford University Press, 2010.

Sinkewicz, Robert E., trans. *Evagrius of Pontus: The Greek Ascetic Corpus.* Oxford: Oxford University Press, 2003.

Small, Jocelyn Penny. "Memory and the Roman Orator." In *Companion to Roman Rhetoric,* edited by William Dominik and Jon Hall, 195–206. Oxford: Blackwell, 2009.

———. *Wax Tablets of the Mind: Cognitive Studies of Memory and Literacy in Classical Antiquity.* London: Routledge, 1997.

Smart, J. J. C. "The Temporal Asymmetry of the World." *Analysis* 14, no. 4 (1954): 79–83.

Smith, Andrew. "Plotinus and the Myth of Love." In *Texts and Culture in Late Antiquity,* edited by J. H. D. Scourfield, 233–46. Swansea: Classical Press of Wales, 2007.

———. *Porphyry's Place in the Neoplatonic Tradition: A Study in Post-Plotinian Neoplatonism.* The Hague: Martinus Nijhoff, 1974.

Smith, Jonathan Z. "Garments of Shame." *History of Religions* 5 (1966): 217–38.

Smith, Morton. *Clement of Alexandria and a Secret Gospel of Mark.* Cambridge, MA: Harvard University Press, 1973.

Smith, Rowland. *Julian's Gods: Religion and Philosophy in the Thought and Action of Julian the Apostate.* London: Routledge, 1995.

Smolin, Lee. *The Life of the Universe.* New York: Oxford University Press, 1997.

Snyder, H. Gregory. *Teachers and Texts in the Ancient World: Philosophers, Poets and Christians.* London: Routledge, 2000.

Sorabji, Richard. *Emotion and Peace of Mind: From Stoic Agitation to Christian Temptation.* Oxford: Clarendon Press, 2000.

———. *Matter, Space and Motion: Theories in Antiquity and Their Sequel.* Ithaca, NY: Cornell University Press, 1988.

———. *The Philosophy of the Commentators, 200–600 AD: A Sourcebook.* Vol. 1, *Psychology.* London: Duckworth, 2004.

————. *The Philosophy of the Commentators, 200–600 AD: A Sourcebook.* Vol. 2, *Physics.* Ithaca, NY: Cornell University Press, 2005.

Spencer, John H. *The Eternal Law: Ancient Greek Philosophy, Modern Physics and Ultimate Reality.* Vancouver: Param Media, 2012.

Spivey, Nigel. *Understanding Greek Sculpture: Ancient Meanings, Modern Readings.* London: Thames and Hudson, 1996.

Sprigge, T. L. S. "Final Causes." *Aristotelian Society Supplementary Volume* 45 (1971): 149–70.

Staal, J. F. *Advaita and Neoplatonism: A Critical Study in Comparative Philosophy.* Madras: University of Madras Press, 1961.

Stace, W. T. *Mysticism and Philosophy.* London: Macmillan, 1961.

Stafford, Emma. "'Without You No-One Is Happy': The Cult of Health in Ancient Greece." In *Health in Antiquity*, edited by Helen King, 120–35. London: Routledge, 2005.

————. *Worshipping Virtues: Personification and the Divine in Ancient Greece.* London: Duckworth, 2000.

Stamatellos, Giannis. "Plotinus on Transmigration: A Reconsideration." *Journal of Ancient Philosophy* 7, no. 1 (2013): 49–64.

Stanford, W. B. *Greek Metaphor: Studies in Theory and Practice.* Oxford: Blackwell, 1936.
————. *The Ulysses Theme.* 2nd ed. Oxford: Blackwell, 1963.

Stanner, W. E. H. "The Dreaming." In *Australian Signpost*, edited by T. A. G. Hungerford, 51–65. Melbourne: F. W. Cheshire, 1956. Reprinted in *Cultures of the Pacific*, edited by Thomas G. Harding and Ben J. Wallace (New York: Free Press, 1970), 304–15.

Stebbing, L. S. *Modern Introduction to Logic.* London: Methuen, 1930.

Stock, R. D. *The Flutes of Dionysus.* Lincoln: University of Nebraska Press, 1989.

Stoneman, Richard. *Palmyra and Its Empire.* Ann Arbor: University of Michigan Press, 1992.

Swinburne, A. G. *Poems and Ballads and Atalanta in Corydon.* Edited by Kenneth Haynes. London: Penguin, 2000.

Taliaferro, Charles. *The Golden Cord: A Short Book on the Secular and the Sacred.* Notre Dame, IN: University of Notre Dame Press, 2013.

Taylor, Jill Bolte. *My Stroke of Insight.* London: Hodder and Stoughton, 2008.

Taylor, Steve. *Waking from Sleep: How Awakening Experiences Occur and How to Make Them Permanent.* London: Hay House, 2010.

Taylor, Thomas, trans. *Selected Works of Porphyry.* London: Thomas Rodd, 1823.

Teixidor, Javier. "Palmyra in the Third Century." In *A Journey to Palmyra: Collected Essays to Remember Delbert R. Hillers*, edited by Eleanora Cussini, 181–226. Leiden: Brill, 2005.

Tesarz, J., A. K. Schuster, M. Hartmann, A. Gerhardt, and W. Eich. "Pain Perception in Athletes Compared to Normally Active Controls: A Systematic Review with Meta-analysis." *Pain* 153, no. 6 (2012): 1253–62.

Thomas, R. S. *Neb.* In *R. S. Thomas: Autobiographies*, edited and translated by Jason Walford Davies. London: Dent, 1997.

Thoreau, W. D. *Walden: The Portable Thoreau.* Edited by Carl Bode. Harmondsworth, UK: Penguin, 1977.

Tieleman, Teun. "Plotinus on the Seat of the Soul: Reverberations of Galen and Alexander in Ennead IV.3 [27].23." *Phronesis* 43, no. 4 (1998): 306–25.

Tolkien, J. R. R. *The Return of the King.* Vol. 3 of *The Lord of the Rings.* 2nd ed. London: Allen and Unwin, 1966.

———. *The Silmarillion.* Edited by Christopher Tolkien. London: HarperCollins, 1998.

Tolle, Eckhart. *A New Earth: Create a Better Life.* London: Penguin, 2005.

———. *The Power of Now.* London: Hodder and Stoughton, 2005.

Traherne, Thomas. *Centuries of Meditations: Poems, Centuries and Three Thanksgivings.* Edited by Anne Ridler. London: Oxford University Press, 1966.

Tsakiridou, Cornelia A. *Icons in Time, Persons in Eternity: Orthodox Theology and the Aesthetics of the Christian Image.* Farnham, UK: Ashgate, 2013.

Turner, Denys. *Eros and Allegory: Medieval Exegesis of the Song of Songs.* Cistercian Studies 156. Kalamazoo, MI: Cistercian Publications, 1995.

Turner, John D. "Gnosticism and Platonism: The Platonizing Sethian Texts from Nag Hammadi in Their Relation to Later Platonic Literature." In *Gnosticism and Neoplatonism,* edited by R. T. Wallis and J. Bregman, 425–59. Studies in Neoplatonism, vol. 6. New York: SUNY Press, 1992.

Uexkuell, Jakob von. "A Stroll through the Worlds of Animals and Men." In *Instinctive Behaviour,* edited by C. H. Schiller, 5–80. New York: International University Press, 1957.

———. *Theoretical Biology.* New York: Harcourt, Brace, 1926.

Ustinova, Yulia. *Caves and the Ancient Mind: Descending Underground and the Search for Ultimate Truth.* New York: Oxford University Press, 2009.

Uzdavinys, Algis. "Animation of Statues in Ancient Civilizations and Neoplatonism." In Vassilopoulou and Clark, *Late Antique Epistemology,* 118–40.

———, ed. *The Heart of Plotinus.* Bloomington, IN: World Wisdom, 2009.

———. *Philosophy and Theurgy in Late Antiquity.* San Rafael, CA: Sophia Perennis, 2010.

Van den Berg, J. H. *The Phenomenological Approach to Psychiatry.* Springfield, IL: C. C. Thomas, 1955.

Van den Berg, R. M. "Proclus and the Myth of the Charioteer." *Syllecta Classica* 8 (1997): 149–62.

Van Nuffelen, Peter. *Rethinking the Gods: Philosophical Readings of Religion in the Post-Hellenistic Period.* Cambridge: Cambridge University Press, 2011.

———. "Words of Truth: Mystical Silence as a Philosophical and Rhetorical Tool in Plutarch." *Hermathena* 182 (2007): 9–34.

Vassilopoulou, Panayiota. "Creation or Metamorphosis: Plotinus on the Genesis of the World." In *Neoplatonism and Western Aesthetics,* edited by Aphrodite Alexandrakis and Nicholas J. Moutafakis, 207–28. New York: SUNY Press, 2002.

———. "From a Feminist Perspective: Plotinus on Teaching and Learning Philosophy." *Women: A Cultural Review* 14 (2003): 130–43.

———. Introduction to Vassilopoulou and Clark, *Late Antique Epistemology,* 1–17.

———. "Plotinus' Aesthetics: In Defence of the Lifelike." In *Routledge Handbook of Neoplatonism,* 484–503. London: Routledge, 2014.

———. "Plotinus and Individuals." *Ancient Philosophy* 26, no. 2 (2006): 371–83.

————. "Sages of Old, Artists Anew." *Classical Bulletin* 81 (2005): 35–49.

————. "Teaching Philosophy through Metaphor." In *Teaching Philosophy*, edited by Andrea Kenkmann, 116–33. London: Continuum, 2009.

Vassilopoulou, Panayiota, and Stephen R. L. Clark, eds. *Late Antique Epistemology: Other Ways to Truth.* Basingstoke, UK: Palgrave Macmillan, 2009.

Vassilopoulou, Panayiota, and Jonardon Ganeri. "The Cathartic Potion of Living To-gether." *Philosophy Now* 50 (2005): 36–9.

————. "The Geography of Shadows: Souls and Cities in P. Pullman's 'His Dark Materials.'" *Philosophy and Literature* 35 (2011): 269–81.

————. "The Metaphor of Life." *Framework: The Finnish Art Review* 4 (2005): 8–12.

Vaughan, Henry. *Collected Poems.* Edited by Alan Rudrum. Harmondsworth, UK: Penguin, 1976.

Vernant, Jean-Pierre. "Hestia-Hermès: Sur l'expression religieuse de l'espace et du mouvement chez les Grecs." *L'homme* 3 (1963): 12–50.

Verney, Stephen. *The Dance of Love.* Glasgow: Collins, 1989.

Vogel, Cornelia J. de. "Greek Cosmic Love and the Christian Love of God: Boethius, Dionysius the Areopagite and the Author of the Fourth Gospel." *Vigiliae Christianae* 35 (1981): 57–81.

Volf, Miroslav. *The End of Memory: Remembering Rightly in a Violent World.* Grand Rapids, MI: William B. Eerdmans, 2006.

Wakoff, Michael. "Awaiting the Sun: A Plotinian Form of Contemplative Prayer." Forthcoming.

Wald, George. *Self-Intellection and Identity in the Philosophy of Plotinus.* Frankfurt: Peter Lang, 1990.

Walker, D. P. *Spiritual and Demonic Magic from Ficino to Campanella.* Stroud, UK: Sutton, 2000.

Ward, Keith. *God, Chance and Necessity.* Oxford: Oneworld, 1996.

Ward, Michael. *Planet Narnia: The Seven Heavens in the Imagination of C. S. Lewis.* New York: Oxford University Press, 2008.

Ware, Kallistos. "How Do We Enter the Heart?" In Cutsinger, *Paths to the Heart*, 2–23.

Warren, Edward. "Memory in Plotinus." *Classical Quarterly* 15 (1965): 252–60.

Waterfield, Robin. *The First Philosophers: The Presocratics and Sophists.* Oxford: Oxford University Press, 2000.

Watson, Alaric. *Aurelian and the Third Century.* London: Routledge, 1999.

Watson, Gerard. *Phantasia in Classical Thought.* Galway: Galway University Press, 1988.

Watts, Alan. *The Book on the Taboo against Knowing Who You Are.* London: Souvenir Press, 2011.

Watts, Edward J. *City and School in Late Antique Athens and Alexandria.* Berkeley: University of California Press, 2006.

Wear, Sarah Klitenic, and John Dillon. *Dionysius the Areopagite and the Neoplatonist Tradition: Despoiling the Hellenes.* Aldershot, UK: Ashgate, 2007.

Webb, Ruth. *Demons and Dancers: Performance in Late Antiquity.* Cambridge, MA: Harvard University Press, 2009.

Weil, Simone. *Gravity and Grace.* Translated by Emma Craufurd. Edited by Gustav Thibron. Lincoln: University of Nebraska Press, 1952.

———. *Intimations of Christianity*. Translated by E. C. Geissbuhler. London: Routledge and Kegan Paul, 1957.

———. *Notebooks*. Translated by A. Wills. London: Routledge and Kegan Paul, 1956.

West, Martin L. *Ancient Greek Music*. Oxford: Clarendon Press, 1992.

———. *The Orphic Poems*. Oxford: Clarendon Press, 1983.

Wilberding, James. "'Creeping Spatiality': The Location of *Nous* in Plotinus' Universe." *Phronesis* 50 (2005): 315–34.

———. *Plotinus' Cosmology: A Study of Ennead II.1 (40); Text, Translation, and Commentary*. New York: Oxford University Press, 2006.

Wildberg, Christian. "Dionysus in the Mirror of Philosophy: Heraclitus, Plato, and Plotinus." In *Dionysus and Ancient Polytheism*, edited by Renate Schleiser, 205–32. Berlin: De Gruyter, 2011.

———. "A World of Thoughts: Plotinus on Nature and Contemplation (Enn. III.8 [30] 1–6)." In *Physics and Philosophy of Nature in Greek Neoplatonism*, edited by Riccardo Chiaradonna and Franco Trabattoni, 121–44. Philosophia Antiqua, vol. 115. Leiden: Brill, 2009.

Williams, Charles. *Descent into Hell*. London: Faber, 1937.

———. *Shadows of Ecstasy*. London: Gollancz, 1933.

Williams, Craig A. *Roman Homosexuality: Ideologies of Masculinity in Classical Antiquity*. New York: Oxford University Press, 1999.

Williams, Michael Allen. *Rethinking Gnosticism: An Argument for Dismantling a Dubious Category*. Princeton, NJ: Princeton University Press, 1996.

Wilson, Colin. *Existential Criticism: Selected Book Reviews*. Edited by Colin Stanley. Nottingham, UK: Paupers' Press, 2009.

———. *The Mind Parasites*. London: Barker, 1967.

———. *The Philosopher's Stone*. London: Barker, 1969.

Winchell, Alexander. *World Life; or, Comparative Geology*. Chicago: S. C. Griggs, 1883.

Wisdom, John O. *The Unconscious Origin of Berkeley's Philosophy*. London: Hogarth Press, 1953.

Witt, R. E. *Isis in the Graeco-Roman World*. London: Thames and Hudson, 1971.

Wittgenstein, Ludwig von. *Tractatus Logico-Philosophicus*. Translated by D. F. Pears and Brian McGuinness. London: Routledge and Kegan Paul, 1971.

Wohl, Victoria. "The Eye of the Beloved: Opsis and Eros in Socratic Pedagogy." In *Alcibiades and the Socratic Lover-Educator*, edited by Marguerite Johnson and Harold Tarrant, 45–60. Bristol: Bristol Classical Press, 2012.

Wolfson, H. A. *Philo: Foundations of Religious Philosophy in Judaism, Christianity and Islam*. Cambridge, MA: Harvard University Press, 1948.

Wood, Ananda. *From the Upanishads*. Pune, India: Ananda Wood, 1996.

Wren-Lewis, John. "The Darkness of God: A Personal Report on Consciousness Transformation through an Encounter with Death." *Journal of Humanistic Psychology* 28 (1988): 105–22.

———. *God in a Technological Age*. Cincinnati, OH: Forward Movement, 1967.

———. "A Mystical Awakening." In *Our Childhood's Pattern: Memories of Growing Up Christian*, edited by Monica Furlong. London: Mowbrays, 1995.

Xenophon. *Memorabilia, Oeconomicus, Symposium, Apology*. Translated by E. C.

Marchant and O. J. Todd. Loeb Classical Library. Cambridge, MA: Harvard University Press, 1923.

Yates, Frances A. *The Art of Memory*. London: Routledge, 1966.

———. *Giordano Bruno and the Hermetic Tradition*. London: Routledge and Kegan Paul, 1964.

Yeats, W. B. *Collected Poems*. London: Wordsworth, 2008.

Zerubavel, Eviatar. *The Seven Day Circle: The History and Meaning of the Week*. Chicago: University of Chicago Press, 1989.

Zimmer, H. R. *The King and the Corpse: Tales of the Soul's Conquest of Evil.* Edited by Joseph Campbell. Princeton, NJ: Princeton University Press, 1975.

Zizioulas, John. *Being as Communion: Studies in Personhood and the Church*. 2nd ed. London: Darton Longman and Todd, 2010.

Zosimus. *A New History*. Translated by Ronald T. Ridley. Sydney: Australian Association for Byzantine Studies, 1982.

Made in the USA
Middletown, DE
05 August 2021